MANIFESTATIONS OF COHERENCE AND INVESTOR–STATE ARBITRATION

Coherence is highly valued in law. It is especially sought after in investor–state dispute settlement, where charges of incoherence in arbitral awards have long been raised by states and scholars. Yet coherence is a largely underexplored notion in international law. Often, coherence is treated as a mere ideal to strive towards or simply as a different way to describe the legal consistency of judicial outcomes. This book takes a different approach. It views coherence as an independent concept having two dimensions: a substantive and a methodological one. Both are critical for legal reasoning by international courts and tribunals, including by investor–state tribunals, and the book illustrates through several case studies some of the ways this conclusion is borne out in practice. A fuller understanding of coherence in international law has implications for the way we should understand the concept of law, the practice of legal reasoning, and judicial professional ethics.

Charalampos Giannakopoulos is a post-doctoral fellow at the Centre for International Law, National University of Singapore. He received his doctorate from the Graduate Institute of International and Development Studies, and has been a Grotius Research Scholar at the University of Michigan Law School, as well as a legal consultant at the United Nations Conference on Trade and Development (UNCTAD).

MANIFESTATIONS OF COHERENCE AND INVESTOR–STATE ARBITRATION

CHARALAMPOS GIANNAKOPOULOS

Centre for International Law, National University of Singapore

CAMBRIDGE
UNIVERSITY PRESS

CAMBRIDGE
UNIVERSITY PRESS

Shaftesbury Road, Cambridge CB2 8BS, United Kingdom

One Liberty Plaza, 20th Floor, New York, NY 10006, USA

477 Williamstown Road, Port Melbourne, VIC 3207, Australia

314–321, 3rd Floor, Plot 3, Splendor Forum, Jasola District Centre, New Delhi – 110025, India

103 Penang Road, #05–06/07, Visioncrest Commercial, Singapore 238467

Cambridge University Press is part of Cambridge University Press & Assessment, a department of the University of Cambridge.

We share the University's mission to contribute to society through the pursuit of education, learning and research at the highest international levels of excellence.

www.cambridge.org
Information on this title: www.cambridge.org/9781009153850

DOI: 10.1017/9781009153874

First published 2022

A catalogue record for this publication is available from the British Library.

ISBN 978-1-009-15385-0 Hardback

CONTENTS

PREFACE AND ACKNOWLEDGEMENTS

This book is a product of my doctoral studies, which I undertook at the Graduate Institute of International and Development Studies. Interestingly, coherence was not the topic I had initially chosen to pursue. This was, rather, general principles of law and their use in investor–state arbitration. I came to coherence almost by accident. Coherence kept turning up in my readings, often in vague and underanalysed ways but undoubtedly as an important concept.

Indeed, coherence is a largely underexamined concept in international law. It is frequently seen as a good thing and as an ideal towards which to strive, but there appears to be little study on any other aspects of it or on any implications that it may have in the legal field. International lawyers agree that coherence is a desirable goal to pursue but tend to stop there and do not scrutinise the matter further. Legal reasoning is therefore an especially fruitful area for one to examine coherence. In international investment law in particular, the relevance and potential practical implications of coherence for legal reasoning are demonstrated in the debate on investor–state dispute settlement reform taking place at Working Group III of the United Nations Commission on International Trade Law (UNCITRAL). The Working Group's mandate is to improve, among other concerns, the coherence of investor–state awards.

The present study thus seeks to take the first steps towards unpacking coherence and identifying its implications – both theoretical and practical – for legal reasoning in international law. While my primary focus in this book is on investor–state arbitration, my intention has been to also contribute to the international legal field more generally. Indeed, the remarks made in the book can be extrapolated and made to cover general international law with only minor modifications. At the same time, I also wanted my examination of coherence to be attuned to the latter's theoretical dimensions. This has often resulted in the book's chapters having to perform a balancing act between theory and practice, as well as between international investment and general international law. Every effort has been made for all of these aspects to complement each other as much as possible. My overall hope is for this study to create greater awareness about coherence and its manifold manifestations in international law and legal reasoning.

In seeing this project to completion, I have collected a few debts of gratitude that I wish to acknowledge here. First and foremost, I am grateful to Zachary Douglas for giving me the opportunity to embark on the doctoral adventure in the first place. I am grateful to Thomas Schultz and George Letsas for kindly agreeing to serve as examiners. Andrea Bianchi, Joost Pauwelyn, and Fuad Zarbiyev have all influenced significant parts of this book with their teaching. While at the Graduate Institute, I was fortunate to benefit from the institute's financial assistance throughout my studies. On several occasions, I had the opportunity to work at the Investment Agreements Section at the United Nations Conference on Trade and Development (UNCTAD), which greatly improved my understanding of investment treaties. I am grateful to Elisabeth Tuerk, Diana Rosert, and Hamed El-Kady for their continued trust.

For general discussions on the topic and comments on earlier drafts, I am thankful to Ayelet Berman, Tomer Broude, N. Jansen Calamita, Anastasios Gourgourinis, Alexandros Kolliopoulos, Panos Merkouris, Suresh Nanwani, Steven Ratner, Yahli Shereshevsky, and Joseph Weiler. Finally, the Investment Law and Policy team at the NUS Centre for International Law has been an ideal and hospitable place to conduct additional research and to finalise the book for publication.

The book is dedicated to my family. The biggest debt of gratitude is owed to them. None of the above would have been possible without their continued support and encouragement.

TABLE OF CASES

International Court of Justice

Aegean Sea Continental Shelf Case (Greece v. *Turkey)*, Judgment of 19 December 1978, ICJ Rep (1978) 3   111

Case Concerning the Barcelona Traction, Light and Power Company, Limited (New Application: 1962, Belgium v. *Spain), Second Phase*, Judgment of 5 February 1970, ICJ Rep (1970) 3   239

Case Concerning Border and Transborder Armed Actions (Nicaragua v. *Honduras), Jurisdiction and Admissibility*, Judgment of 20 December 1988, ICJ Rep (1988) 69   246

Case Concerning the Continental Shelf (Tunisia/Libyan Arab Jamahiriya), Judgment of 24 February 1982, ICJ Rep (1982) 18   68

Case Concerning Kasikili/Sedudu Island (Botswana/Namibia), Judgment of 13 December 1999, ICJ Rep (1999) 1045   98, 125

Case Concerning the Land and Maritime Boundary between Cameroon and Nigeria (Cameroon v. *Nigeria), Preliminary Objections*, Judgment of 11 June 1998, ICJ Rep (1998) 275   246

Case Concerning Maritime Delimitation and Territorial Questions between Qatar and Bahrain (Qatar v. *Bahrain), Jurisdiction and Admissibility*, Judgment of 1 July 1994, ICJ Rep (1994) 112   116

Case Concerning Maritime Delimitation and Territorial Questions between Qatar and Bahrain (Qatar v. *Bahrain), Jurisdiction and Admissibility*, Judgment of 15 February 1995, ICJ Rep (1995) 6   117

Case Concerning Military and Paramilitary Activities in and against Nicaragua (Nicaragua v. *United States of America), Merits*, Judgment of 27 June 1986, ICJ Rep (1986) 14   98

Case Concerning Oil Platforms (Islamic Republic of Iran v. *United States of America)*, Judgment of 6 November 2003, ICJ Rep (2003) 161   129, passim

Case Concerning Pulp Mills on the River Uruguay (Argentina v. *Uruguay)*, Judgment of 20 April 2010, ICJ Rep (2010) 14   136

Case Concerning Right of Passage over Indian Territory (Portugal v. *India), Merits*, Judgment of 12 April 1960, ICJ Rep (1960) 6   215

Permanent Court of International Justice

International Tribunal for the Law of the Sea

Investor–State Dispute Settlement

Unless otherwise indicated, ISDS decisions and other documents associated with ISDS cases are available online at https://icsid.worldbank.org/, http://italaw.com/, www.uncitral.org/transparency-registry/registry/index.jspx, or https://investmentpolicy.unctad.org/investment-dispute-settlement.

Tulip Real Estate and Development Netherlands B.V. v. *Republic of Turkey*, ICSID Case No. ARB/11/28, Decision on Annulment, 30 December 2015 128

United Parcel Service of America Inc. v. *Government of Canada*, UNCITRAL Rules, Award on the Merits, 24 May 2007 173–177

Vattenfall AB and Others v. *Federal Republic of Germany*, ICSID Case No. ARB/12/12, Decision on the *Achmea* Issue, 31 August 2018 127

Venezuela Holdings, B.V., et al (case formerly known as Mobil Corporation, Venezuela Holdings, B.V., et al.) v. *Bolivarian Republic of Venezuela*, ICSID Case No. ARB/07/27, Decision on Jurisdiction, 10 June 2010 229, 233–234

Venoklim Holding B.V. v. *Bolivarian Republic of Venezuela*, ICSID Case No. ARB/12/22, Award, 3 April 2015 238

Vladislav Kim and Others v. *Republic of Uzbekistan*, ICSID Case No. ARB/13/6, Decision on Jurisdiction, 8 March 2017 198–203

Waste Management, Inc. v. *United Mexican States*, ICSID Case No. ARB(AF)/98/2, Arbitral Award, 2 June 2000 (*Waste Management I*) 204

Wena Hotels Ltd. v. *Arab Republic of Egypt*, ICSID Case No. ARB/98/4, Award, 8 December 2000 (2002) 41 *International Legal Materials* 896 91

Windstream Energy LLC v. *Government of Canada*, PCA Case No. 2013-22, Award, 27 September 2016 97

Wintershall Aktiengesellschaft v. *Argentine Republic*, ICSID Case No. ARB/04/14, Award, 8 December 2008 112, 161

International Arbitration

Affaire des biens britanniques au Maroc espagnol (Espagne c. *Royaume-Uni)*, Award, 1 May 1925, Vol II *RIAA* 615 88

Amoco International Finance Corporation v. *The Government of the Islamic Republic of Iran, National Iranian Oil Company, National Petrochemical Company and Kharg Chemical Company Limited*, Partial Award No 310-56-3, 14 July 1987, (1988) 27 *International Legal Materials* 1314 127

Arbitration Regarding the Iron Rhine ('Ijzeren Rijn') Railway (Belgium/Netherlands), Award of the Arbitral Tribunal, 24 May 2005, Vol XXVII *RIAA* 35 98

Cayuga Indians (Great Britain) v. *United States*, Decision, 22 January 1926, Vol VI *RIAA* 173 68

Georges Pinson (France) v. *United Mexican States*, Decision No 1, 19 October 1928, French-Mexican Claims Commission, Vol V *RIAA* 327 113, 127

Island of Palmas Case (Netherlands/United States of America), Award, 4 April 1928, Vol II *RIAA* 829 215, 232

Libyan American Oil Company (LIAMCO) v. *Government of the Libyan Arab Republic*, Award, 12 April 1977, 62 *ILR* 140 73

Petroleum Development (Trucial Coast) Ltd v. *The Sheikh of Abu Dhabi*, (1952) 1 *International and Comparative Law Quarterly* 247 216

Iran-United States Claims Tribunal

World Trade Organisation

European Court of Human Rights

Domestic Courts

TABLE OF INTERNATIONAL CONVENTIONS

TABLE OF INTERNATIONAL INVESTMENT AGREEMENTS

TABLE OF PROCEDURAL RULES

ABBREVIATIONS

BIT	bilateral investment treaty
CETA	Comprehensive Economic and Trade Agreement
CITES	Convention on International Trade in Endangered Species of Wild Fauna and Flora
CPTPP	Comprehensive and Progressive Agreement for Trans-Pacific Partnership
DSU	Dispute Settlement Understanding
ECHR	European Convention on Human Rights
ECT	Energy Charter Treaty
ECtHR	European Court of Human Rights
EU	European Union
FCTC	Framework Convention on Tobacco Control
FET	fair and equitable treatment
FTA	free trade agreement
GATS	General Agreement on Trade in Services
GATT	General Agreement on Tariffs and Trade
ICC	International Chamber of Commerce
ICFA	Investment Cooperation and Facilitation Agreement
ICJ	International Court of Justice
ICJ Rep	International Court of Justice Reports
ICSID	International Centre for Settlement of Investment Disputes
ICSID Rep	International Centre for Settlement of Investment Disputes Reports
ILC	International Law Commission
ILR	International Law Reports
IPA	Investment Protection Agreement
Iran-US CTR	Iran-United States Claims Tribunal Reports
ISDS	investor–state dispute settlement
ITLOS	International Tribunal for the Law of the Sea
LCIA	London Court of International Arbitration
MERCOSUR	Mercado Común del Sur (Southern Common Market)
MFN	most-favoured-nation

OSPAR Convention	Convention for the Protection of the Marine Environment of the North-East Atlantic
Recueil des cours	Recueil des cours de l'académie de droit international de la Haye (Collected Courses of the Hague Academy of International Law)
RIAA	Reports of International Arbitral Awards
SCC	Stockholm Chamber of Commerce
SIAC	Singapore International Arbitration Centre
UN	United Nations
UNCITRAL	United Nations Commission on International Trade Law
UNCLOS	United Nations Convention on the Law of the Sea
UNCTAD	United Nations Conference on Trade and Development
UNECE	United Nations Economic Commission for Europe
UNTS	United Nations Treaty Series
VCLT	Vienna Convention on the Law of Treaties
WHO	World Health Organisation
WTO	World Trade Organisation

Introduction

Coherence is often described as an ideal towards which to strive. We tend to place value on coherence because it implies that something, or someone, makes sense and is intelligible. Being incoherent, by contrast, causes frustration and confusion. Coherence is thus thought to be a highly desirable attribute to have in virtually every aspect of one's life. It is sought after in the way one talks, writes, thinks, forms justified beliefs, or acts. Coherence figures prominently in contemporary approaches to ethics and the structure of epistemic justification across different disciplines, including in theories about the nature of truth as well as about theoretical and practical reasoning.[1] We typically wish for our various fields of knowledge, our science, and the ordering systems of our societies to be coherent. The legal field is no exception. Indeed, there appears to be large consensus that the concept of coherence suits law and legal reasoning particularly well.[2]

This book does not deal with coherence at large. It does not, for example, seek to present a comprehensive account of coherence across disciplines.[3] Its scope of inquiry is rather limited to the international legal field. Further still, it only seeks to investigate some of the implications emanating from having expectations of coherence in law, with a particular focus on the inner workings of a specific domain of public international law, that is, international investment law and the practices of ISDS tribunals.

This introductory chapter serves to set the stage for the book's investigation. To that end, it outlines the impetus behind the choice of coherence as a subject for inquiry (Section I.1), the principal, so-called

[1] See Y. Radi, 'Coherence', in J. d'Aspremont and S. Singh (eds.), *Concepts for International Law: Contributions to Disciplinary Thought* (Cheltenham: Edward Elgar, 2019) 105, 105.
[2] Ibid., 107 (and references therein).
[3] For an effort in that direction, see A. Amaya, *The Tapestry of Reason: An Inquiry into the Nature of Coherence and Its Role in Legal Argument* (Oxford: Hart, 2015).

'bottom-up' perspective from which the subject of coherence is examined in the book (Section I.2), the core thesis advanced in relation to the nature of coherence and its role in judicial reasoning in ISDS (Section I.3), and the division of labour amongst the book's chapters (Section I.4).

I.1 Three Reasons to Investigate Coherence

The impetus for this book's inquiry rests on three kinds of interconnected considerations. In the first place, over the past several years states and commentators have expressed widespread concern about instances of perceived incoherence in international investment law and in the decisions produced by ISDS tribunals in particular.[4] In their discussions on ISDS reform at UNCITRAL's Working Group III, state delegations have overwhelmingly identified a perceived lack of coherence in ISDS decisions as a key cause for concern, alongside related concerns about a lack of consistency, predictability, and correctness.[5] Delegations participating in Working Group III thus seek to take steps to enhance coherence in ISDS in an effort to improve the overall regime's legitimacy and to strengthen its rule of law footprint.[6]

However, in the second place, coherence remains a largely under-theorised concept in practice and its exact content is opaque in the ISDS context. For instance, discussion in the literature tends to be structured around the imperative of consistency of arbitral outcomes.[7] Moreover, scholarship making direct reference to the idea of coherence

[4] It is to be noted, however, that this book takes no strong views as to whether international investment law or ISDS are in fact incoherent. Putting such a statement forward would require an empirical examination of coherence in international investment law and ISDS. Yet, as explained in Section I.2, such examination appears premature at this stage, given the general absence of debate or consensus with respect to the content of the concept of coherence and with respect to its implications vis-à-vis legal reasoning.

[5] E.g., see UNCITRAL Working Group III (Investor–State Dispute Settlement Reform), 'Possible Reform of Investor–State Dispute Settlement (ISDS): Consistency and Related Matters', UN Doc A/CN.9/WG.III/WP.150 (28 August 2018).

[6] UNCITRAL, 'Report of Working Group III (Investor–State Dispute Settlement Reform) on the Work of its Thirty-fourth Session (Vienna, 27 November–1 December 2017) – Part II', UN Doc A/CN.9/930/Add.1/Rev.1 (26 February 2018), 3 (para 11).

[7] E.g., K. Diel-Gligor, *Towards Consistency in International Investment Jurisprudence: A Preliminary Ruling System for ICSID Arbitration* (Leiden: Brill/Nijhoff, 2017); Y. Banifatemi, 'Consistency in the Interpretation of Substantive Investment Rules: Is It Achievable?', in R. Echandi and P. Sauvé (eds.), *Prospects in International Investment Law and Policy* (Cambridge: Cambridge University Press, 2013) 200.

tends to simply state that coherence is desirable[8] and often regards coherence as exclusively synonymous or interchangeable with concepts such as legal certainty, predictability, and legal authority.[9] Further, despite its centrality in UNCITRAL's Working Group III, coherence is a generally under-examined subject in that context as well. In the Working Group's discussions, coherence is neither given an independent content compared to the three other causes for concern (in fact, coherence is often lost in discussions about the consistency of outcomes) nor is its relationship with these other causes for concern made clear (thus, e.g., coherence is often seen as coterminous with predictability and its potential relationship to correctness has not been examined in much detail).[10]

[8] E.g., see F. Baetens, 'Judicial Review of International Adjudicatory Decisions: A Cross-Regime Comparison of Annulment and Appellate Mechanisms' (2017) 8 *Journal of International Dispute Settlement* 432; E.-U. Petersmann, 'The Judicial Task of Administering Justice in Trade and Investment Law and Adjudication' (2013) 4 *Journal of International Dispute Settlement* 5; Z. Douglas, 'The MFN Clause in Investment Arbitration: Treaty Interpretation Off the Rails' (2011) 2 *Journal of International Dispute Settlement* 97, 99; S. W. Schill, 'Allocating Adjudicatory Authority: Most-Favoured-Nation Clauses as a Basis of Jurisdiction – A Reply to Zachary Douglas' (2011) 2 *Journal of International Dispute Settlement* 353, 357; D. McRae, 'The WTO Appellate Body: A Model for an ICSID Appeals Facility?' (2010) 1 *Journal of International Dispute Settlement* 371.

[9] E.g., C. Schreuer, 'Coherence and Consistency in International Investment Law', in Echandi and Sauvé (n. 7) 391, 391:

> Coherence and consistency are desirable qualities in any legal system. A legal system is coherent if its elements are logically related to each other and if it shows no contradictions. A legal system is consistent if it treats identical or similar situations in the same way and if it gives equal treatment to the participants in the system.

Similarly, C. Schreuer, 'Diversity and Harmonization of Treaty Interpretation in Investment Arbitration', in M. Fitzmaurice, O. Elias, and P. Merkouris (eds.), *Treaty Interpretation and the Vienna Convention on the Law of Treaties: 30 Years On* (Leiden: Martinus Nijhoff, 2010) 129, 139 ('The need for a coherent case law is evident. It strengthens the predictability of decisions and enhances their authority.').

[10] E.g., see UNCITRAL, 'Report of Working Group III (Investor–State Dispute Settlement Reform) on the Work of its Thirty-fifth Session (New York, 23–27 April 2018)', UN Doc A/CN.9/935 (14 May 2018), 5–8 (paras 20–44), where, under the general heading 'coherence and consistency', coherence is scarcely mentioned as an independent concept and is often lost in discussions regarding consistency, certainty, and predictability. See also, UNCITRAL Working Group III (n. 6), 3ff (paras 9ff).

Further, see A. Roberts and Z. Bouraoui, 'UNCITRAL and ISDS Reforms: Concerns about Consistency, Predictability and Correctness', *EJIL: Talk!* (5 June 2018), reporting on the interventions made by individual state delegations on consistency and coherence during the early Working Group III sessions, many of which seem to have regarded the two concepts as interchangeable.

Crucially, under-theorisation is not unique to the context of ISDS and its potential reform. The same applies with respect to general international law, wherein one often finds at most passing references to coherence. For instance, one finds in the ILC's work on the fragmentation of international law references to the existence of a link between coherence and the principle of systemic integration under Article 31(3)(c) of the VCLT.[11] Yet, even in such references, coherence seems to be regarded primarily as coterminous to mere legal security and predictability.[12] That is to say, coherence tends to be regarded as a formal principle devoid of any independent substantive content of its own.[13]

Furthermore, in the third place, a review of the international law literature also shows that coherence is frequently approached in a methodologically monolithic manner. The common way in which coherence is viewed can be described as 'top-down', whereby one looks at whether international law coheres as a system on the whole, or at whether particular, specialised regimes of international law cohere, either between themselves or with general international law.[14] That is unfortunate since law is a field where expectations of coherence seem to apply at every corner one looks – in the legal system on the whole, in individual pieces of legislation and individual legal norms, as well as in pronouncements by judicial bodies. This means that there are in principle multiple levels of inquiry into the subject of coherence in ISDS: not only between international investment law and other regimes or strictly within international investment law itself ('top-down') but also in relation to the

[11] International Law Commission, 'Fragmentation of International Law: Difficulties Arising from the Diversification and Expansion of International Law – Report of the Study Group of the International Law Commission', UN Doc A/CN.4/L.682 (13 April 2006), 211 (para 419) ('This is all that article 31(3)(c) [of the VCLT] requires; the integration into the process of legal reasoning – including reasoning by courts and tribunals – of a sense of coherence and meaningfulness.').

[12] See ibid., 248 (para 491) ('Fragmentation puts to question the coherence of international law. Coherence is valued positively owing to the connection it has with predictability and legal security.').

[13] See, e.g., the following passage, ibid.: 'Coherence is, however, a formal and abstract virtue. For a legal system that is regarded in some respects as unjust or unworkable, no added value is brought by the fact of its being coherently so.'

[14] E.g., see S. Gáspár-Szilágyi, D. Behn, and M. Langford (eds.), *Adjudicating Trade and Investment Disputes: Convergence or Divergence?* (Cambridge: Cambridge University Press, 2020); M. Andenas, M. Fitzmaurice, A. Tanzi, and J. Wouters (eds.), *General Principles and the Coherence of International Law* (Leiden: Brill/Nijhoff, 2019); M. Andenas and E. Bjorge (eds.), *A Farewell to Fragmentation: Reassertion and Convergence in International Law* (Cambridge: Cambridge University Press, 2015).

process of legal reasoning used by investment tribunals ('bottom-up').[15] The latter, 'bottom-up' outlook does not appear to have been commonly or extensively explored. While some scholars have moved in that direction in the ISDS context, for instance, by correctly pointing out that the question of coherence is also strongly related to the theory of legal reasoning and interpretation,[16] the broader implications of positing such a link have yet to be examined.

I.2 Coherence, from the 'Bottom-up'

Based on the above, the current understanding of the concept of coherence in international law and international investment law seems to be incomplete and monolithic. It is incomplete because coherence is not given an independent meaning from related but distinct concepts such as consistency, correctness, or predictability. This causes terminological confusion as different concepts are used interchangeably.[17] The current understanding of coherence is also monolithic because most inquiries into the subject are done from a 'top-down' perspective that looks, either

15 The in-principle availability of 'top-down' and 'bottom-up' approaches to addressing coherence is not unique to international investment law and ISDS. For an example coming from the domain of regulatory convergence in international trade law, see R. Polanco and P. Sauvé, 'The Treatment of Regulatory Convergence in Preferential Trade Agreements' (2018) 17 *World Trade Review* 575.

16 E.g., see G. Zarra, 'The Issue of Incoherence in Investment Arbitration: Is There Need for a Systemic Reform?' (2018) 17 *Chinese Journal of International Law* 137, 167; J. Kurtz, 'Building Legitimacy through Interpretation in Investor–State Arbitration: On Consistency, Coherence, and the Identification of Applicable Law', in Z. Douglas, J. Pauwelyn, and J. E. Viñuales (eds.), *The Foundations of International Investment Law: Bringing Theory into Practice* (Oxford: Oxford University Press, 2014) 257, 274–280; V. Vadi, 'Towards Arbitral Path Coherence and Judicial Borrowing: Persuasive Precedent in Investment Arbitration' (2008) 5 *Transnational Dispute Management* 1; and generally, Radi (n. 1).

17 By contrast, as defined and used in this book: (i) coherence relates to the degree to which a set of legal propositions are rationally related to each other and to the ordering values or ordering principles that are thought to justify them (axiological compatibility), thus having a dual dimension that is both substantive and methodological; (ii) consistency relates to the absence of contradictions between a set of legal propositions; (iii) predictability relates to the law's ability to readily supply an answer to each and every question that may be raised presently or in the future; and (iv) correctness relates to the law's ability to supply determinately and demonstrably accurate answers to questions that may be raised presently or in the future. Furthermore, as understood in the book, coherence often incorporates elements of consistency, predictability, and correctness. But there exists no equivalency or logical entailment between coherence and the latter three concepts.

for so-called 'global' coherence between different regimes of international law (e.g., between international investment and international trade law), or for so-called 'local' coherence within a specialised regime of international law (e.g., within international investment law).

It is submitted that the 'top-down' outlook would not be an appropriate direction for the inquiry of this book to take. The principal reason for this is the absence of a single legislative will behind the creation of international law. International treaties and customary international law often come about as a result of conflicting motives and objectives. At times, they may even be the result of spontaneous reactions by states to external events.[18] Further to this, the diversification of international law into a variety of functional regimes makes it unlikely that the same goals, values, or governing principles are shared throughout beyond a minimum core.[19] Similar considerations apply if one elects to look only within international investment law itself. International investment law is heavily fragmented substantively (and to some extent also procedurally), comprising thousands separate, individual treaties. Therefore, one cannot readily assume that all states who have ever signed an investment treaty did so sharing the same *ex ante* understanding about guiding values or governing principles.[20] In short, rather than being imposed from the top or found determinately at a prior moment in time, a common understanding on guiding values and governing principles in international investment law must instead be constructed case by case in the course of the regime's existence and operation.

Consequently, this book adopts the aforementioned 'bottom-up' outlook for its inquiry into coherence. Such an outlook is further warranted considering the important role that arbitrators as decision-makers play in ISDS practice. Because of international investment law's fragmented and diffuse nature, arbitrators have become de facto agents of convergence in the system contributing to its intelligibility and gradual development over time. Given this, the book undertakes a jurisprudential examination

[18] ILC Fragmentation Report (n. 11), 23 (para 34).

[19] Cf. M. Koskenniemi, 'The Fate of Public International Law: Between Technique and Politics' (2007) 70 *Modern Law Review* 1, 15–19.

[20] As an additional remark, considering the largely piecemeal reaction of states vis-à-vis their expressed concerns about international investment law and ISDS, as well as the current unfavourable climate towards substantive reform in the UNCITRAL Working Group III discussions, one cannot readily assume that states would be willing to enter into a single international instrument covering both the substantive and the procedural aspects of international investment protection either.

of the interplay between coherence and judicial reasoning in ISDS, as opposed to a survey approach exclusively examining investment treaties and relevant arbitral case law in an effort to determine whether these exhibit coherence to some degree.[21] The latter approach is not followed here for the added reason that it seems to put the cart before the horse in this particular context. Focusing solely on surveying investment treaties and arbitral awards for their degree of coherence *inter se* begs the question of what coherence is and what its implications are in a judicial setting. Thus, if one hopes to engage into a reassessment of ISDS with a view to enhancing its coherence, one must first form a full picture of the content of coherence and its implications with respect to legal reasoning by international courts and tribunals. This requires both theorising coherence as a concept and identifying its manifestations in judicial reasoning.

Given the choice of a 'bottom-up' outlook, the core question with which the book grapples is therefore the following:

> How do considerations of coherence manifest in international adjudication and in ISDS in particular?

Answering this question involves the examination of several other lines of inquiry, which may also be formulated as additional sub-questions to be answered. These are:

(1) What is the content of coherence? What is its relation to legal reasoning by international courts and tribunals and what role, or roles, does it play therein?
(2) Is there a role for coherence during legal interpretation by international courts and tribunals, both with respect to the interpretation

[21] Generally, cf. L. Moral Soriano, 'A Modest Notion of Coherence in Legal Reasoning. A Model for the European Court of Justice' (2003) 16 *Ratio Juris* 296, 297, who describes this analytical process as follows: '[P]rior to asking whether the rule contained in a decision coheres with the legal system, one should ask whether the reasoning itself coheres.' According to Moral Soriano, scrutinising the coherence of judicial reasoning can still promote overall coherence in the legal system, albeit the way this is done is indirect. In particular, Moral Soriano argues (ibid., 300), overall systemic coherence is still promoted for two reasons: firstly, because an adjudicator cannot proceed to decide a case except by connecting together various parts of the legal system, even though these may not have an immediately apparent relation and, secondly, because in his or her decisions the adjudicator must also connect the norms of the legal system with political, constitutional, and moral theories, thus bringing together reasons that help to justify and support the legal system as a whole.

of international treaties as well as more broadly (e.g., analogical reasoning in ISDS)?

(3) Is there a role for coherence in the justification of decisions in international adjudication? What lessons may be drawn from a jurisprudential examination of coherence with respect to how investment arbitrators as dispute-resolving actors should discharge their duties?

Put differently, the book principally seeks to determine (i) how the concept of coherence manifests in the legal reasoning of international courts and tribunals, with a particular focus on ISDS tribunals (i.e., by way of what kind of methodology or arguments) and (ii) what could a search for coherence mean for the moral and ethical dispositions of arbitrators when deciding investment disputes. Importantly, this is not a purely descriptive inquiry. It has a normative core as it rests on certain presuppositions about the nature of law and the character of legal reasoning. These presuppositions must be made clear and be subjected to argument in the course of the inquiry.

I.3 The Thesis in a Nutshell

The book argues that the concept of coherence has a simultaneous dual dimension. One dimension of coherence is substantive (or ontological), referring to the determinate correctness or accuracy of the object to which coherence attaches. In this dimension, coherence is often seen as an ideal towards which to strive. The other dimension of coherence is methodological (or epistemic), referring to the demonstrable correctness or accuracy of the object to which coherence attaches. In this second dimension, coherence is seen as a process to be followed in order to reach and justify a decision or commit to a course of action vis-à-vis the object of one's inquiry in each case. It is argued that this interplay between substance and method is critical for legal reasoning by international courts and tribunals, including by ISDS tribunals. This is because legal reasoning is practical rather than simply theoretical. Legal reasoning is practical because it (i) seeks to commit one to a particular course of action to resolve a legal problem and (ii) is defeasible, meaning that it can be challenged and set aside not only on grounds of logical invalidity but also on grounds of implausibility and lack of persuasiveness.

Accordingly, on the substantive side, an expectation of coherence in law implies that law cannot be seen as being entirely distinct from moral considerations. Under the rubric of coherence, elements such as respect for the law's authority and its planning function, on the one hand, meet and become combined with demands that the law leads to morally just outcomes, on the other. Coherence describes the best possible combination of the above elements. This operation is akin to a balancing act and is performed by anyone who reasons about the law. In the context of international investment law, this operation is frequently performed by the arbitrators chosen to hear disputes between investors and states. Further, on the methodological side, coherence implies two key mental processes, namely, framing and contextualisation. Framing identifies the contours of the legal problem to be addressed. It singles out the legal questions to be answered and the goal(s) to be achieved on each occasion. Contextualisation places these issues against a larger normative context that will contribute to their eventual resolution. In ISDS, such context includes the various norms, past practices, and guiding principles found in the legal system, as well as the arbitrator's appreciation of the institutional role that he or she performs within that same system.

Thus understood, coherence is an endemic feature of arbitral decision-making in ISDS, and its manifestations therein are pervasive. Because of this, searching for coherence creates a particular kind of moral responsibility in arbitrators as dispute-resolving actors. Moral responsibility is here understood as encompassing certain desirable judicial dispositions, described in the book as 'virtues' to be practised by investment arbitrators during the performance of their judicial duties.

I.4 Outline of the Book's Chapters

In putting forward the above thesis, the book follows a three-step process of proof. Firstly, it demonstrates that, contrary to conventional wisdom, coherence is not a mere formal concept that is devoid of substantive content but that it has a dual dimension that is at once substantive and methodological. Secondly, it shows that coherence in its dual dimension is necessarily implied in judicial interpretation and argumentation in international law. Thirdly, it delves deeper by pointing out that, in addition to describing the quality of the judicial outcome itself, coherence also describes a general judicial attitude of reflexivity. Reflexivity helps justify judicial outcomes and further paves the way for recognising duties of professional moral responsibility to arbitrators.

The steps of the proof are reflected in the organisation of chapters. The book consists of seven substantive chapters that can be divided thematically as follows: conceptual foundations (Chapters 1–3), interpretation (Chapters 4–5), and justification (Chapters 6–7).

Chapters 1–3 provide a workable understanding of the concept of coherence and flesh out its relationship with legal reasoning. Questions to be answered in these chapters include: What kind of a concept is coherence? Are there any criteria normally associated with coherence? How strongly must individual elements fit together in a legal setting in order for the whole to be regarded as coherent? What roles does coherence play within legal reasoning?

Chapters 4–5 establish the link between considerations or presumptions of coherence and legal interpretation. Questions to be answered in these chapters include: Is there a connection between coherence and the VCLT rule of interpretation? What does coherence imply for the way ISDS tribunals use analogies?

Chapters 6–7 delve deeper into the relationship between coherence and judicial justification and, in so doing, also offer a synthesis of the book's main arguments and conclusions. Questions to be answered in these chapters include: Does coherence mandate reflexivity by arbitrators and, if yes, does this lead to a particular deliberative technique? What lessons could one draw regarding the professional moral responsibility of arbitrators as dispute-resolving actors?

A Coda then briefly brings the discussion back to ISDS reform and attempts a tentative assessment of the direction taken by the discussions at Working Group III, in light of the book's overall findings. This is followed by an Epilogue.

1

The Content of Coherence

1.1 Introduction

Coherence is a rather elusive concept to grasp. We have seen in the Introduction that coherence is conceptually under-theorised and under-scrutinised in international law and international investment law. Conventional wisdom seems to regard coherence as synonymous, or at least coterminous, with concepts such as legal certainty, consistency, or predictability. No doubt, links between the latter concepts and coherence do exist; however, reducing the meaning of coherence to these notions seems to be a mistake. This is not only because we tend to distinguish between the above concepts in ordinary language but also because it would seem redundant to have different words mean the exact same thing or serve identical purposes.

Therefore, before examining coherence in a legal setting, one needs to engage, as a preliminary matter, in an examination of the concept of coherence itself. Put differently, the question that must be asked at the outset is what kind of a concept coherence is, followed by an attempt to form an understanding of this concept's content. This foundational inquiry is precisely the aim of the present chapter. Because coherence is an elusive concept, a combination of ordinary understanding of the term and a theoretical assessment of it seems to be the appropriate way to go in creating a workable conception of coherence for our purposes.

The chapter's analysis proceeds as follows. To better frame the discussion, a brief introduction on concepts and concept types is first offered in Section 1.2. Three different concept types are identified: criterial concepts, natural-kind concepts, and interpretative concepts. As coherence is clearly not a natural-kind concept, Section 1.3 analyses coherence as a potential candidate concept of the criterial kind. It identifies three elements often associated with, and deemed necessary for, the existence of coherence in a legal setting: consistency, correctness, and comprehensiveness. Incidentally, these are also key concerns regarding the existing ISDS regime as expressed by state delegations and scholars. The section ultimately concludes that none of the three elements is necessary for coherence to exist in non-ideal practical situations. Based on this examination, Section 1.4 then shifts perspectives and characterises coherence as a concept of the interpretative kind. In so doing, the section illustrates the dual, substantive, and methodological dimension of coherence. Section 1.5 concludes by summarising the chapter's key findings and by setting the stage for the later steps of the inquiry.

1.2 A Primer on Concept Types

Concepts are useful tools for understanding the world around us, and we have several of these tools at our disposal. Following Dworkin, it is possible to identify three main types of concepts used in everyday life: criterial concepts, natural-kind concepts, and interpretative concepts.[1] People share and debate meaningfully about each type of concept in a different way.

Criterial concepts are those for which, for people to share them, there is a need for a series of shared criteria to identify instances of these concepts.[2] The concept of an equilateral triangle is an example of a criterial concept. In geometry, an equilateral triangle is a shape identified by three criteria: it has three equal sides, three equal angles, and three equal altitudes. If a shape has three equal sides, three equal angles, and three equal altitudes, then the shape in question is an equilateral triangle. And conversely, if we are told that the shape before us is an equilateral triangle, we would be justified in expecting it to have the above characteristics. A concept can be a 'vague' criterial too, when, even though people mainly agree about the correct criteria for its application, they tend to differ on a range of applications of these criteria that each person regards as marginal.[3] For instance, people may generally agree on the criteria that constitute the concept of a book (e.g., a series of pages bound together); but in this case, there exists vagueness at the margins of this

[1] R. Dworkin, *Justice for Hedgehogs* (Cambridge, MA: Harvard University Press, 2011), chapter 8.

[2] Ibid., 158.

[3] Ibid., 158–159.

criterion and therefore people may disagree on whether the concept obtains in certain situations (e.g., at what precise moment in binding pages together does a 'booklet' become a 'book'?).

The second type of concept are those of the natural kind. Natural-kind concepts have a fixed identity in nature. This is an essential structure – such as a specific chemical or molecular composition – without which they would not be the kind of thing that they are.[4] 'Tiger', 'lion', 'wood', and 'rock' are examples of concepts of this type. People share a natural-kind concept, therefore, not when they have a series of shared criteria that they can use to identify instances of that concept but when they have a physical or biological account of the concept's essential nature.

The third type of concept – interpretative concepts – is different still. Whereas the ability to share a criterial or a natural-kind concept depends on the existence of a decisive test of some kind, this is not the case for interpretative concepts. The latter type of concept can be shared even when there exists disagreement regarding the correct criteria of their application or on their inherent nature. According to Dworkin, an interpretative concept is shared by people participating in a practice that seeks to identify instances of that concept by appealing to the purpose that this concept has or the value that it serves.[5] Therefore, when people disagree about the specific criteria or the particular instances of application of an interpretative concept, they do not talk past each other. Rather, they disagree about the value or purpose of that concept. The concept of 'justice' is an example of an interpretative concept. People of all moral and political orientations can debate meaningfully about justice, despite frequently disagreeing about its criteria and about particular instances of justice or injustice.[6] People thus share the *concept* of justice but often disagree about particular *conceptions* of it. That is, they disagree about particular *interpretations* of what 'justice' mandates in specific situations.[7]

[4] Ibid., 159; also, R. Dworkin, *Justice in Robes* (Cambridge, MA: Harvard University Press, 2006), 224.

[5] Dworkin (n. 1), 160ff.

[6] Dworkin (n. 4), 224–225.

[7] See J. Rawls, *A Theory of Justice*, revised ed. (Cambridge, MA: Harvard University Press, 1999), 9 (emphases added): 'The *concept* of justice I take to be defined, then, by the role of its principles in assigning rights and duties and in defining the appropriate division of social advantages. A *conception* of justice is an interpretation of this role.'

Coherence is clearly not a natural-kind concept. It does not exist in nature, independently of people's thoughts and beliefs. It is less clear, however, whether coherence is a criterial or an interpretative concept. On the one hand, seen in the abstract, coherence does not appear to spark significant political or normative disagreements among people. We do not normally disagree, for instance, that coherence is desirable and valuable. This may suggest that coherence is not an interpretative but a criterial concept. On the other hand, we may well disagree about whether it is possible to fully achieve coherence, about whether this or that element is a characteristic element of coherence, or about the strength with which the individual aspects of a whole must fit together if the whole is to be described as coherent. These disagreements can be significant, but it remains to be seen whether they ultimately preclude us from sharing the concept of coherence in an independent manner. Indeed, if they do not, this would militate against coherence being a criterial concept.

Resolving the question of the conceptual nature of coherence at the outset is important to fully appreciate its role and implications in judicial reasoning during the later parts of the book. It is, moreover, important to resolve this question here in the context of the legal field and not in the abstract. Accordingly, the thesis that this chapter will pursue is that, despite often having criteria associated with it, coherence in a legal setting is an interpretative and not a criterial concept. To that end, Section 1.3 begins by examining concepts that are related to coherence in law and are commonly identified as its criteria (i.e., consistency, correctness, and comprehensiveness). Section 1.3 ultimately concludes that the presence of any of these related concepts is not necessary for coherence to exist in law.

1.3 Coherence and Related Concepts

Let us begin with a rather brief and loose definition of coherence given by Neil MacCormick, which may be roughly stated as follows: a lack of coherence results in a failure to make sense. An incoherent set of guiding norms of conduct, for instance, might be such that each could be fulfilled without infringing on any other, yet the whole would still seem to make no sense as constituting or mapping out a reasonable order of conduct.[8]

[8] N. MacCormick, *Rhetoric and the Rule of Law* (Oxford: Oxford University Press, 2005), 189, 230, 231.

According to similar statements by other authors, an object of inquiry would be coherent if it hangs together well, if its parts fit and are mutually supportive, if it is intelligible, or if it flows from or expresses a unified viewpoint; whereas, the object would be incoherent if it is unintelligible, self-contradictory, fragmented, or disjointed.[9]

A humorous example, again used by MacCormick, helps to make the point stand out clearer. Let us suppose, MacCormick says, that there exists a house where the cleaning rules are as follows: leave everything as untidy as possible on Mondays, Wednesdays, and Fridays, but tidy everything up to the highest perfection on Tuesdays, Thursdays, and Saturdays (with Sundays being reserved for resting). These rules can be easily observed, but they surely give rise to an unreasonable, indeed absurd, way of living since they do not seem to serve any immediately discernible end – in short, they make no sense. The image of coherence painted by this example and the general definitions above is that of a network, or interdependent web, between propositions and their justification standing or falling together as a unit.[10] It is therefore possible to restate the quality of being coherent as a function of the ability to 'make sense', as being the degree to which a set of propositions are rationally related to each other and to the ordering values or principles that are thought to justify them (which MacCormick usefully summarised in the following phrase: 'axiological compatibility among two or more rules').[11]

A key notion in the above statement is that of rationality, denoting the ability to justify one's choice of propositions and of ordering values or principles. This is appropriate since rationality is also a key feature in the legal field and in adjudication especially. For the purposes of this chapter, there is no need to go into detail on what rationality demands in the

[9] K. Kress, 'Coherence', in D. Patterson (ed.), *A Companion to Philosophy of Law and Legal Theory*, 2nd ed. (Malden, MA: Wiley-Blackwell, 2010) 521, 521; J. Raz, 'The Relevance of Coherence' (1992) 72 *Boston University Law Review* 273, 276.

[10] See Raz (n. 9), 287: '[W]e attribute beliefs, goals, and actions to people, not singly but in interdependent clumps. This interdependence means nothing other than a presumption of coherence.' For a similar understanding of coherence in a different discipline (text linguistics), see R.-A. de Beaugrande and W. U. Dressler, *Introduction to Text Linguistics* (London; New York: Longman, 1981), chapter V, para 23: 'Coherence will be envisioned as the outcome of combining concepts and relations into a network composed of knowledge spaces centred around main topics.'

[11] See the analysis in MacCormick (n. 8), 189–193, 230–231.

context of judicial justification. This is a task to be undertaken in Chapter 2. For the moment, it would be sufficient to note the following: first, that the concept of coherence has a link to justification, and second, that rationality in the legal context conjures up images of consistency (absence of contradictions), correctness of outcomes, and comprehensiveness of scope (predictability). Incidentally, these are also elements that scholars in the field of philosophy have considered as being possible criteria of coherence,[12] in addition to being clearly identified as causes of concern by state delegations participating in the ISDS reform debate.

In summary, to the extent that coherence is a function of the degree to which propositions are rationally related to each other and to ordering values or principles, the elements of consistency, correctness, and comprehensiveness may be regarded as determinants or 'criteria' of coherence. The remainder of this section thus examines the relationship and linkages between coherence and each of the three proposed criteria of it. To what extent are these necessary for coherence to exist?

1.3.1 Consistency (Non-contradiction)

Consistency is the first and most frequently invoked requirement of coherence. In the context of ISDS, so-called unjustifiable inconsistencies in arbitral awards is a key cause of concern for states, finding itself at the forefront of the discussions during the reform debate.[13] Conventional wisdom in both international investment law and general public international law seems to treat the concepts of coherence and consistency as synonymous or interchangeable in practice. However, upon closer inspection, this supposed necessary link between the two concepts is not borne out.

Consistency is satisfied in the absence of contradictions.[14] A series of propositions are mutually consistent if each can, without contradiction,

[12] See Kress (n. 9), 521.

[13] UNCITRAL, 'Report of Working Group III (Investor–State Dispute Settlement Reform) on the Work of Its Thirty-Sixth Session (Vienna, 29 October–2 November 2018)', UN Doc A/CN.9/964 (6 November 2018), 6–8 (esp. paras 28, 31, 39–40).

[14] L. A. Kornhauser and L. G. Sager, 'Unpacking the Court' (1986) 96 *Yale Law Journal* 82, 103 ('Of the two concepts [of consistency and coherence], consistency is easier to grasp and imposes a less stringent requirement. For our purposes, consistency is simply the state of non-contradiction, and two legal rules are inconsistent if and only if they are contradictory').

be asserted in conjunction with every other proposition and with their conjunction.[15] Consistency is thus an absolute and logical property. Two propositions either are or are not consistent. When we refer to inconsistencies in judicial decision-making, then, we more properly refer to decisions that reach opposing conclusions, despite having applied treaties with the same or very similar language and having addressed the same or very similar set of facts.

An often-quoted example of such an inconsistency in ISDS are the opposing outcomes in the *Lauder* v. *Czech Republic* and *CME* v. *Czech Republic* cases.[16] The *CME* case was brought under the Czech Republic-Netherlands BIT (1991) and the *Lauder* case was brought under the Czech Republic-United States BIT (1991). The two proceedings involved the same measure, alleged harm, and claimant from an economic perspective (Lauder brought a claim in his own name in one proceeding and as a shareholder of CME in the other). The two tribunals came to contradicting decisions. The *Lauder* tribunal partially dismissed the claims and did not order the payment of compensation, whereas the *CME* tribunal found the Czech Republic in full breach of the treaty and ordered the payment of compensation to the investor. Other examples of similar inconsistencies that have emerged over time in ISDS include the divergent interpretations on the applicability of MFN clauses to dispute settlement provisions, when this divergence cannot be traced to the particular wording of each treaty's text;[17] the divergent views about the meaning of the term 'investment' found

[15] MacCormick (n. 8), 190.

[16] *CME Czech Republic B.V.* v. *The Czech Republic*, UNCITRAL Rules, Partial Award, 13 September 2001; and *CME Czech Republic B.V.* v. *The Czech Republic*, UNCITRAL Rules, Final Award, 14 March 2003; *Ronald S. Lauder* v. *The Czech Republic*, UNCITRAL Rules, Final Award, 3 September 2001.

[17] Cf. *Emilio Agustín Maffezini* v. *The Kingdom of Spain*, ICSID Case No. ARB/97/7, Decision of the Tribunal on Objections to Jurisdiction, 25 January 2000 (allowing the use of the MFN clause and thus permitting the investor to circumvent the requirement to have recourse to domestic courts for eighteen months prior to initiating ISDS); with *Salini Costruttori S.p.A. and Italstrade S.p.A.* v. *The Hashemite Kingdom of Jordan*, ICSID Case No. ARB/02/13, Decision on Jurisdiction, 29 November 2004 (disallowing the use of the MFN clause and thus refusing the investor's attempt to create an otherwise non-existent ICSID jurisdiction).

in Article 25(1) of the ICSID Convention;[18] or the no less than four different approaches on the substantive scope of the umbrella clause.[19]

One way to resolve contradictions in law is by introducing a principle of prioritisation (e.g., *lex specialis derogat legi generali*, *lex posterior derogat legi priori*). Another, arguably more pervasive, approach is by way of interpretation.[20] Consider this. It is often said that consistency in a legal context means treating like things alike.[21] If one case is decided one way and a subsequent 'like' case is decided another way, then this would mean that the two tribunals have contradicted each other. This is

[18] Two kinds of divergent views can be identified in this respect:

(1) Whether the meaning of 'investment' in the ICSID Convention must be determined: independently of the definitions contained in individual treaties (known as the objective approach and found, e.g., in *Salini Costruttori S.p.A. and Italstrade S.p.A.* v. *Kingdom of Morocco*, ICSID Case No. ARB/00/4, Decision on Jurisdiction, 31 July 2001 (2003) 42 *International Legal Materials* 609, para 52); or rather by taking the treaty definitions into account (known as the subjective approach and found, e.g., in *Philippe Gruslin* v. *Malaysia*, ICSID Case No. ARB/99/3, Award, 27 November 2000, paras 13.5–13.6).

(2) When following the objective approach, whether all of the *Salini* criteria are relevant or necessary to conclude that an economic project is an 'investment' under the ICSID Convention (particularly controversial has been the criterion of the contribution to the host state's development: e.g., cf. *Malaysian Historical Salvors, SDN, BHD* v. *The Government of Malaysia*, ICSID Case No. ARB/05/10, Award on Jurisdiction, 17 May 2007, para 123; with *Saba Fakes* v. *Republic of Turkey*, ICSID Case No. ARB/07/20, Award, 14 July 2010, para 111).

[19] E.g., see J. Crawford, 'Treaty and Contract in Investment Arbitration' (2008) 21 *Arbitration International* 351.

[20] International Law Commission, 'Fragmentation of International Law: Difficulties Arising from the Diversification and Expansion of International Law – Report of the Study Group of the International Law Commission', UN Doc A/CN.4/L.682 (13 April 2006), 24–25 (para 36).

[21] E.g., C. Schreuer, 'Coherence and Consistency in International Investment Law', in R. Echandi and P. Sauvé (eds.), *Prospects in International Investment Law and Policy* (Cambridge: Cambridge University Press, 2013) 391, 391. On a more general note, the view that consistency means treating like cases alike is sometimes attributed to Dworkin (e.g., see R. Dworkin, *Law's Empire* [Cambridge, MA: Harvard University Press, 1986], 219). As this book draws substantially from Dworkin's theory, it should be clarified that this attribution may not be entirely accurate. Dworkin's use of the word 'consistency' is ambivalent. He distinguishes between 'narrow consistency' (or, sometimes, 'consistency in strategy') and 'consistency in principle'. He seems to regard the former as indicating the absence of contradiction, and the latter as indicating something closer to what has been here described as coherence (i.e., justification by appeal to values/principles). Dworkin also regards his preferred conception of law – law as integrity – as being about consistency in principle and not about mere narrow consistency (see, Dworkin, ibid., 133–135, 219–222).

true, but notice how the key criterion in finding a contradiction in this example is that of 'likeness'. To determine 'likeness', one must first decide that the two cases in question share enough similarities in principle that it is fair and just for both to have the same outcome or to be decided under the same substantive norm or under the same interpretation of the substantive norm. Indeed, this appears to be the reason why we perceive the existence of a contradiction in the *CME* and *Lauder* example mentioned above. Such an inquiry, however, appears to be more about coherence rather than mere consistency. The general point thus being made here is that there exists scope, sometimes considerable scope, for interpretative discretion when dealing with apparent contradictions in law. In other words, something that appears inconsistent may still be coherent, and conversely, an appearance of consistency between two situations, cases, or propositions may end up being illusory if one examines the statement of reasons offered in their support.

The difference between consistency and coherence just sketched out is usefully demonstrated in the treatment of the *Charanne* v. *Spain*[22] decision by the subsequent tribunal in *Eiser* v. *Spain*.[23] The two cases involved the same host state (Spain), the same investment treaty (the ECT), investors in the same sector (renewable energy and, in particular, ownership of solar power plants), and broadly the same measures (a series of energy reforms affecting Spain's renewables sector as a whole). During the *Eiser* hearing, and in response to the investor's FET claim, Spain raised the *Charanne* decision – which had dismissed the investor's claims – as governing authority for how the *Eiser* case should be decided.[24] Finding against Spain, the *Eiser* tribunal distinguished the circumstances of the *Charanne* case from the ones before it. In particular, it held that the factual and legal situation before it differed fundamentally from that addressed in *Charanne*, that the measures complained of in

[22] *Charanne B.V. and Construction Investments S.à.r.l.* v. *Spain*, SCC Case No. V 062/2012, Award, 21 January 2016.

[23] *Eiser Infrastructure Limited and Energía Solar Luxembourg S.à r.l.* v. *Kingdom of Spain*, ICSID Case No. ARB/13/36, Award, 4 May 2017. It is noted here that the *Eiser* award has been annulled in its entirety (see *Eiser Infrastructure Limited and Energía Solar Luxembourg S.à r.l.* v. *Kingdom of Spain*, ICSID Case No. ARB/13/36, Decision on the Kingdom of Spain's Application for Annulment, 11 June 2020). However, the award was annulled on the grounds of improper constitution of the tribunal and of serious departure from a fundamental rule of procedure, under Article 52(1)(a) and (d) of the ICSID Convention. Both grounds are thus unrelated to the substance or the reasoning of the award, which is the focus of the example here.

[24] *Eiser* v. *Spain*, Award, para 53.

Charanne had far less dramatic effects on that investment, and that the damage claimed by the investor in *Charanne* was far less sweeping.[25] In the *Eiser* tribunal's words:

> [The *Charanne* tribunal] decision did not address . . . the key actions at issue in this case. Instead, the case addressed much less sweeping changes to the photovoltaic regulatory regime, changes that produced far less drastic economic consequences for the *Charanne* claimants.[26]

At the same time, it is important to note that the *Eiser* tribunal still considered that the statements of principle expressed in *Charanne* with respect to the ECT's FET provision were well-founded. In particular, the *Eiser* tribunal agreed with the view expressed in *Charanne* that any changes to a state's regulatory regime may not be random or unnecessary or suddenly and unexpectedly remove the essential features of the regulatory framework previously in place.[27] In other words, both tribunals agreed on the level of abstract principle (i.e., on the relevant considerations when changing one's regulatory regime); yet according to the *Eiser* tribunal, the two cases had enough key differences between them that a different outcome was warranted. Cast in this light, the contradiction in outcomes between the two decisions is only apparent and upon closer inspection they seem to cohere with each other, at least on the FET point.

The *Charanne*/*Eiser* example thus confirms that the mere fact that two propositions appear contradictory is not necessarily evidence of them being incoherent, since the contradiction may be explained (or interpreted) away by appeal to a guiding value or principle.[28] By the same token, an appearance of consistency does not necessarily indicate coherence either. Consider, for example, a hypothetical scenario where the *Charanne* and *Eiser* tribunals, this time faced with the exact same series of challenged measures, rendered the same outcome with respect to Spain's FET liability. Their decisions would still not be coherent if each tribunal used a different set of guiding values or governing principles to

[25] Ibid., 367–368.

[26] Ibid., para 369.

[27] Ibid., para 370.

[28] See also, P. Webb, 'Factors Influencing Fragmentation and Convergence in International Courts', in M. Andenas and E. Bjorge (eds.), *A Farewell to Fragmentation: Reassertion and Convergence in International Law* (Cambridge: Cambridge University Press, 2015) 146, 151 ('Convergence does not equate to uniformity; as long as disparities in treatment of the same or similar legal issues are explained and justified, the end result can still be convergence').

construe the investor's legitimate expectations while interpreting the FET standard.[29]

So far, we have talked about apparent contradictions causing apparent inconsistency. What if the contradictions are true and cannot be explained or interpreted away?[30] It seems clear that a series of propositions mired with such true contradictions would be incoherent as they would likely not point towards a common set of guiding norms of conduct. But this observation cannot take us very far. What if contradictions are not widespread but instead localised or partial? Is coherence necessarily affected as a result?

The answer seems to be negative. Kress has pointed out that some consistency at some point in time is a necessary condition for coherence in theory but not necessarily so in practice.[31] Therefore, the existence of some inconsistencies does not necessarily mean that the whole is incoherent because of them.[32] We would not, for example, say that a state's

[29] E.g., cf. *Técnicas Medioambientales Tecmed, S.A.* v. *The United Mexican States*, ICSID Case No. ARB(AF)/00/2, Award, 29 May 2003, para 154; and *MTD Equity Sdn. Bhd. and MTD Chile S.A.* v. *Republic of Chile*, ICSID Case No. ARB/01/7, Award, 25 May 2004, paras 113–114 (both imposing duties of total transparency, stability and predictability of the legal environment as components of legitimate expectations); with *Philip Morris Brands Sàrl, Philip Morris Products S.A. and Abal Hermanos S.A.* v. *Oriental Republic of Uruguay (formerly FTR Holding S.A., Philip Morris Products S.A. and Abal Hermanos S.A.* v. *Oriental Republic of Uruguay)*, ICSID Case No. ARB/10/7, Award, 8 July 2016, paras 429–430 (relying instead on a theory of detrimental reliance to determine the legitimacy of an investor's expectations).

[30] The qualifier 'true' is precisely meant to exclude situations, such as the one between the *Eiser* and *Charanne* decisions described above, where contradictions are more apparent than real and can thus be resolved by an appropriate interpretation of the norm(s) concerned. By way of example, it is not contradictory to simultaneously assert a state's power to regulate and its duty to treat investors fairly and equitably, for instance, by not frustrating their legitimate expectations, if one construes legitimate expectations under a standard of reasonableness. By contrast, an example of a true contradiction would be between a norm that provides for a duty to do *x* and one that provides for a liberty to abstain from doing *x*. The duty and the liberty cannot logically co-exist, and the contradiction cannot be interpreted away.

[31] Kress (n. 9), 528.

[32] Cf. MacCormick (n. 8), 190 (footnote omitted):

> Complete consistency is not a necessary condition of coherence, since unlike consistency, coherence can be a matter of degree. A story can be coherent on the whole and as a whole, though it contains some internal inconsistencies – and in this case, the sense of the overall coherence of the story may be decisive for us in deciding which among pairs of inconsistent propositions to disregard as anomalies in an overall coherence account or opinion.

entire legal system lacks coherence just because the decisions produced by that state's courts may on occasion truly contradict each other. In the same vein, despite occasional true contradictions in ISDS awards, lawyers are still able to praise or criticise tribunals for the decisions they produce. Giving praise and rendering critical assessments are only possible on an assumption of coherence about what international investment law requires and about how a particular case ought to be decided.

In that sense, inconsistency at some point in time can be regarded as necessary case-by-case experimentation in the face of legal uncertainty or novelty, ultimately aiming towards the development of a coherent approach. By the same logic, we may also conclude that complete consistency or complete consistency over time are not necessary requirements for coherence either. In fact, complete consistency over time may not even be desirable in law.[33] Being a logical proposition, consistency tends to be agnostic towards the merits of the elements that are made consistent.[34] Ironically, then, in some circumstances greater consistency may perpetuate or foster injustice. It follows that the coherence of law is not necessarily undermined by the presence of inconsistencies over time. The need for change, evolution, and progressive development are indeed well-recognised in the legal field. If we were to require consistency over time as a necessary condition for coherence, then we would reach the counter-intuitive conclusion that any change in the settled law of a system – even if morally beneficial – would automatically count against that system's overall coherence. To the contrary, rather, some inconsistencies over time may in fact help to strengthen overall coherence depending on the reasons offered for the divergence. This is a point of particular importance in ISDS, where development often takes place case by case and not by way of a preordained legislative plan.

1.3.2 Correctness (Right Answers)

The ability to arrive at right answers is often regarded as an additional requirement associated with coherence. The requirement of correctness

[33] A similar point is made by J. Arato, C. Brown, and F. Ortino, 'Parsing and Managing Inconsistency in Investor–State Dispute Settlement' (2020) 21 *Journal of World Investment and Trade* 336, 339.

[34] See T. Schultz, 'Against Consistency in Investment Arbitration', in Z. Douglas, J. Pauwelyn, and J. E. Viñuales (eds.), *The Foundations of International Investment Law: Bringing Theory into Practice* (Oxford: Oxford University Press, 2014) 297.

states that a coherent whole should be able to determine the single correct outcome in particular cases.[35] Transposing the criterion of correctness to the legal field, we may then say that if law is to be a coherent whole it must provide us with the determinately correct answer to each and every legal question raised. Given the remarks made above on the nuanced differences between consistency and coherence, such a strong presupposition regarding the link between coherence and correctness seems to need some elaboration and nuance also. This is even more so considering that correctness in law cannot be simply reduced to an outcome (e.g., 'the law demands *x* to be done'; 'party A must bear liability'). Correctness in law, rather, seems to be a combination of the outcome and the reasons offered in support of the outcome.

There does exist correlation between coherence and correctness in law, but there are reasons to doubt that it extends to causation. The key to understanding why that is so lies in the proper understanding of the term 'determinate' – seen in the phrase 'determinately correct answer' above – and in its contradistinction with the notion of demonstrability. In philosophical parlance, determinacy is a species of ontological objectivity describing the way things really are – their nature and existence – in this case by making particular reference to their ability to produce accurate answers.[36] A question therefore has a determinate answer whenever there exists a reason or a series of reasons compelling that answer. To say that the answer is determinate in the sense of compelled means that the reasons offered in its support carry the greatest weight out of all other competing plausible reasons.[37] Conversely, the answer to a question is indeterminate whenever the reasons that can be offered for or against a plausible answer are all of equal strength and weight, so that no choice is ultimately better than any other.[38] Determinacy and indeterminacy are

[35] Kress (n. 9), 528. Kress calls this, the 'completeness' requirement of coherence.

[36] See M. H. Kramer, *Objectivity and the Rule of Law* (Cambridge: Cambridge University Press, 2007), chapter 1.

[37] See R. Dworkin, 'Objectivity and Truth: You'd Better Believe It!' (1996) 25 *Philosophy and Public Affairs* 87, 129–131. For a more in-depth examination on the various strengths of a statement of reasons see Section 2.2.2.

[38] The indeterminacy thesis applied in the legal context is a sceptical view about the law. In the domain of international law, this thesis has been expressed, e.g., in M. Koskenniemi, *From Apology to Utopia: The Structure of International Legal Argument*, reissue with a new epilogue (Cambridge: Cambridge University Press, 2005); and D. Kennedy, 'Theses about International Law Discourse' (1980) 23 *German Yearbook of International Law* 353. For an argument against the indeterminacy thesis in law, see Dworkin (n. 37).

properties that obtain in degrees.[39] The stronger the reasons offered the more they would determine the answer that derives from them. Conversely, the weaker the reasons the less they would determine the answer they seek to support.

The above holds true for the determinacy of law also. Law has an arguable character, meaning that any statement about its content is in reality an argument supported by reasons whose relative strength may vary.[40] Evaluating the relative strength of competing legal arguments is bound to be a matter of degree and calling for judgment.[41] This further means that, barring instances of clear and obvious mistakes,[42] correctness in law often tends to be in the eye of the beholder. To clarify, the intention behind such a statement is not to advocate for a sceptical view about law – that is to say, a view that regards law as hopelessly indeterminate. Rather, the point is simply made to note that it may not always be easy to identify cases where errors of law have been made, since, usually, one characterises a case as 'wrongly decided' because one disagrees with the normative choices underlying the court's reasoning and not because there has been an obvious error of law in the judgment.[43] This holds especially true in international investment law where the core standards of investment protection tend to be evaluative in character and rather vaguely drafted, thus leaving a generally wide margin of discretion to arbitrators.

Determinacy can be contrasted to demonstrability. The latter term denotes the ability to demonstrate the correctness of a proposition to the

[39] Kramer (n. 36), 15.

[40] See J. B. White, 'Law as Language: Reading Law and Reading Literature' (1981–1982) 60 *Texas Law Review* 415, 436: '[T]he law can more properly be seen not as a set of commands or rules, even with a set of restatable principles or values behind them, but as the culture of argument and interpretation through the operations of which the rules acquire their life and ultimate meaning.'

[41] MacCormick (n. 8), 14.

[42] For instance, the confluence of treaty-based and customary law-based defences of necessity in international law (found, e.g., in *CMS Gas Transmission Company* v. *The Republic of Argentina*, ICSID Case No. ARB/01/8, Award, 12 May 2005) is an example of a clear error of law, given that the law of state responsibility comprises secondary rather than primary norms. It has moreover been recognised as such by the *CMS* annulment committee (see *CMS Gas Transmission Company* v. *The Republic of Argentina*, ICSID Case No. ARB/01/8, Decision of the *Ad Hoc* Committee on the Application for Annulment of the Argentine Republic, 25 September 2007, paras 128–136).

[43] See E. Sardinha, 'The Impetus for the Creation of an Appellate Mechanism' (2017) 32 *ICSID Review – Foreign Investment Law Journal* 503, 514 (reporting on a view previously expressed by arbitrator J. Christopher Thomas).

satisfaction of everyone or virtually everyone.[44] Rather than being an ontological state, demonstrability refers to the epistemic state of rational agents having formed a justified belief on the correctness of the proposition in question. Like determinate correctness, demonstrable correctness is also a matter of degree.[45] Some answers may be more demonstrably correct than others. In addition, propositions that were once subject to uncertainty or disagreement may not be so presently and vice-versa. Notwithstanding this similarity, determinate and demonstrable correctness are non-equivalent properties given their different natures. One does not entail the other. A determinately correct answer may not be accepted by everyone as such and, conversely, an answer that everyone accepts as correct may not be determinately so (e.g., perhaps there exist stronger reasons pointing towards a different answer, yet these reasons are still in the minority). A further difference between the two is that, given its nature, demonstrability primarily depends on the methods used to arrive at a particular conclusion as opposed to only being concerned with the substance of the reasons offered in support of said conclusion.[46]

Both determinate and demonstrable correctness can be linked to coherence. However, since it was said that determinate and demonstrable correctness are not absolutes but matters of degree, the link to coherence must be the following. One person's 'correct' interpretation or decision may still be thought to cohere better than another's, given the justification offered for each interpretation or decision and given the method used to arrive at them. Consequently, on the one hand, the existence of a coherent process of reasoning would mean that the outcome of it has a claim to correctness but also, on the other hand, such claim would not be absolute, since another person's process of reasoning may have been performed better, thus making the latter person's chosen outcome arguably more coherent and with a stronger claim to correctness.

Transposed to law, therefore, an otherwise coherent process of justification may still result in a decision that we may regard as legally incorrect. An adjudicator may use an appropriate method and link the various aspects of the legal system together in a competent manner (e.g., by properly identifying the relevant materials, legal norms, or past practices) but may nonetheless make a substantive, value-laden interpretation of them with which at least some participants in the legal system may not

[44] Kramer (n. 36), 17.
[45] Ibid., 46–47.
[46] Ibid., 47–48.

agree.[47] By the same token, the following would also seem to apply: determining that a judicial decision is coherent cannot be exclusively a function of the extent to which the decision is considered to be correct in its substance. An adjudicator may reach a morally correct decision, which everyone would agree that the law ought to provide, yet do so through contradictory reasoning or through a not well-justified process where the various elements of the legal system have not been linked together adequately or accurately.[48] In such a case, we may be inclined to conclude that the decision would still lack in coherence despite the substantive correctness of the outcome.[49]

1.3.3 *Comprehensiveness of Scope (Predictability)*

Comprehensiveness of scope is yet a third requirement often associated with coherence. Comprehensiveness of scope implies that a coherent object of study is free of gaps and, consequently, that it can readily supply an answer to each and every question that may be raised,[50] perhaps even without much substantive deliberation or analysis. A system can be comprehensive in this way, for instance, by having in place a closing rule of some kind (e.g., 'absent an expressed prohibition there exists a presumption of freedom').[51] Comprehensiveness is thus linked to the ability

[47] As an example of a case in point in the ISDS context, one could look at the disagreement between the majority and the dissent in the 2016 *Philip Morris* v. *Uruguay* award. The case is examined in detail in Section 5.5.2.

[48] Institutional design in international law confirms this assessment. Take the example of the WTO Appellate Body. According to Article 17.13 of the DSU: 'The Appellate Body may uphold, modify or reverse the legal findings and conclusions of the panel.' It is confirmed in the literature that the Appellate Body upholds when it agrees with both the reasoning and the conclusions reached by the Panel, modifies when it agrees with the conclusions but not with the reasoning leading up to them, and reverses when it disagrees with both the reasoning and the conclusions reached (see P. van den Bossche and W. Zdouc, *The Law and Policy of the World Trade Organization: Text, Cases and Materials*, 4th ed. [Cambridge: Cambridge University Press, 2017], 243). It is worth noting here that the same formula is also followed by the EU's investment protection agreements in relation to the powers of the Appellate Tribunals created under them. For instance, see Article 8.28(2) Canada-EU CETA (2016), Article 3.19(2)–(3) EU-Singapore IPA (2018), Article 3.54(2)–(3) EU-Viet Nam IPA (2019).

[49] A case in point in the ISDS context is arguably the decision in *Phoenix Action, Ltd.* v. *The Czech Republic*, ICSID Case No. ARB/06/5, Award, 15 April 2009, which is examined in detail in Section 6.3.5.

[50] Kress (n. 9), 528.

[51] For a version of this in international law, see *The Case of the S.S. 'Lotus' (France* v. *Turkey)*, Judgment of 7 September 1927, PCIJ Series A No 10 (1927) 4, 18. However,

to predict. In a legal setting, predictability is the corollary of the value of legal certainty, as it describes one's ability to anticipate or foresee one's legal situation following certain action or inaction. Legal certainty and predictability are in turn linked to the concept of the rule of law, since they allow the law's addressees to plan their conduct.[52] It thus comes as no surprise to see that a general absence of predictability in the way ISDS decisions turn out is among the reasons why states wish to reform the existing system.

An important feature of comprehensiveness as predictability is that it is a property that obtains in degrees. It may be a reasonable assumption to make that if an object of inquiry is sufficiently comprehensive and thus exhibits a high degree of predictability, then it would also be coherent as a result. However, although there does exist correlation between coherence and comprehensiveness, it is again doubtful whether this also extends to causation. In other words, comprehensiveness does seem to improve the chances of overall coherence but probably cannot guarantee it; and, conversely, coherence does seem to improve the chances of eventually experiencing comprehensiveness (and hence predictability) over time but probably cannot guarantee that either.[53] This conclusion

cf. different readings of the *Lotus* principle, recasting it not as a 'presumption of freedom' but as a 'presumption against freedom', seen under the light of a general principle of coexistence, in A. Hertogen, 'Letting *Lotus* Bloom' (2015) 26 *European Journal of International Law* 901; O. Spiermann, '*Lotus* and the Double Structure of International Legal Argument', in L. Boisson de Chazournes and P. Sands (eds.), *International Law, the International Court of Justice and Nuclear Weapons* (Cambridge: Cambridge University Press, 1999) 131; *Legality of the Threat or Use of Nuclear Weapons*, Advisory Opinion of 8 July 1996, ICJ Rep (1996) 226, Dissenting Opinion of Judge Shahabuddeen, 393–394.

52 See MacCormick (n. 8), 12, stating that:

> The Rule of Law is a signal virtue of civilized societies. Where the Rule of Law obtains, the government of a state . . . is carried on within a framework laid down by law. This gives significant security for the independence and dignity of each citizen. Where the law prevails, you know where you are, and what you are able to do without getting yourself embroiled in civil litigation or in the criminal justice system.

Indeed, a legal norm that gives truly contradictory guidance to its addressees is a flawed legal norm insofar as it renders them unable to plan their conduct. The more norms of this kind there exist in a system of social ordering that purports to be 'legal', the more doubts one is justified in having as to whether that system deserves that label jurisprudentially or morally (see, Kramer [n. 36], 125–130, 158–164).

53 On the non-equivalency between comprehensiveness/predictability and coherence, also see Kress (n. 9), 528.

follows logically from the previous examination of the links between coherence and consistency and coherence and correctness. A few brief remarks would thus suffice here.

Consider, first, the lack of necessary entailment between comprehensiveness and coherence. As we have seen, complete consistency at a time or over time is not a necessary requirement for coherence. Accordingly, the predictability that would normally result from a consistent line of interpretations or applications of the law does not mean that these would necessarily exhibit coherence also. Furthermore, one need not be fully comprehensive in scope, or perfectly predictable at the outset, in order to be coherent. This applies especially in law, considering again the aforementioned need for change and progressive development following the occurrence of novel situations not covered in the existing legal instruments or following a change in collective attitudes and beliefs. Therefore, even when there are gaps in the law, these can still be coherently filled as and when they arise. The latter will apply with greater force if there is clarity within the legal system with respect to guiding values or principles and the interpretation to be given to them.

By the same token, the inverse situation also holds true. There appears to be no necessary entailment between coherence, on the one hand, and predictability or comprehensiveness, on the other hand. Coherence does not preclude the need at times to strike a different path than what past consistent practice may indicate. Nor does coherence preclude the existence of gaps in law, although, as it will be argued in Chapter 3, pronouncing the existence of a legal gap may be more a question of interpretation than an empirical declaration.

1.3.4 Summing up

It is now time to pause and take stock of the above discussion. How do consistency, correctness, and comprehensiveness fare as determinants of coherence? In the abstract, it seems that the occurrence of all three of them is necessary to describe an object of study as coherent in ideal theory. That is to say, the perfect coexistence of all three elements will necessarily render the object of study perfectly coherent in an ideal situation; conversely, the absence of all three elements would render the object incoherent. However, based on the preceding analysis, the same conclusion does not seem to follow in practical, non-ideal situations. The following three points can be summarised here.

The first point is that, although certainly desirable for coherence to exist, consistency does not appear to be a necessary or sufficient requirement of it. That is to say, the presence or absence of consistency does not necessarily mean that coherence obtains or that coherence is forfeit. In fact, consistency seems to be the dependent concept when seen against coherence. Often, it is a sense of coherence that makes us either disregard contradictions as being only apparent or indeed call them out as being true. The second point is that correctness is likewise not necessary as a criterion for coherence. Although there seems to exist correlation between correctness (both determinate and demonstrable) and coherence in law, this does not extend to causation given the law's arguable character and the scope within it for debate and reasonable disagreement. Judicial outcomes may not always be determinately correct, yet they could still exhibit a degree of coherence with some of the system's principles or values and be supported by a competently drafted statement of reasons. Incoherence resulting from a complete disregard of a system's norms, practices, and principles, or resulting from a complete disregard of the ways of structuring and presenting legal arguments, is likely to be a rare occurrence. The third point is that the same considerations also apply by extension with respect to comprehensiveness as a determinant of coherence. Some unpredictability resulting from an absence of comprehensiveness is not necessarily a sign of incoherence. The law is always a work in progress and unpredictable outcomes may be caused by courts using a novel doctrine or a novel theory that are not yet perfectly coherent but are still above an unspecified threshold of coherence.

Harkening back to the question posed at the outset of this section, what do the above conclusions mean for the criterial or interpretative nature of coherence? If coherence in law were criterial then we could only perceive it to the extent, if any, that it entails or is entailed by consistency, correctness, and comprehensiveness as its criteria.[54] That is to say, the conclusion 'coherent or incoherent' would necessarily follow from any statement about the law, so long as we considered that statement to be consistent, correct, or comprehensive (predictable). However, as the

[54] Recall that people share a criterial concept when there is an agreed, defined test for determining instances of that concept. Absent agreement on such a test, people talk about different concepts. A concept is a vague criterial when there exist marginal instances in using the agreed test where people can disagree as to whether the test obtains. In such instances, people still share the criterial concept because they disagree on the extent to which the defining test applies to those marginal cases and not on the contents of the test itself.

discussion above showed, this does not appear to be the case. To the contrary, we are ultimately not precluded from perceiving coherence in practice or from debating about coherence meaningfully, even when some of the above-identified elements are satisfied to a lesser extent or are entirely missing. This militates against coherence being a criterial concept and instead points towards it being an interpretative concept.

1.4 Coherence and the Dimensions of Substance and Method

To recall, people can share an interpretative concept despite on occasion disagreeing on a decisive test for determining when that concept applies. This is possible because assessments of the correct application of interpretative concepts are fixed by what people consider to be the best interpretation of the social practices in which such concepts figure.[55] When using an interpretative concept, one is thus directly engaging in an interpretation of the practice in which that concept is found.[56] Consequently, in the case of the interpretative concept of coherence in law, one must be thought of as engaging in an interpretation of the legal practice itself every time an assessment is made on the coherence of a legal pronouncement.[57] This conclusion will indeed be borne out in greater detail in the course of the book. For present purposes, this section seeks to clearly draw out two critical dimensions of coherence in law, already alluded to in the discussion above, that derive from its interpretative nature. These are the dimensions of substance and method. They will be used to frame the analysis in subsequent chapters.

We begin with the dimension of substance. The elements of consistency, correctness, and comprehensiveness were examined above since they are often associated with coherence as its criteria, at least in ideal situations. It was concluded that they are not necessary for coherence, although there does appear to exist a correlation between them and coherence. That is, one could still make assessments about consistency, correctness, and predictability and use them in an overall argument about coherence. This implies that there exists a threshold below which a proposition is incoherent and above which it is coherent. However, it

[55] Dworkin (n. 1), 160.
[56] Ibid., 163–164.
[57] For coherence as being the result of interpretation, also see M.-E. Conte, 'Coherence in Interpretation', in W. Heydrich, F. Neubauer, and Others (eds.), *Connexivity and Coherence: Analysis of Text and Discourse* (Berlin: Walter de Gruyter, 1989) 275.

was said above that correctness and comprehensiveness are scalar properties that can be fulfilled in degrees. It was also said that consistency is a non-scalar and absolute property but that its existence is nevertheless not required, or indeed possible, or even desirable at times. Identifying the threshold of coherence in the abstract may thus not be possible in practice. This applies especially in law, where exact determinations of coherence or incoherence may be precarious without considering the facts of a situation and the arguments put forward by the parties involved. In short, there will inevitably exist borderline cases where people will reasonably disagree as to the coherence of a judicial pronouncement.

However, in so disagreeing about whether coherence obtains, people must still offer reasons to justify their assessment if they hope to persuade others. Statements about the law's content being in fact arguments, they must be supported by reasons attesting to their authoritativeness or moral imperativeness. Indeed, as Chapter 3 will point out in greater detail, authoritativeness and moral imperativeness are inherent dimensions of the legal practice.[58] This introduces a substantive dimension to coherence. Coherence in law is therefore intimately linked to the law's arguable character and the elements of authoritativeness and moral imperativeness. In its substantive dimension, coherence is often seen as an ideal towards which law-interpreters and law-appliers must strive. At the same time, it is likely to also be an unattainable ideal.

One can appreciate an additional dimension of the interpretative nature of coherence alongside its substantive dimension, if one delves deeper on the question of the scalability of the property of being coherent, which is to say, of the extent to which the property itself obtains by degrees. The fact that coherence is linked to the arguable character of the law may lead one to the conclusion that the concept of coherence is itself also a matter of degree. This conclusion is seemingly further buttressed by the fact that it is common in everyday speech to refer to something as being 'more (or less) coherent' than something else.

[58] Chapter 3 argues further that a better way to look at law is through the lens of interpretivism. Yet, for present purposes, one need not commit to interpretivism to accept the statement about authoritativeness and moral imperativeness being inherent dimensions of the legal practice. In fact, Chapter 3 also shows that legal positivism clearly recognises that adjudicators must reach to morality for the correct answer, at least when they are faced with a genuinely hard case.

Such a conclusion should be resisted. It is not the case that, just because some of the elements of an object *x* are scalable, then *x* itself is also scalable.[59] According to Thomas Schultz, we can see why that is not the case if we distinguish between the existence of *x* and the purposeful enterprise of seeking to do *x*. The two, Schultz argues, are not necessarily equitable.[60] The purposeful enterprise of doing *x* may be done more or less well, so that the outcome of this process may be more or less good, clear, or straightforward, but it can still be the case that the outcome itself is or is not *x*. For example, a 200-page-long fictional narrative is more clearly a 'novel' than a 50-page-long one, but at the end of the day both either are or are not 'novels'. The 50-page-long fictional narrative cannot be 'less of a novel' than the 200-page-long one, although upon reflection it may be more accurate to call it a 'novella' rather than a 'novel' given its size.[61]

The concept of coherence works similarly. The purposeful enterprise of an adjudicator seeking to make a coherent interpretation of the law and render a coherent decision can be done more or less well, yet the outcome of this exercise will eventually be characterised as coherent or incoherent. The gradual nature of the evolution of the manner in which the enterprise is conducted does not mean that the outcome of it obtains by degrees also. The evolution rather reaches a certain threshold and then the difference in degree becomes a difference in kind, much like ice turns to water and eventually to steam by the introduction of heat.[62] This threshold, we have already seen, cannot be identified in the abstract. Because the law has an arguable character, determining whether the threshold of coherence has been crossed in each case is bound to be a matter of judgment and even be the subject of reasonable disagreement.

Notice, however, that in introducing the element of the 'purposeful enterprise' of seeking to make a coherent interpretation, we have shed light on an additional dimension of the interpretative concept of coherence: coherence as a method and a process. The latter dimension

[59] T. Schultz, *Transnational Legality: Stateless Law and International Arbitration* (Oxford: Oxford University Press, 2014), 69.

[60] Ibid.

[61] Ibid. Cf., also, another example used by Schultz, ibid., 70: '[T]he differences in musical achievement between Madonna and Ludwig van Beethoven are clear (to most people), but we cannot say that the 9th Symphony is "more" music than *Ray of Light*.'

[62] Ibid., 70.

complements the dimension of substance.[63] Suppose, for example, that one were to ask whether ISDS awards exhibit coherence. Based on the discussion in this chapter, we may be inclined to answer in the affirmative. In most cases, most decisions do seem to cross the threshold of coherence. They generally do 'make sense', they generally do attempt to connect the various elements of the international legal system and make them converge, and they generally do exhibit internal unity in their reasoning. But saying this should not signal the end of the matter or the end of our interest into coherence in law and into its various manifestations.

Legal reasoning is the means through which adjudicators arrive at and justify conclusions on points of law. Legal reasoning, we shall see in more detail in Chapter 2, is also a purposive enterprise and may thus be deployed more or less well, which would in turn bear on whether the outcome of it can be described as coherent or incoherent. Therefore, even in cases where one believes that the unspecified minimum threshold for coherence has been achieved from a substantive standpoint, the method used to reach the outcome matters still. The better this process has been undertaken, the more *clearly* coherent, and therefore the more robust or persuasive, the outcome would be perceived to be.

The manifestations of these two dimensions of coherence are ubiquitous in law and the judicial function. Indeed, as the subsequent chapters of this book will show, coherence manifests in a variety of ways in the structure of legal reasoning, in treaty interpretation, in analogical reasoning in ISDS, in the justification of decisions, as well as in the professional moral responsibility of arbitrators as dispute-resolving actors.

1.5 Conclusion: Expanding the Debate on Coherence

This first chapter has served the foundational aim of engaging into a theoretical examination of the concept of coherence. This has been necessary to better anchor the analysis that is to be undertaken in later chapters. In so doing, the chapter adopted the 'bottom-up' outlook identified in the Introduction and has thus principally looked at

[63] For a similar in spirit use of coherence as both an end (i.e., substance) and a means (i.e., process/method), cf. P. Mumford, 'Regulatory Coherence: Blending Trade and Regulatory Policy' (2014) 10 *Policy Quarterly* 3.

coherence from the point of view of legal reasoning. Five main conclusions from this examination are briefly summarised below.

Firstly, in general terms, the property of being coherent can be defined as the extent to which a set of propositions exhibit 'axiological compatibility'. This indicates that a set of propositions cohere when they are rationally related to each other and to the ordering values or ordering principles that are thought to justify them. Thus, the image that the property of being coherent conjures up is that of a network, or interdependent web, among propositions and their justification, standing or falling together as a unit.

Secondly, coherence in law is better regarded as an interpretative rather than a mere criterial concept. In essence, this means that, despite often having certain criteria associated with it, these are not necessary for coherence to exist. In particular, the three elements often associated with coherence as its criteria (namely, consistency, correctness, and comprehensiveness) only appear to be necessary for coherence in ideal situations. In non-ideal practice, we are ultimately not precluded from perceiving coherence, or from debating about coherence meaningfully, even when some of these elements are satisfied to a lesser degree or are entirely missing. This further means abandoning existing conventional wisdom to the extent that it regards coherence as a mere formal principle or simply as a concept synonymous with consistency or predictability.

Thirdly, because the properties of coherence, consistency, correctness, and comprehensiveness do not necessarily advance all together, determining whether the threshold of coherence has been crossed in each case is a matter of judgment and can be the subject of reasonable disagreement. Moreover, because coherence is an interpretative concept, one's determination of coherence or incoherence in law is an interpretation of the legal practice one finds himself or herself in. This follows logically also from the fact that law itself has an arguable character.

Fourthly, coherence in law relates not only to the substance of a legal outcome but also to the process and method through which that outcome was achieved. Even when the threshold of coherence has been crossed from the standpoint of substance, the process matters still. The better the process has been performed, the more coherent the outcome would be perceived to be (i.e., the more persuasive it would be and with a stronger claim to correctness).

Fifthly, to the extent that a better process of reasoning may result in stronger or more robust grounds upon which to base legal conclusions, a greater collective emphasis on coherence may be hoped to eventually coalesce into determinately and demonstrably correct answers to at least some of the legal questions raised in ISDS. Consequently, if concerns about coherence in ISDS are to be taken seriously, then one must push forward and identify the full implications of the drive to achieve coherence in this context, notwithstanding the fact that in reality absolute or perfect coherence is likely to be an unattainable ideal. To that end, the interplay between substance and method in the structure of legal reasoning is a critical point. Chapter 2 takes that up in greater detail.

2

Coherence and Legal Reasoning

2.1 Introduction

Chapter 1 examined the concept of coherence in law in a rather general and abstract manner. Among the key takeaways were the following: coherence is not a mere formal principle that is devoid of any independent content; rather, coherence appears to have a dual dimension that is at once substantive and methodological; and there also appears to exist a strong link in principle between coherence and legal reasoning. The present chapter picks up from this point and aims, firstly, to analyse how and why the two dimensions of coherence fit within the structure of legal reasoning and, secondly, to clarify the standard of rationality and rational justification that coherence implies in a legal context. In many respects, therefore, the analysis of this chapter dovetails with the analysis undertaken in Chapter 1.

Three main conclusions are accordingly drawn in this chapter with respect to coherence and legal reasoning. A first conclusion is that legal reasoning is an instance of practical reasoning and practical deliberation. What this means, ultimately, is that when one reasons and argues about the content of the law, one does not seek to discover truth in the same sense as when forming an opinion about the way things are in nature. Rather, the aim is to formulate a reasoned opinion and commit oneself to a specific course of action given the presence of a legal problem. A second conclusion is that, when understood as practical reasoning, legal reasoning exhibits certain coherence-related features. These are a web-like structure, the fact that rationality in it does not depend only on logical entailment but also on plausibility (or fit), and a purposive nature. A third conclusion is that coherence functions as a substantive and a methodological principle during legal reasoning, thus confirming the dual dimension identified in Chapter 1.

In terms of structure, the analysis of the present chapter proceeds as follows. Section 2.2 begins by setting out two points of departure, namely, that legal reasoning must be normative and that there exists multiple possible standards of rationality that may be imposed on it. Section 2.3 examines the key characteristics, similarities, and differences of the two principal formats of reasoning – the 'theoretical' and the 'practical' – and categorises legal reasoning under the latter format. Following that, Section 2.4 identifies three coherence-related features of legal reasoning and offers a preliminary sketch of the dual role that coherence in its two dimensions plays therein. Section 2.5 summarises and concludes.

2.2 Two Points of Departure

Adjudication brings about the exercise of coercive force in various forms. For example, in criminal law adjudication a perpetrator may be sentenced to prison, in contract law adjudication the defaulting party to a contract may be ordered to perform the contract's agreed terms, and in ISDS a host state may be ordered to compensate a foreign investor because it unlawfully expropriated the latter's property. As a practice, therefore, adjudication is dependent on the notion of justification. Justification in turn entails some form of rationality. Rationality is thus an integral part of adjudication, wherein it manifests as a general duty to state one's reasons in the form of legal reasoning.[1]

Accordingly, our examination of coherence and legal reasoning begins by setting out two necessary points of departure regarding reasoning in a legal context. The first point to be made in this respect is that, to be justificatory, legal reasoning must be normative rather than merely causal. The second point to be made is that there are various standards of rationality that one can expect from adjudicators. Each point is taken in turn below.

2.2.1 *Legal Reasoning Is Normative Rather than Causal*

To be able to perform its role, legal reasoning must be normative rather than merely causal. Put differently, legal reasoning must be able to justify

[1] Indicatively, see Article 56(1) ICJ Statute; Article 30(1) ITLOS Statute; Articles 53(2), 58(2)(e), 61(4), 72(7)(a)(ii), 74(5), and 83(4) Rome Statute of the International Criminal Court; Article 11 DSU (where the phrase 'objective assessment' used therein has been interpreted to include a duty to state reasons); Article 45 ECHR; Article 48(3) ICSID Convention; Article 32(2) ICC Rules (2021). However, see also arbitration rules where the duty to state reasons can be dispensed with, following an agreement of the disputing parties to that effect, e.g.: Article 34(3) UNCITRAL Rules (2013); Rule 30.4 SIAC Investment Arbitration Rules (2017); Article 26.2 LCIA Rules (2020); Article 42(1) SCC Rules (2017).

the outcome reached in each case rather than simply being able to provide a statement of that outcome's causes.[2] This is an important clarification to make since, as a general proposition, an action may be intelligibly explained merely by stating its causes. For instance, the fact that person A hit person B may be explained as the result of reasons *x* or *y*, where *x* is because A did not like the way that B looked at him, and *y* is because B assaulted A without any prior form of provocation on A's part. In both instances, A's action is explainable since *x* and *y* are the factors that caused it – but only if it was actually motivated by reason *y* is A's action in some way justifiable on legal or moral grounds. Oversimplified as this example is, it nonetheless shows that reasons as causes and reasons as justifications are two categories that, although they may overlap on occasion, are nevertheless analytically distinct. Moreover, it is only the latter category of reasons (i.e., reasons as justifications) that have a direct link with legitimacy. Whatever triggers one to do something, one is impelled to not merely explain but rather to justify doing so on grounds that others in his or her community would accept as legitimate and would find persuasive.[3]

The fundamental requirement that legal reasoning must be justificatory finds practical expression in ISDS in the uniformly embraced view that an arbitral award that is motivated by so-called 'frivolous' or absurd reasons would amount to an award motivated by no reasons at all.[4] For

[2] W. Lucy, 'Adjudication', in J. L. Coleman, K. E. Himma, and S. J. Shapiro (eds.), *The Oxford Handbook of Jurisprudence and Philosophy of Law* (Oxford: Oxford University Press, 2004) 206, 221–222.

[3] See O. Schachter, 'International Law in Theory and Practice: General Course in Public International Law' (1982) 182 *Recueil des cours* 9, 59, expressing a similar idea:

> The fact that governments are generally motivated by self-interest does not preclude them from advancing objective legal grounds for the desired outcome. Motivation and justification are analytically distinct. Whatever their motives for acting, governments are impelled to justify their position on grounds other than their interests. They have to do so if their views are to be persuasive to others.

[4] In arbitral jurisprudence, e.g., see *Maritime International Nominees Establishment (MINE)* v. *Republic of Guinea*, ICSID Case No. ARB/84/4, Decision on the Application by Guinea for Partial Annulment of the Arbitral Award, 6 January 1988 (1990) 5 *ICSID Review – Foreign Investment Law Journal*, 95, para 5.09; *CDC Group plc* v. *Republic of the Seychelles*, ICSID Case No. ARB/02/14, Decision of the *Ad Hoc* Committee on the Application for Annulment of the Republic of Seychelles, 29 June 2005, para 70; *AES Summit Generation Limited and AES-Tisza Erömü Kft* v. *The Republic of Hungary*, ICSID Case No. ARB/07/22, Decision of the *Ad Hoc* Committee on the Application for Annulment, 29 June 2012, para 54; *MCI Power Group L.C. and New Turbine, Inc.* v. *Republic of Ecuador*, ICSID Case No. ARB/03/6, Decision on Annulment, 19 October 2009, para 84; *Hussein Nuaman*

example, if a tribunal openly decides a dispute out of bias, prejudice, mere intuition, or habit, then its reasoning can be described as frivolous given its non-normative and non-justificatory character. This does not mean that a judicial outcome reached by frivolous reasons is by necessity wrong in its substance. It does mean, however, that the outcome cannot be considered as being appropriately and legitimately justified from a legal point of view given the nature of the reasons offered in its support.[5]

Clarifying as a preliminary matter that legal reasoning must be normative rather than merely causal is important for our examination of the role of coherence in legal reasoning. This is because, in principle, coherence can be relevant with respect to causal explanations as well. One could argue, for example, that the plausibility or probable truthfulness of a narrative of merely causal and factual explanations for a judicial decision would also depend on their degree of internal coherence.[6] While this would appear to be true, it would also risk that the nature of coherence thus used would be, at least some times, closer to that of a merely formal concept, equivalent to logical consistency and non-contradiction. This is an understanding of coherence that was explicitly rejected in Chapter 1 at least as it pertains to law.

2.2.2 *The 'Rationality Ladder'*

Legal reasoning is the means through which adjudicators arrive at, and justify, conclusions on points of law. Legal reasoning does so by seeking

Soufraki v. *The United Arab Emirates*, ICSID Case No. ARB/02/7, Decision of the *Ad Hoc* Committee on the Application for Annulment of Mr Soufraki, 5 June 2007, paras 125–126. In literature, e.g., see C. Schreuer, L. Malintoppi, A. Reinisch, and A. Sinclair (eds.), *The ICSID Convention: A Commentary*, 2nd ed. (Cambridge: Cambridge University Press, 2009), 997 (para 344) ('No doubt frivolous, perfunctory or absurd arguments by a tribunal would not amount to "reasons"'); A. Broches (ed.), 'Observations on the Finality of ICSID Awards', in *Selected Essays: World Bank, ICSID, and Other Subjects of Public and Private International Law* (Dordrecht: Martinus Nijhoff, 1995) 295, 342 ('[a] reason may be said to be frivolous when it is manifestly irrelevant and known to be so by the tribunal').

[5] It can be argued that the concept of 'frivolous reasons' may also be broad enough to encompass a review of the quality or acceptability of the reasons offered in support of a decision. Following Broches' more capacious definition of frivolity in n. 4, it is conceivable that the term can also be used to disregard even normative reasons that do not pass muster under substantive review. For instance, the fact that A justifies hitting B on the grounds that B is a person of bad character who deserved the punishment is itself a normative (moral) reason. However, this reason would surely be regarded as manifestly irrelevant, and thus frivolous, when presented by A before a court of law.

[6] See N. MacCormick, *Rhetoric and the Rule of Law* (Oxford: Oxford University Press, 2005), chapter 11, describing this kind of coherence as 'narrative coherence'.

to bring the various bits of a legal system together in support of an outcome. A question that may be asked in this respect is how strong or robust must one's reasons be for the outcome to be regarded as rational? Or, stated differently, what is the standard of rationality to which adjudicators should conform? Depending on the answer to this question, the scope and extent of our examination of the exact role of coherence in legal reasoning may differ.

According to William Lucy, there can be three standards of rationality in adjudication, each being more stringent than the last, somewhat like ascending steps on what he describes as a 'rationality ladder'.[7] These steps are as follows: having reasons, sorting reasons, and weighing reasons.

Having reasons is the lowest step on the ladder. Here, a decision to do *x* is rational simply if a court or tribunal believes that there are reasons for deciding *x*, such reasons being compatible with the existence of possible countervailing reasons. The only conditions are that the court or tribunal must be aware of these reasons and must be able to articulate them when asked why it decided *x*. The requirement of having reasons rules out some types of reasoning from the judicial process. It was said before that reasoning in adjudication must be justificatory rather than causal. Thus, if a court or tribunal decides *x* on a purely unreflective manner, or out of bias, prejudice, intuition, or habit, then its reasoning is frivolous, which means that the court or tribunal really had no legitimate reasons for deciding *x*. The requirement of having reasons does not however exclude much else since it is nothing more than a minimal requirement. Thus, if a court or tribunal decides to do *x* because 'everyone else does *x* in this situation' (e.g., there exists a consistent line of cases on the matter and the tribunal considers that the case before it is similar to those preceding cases), then this is the product of some minimal reflection and would count as having reasons for doing *x*.[8]

[7] Lucy (n. 2).

[8] Ibid., 229–230. Implicitly confirming that simply 'having reasons' is a minimal requirement of rationality in ISDS, at least in the context of ICSID annulment, see *Enron Corporation and Ponderosa Assets, L.P.* v. *Argentine Republic (also known as: Enron Creditors Recovery Corp. and Ponderosa Assets, L.P.* v. *The Argentine Republic)*, ICSID Case No. ARB/01/3, Decision on the Application for Annulment of the Argentine Republic, 30 July 2010, paras 93–95 (some emphases in original, some emphases added):

> [T]he Tribunal said that although decisions of other ICSID tribunals are not binding precedents, 'the conclusions of the Tribunal follow the same line of

The immediately higher step above having reasons is that of sorting reasons. Here it is not enough for the decision-maker to be aware of, and able to articulate, the reasons for deciding *x*. Rather, the decision-maker is also required to take additional steps to determine that his or her reasons for *x* are genuine. This means that the decision-maker has knowledge of the range of possible reasons for doing *x*.[9] Another way of describing the requirement to sort reasons is by saying that the decision-maker must have adequate reasons for his or her decisions. For Joseph Raz, the claim that a reason *y* is adequate for action *x* contains two elements: (i) that *y* is a sufficient reason in the sense that it makes *x* intelligible and (ii) that *y* is not defeated, wholly or partly, by other conflicting reasons that ultimately render doing *x* wrong, irrational, or unreasonable.[10] Sorting reasons does not mean that there will always be a variety of reasons for a particular decision. According to Lucy, sorting may also take place when there is only one candidate reason for *x* and the judge nonetheless takes steps to ensure that this reason is indeed a genuine or an adequate one in a legal setting.[11]

As a requirement of rationality, sorting reasons is more demanding than merely having reasons as it includes a process of evaluation of the reasons that are offered for or against a decision. Sorting reasons would

> reasoning ... because the circumstances of the various cases are comparable, and in some respects identical.' ...
>
> There is nothing to prevent a tribunal from agreeing with, and incorporating by reference as its own, reasoning found in any other source, provided that it is ultimately *sufficiently clear* what are the tribunal's reasons ...
>
> Provided that the tribunal's own reasons are *sufficiently apparent*, it is not necessary for a tribunal in adopting the reasoning of the earlier decision to distinguish specifically between those passages in the earlier decision that it adopts as its own reasoning, and those passages in the earlier decision that it considers inapplicable to its own decision.

9 Lucy (n. 2), 230.

10 J. Raz, *Engaging Reason: On the Theory of Value and Action* (Oxford: Oxford University Press, 2002), 96–97. Raz uses the following example:

> [O]ther things being equal, that Julie has promised John to help him when he moves house is an adequate reason for her to do so. Other things being equal, if she helps him because she promised her action will be intelligible and not wrong. We could distinguish two elements in a claim that something (Julie's promise) is an adequate reason for an action (the promised action). First the reason (the promise) is a sufficient reason in that it makes the action it is a reason for intelligible. Second, given that it is not defeated by (wholly or partly) conflicting reasons, it is an adequate reason for the action, for conforming to it is not wrong or unreasonable or irrational.

11 Lucy (n. 2), 230.

not, for example, allow for reasoning in the form of 'the decision ought to be *x* because everyone decides *x* in situations similar to this one', if the court or tribunal did not even attempt to establish for its own that this is indeed a genuine reason. For instance, the court or tribunal could further reason that following the consistent line of past cases on this issue would ensure legal certainty, which is generally recognised as a desirable value in law. That would count as sorting and as having a genuine reason to decide *x* in this case. But the exact same articulation for doing *x* ('because everyone does so') would not be genuine if the court or tribunal decided to use it, not because it would secure legal certainty but simply as a matter of practical efficiency or in the interest of a speedy resolution of the case.

The third, and final, step in our 'rationality ladder' involves weighing reasons. This account of rationality adds one additional requirement to the previous ones, namely, the weighing of the genuine or adequate reasons for doing *x*. Accordingly, a court's decision to do *x* would be rational only on the basis of the strongest, weightiest reason or collection of reasons for doing *x*, taken among the class of genuine or adequate reasons for *x*.[12] Weighing reasons is only conceivable in cases where there is a plurality of genuine reasons supporting a conclusion. In adjudication, this type of situation is commonly described as a hard case, which is to say, a case where deciding either way is plausible and not obviously wrong. In hard cases, even people who are well-informed about the law may find themselves in reasonable disagreement.[13]

Weighing reasons for a decision places a decision-maker within the domain of compelling reasons. Compelling reasons for *x* require choosing or doing *x* on pain of irrationality.[14] Therefore, to say that *y* is a compelling reason for *x* not only means that *y* rationally requires *x* but also that there is no better justification for *x* other than *y*, even though there may also exist a range of other conceivable and adequate justifications for it. For instance, a court or tribunal may have a compelling reason to decide *x* following the consistent line of past cases that point to *x*, because doing so would enhance legal certainty and because adopting a contrary, yet plausible, interpretation that does not track with past practice would not be conducive towards the maintenance of legal

[12] Ibid., 230–231.

[13] See R. Dworkin, *Law's Empire* (Cambridge, MA: Harvard University Press, 1986), 255–256.

[14] Lucy (n. 2), 231.

certainty. The general point that this example illustrates is that, from the point of view of ensuring legal certainty, following past practice is a compelling reason for deciding *x* in this instance and not doing so would be considered irrational.

What should be the standard of rationality to which we should hold adjudicators? At a minimum, between having and sorting reasons adjudicators must be required to always ensure the latter.[15] This is not to say, however, that the possibility of weighing/having compelling reasons should be discarded altogether. Decisions in hard cases tend to require additional justification because, in deciding them, adjudicators must take a clearer stand on what the content of the law is. Therefore, when in doubt about which proposition of law is applicable or about which out of a range of possible interpretations of the same proposition of law is the best, adjudicators inadvertently have a choice to make. This choice they must justify. It is therefore not unreasonable to expect adjudicators to try and identify compelling reasons for their judgments, particularly in so-called hard cases.

Having arrived at this conclusion, a series of further questions arise. How is rationality ensured in the context of legal reasoning? What is the format of legal reasoning that enables adjudicators to form compelling, or at minimum adequate, reasons for a decision? And how does the ideal of coherence fit within this format? These are the questions that the remainder of this chapter seeks to answer.

2.3 Is the Format of Legal Reasoning 'Theoretical' or 'Practical'?

An inquiry into the role played by coherence in legal reasoning and legal argumentation must begin with an understanding of the basic format through which legal reasoning and legal argumentation operate. There are two principal formats to consider in this respect: the theoretical and

[15] Indeed, on the requirement of merely having reasons, Lucy (n. 2), 230, says [footnote omitted]:

> Applied to judicial decision-making, this requirement would seem to be far too lenient. Although it would rule out much that we expect to be excluded from adjudication – judges openly tracking their prejudices, arriving at decisions solely by fiat rather than reason – it does not seem sufficient to allow adjudication to come close to living up to its publicity, both in the academy and the wider world. If courts are forums of principle, and if law schools do indeed preach 'faith in the power of reason', then a more demanding account of rationality must be sought.

the practical. Both formats of reasoning share certain similarities but differ in fundamental ways – principally in their respective conditions of validity and in the outcomes that each seeks to achieve. The thesis that this section advances is that legal reasoning, and legal argumentation more generally, track closer to the format of practical reasoning rather than that of theoretical reasoning. This has important implications for the role played by coherence therein, as elaborated later in Section 2.4.

2.3.1 Characteristics of Theoretical Reasoning

2.3.1.1 A Remarkable Discovery

In 2017, BBC published the story of a discovery so remarkable that it promised to 'rewrite the textbooks' on palaeoanthropology. In June of that year, a team of researchers announced that fossils of five early humans were found in North Africa.[16] The fossils were carbon-dated to be between 300,000 and 350,000 years old. Examination of the skulls and the tools found on the dig site indicated that the remains belonged to *Homo sapiens*. Until that time, the mainstream view had been that *Homo sapiens* evolved suddenly from more primitive humans in East Africa, approximately 200,000 years ago, and that only then did they begin spreading throughout Africa and eventually to the rest of the planet. The mainstream view was in turn based on the fact that the earliest human fossils until that time were from a region in eastern Africa and were dated to be approximately 195,000 years old. But this new discovery appeared to shatter the mainstream view. The newly discovered fossils seemed to be suggesting, instead, that our species evolved more gradually all across the African continent 100,000 years earlier than previously recognised.

The above example is paradigmatic of what is known as theoretical reasoning. Theoretical reasoning is reasoning principally about questions of fact, explanation, and prediction.[17] When one is engaged in theoretical argumentation, one adduces reasons for or against forming a belief about what is or is not the case in reality.[18] As such, theoretical reasoning has a

[16] BBC News, '"First of Our Kind" Found in Morocco', 7 June 2017, available at www.bbc.com/news/science-environment-40194150.

[17] R. Jay Wallace, 'Practical Reason', in E. N. Zalta (ed.), *The Stanford Encyclopedia of Philosophy* (Spring 2020 edition), available at https://plato.stanford.edu/entries/practical-reason/.

[18] N. MacCormick, 'Argumentation and Interpretation in Law' (1993) 6 *Ratio Juris* 16, 16. MacCormick uses the term 'speculative' to refer to theoretical reasoning.

backward-looking and a forward-looking dimension. It is backward-looking when it looks at events that have already occurred and asks why or how they have occurred. It is forward-looking when it uses past observations and the rules of logic to attempt a true determination about what is going to happen in the future.

This way of defining the contours of theoretical reasoning may seem to make its application to legal reasoning inappropriate. We have said that legal reasoning must be normative rather than simply explanatory or causal. If theoretical reasoning is only good for questions of fact and their explanation, then that would mean that theoretical reasoning is not appropriate for judges and arbitrators to use. This would be an easy but misleading conclusion. There is nothing preventing theoretical reasoning from being concerned with determining the truth condition of normative questions too.[19] All that is required is that the premises from which one begins to reason are normative rather than merely empirical in character. Accordingly, if there are ways in which legal reasoning departs from the model of theoretical reasoning, these ways must be sought elsewhere. We begin to identify such ways below, by considering the particular format and conditions of validity of a theoretical inference. The decision in the ISDS case of *Soufraki* v. *United Arab Emirates* will be used to illustrate the points made.

2.3.1.2 'If *P* Then *Q*' Syllogisms and the *Soufraki* Decision

The idea that legal reasoning is based on logic is one that enjoys general support in legal theory, including in international legal theory. Indeed, the traditional understanding of legal reasoning in its simplest form is that of a logical deduction.[20] This deduction consists of a syllogism with

[19] Jay Wallace (n. 17).

[20] E.g., see G. Abi-Saab, 'Cours général de droit international public' (1987) 207 *Recueil des cours* 9, 214 (emphasis in original):

> L'essence de la fonction juridictionnelle est ainsi d'assurer la continuité, ou d'établir le lien, entre la règle générale et la situation particulière; un processus qui peut être envisagé . . . déductivement, en partant de la règle vers le fait, du général vers le particulier; c'est le processus qu'on appelle d'habitude *interprétation* ou l'une de ses variantes.

Alongside this deductive process, Abi-Saab (ibid., 214–215) also identifies an inductive process. He describes the latter as the 'juridical qualification' of particular fact-situations on the basis of a general rule. In international law, induction is said to take place when one seeks to ascertain the existence and content of a norm of customary international law or of a general principle of law recognised by the community of nations. Since this book

an open hypothetical in the format 'if p then q', where p stands for a proposition of law and q stands for the consequence that follows from it.[21] The role of the adjudicator on this view is to input to the formula the relevant set of facts that match the applicable proposition of law, in order to get the legally prescribed solution.

Consider but a single example from ISDS demonstrating how this may work in practice. In *Soufraki* v. *United Arab Emirates*, the claimant was an Italian national by birth and was able to produce certificates in proof of that fact during the proceedings. However, unbeknownst to him, under Italian law he had automatically lost the Italian nationality because of acquiring Canadian nationality at some point in his life. Italian law allowed Soufraki to reacquire the Italian nationality, either by making an application to that effect or by taking up residence in Italy for one year. He maintained that he had fulfilled the latter requirement, but upon reviewing the evidence the tribunal concluded that this was not the case.[22] There was a question at this point as to whether the tribunal should nonetheless accept the certificates of nationality that were produced. The tribunal asserted its competence to make its own objective determination on the matter of Soufraki's nationality.[23] It held that the certificates, though a prima facie evidence of nationality, could not be relied upon in that instance, since it was clear from the record that the Italian authorities that had issued them were not aware of the fact that Soufraki had lost the Italian nationality in the first place.[24] As a result, the tribunal concluded that it did not have jurisdiction over the case.

On the face of it, the *Soufraki* case did not seem to be a particularly challenging one for the tribunal, in the sense that both the facts and the applicable law were undoubtedly clear, unambiguous, and relevant. The tribunal's process of reasoning follows a clear deductive path when reconstructed, which can be roughly schematised as follows:

does not address the latter sources of international law directly, the term 'deduction' rather than 'induction' will most often be used. However, it bears noting that, even when performing inductive reasoning, the fundamentally syllogistic 'if p then q' format remains.

21 N. MacCormick, *Legal Reasoning and Legal Theory* (Oxford: Clarendon Press, 1978), 23.

22 *Hussein Nuaman Soufraki* v. *The United Arab Emirates*, ICSID Case No. ARB/02/7, Award, 7 July 2004, paras 49–52, 69–71, 80–81.

23 Ibid., para 55.

24 Ibid., paras 63–68.

Overall premise 1: An ICSID tribunal has *ratione personae* jurisdiction over an investment dispute provided that the dispute involves nationals of either contracting party to the applicable investment treaty.

Overall premise 2: The BIT between Italy and the United Arab Emirates only applies with respect to nationals of Italy or the United Arab Emirates who, in their capacity as investors, raise a complaint against the other state.

Overall premise 3: A tribunal has the power to determine for itself the existence of its own jurisdiction (*competence-competence*).

Factual determination: Soufraki, an Italian national by birth, lost his Italian nationality automatically under the applicable laws of Italy by reason of acquiring Canadian nationality.[25]

> *Intermediate premise*: Under the laws of Italy, Soufraki could have reacquired the Italian nationality by taking up residence in Italy for a period of one year.
>
> *Intermediate factual determination*: Soufraki failed to take up residence in Italy for the requisite period of one year.
>
> *Intermediate conclusion*: Therefore, Soufraki is not an Italian national under the relevant Italian laws.

Overall conclusion: Soufraki not being an Italian national, he cannot rely on the BIT for protection and the tribunal must, therefore, decline jurisdiction on *ratione personae* grounds.

According to the theoretical format of reasoning, legal reasoning in all cases can be described as a chain of deductively valid 'if *p* then *q*' syllogisms similar to the one above, which results in the final outcome reached in each case being deductively valid too. The harder the case, the more complex the chain of syllogisms that will be required.

However, it is worth pondering a bit longer on what it means to say that an outcome reached through the deduction 'if *p* then *q*' is a 'valid' one. In answering this question, one needs to further distinguish between an argument's formal validity and the validity (or accuracy) of the

[25] This factual determination is itself the outcome of another implicit deductive syllogism, consisting of a major premise addressing the current state and content of Italian law and a minor premise addressing the fact of acquisition of Canadian nationality by Soufraki. This syllogism has been omitted here in the interest of ease of presentation.

argument's propositions. As MacCormick remarked, a deductive argument purports to show that one proposition (the conclusion of the argument) is compelled by some other proposition or propositions (the premises of the argument).[26] A deductive argument is thus valid if its form is such that the premises do in fact imply or entail the conclusion, so that it would be self-contradictory for anyone to assert the premises but deny the conclusion. All that a formally valid 'if *p* then *q*' deduction tells us, therefore, is that, if *p* is true then it must logically and compellingly follow that *q* is also true.[27] Importantly, the actual accuracy or truthfulness of the premises and the conclusion do not have a bearing on the formal validity of the theoretical argument.

Vincent Descombes uses the following example to illustrate the above point.[28] Suppose I want to find my keys and to do so I use the following proposition: 'The keys are either in my pocket or in the drawer.' If the keys are not in my pocket, then it logically follows that they are in the drawer. If, however, the keys are not to be found in the drawer either, then this does not mean that my syllogism was logically (read: formally) invalid. The syllogism itself is irreproachable since it had the capacity to lead to a true outcome. The problem in this case rather lies with the original premise used. To reach the correct outcome (i.e., finding my keys) I need to reject the original premise and replace it with one that is in fact true (e.g., 'the keys are either in my pocket, in the drawer, or on the desk'). The truthfulness or accuracy of the premises therefore matters, but it matters for what we may call the substantive validity of the deduction. If the conclusion of a theoretical inference does not match reality, then we have good reason to question our choice of premises in a manner not dissimilar to how the astonished palaeoanthropologists did in the news report mentioned at the beginning of this section.

To summarise, a theoretical inference may be invalidated in two ways: firstly, by challenging the validity of the moves made from the premises to the conclusion for not following the rules of logical consequence or entailment; secondly, by challenging the truthfulness or accuracy of the premises or the conclusion. But does the way lawyers reason and

[26] MacCormick (n. 21), 21–22.

[27] Ibid., 23.

[28] V. Descombes, *Le raisonnement de l'ours: et autres essais de philosophie pratique* (Paris: Seuil, 2007), 117–118.

argue actually track the mode of theoretical reasoning just described? How would a lawyer attempt to challenge an opposing counsel's reasoning?

2.3.2 *Characteristics of Practical Reasoning*

2.3.2.1 A Return to *Soufraki*

Let us return to the *Soufraki* case for a moment. Restated briefly, the decision is based on three major premises (i.e., jurisdiction is based on nationality; Soufraki must be an Italian national; *competence-competence*), and one minor premise (i.e., Soufraki is not an Italian national), all logically leading to the conclusion that the case must be dismissed for lack of jurisdiction *ratione personae*. Based on what was said above, we cannot doubt that the logic of the tribunal's syllogism is formally valid. Similarly, we cannot doubt the accuracy of the premises either. They all correspond to what was true in fact and to what international lawyers know to be true in terms of applicable international investment law. Does this automatically mean that the decision is also correct from a legal standpoint? Not everyone has thought so. Commenting on the case, Zachary Douglas offers the following critique of it.

Douglas takes issue with the fact that the tribunal treated the question of Soufraki's nationality as an evidentiary matter. That is, he takes issue with the fact that the question of nationality was treated as a question of fact and not as a question of law.[29] Instead, Douglas argues, the tribunal should have accepted the official certificates produced by Soufraki as fulfilling the criterion of nationality. His full argument on this point reads as follows:

> It was not open to the Tribunal to treat the nationality requirement in article 25(2)(a) [of the ICSID Convention] and the BIT as a question of fact and thereby to consider Soufraki's status in the Italian legal order as an evidential matter that could be suppressed by reference to other evidence. For the Tribunal to decline jurisdiction in spite of Soufraki's status in the Italian legal order, it had to rule that the nationality requirement in article 25(2)(a) and the BIT is an autonomous test so that factors *in addition* to Soufraki's possession of Italian nationality should be taken

[29] Z. Douglas, 'Other Specific Regimes of Responsibility: Investment Treaty Arbitration and ICSID', in J. Crawford, A. Pellet, and S. Olleson (eds.), *The Law of International Responsibility* (Oxford: Oxford University Press, 2010) 815, 824.

> into account. This was the approach taken by the International Court in the *Nottebohm* case when it imported a 'genuine link' requirement into the nationality of claims rule in diplomatic protection. In other words, it was not permissible for the tribunal to question Soufraki's status in the Italian legal order, but it was open to the tribunal to decide whether his Italian nationality could be invoked against the UAE for the purposes of an international claim under the ICSID Convention. But although this route was open, it would not have been a welcome precedent either. There is little evidence that the drafters of the ICSID Convention had envisaged that the nationality requirements for natural or juridical persons should be interpreted against the background of diplomatic protection rules or any other notion of 'dominant' or 'effective' nationality.[30]

Notice what the above critique is doing. It does not challenge the accuracy of any of the original premises used or the logical consequence of the tribunal's syllogism, yet it still claims that the tribunal made an error of law. To that end, the critique points to two things in particular: (i) that, in order to treat the question of nationality as a question of fact, the tribunal should have first established that ISDS tracks closer to a paradigm of diplomatic protection, so that Article 25(2)(a) of the ICSID Convention could be interpreted as providing for an autonomous test of nationality and (ii) that, even if the tribunal were to do so, treating the issue of nationality as a question of fact still seems contrary to the intentions of the ICSID Convention drafters, who did not see an equivalency between the Convention and diplomatic protection. The thrust of the critique is that the tribunal should have added, or at the very least implied, two additional premises within its reasoning. Also note that, if it were to do so, the tribunal need not have rejected any of its original premises. Those would still stand and even Douglas' critique nowhere implies otherwise.

We have just seen a new, third way of challenging inferences on points of law that takes place through the expressed or implied inclusion of missing premises in one's syllogism. Supposing for the sake of argument that Douglas' critique is correct, then the *Soufraki* decision was wrongly decided even though the syllogism used by the tribunal was a formally valid one and all of the original premises were correct. Such a way of arguing about the content of the law and challenging others' views about it is a staple not of theoretical but of a different kind of reasoning, called practical.[31]

30 Ibid. (emphasis in original).
31 Descombes (n. 28), 118–119.

2.3.2.2 In What Way Is Legal Reasoning 'Practical'?

Identifying the way in which legal reasoning is practical is essentially the same sort of inquiry as seeking to identify the way in which practical reasoning differs from theoretical reasoning. Thus, the latter question is answered first below. If we were to extrapolate from the different ways one can challenge a theoretical and a practical inference examined above, it is possible to distinguish three points on which theoretical and practical reasoning differ in fundamental ways.

In the first place, the outcome of practical reasoning is an action rather than simply the formation of an opinion or belief about the way things are.[32] In practical contexts, actors adduce arguments that are either reasons for or against doing something, or reasons for or against holding an opinion about what ought to be, or may be, or can be done.[33] Put differently, practical reasoning attaches to a project that the actor has and seeks to identify the course of action that would lead to a satisfactory completion of that project.[34] Suppose, for example, that I find myself working at the office during a particularly warm day and I feel some discomfort. The answer to a theoretical problem is one that describes what the case is in reality (e.g., the weather is warm, and the air-conditioning is off) or describes what the case is by making an evaluation of it (e.g., it is not good that the air-conditioning is off given the warm weather). The answer to a practical problem, by contrast, is one that tells me what ought to, can, or may be done (or not done) given the situation as it is or as it is evaluated to be (e.g., I must turn on the air-conditioning, because the air-conditioning is off, and because it is not good that it is off given the warm weather).[35] The observation leads to an assessment that then moves me into specific action given my intended plan (presumably, to keep cool).[36]

[32] See A. J. Kenny, 'Practical Inference' (1966) 26 *Analysis* 65, 73 ('[T]he purpose of practical reasoning is to get done what we want; just as the purpose of theoretical reasoning is to discover truth.').

[33] MacCormick (n. 18), 16–17; also Jay Wallace (n. 17): 'Practical reason . . . is concerned not with the truth of propositions but with the desirability or value of actions.'

[34] Descombes (n. 28), 21.

[35] Cf. ibid., 103–105.

[36] It follows, then, that an inference through which an actor merely forms a normative prescription is still theoretical because, by itself, the normative prescription does not tell the actor how to act (see Descombes, ibid., 110–114). The categorical prescription 'one must not tell lies under any circumstances' does not tell the actor how to respond in a difficult situation, for instance, when he is asked by the secret police of an oppressive regime about the whereabouts of his friend, whom he is hiding in his house. The

In the second place, whereas the outcome of a theoretical inference, properly conducted, will be the same for everyone, this is not a guarantee in a practical inference.[37] Two actors may both reason correctly from a logical point of view but still arrive at different courses of action. For instance, from the same, assumed valid, theoretical inferences that 'the weather is warm and the air-conditioning is off' or 'it is not good that the air-conditioning is off given the warm weather', one person may choose to turn the air-conditioning on while another may choose to keep it off but open the window instead. In both instances, the actors' intended plans are fulfilled – both are kept cool either because the air-conditioning is now on or because of the breeze that the open window lets in the room.

It thus follows that, in the third place, and unlike theoretical reasoning, practical reasoning frequently does not seek to designate one single outcome that must be followed on pain of irrationality. Rather, the practical problem is often one in which the actor must choose the best, or at least better, course of action out of various available options. Resolving a practical problem thus requires the actor to deliberate in order to prioritise or reconcile competing ends as well as the requirements underpinning each of the available courses of action to meet these ends.[38] Reconciling and prioritising may lead the actor to choose a different course of action and to even change or amend his or her original goals. Or, as said by Descombes, practical deliberation requires the actor to simultaneously determine: how to do what seems like a good idea of doing; as well as whether it really is a good idea to do it.[39]

Rationality in a practical inference is then a function of the degree to which a desirable end *x* is achieved by a course of action *y*, subject to any competing or countervailing reasons for not doing *y* given the possible existence of an additional, also desirable, end *z*. By enlarging the scope of

prescription notwithstanding, the actor still has to decide whether to flatly lie (presumably, because in this case protecting the life of his friend trumps the duty to tell the truth) or to instead offer an evasive and deflecting answer (presumably, in an attempt to reconcile the competing duties). In other words, to be 'practical' an inference must actually result in the actor committing to a specific course of action.

37 Descombes, ibid., 23 (emphasis in original): '[E]n matière théorique, nous avons la garantie qu'un conflit entre deux descriptions d'une même situation n'est qu'une apparence: ou bien l'une (au moins) de deux propositions que nous voulons soutenir n'est pas vraie, ou bien il y a une manière de les comprendre qui lève la contradiction (et il faut ici appliquer la technique du *distinguo*). En matière pratique, nous n'avons nullement cette garantie.'

38 Ibid., 23–24.

39 Ibid., 26.

the debate in this way, the rationality of a practical inference may be affirmed or challenged.[40] By way of example, my desire to keep cool on a warm day makes the decision to turn on the air-conditioning logical and rational. Upon reflection, however, I may decide that my desire to keep cool will have to be reconciled with my equally strong desire to maintain a low carbon footprint in my daily activities. I may even decide that maintaining a low carbon footprint must take priority because of climate change. In this case, turning on the air-conditioning is incompatible with my amended goal, thus making it a less desirable course of action than simply opening the window. I may therefore conclude that what I ought to do in this case – what I am compelled to do given my amended objectives – is to open the window.

Legal reasoning, too, is practical in the three ways just described. Returning once again to the critique of the *Soufraki* decision offered by Douglas, we note the following. The critique points to two missing premises in the tribunal's original reasoning: a doctrinal premise (i.e., the relevance of the applicable rules of general international law on the nationality of claims) and a premise regarding the VCLT (i.e., the relevance of the intentions of the ICSID Convention drafters). The introduction of these two premises enlarges the scope of deliberation by inviting us to consider the impact on the decision of two previously unexplored contexts, thus resulting in two possible and plausible courses of action (i.e., assumption or rejection of jurisdiction), rather than the single course of action mandated by the tribunal's original premises. Following Douglas' critique, the task that the tribunal would have before it would no longer be one of merely inputting law and facts into an 'if *p* then *q*' formula. Its task rather would be one of weighing competing courses of action, and the reasons supporting these courses of action, in an effort to reconcile competing objectives (i.e., respecting the nationality requirements in ISDS, maintaining consistency with international law doctrine, being faithful to the intentions of the ICSID Convention drafters).

2.4 Coherence and the Format of Practical Legal Reasoning

Having concluded that legal reasoning and legal argumentation are instances of practical reasoning and practical deliberation, what role does coherence play therein? And does this role correspond to the dual dimension of coherence identified in Chapter 1? This section argues that,

[40] Ibid., 27.

indeed, coherence simultaneously serves as a substantive and a methodological consideration in legal reasoning, which is in keeping with its identified dual dimension. Moreover, legal reasoning itself exhibits at least three coherence-related features as identified in Chapter 1, namely: (i) a web-like structure; (ii) the dimension of plausibility (or fit) alongside the dimension of logic; and (iii) a purposive character.

2.4.1 Three Coherence-Related Features of Legal Reasoning

2.4.1.1 A Web-Like Structure

A first coherence-related feature of legal reasoning that can be drawn out is that the process of legal argumentation does not actually resemble a chain of demonstrative reasoning, even though it is often presented as being such. Reasons adduced for a legal outcome are, to use John Wisdom's famous phrase, less like the links of a chain and more like the legs of a chair.[41] Using a different analogy, we may say that legal reasoning exhibits a web-like structure. Such an image corresponds to what the concept of coherence implies in terms of justification, which is to say, justification that is not linear but based on a web or network of convictions.[42] In such a model, legal arguments severally cooperate to support a conclusion in a manner that is horizontally, rather than vertically, extensive.[43] The cumulative weight of one cluster of arguments is then weighed against the cumulative effect of another cluster.[44] The strength of a legal inference thus comes from the number of premises

[41] J. Wisdom, 'Gods' (1944) 45 *Proceedings of the Aristotelian Society* 185, 194.

[42] See L. Moral Soriano, 'A Modest Notion of Coherence in Legal Reasoning: A Model for the European Court of Justice' (2003) 16 *Ratio Juris* 296, 310–311, using the similar metaphor of 'nets' of arguments.

[43] Wisdom (n. 41), 194; similarly, J. Bell, 'The Argumentative Status of Foreign Legal Arguments' (2012) 8(2) *Utrecht Law Review* 8, 10 (footnote omitted):

> I do not believe that the justification of judicial decisions typically depends on a single argument, but that it depends on an accumulation of arguments. The model of legal reasoning I have in mind is one that depends on a combination of reasons, each of which may be insufficient to justify the decision in its own right, but, taken together, they provide support for the decision. The analogy is with individual threads of fibre. On its own, a single thread cannot hold up a weight, but twisted in combination with other threads, it forms a cord which can carry a substantial weight.

[44] Wisdom (n. 41), 194.

used in a cluster and, arguably more critically, from the degree of mutual supportiveness that these premises exhibit.[45]

Using the *Soufraki* case study, we can represent this model schematically in the manner depicted in Figure 2.1. The left side of the graph shows the expressed and missing premises (according to Douglas' analysis) of the *Soufraki* decision. It also shows the expressed and implied supportive links between these premises that led to the tribunal's conclusion. The right side of the graph reconstructs an idealised reasoning for the tribunal following Douglas' analysis, pointing out the areas where supportive links may and may not be drawn among the premises used.

2.4.1.2 Fit Alongside Logical Entailment

A second feature of legal reasoning emerging from the preceding discussion is that its rational character does not depend only on logical entailment among the premises used and the conclusion reached. This feature follows from the conception of rationality that is applicable in practical argumentation. Briefly repeated here, the essence of rationality in practical argumentation is as follows. Having shown that it would be a good course of action to do *x* (because doing *x* would promote goal *y*, which would be desirable for its own sake or for the state of affairs it would bring about),[46] it is still upon the actor to establish the rationality of doing *x* by considering whether there are reasons to not do *x* in the particular case – for instance, because they put the desirability of goal *y* into doubt favouring instead another goal *z*, or because they instruct the actor to interpret *y* in a different way thus resulting in an understanding of it that is different from what was originally conceived.[47]

Therefore, the way for the adjudicator to scrutinise his or her choice of premises, and to thus bolster the rationality of his or her reasoning, is through the positing, interpreting, and reinterpreting of desirable ends, as well as through an assessment of the degree to which these ends are satisfactorily achieved by the chosen course of action.[48] Such description once again corresponds to what coherence implies. As defined in Chapter 1, coherence describes a situation where a series of elements

[45] Soriano (n. 42), 311 ('[W]hat matters is not the number of reasons (the number of legs of a chair) but rather the connection between reasons'.).

[46] MacCormick (n. 18), 17–18, respectively calls these deontological (or rightness) reasons and teleological (or goal) reasons.

[47] See Descombes (n. 28), 27.

[48] Kenny (n. 32) calls this the 'logic of satisfactoriness', which he argues applies in practical inferences.

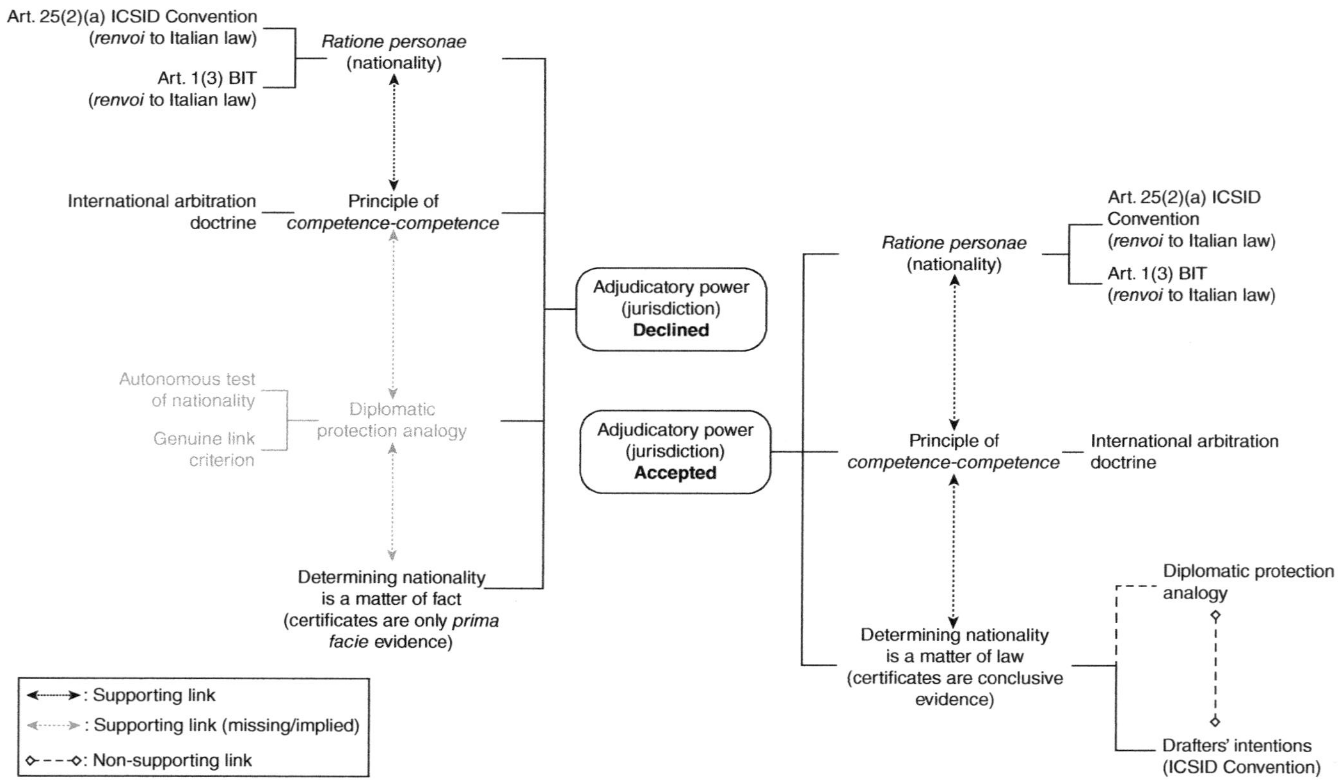

Figure 2.1 Network of reasons – The *Soufraki* v. *United Arab Emirates* decision, reconstructed (left) and idealised (right)

are linked together, mutually support each other, and express a unified viewpoint. It follows, then, that the degree to which a practical legal inference is compelling comes not only from its overall logical consequence but also from the interactions and the degree of mutual supportiveness between (i) the various premises that are employed (i.e., the 'chair legs' in Wisdom's metaphor) and (ii) the expressed or implied reasons acting in support of these premises. The strength of these supportive links among premises, and between premises and their reasons, can itself be based on logic or plausibility (i.e., fit).[49] A logical link would exist, for instance, when such reasons are non-contradictory and when the intended premise can be inferred from them deductively or inductively.[50] A plausible link, or an element of fit, would exist when the reasons adduced make the premise they seek to justify believable and acceptable to the legal community.[51]

Such a conclusion also tracks with the assertion made in Chapter 1 that an otherwise coherent process of reasoning would still result in an outcome with a non-absolute claim to correctness. That assertion can now be complemented in the following manner. The outcome's claim to correctness, which is to say it being supported by compelling reasons, is not absolute because the adjudicator may have omitted to take into account additional contexts or premises that would undercut the ones originally used (methodological dimension of coherence) or because the reasons the adjudicator used to support the premises failed to do so either logically or plausibly (substantive dimension of coherence).

2.4.1.3 A Purposive Activity

Flowing from the above remarks is the third coherence-related feature of legal reasoning. At its core, legal reasoning is a purposive activity. This is not an altogether novel idea in international law. In its report on the fragmentation of international law, the ILC clearly acknowledged that legal argumentation cannot be regarded 'merely as a mechanic application of apparently random rules, decisions or behavioural patterns but as the operation of a whole that is directed toward some human objective'.[52]

[49] Soriano (n. 42), 310.

[50] A. Aarnio, *The Rational as Reasonable: A Treatise on Legal Justification* (Dordrecht: D. Reidel, 1987), 199–200; also Soriano (n. 42), 310.

[51] Cf. Aarnio (n. 50), 190, 200–201.

[52] International Law Commission, 'Fragmentation of International Law: Difficulties Arising from the Diversification and Expansion of International Law – Report of the Study Group of the International Law Commission', UN Doc A/CN.4/L.682 (13 April 2006), 23 (para

Thus, purposiveness is, alongside the web-like structure and the dimension of fit, an additional coherence-related feature of legal argumentation.[53] That said, the statement about the purposive nature of legal reasoning needs to be unpacked and clarified for the avoidance of confusion. Confusion may arise because both types of reasoning identified in this chapter – the theoretical and the practical – are purposive. Therefore, if legal reasoning is practical rather than merely theoretical, then we must identify how the purposive character of the former differs from that of the latter.

The key difference between theoretical and practical reasoning in terms of their purposive character has been alluded to Section 2.3.2 and is the following. Theoretical reasoning rests on a means-ends logic of inference where the ends tend to be clearly defined and certain.[54] Recall that theoretical reasoning concerns questions of fact, explanation, and prediction. Therefore, the kind of reasons that theoretical argumentation deals in are reasons that speak for or against certain propositions being true or worthy of acceptance.[55] The end is also clear and certain in theoretical reasoning: truth of a proposition or acceptance of a proposition as a matter of belief. The intellectual challenge when engaging in theoretical reasoning, therefore, is to identify among the range of plausible reasons the one(s) that best achieve this end. Put differently, theoretical reasoning is primarily a process of problem solving.[56]

By contrast, practical argumentation deals in reasons that speak for or against a particular course of action, by characterising it as good or worthy of performance.[57] This is still a means-ends logic of inference but with an important difference. When one contemplates possible courses of action in practice, one often comes up against phenomena such as complexity, uncertainty, instability, uniqueness, or value-conflict.[58] In these situations, the ends cannot be always taken as given, that is to say, they cannot be always accepted without some prior attempt at

34). In a later passage (ibid.), the ILC reaffirms the same: 'Much legal interpretation is geared to linking an unclear rule to a purpose and thus, by showing its position within some system, to providing a justification for applying it in one way rather than another.'

[53] MacCormick (n. 6), 230 ('Coherence stipulates that norms should not merely not contradict each other, but should also hang together purposively.').

[54] See D. A. Schön, *The Reflective Practitioner: How Professionals Think in Action* (New York: Basic Books, 1983), 39–42 (describing a similar process under the substantially similar term 'Technical Rationality').

[55] Jay Wallace (n. 17).

[56] Schön (n. 54), 39–42.

[57] Jay Wallace (n. 17).

[58] Schön (n. 54), 39.

identifying their desirability or appropriateness as ends to be achieved.[59] This is a task that the actor who does the reasoning must perform for himself or herself.[60] In other words, in addition to being concerned with problem solving, reasoning in these situations must also address the issue of problem setting. According to Donald Schön, problem setting is the process by which 'we define the decision to be made, the ends to be achieved, [and] the means which may be chosen' to do so.[61] He continues:

> When we set the problem, we select what we will treat as the 'things' of the situation, we set the boundaries of our attention to it, and we impose upon it a coherence which allows us to say what is wrong and in what directions the situation needs to be changed. Problem setting is a process in which, interactively, we *name* the things to which we will attend and *frame* the context in which we will attend to them.[62]

The above remarks about problem setting apply in law also. Indeed, it is far from certain that the law has clearly defined ends.[63] For instance, seen from a functional point of view, the law may be used to pursue multiple policy goals. The multiple ends served by international investment law and ISDS are a case in point. Investment treaties, among other things, are meant to protect individual investors and their investments, stimulate investment flows, and contribute to countries' economic development.[64] For its part, ISDS is meant to serve as an additional guarantee

[59] See, ibid., 41, pointing out that

> [w]hen ends are fixed and clear, then the decision to act can present itself as an instrumental problem. But when ends are confused and conflicting, there is as yet no 'problem' to solve. A conflict of ends cannot be resolved by the use of techniques derived from applied research. It is rather through the non-technical process of framing the problematic situation that we may organize and clarify both the ends to be achieved and the possible means of achieving them.

[60] See Descombes (n. 28), 132–136.

[61] Schön (n. 54), 40.

[62] Ibid. (emphases in original).

[63] Cf. ILC Fragmentation Report (n. 52), 23 (para 34): '[Legal reasoning] cannot be understood as reaffirming something that already "exists" before the systemic effort itself. There is no single legislative will behind international law. Treaties and custom come about as a result of conflicting motives and objectives – they are "bargains" and "package-deals" and often result from spontaneous reactions to events in the environment.'

[64] E.g., see the preambles of:

- Canada-EU CETA (2016) (contains several mentions to the importance of promoting non-economic policies simultaneously with the economic priorities of the parties and, in a direct reference to its investment chapter, clarifies that: '[T]he provisions of this

of protection for investors and, by extension, also as an additional incentive to invest in a foreign jurisdiction[65] as well as to make the resolution of investment disputes less political for states, by removing them from the domain of diplomatic protection.[66] Such goals cannot be taken as indivisible wholes or without argument in the resolution of investment disputes. Rather, they require interpretation, prioritisation, and at times even compromise. What is more, even if one were to focus on purely doctrinal goals often associated with law (e.g., legal certainty/predictability, substantive/moral correctness) and arbitration (e.g., justice between the parties, procedural justice) and sought to determine how

Agreement protect investments and investors with respect to their investments, and are intended to stimulate mutually-beneficial business activity, without undermining the right of the Parties to regulate in the public interest within their territories');

- Morocco-Nigeria BIT (2016) (recognises 'the important contribution investment can make to the sustainable development of the state parties, including the reduction of poverty, increase of productive capacity, economic growth, the transfer of technology, and the furtherance of human rights and human development');
- Brazil-Malawi ICFA (2015) (recognises 'the essential role of investment in promoting sustainable development, economic growth, poverty reduction, job creation, expansion of productive capacity and human development');
- Canada-Republic of Korea FTA (2014) (clearly records the parties' recognition that the mutual promotion and protection of investments 'will be conducive to the stimulation of mutually beneficial business activity');
- Greece-United Arab Emirates BIT (2014) (records, first, the parties' expectation that the promotion and protection of investments will lead to their economic development and prosperity, and then further clarifies that: '[T]hese objectives should be achieved in a manner consistent with the protection of public health, safety, the environment and sustainable development as well as with the promotion of internationally recognized labour rights as provided for and applied by the national laws and regulations of each Contracting Party').

[65] See first recital of the preamble of the ICSID Convention referring to 'the need for international cooperation for economic development, and the role of private international investment therein'; Report of the Executive Directors on the Convention on the Settlement of Investment Disputes between States and Nationals of Other States, in ICSID Convention, Regulations and Rules (ICSID, April 2006) 35, 40–41 (paras 9, 12–13); A. Broches, 'The Convention on the Settlement of Investment Disputes between States and Nationals of Other States' (1972) 136 *Recueil des cours* 331, 348.

[66] See *Corn Products International, Inc.* v. *United Mexican States*, ICSID Case No. ARB(AF)/04/1, Award, 18 August 2009, Separate Opinion of Andreas F. Lowenfeld, para 1 ('The essence of each of these arrangements [i.e., ICSID Convention, Bilateral Investment Treaties, Chapter Eleven of the NAFTA] is that controversies between foreign investors and host states are insulated from political and diplomatic relations between states'). But, for a critical review of the goal of depoliticisation in ISDS, see M. Paparinskis, 'Limits of Depoliticisation in Contemporary Investor–State Arbitration', in J. Crawford and S. Nouwen (eds.), *Select Proceedings of the European Society of International Law: Volume 3* (Oxford: Hart, 2012) 271.

these should be promoted through legal reasoning, one would still need to perform an act of interpretation of these goals in light of the circumstances of each case and the arbitrator's institutional role in the regime.[67]

2.4.2 The Role of Coherence in Legal Reasoning: A Preliminary Sketch

Having shown that legal reasoning exhibits certain coherence-related features (i.e., a web-like structure, the dimension of fit, and a purposive character), what is, then, the role of coherence in legal reasoning? Based on the foregoing analysis, coherence seems to play the same dual role in legal argumentation emanating from its two dimensions. That is, coherence in legal reasoning at once acts as a substantive, axiological principle and as a method to be followed by the adjudicator. Much of the remainder of this book is dedicated to showing how this dual role of coherence manifests in ISDS. Therefore, for the time being, a few preliminary remarks setting out this dual role would suffice.

We have seen that from the two formats of reasoning – the theoretical and the practical – that could be used to account for the way judges and lawyers deliberate, it is the latter that better describes this process. We have further seen that practical deliberation presupposes the existence of an objective, which the actor who deliberates strives to achieve, but which is not always free of ambiguities or of the need for itself to be interpreted. Moreover, having identified an appropriate objective, the adjudicator must then identify a course of action that can achieve that objective in a satisfactory manner, subject to the possible existence of any contrary or countervailing reasons or objectives.

Coherence has a role to play at both of these stages. On the one hand, when faced with a dispute, adjudicators must frame the legal question at issue, identify and interpret the governing values, principles and other norms of conduct which will guide their decision, and, in so doing, also reflect on their institutional role (and on the limits of this role) in the legal system in which they find themselves.[68] Moreover, they must do this in a manner that is acceptable to the legal community of that system. Their interpretation of the above elements must thus correspond to, or cohere with, the knowledge and value systems of that community.[69]

[67] A more detailed discussion on aspects of these two broad categories of issues is undertaken, respectively, in Chapters 3 and 7.

[68] Cf. Descombes (n. 28), 118–119.

[69] Cf. Aarnio (n. 50), 189–190.

Coherence here operates in a clearly normative way as a substantive, axiological principle.[70] It assists adjudicators in formulating, even if in the abstract, the end, purpose, or state of affairs to be achieved and the reasons supporting it.

On the other hand, having come up with this abstract end, purpose or state of affairs to be achieved, adjudicators must then proceed by following an iterative process whereby they identify concrete courses of action to fit the identified end, purpose, or state of affairs; consider the impact on the chosen actions of any contrary or countervailing ends, purposes, or states of affairs; in the process, potentially reassess the desirability of the end, purpose, or state affairs originally identified; and, if so, reformulate amended courses of action as appropriate to fit the reassessed end, purpose, or state of affairs to be achieved. The idea of coherence here takes on a methodological hue. It describes a process of internal and collective deliberation. More generally, it describes a process of structuring all relevant elements into a narrative form that seems at least plausible, if not compelling, and ultimately persuasive to the disputing parties and to the community at large.

2.5 Conclusion

This chapter sought to elaborate on the link that exists between coherence and legal reasoning. In the process, it was shown that legal reasoning tracks closer to the paradigm of practical reasoning rather than to the paradigm of theoretical reasoning. This means that reasoning and arguing about the law's content does not aim at discovering legal truth or at simply forming a belief about the way things are. Rather, the aim is to formulate a reasoned opinion and commit oneself to a specific course of action given the presence of a legal problem in need of resolution.

Once legal reasoning is viewed in this light, it is also possible to discern that it exhibits certain coherence-related features, such as (i) a web-like structure, whereby legal arguments severally cooperate in clusters to support a conclusion in a manner that is horizontally, rather than vertically, extensive; (ii) an understanding of rationality that does not depend only on logical connections among premises but also includes the element of plausible connections (i.e., fit) among premises and between

[70] Recall again MacCormick (n. 6), 231 ('Coherence is axiological compatibility among two or more rules, all being justifiable by reference to some common principle or value.').

the premises chosen and the reasons supporting them; and (iii) a purposive character, whereby a chosen objective guides the process yet such objective is not necessarily free of ambiguities or of the need for itself to be interpreted. These features thus reconfirm the dual – substantive and methodological – dimension of coherence and the similar role that it plays in legal reasoning by courts and tribunals.

Pausing for a moment, three kinds of conceptual questions regarding coherence have been addressed thus far. We may call these the 'what', 'why', and 'how' questions. Chapter 1 addressed the 'what' question, by providing answers to questions such as the kind of concept that coherence is, its content, and its link in principle to legal reasoning. The present chapter addressed the 'why' and 'how' questions, by setting out the reasons why coherence is linked to legal reasoning as well as the role that it plays therein. An additional series of conceptual issues to be addressed pertain to the 'where' question. Where in the course of legal reasoning by courts and tribunals does coherence fit? What is the model of coherence that applies therein? Chapter 3 takes up such questions.

3

Two Models for Coherence

3.1 Introduction

Having established the general contours and the dual dimension of coherence in Chapters 1 and 2, this chapter enquires into the place within legal reasoning where coherence fits. This is necessary because different models of coherence may be offered in this respect depending on the view one holds about the law and about legal reasoning. To that end, the chapter presents and contrasts two views about how legal reasoning is deployed – the positivist view and the non-positivist (in particular, interpretivist) view. Both views agree that the law carries expectations with respect to the achievement of certain values, notably, legal certainty, on the one hand, and substantive correctness (justice), on the other. They disagree, however, about the relationship between those two values when it comes to legal reasoning, hence the different models for coherence that each view gives rise to.

The positivist view gives rise to a model of 'double coherence', whereas the non-positivist view gives rise to a model of 'single coherence'. This chapter ultimately sides with the interpretivist/single coherence view. Two grounds are offered for this conclusion. Firstly, after scrutiny, the core assumptions of the positivist view regarding the different processes of legal reasoning allegedly at play when one is deciding easier and harder cases do not seem to hold. Secondly, following the positivist view may result in certain methodological pitfalls for adjudicators that the non-positivist view seems to avoid.

The analysis proceeds as follows. Section 3.2 introduces the two core values at stake when resolving disputes, namely, certainty and substantive correctness (justice). Section 3.3 presents the positivist and non-positivist views on legal reasoning, whereas Section 3.4 critically assesses both views ultimately siding with the latter. Section 3.5 summarises and concludes.

3.2 The Two Dimensions of Law

Calling something 'law' carries certain expectations, among which is the expectation of exhibiting certain characteristics.[1] For our purposes, two such characteristics, representing fundamental legal values, are important: certainty and correctness. Taken together, these give rise to what Robert Alexy has described as the law's 'dual nature'.[2] For Alexy, saying that law has a dual nature means that it has both a factual/social dimension, which is represented by the elements of authoritative issuance and efficacy, and an ideal dimension, which is represented by an expectation of moral correctness with respect to the outcomes that the law produces.[3]

Certainty and correctness are values that all legal systems are expected to fulfil, and, by extension, they are also values that adjudicators must promote when deciding cases in accordance with the law.[4] These values must thus figure in some form or another in legal reasoning. Since we have already seen that coherence indeed plays a role in legal reasoning, we must now determine the model of coherence to which the interaction of these two values gives rise. In this context, the aim in this section is, first, to briefly present the contours of the two values of certainty and correctness and, second, to broadly clarify their content so as to assist the analysis in the later parts of this chapter.

3.2.1 Certainty

The value of certainty gives expression to the factual and social dimension of law. Certainty is thus linked to the law's authoritative issuance

[1] See T. Schultz, *Transnational Legality: Stateless Law and International Arbitration* (Oxford: Oxford University Press, 2014), 49:

> Calling a regime 'law' . . . has certain implications: it creates expectations of predictability and of justice; it engenders moral reasons to obey the regime; it gives the regime increased authority; it accords power to those who produce or control the regime or some of its norms; it facilitates policies of laissez-faire with regard to that regime; and overall it fashions the lawyers' appropriate field of expertise. Affixing the label of law to given rule systems is not a neutral matter of merely settling the semantics.

[2] R. Alexy, 'Legal Certainty and Correctness' (2015) 28 *Ratio Juris* 441, 441.

[3] Ibid.

[4] See also T. Schultz, 'The Three Pursuits of Dispute Settlement' (2010) 1 *Czech & Central European Yearbook of Arbitration* 227, 241–242, using the binary 'procedural justice/ substantive justice' to refer, respectively, to the substantively equivalent characteristics of predictability and the pursuit of societal values. The topic is revisited in Chapter 7.

and to its efficacy. According to Joseph Raz, the law is authoritative when it allows its addressees to settle their disagreements by reference to the social facts that are prevalent in the legal system in question.[5] In this way, law reduces the scope for intractable moral disagreements between individuals about the proper course of action to take in everyday life[6] and thus enables them to plan their conduct with a reasonable degree of foresight and predictability.[7] Scott Shapiro has made a similar claim, seeing law as a social planning activity and specific laws as plans or plan-like norms resulting in overall social efficacy.[8] As Shapiro argues:

> Laws guide conduct in the same way that plans do, namely, by cutting off deliberation and directing the subject to act in accordance with the plan. By settling matters in favor of the directed action, laws cut down on deliberation and bargaining costs and compensate for cognitive incapacities and informational asymmetries, thereby enabling community members to achieve goals and realize values that would otherwise be beyond their grasp.[9]

Given the importance of the value of certainty, arguments based on authority have a special place in law and in judicial decision-making. In international law too, arguments from authority are prominent, including in particular arguments: (i) that states have produced law regulating the matter in dispute either by having negotiated a treaty to that end or through their long-standing international and domestic practice (i.e., customary international law and general principles of law); (ii) that

[5] J. Raz, *Ethics in the Public Domain: Essays in the Morality of Law and Politics*, rev. ed. (Oxford: Clarendon Press, 1995), 215–220.

[6] Raz, ibid., 219, uses the following example to describe the function that the authoritativeness of law plays in everyday life:

> If I decide what would be the best life insurance to buy, it is no good trying to remind me of my decision by saying that I decided to buy the policy which it is best to buy. It means that I have to decide again in order to know what I decided before, so the earlier decision might just as well never have happened.

[7] Cf. also a similar view from a non-positivist perspective in L. L. Fuller, *The Morality of Law*, rev. ed. (New Haven: Yale University Press, 1969), 210 ('[Law] is basically a matter of providing the citizenry with a sound and stable framework for their interactions with one another . . ..'), 229 (describing the function of law as one of 'furnish[ing] dependable guideposts for self-directed action').

[8] S. J. Shapiro, *Legality* (Cambridge, MA: Harvard University Press, 2011), chapter 7.

[9] Ibid., 274–275. From this starting point, Shapiro then argues in favour of an exclusive version of legal positivism which, as will be seen later on, is the thesis that the existence and content of law cannot under any circumstances be determined by facts whose very existence the law aims to settle in the first place (i.e., moral facts).

international courts have treated similar matters in the past or that there exists concordant judicial practice on how a matter must be decided; or (iii) that other kinds of legally relevant actors, such as the epistemic community of international lawyers, share a view that should be heeded in the case at hand. To be sure, not all of these types of arguments from authority have the same formal degree of persuasive force.[10] It is clear, however, that legal argumentation in international law can never proceed acceptably without having some basis in some type of argument from authority.[11]

3.2.2 *Correctness*

The fact that arguments from authority always have a special place in legal argumentation does not mean that these are the only prevalent or acceptable kinds of arguments. There exists an ideal dimension next to the social dimension of law that mandates that legal outcomes must also be correct in substance.[12] The expectation of substantive correctness in

10 Traditionally, doctrine regards international treaties, customary international law, and general principles of law as 'formal' sources, giving rise to binding law and thus commanding the highest degree of authoritativeness and persuasiveness. By contrast, judicial decisions and the views of the epistemic community of international lawyers (commonly referred to as the 'writings of publicists') are regarded as 'material' sources of international law, thus commanding a lesser degree of authoritativeness at least in theory. That notwithstanding, studies indicate that judicial decisions, and especially decisions of the ICJ, have proven to be a powerful tool for the consolidation and gradual evolution of international law in practice (e.g., see A. Pellet and D. Müller, 'Article 38', in A. Zimmermann, C. J. Tams, and others [eds.], *The Statute of the International Court of Justice: A Commentary*, 3rd ed. [Oxford: Oxford University Press, 2019] 819, 954 [paras 324ff]). This means that their persuasive force tends to be rather high in practice. Furthermore, reference to past decisions is an argument from authority that is particularly prominent in the context of ISDS too. With respect to the writings of publicists, a 2008 study by Fauchald indicates that this has also been a frequent authoritative source in ISDS, at least in the earlier days of the regime. According to Fauchald, writings of publicists have been used on occasion: as an essential interpretative argument, as a starting point for further legal analysis, or to establish tests to be used as conditions for applying rules (see O. K. Fauchald, 'The Legal Reasoning of ICSID Tribunals – An Empirical Analysis' (2008) 19 *European Journal of International Law* 301, 351–353).

11 Indeed, this is a general feature of law, e.g., see N. MacCormick, 'Argumentation and Interpretation in Law' (1993) 6 *Ratio Juris* 16, 18.

12 See Shapiro (n. 8), 258 ('A reasonable legal system is one that strikes a balance between clarity, predictability, and constraint on the one hand, and correctness, flexibility, and discretion on the other.').

law typically takes the form of an expectation of justice.[13] Such an expectation applies both at the point of lawmaking and at the point of judicial resolution of concrete disputes. The same expectation of justice is ingrained in the practice of international law too, where it is often expressed under the equivalent term 'equity'.[14] In *North Sea Continental Shelf*, the ICJ gave expression to precisely this expectation by saying that '[w]hatever the legal reasoning of a court of justice, its decisions must by definition be just, and therefore in that sense equitable'.[15] The Court later confirmed the same position in *Tunisia/Libya* by stating that 'when applying positive international law, a court may choose among several possible interpretations of the law the one which appears, in the light of the circumstances of the case, to be closest to the requirements of justice'.[16]

Seen in the abstract, substantive correctness as justice describes the expectation of the participants in a legal system that the system gives rise to a correct distribution of entitlements, benefits, and burdens among them.[17] It is to be noted, however, that what constitutes a correct, or just, allocation will likely differ from one legal system to the next and, in the case of international law, even from one branch of international law to the next. The same applies by extension to the question of how the

[13] E.g., R. Alexy, 'Law and Correctness' (1998) 51 *Current Legal Problems* 205, 211; see also, H. L. A. Hart, 'Positivism and the Separation of Law and Morals' (1958) 71 *Harvard Law Review* 593, 622; Schultz (n. 1), 19, 49.

[14] For a historical source linking equity to the notion of justice, see *Cayuga Indians (Great Britain) v. United States*, Decision, 22 January 1926, Vol VI *RIAA* 173, 179–180 (where the tribunal made multiple direct references to the fact that international law is to be applied with equity in the sense of justice), 189–190 (where the tribunal: (i) refused to apply for reasons of equity the US defence of laches against the Canadian Cayuga Indians even though the defence could have been raised against Great Britain as the espousing state of the claims and (ii) apportioned the annuity owed to the Canadian Cayugas by the United States in an equitable way).

[15] *North Sea Continental Shelf Cases (Federal Republic of Germany/Denmark; Federal Republic of Germany/Netherlands)*, Judgment of 20 February 1969, ICJ Rep (1969) 3, para 88.

[16] *Case Concerning the Continental Shelf (Tunisia/Libyan Arab Jamahiriya)*, Judgment of 24 February 1982, ICJ Rep (1982) 18, para 71.

[17] Alexy (n. 13), 211:

> As a general or abstract claim, the claim to justice does not aim at a specific conception of justice, but only at a correct distribution of goods and burdens and the correct balance of guilt and punishment, and damage and compensation. Abstract justice is nothing else but correctness concerning distribution and balance.

expectation of correctness translates into judicial reasoning in different legal systems or in the different branches of international law. Given this, although the abstract claim to justice has usefulness as a universal claim about law in general, it also has limitations when one delves into particulars. For present purposes, there is no need to enter into a more detailed examination of what the claim to justice could mean for judicial reasoning in the ISDS context. Subsequent chapters will address aspects of this question as they may arise in the course of the discussion. The analysis here can thus proceed on the basis of the more abstract version of the claim to justice just identified.

3.3 Two Models for the Place of Coherence within Legal Reasoning

It is time for a brief recapitulation and stocktaking of the main points made until now. Recall from Chapters 1 and 2 that coherence has a role to play in legal reasoning. It is clear from the discussion in this chapter that in deciding disputes adjudicators must strive to give effect to both the factual/social and the ideal dimension of law. It is moreover equally clear that, although these two dimensions can often be seen as advancing together, there may be times when they come into conflict with each other. What is then the model for coherence to which the interaction of these two dimensions of law gives rise?

This section distinguishes two approaches to answering this question: (i) the positivist approach, which gives rise to what can be called a 'double coherence' model, and (ii) the non-positivist approach, which gives rise to what can be called a 'single coherence' model. Central to both approaches are opposing views on how one should conceptualise the interaction between the social and the ideal dimensions of law or, put differently, on how one should understand the relation between law and morality. The precise content of each approach is presented in turn below. A critical assessment of them is undertaken in Section 3.4.

3.3.1 *The Positivist Approach and the Model of 'Double Coherence'*

3.3.1.1 Legal Positivism and the Relationship between Law and Morality

A central tenet of legal positivism is the separability thesis, which advocates a very clear conceptual distinction between law and morality. The word 'conceptual' is key. The separability thesis does not advocate a complete separation between law and morality.[18] Positivism does not deny that morality (e.g., in the form of values or moral principles) is important for law, nor does it claim that the law's merits are unimportant or peripheral to the law's project. What positivism denies, rather, is that morality is as such a constitutive part of the processes that make the law. Put differently, positivism denies that morality figures among the processes that grant a specific norm its legality.[19] Summed up in a famous aphorism attributed to John Austin, both the existence and content of law depend on social facts alone and not on the law's merits.[20]

Taking a closer look at the separability thesis, however, one notices that there are in fact two questions hiding behind it that require some unpacking. The first question has to do with determining the criteria of legality (i.e., whether morality has a place among the processes that make law). The second question has to do with how adjudicators should go about deciding disputes, especially hard or controversial disputes, where clear guidance from the formal sources of law seems to be lacking (i.e., whether morality, considerations of justice, and other so-called 'extra-legal' factors have any relevance in this process). Positivists disagree even among themselves about the answer to the first question, but they converge on their views regarding the answer to the second question.

Two versions of legal positivism can therefore be distinguished. According to the exclusive or 'hard' version, there is no relation between law and morality, period.[21] In this version, tests of legality must always distinguish between law and non-law exclusively on the basis of a norm's

[18] L. Green, 'Positivism and the Inseparability of Law and Morals' (2008) 83 *New York University Law Review* 1035.

[19] For an example of such an outlook in international law, see *South West Africa (Ethiopia* v. *South Africa; Liberia* v. *South Africa), Second Phase*, Judgment of 18 July 1966, ICJ Rep (1966) 6. There, the ICJ refused to grant any legal effect (taking the form of legal rights and obligations) to the concept of 'humanitarian considerations' and to the principle of the 'sacred trust'. As the Court said at paras 49–51 of its judgment, moral principles may constitute the inspirational bases for rules of law but do not in themselves amount to rules of law. This means that they can be taken into account only insofar as they have been given sufficient prior expression in legal form.

[20] See J. Austin, *The Province of Jurisprudence Determined*, ed. by W. E. Rumble (Cambridge: Cambridge University Press, 1995), 157 ('The existence of law is one thing; its merit or demerit is another. Whether it be or be not is one enquiry; whether it be or be not conformable to an assumed standard, is a different enquiry.').

[21] J. Raz, *The Authority of Law: Essays on Law and Morality*, 2nd ed. (Oxford: Oxford University Press, 2009), 45–50. For an additional defence of the exclusive version of legal positivism by the same author, see Raz (n. 5), chapter 10.

social source without resort to moral reasoning whatsoever.[22] That could be done by tracing a norm to one of the recognised formal sources of law or by finding evidence of widespread agreement amongst the legal system's officials with respect to the existence and content of a norm, even if that norm does not take the form of one of the sources of law in that system.[23] Conversely, according to the inclusive or 'soft' version of positivism, the case rather is that there exists no necessary connection between legality and morality. The inclusive version still maintains that the existence and content of law is ultimately determined by social facts. It does not deny, however, as the exclusive version does, that the ultimate tests of legality could incorporate criteria of a moral nature.[24] Such a thing is possible and indeed acceptable so long as the master rule of legality – the 'rule of recognition' according to Hart – itself has a social pedigree.[25] Put differently, according to the inclusive version, there can exist a legal system where legality would be wholly or partly determined by the dictates of morality but only if the officials in that system have agreed that this is indeed the case.

The separability thesis carries over to the interpretation and application of law by courts, yet it does so with important differences. A change in the process of reasoning occurs when we move from the criteria of legality and towards adjudication.[26] Identifying the existence of legal norms according to the separability thesis leads logically to the conclusion that the law would inevitably include gaps that adjudicators would have to fill, even if that may mean having at times to reach beyond the law to do so. Accordingly, whereas the proponents of each version of

[22] S. J. Shapiro, 'The "Hart-Dworkin" Debate: A Short Guide for the Perplexed', in A. Ripstein (ed.), *Ronald Dworkin* (Cambridge: Cambridge University Press, 2007) 22, 31–32.

[23] On such an expanded understanding of the law's social 'sources', see Raz (n. 21), 47–78.

[24] See 'Postscript', in H. L. A. Hart, *The Concept of Law*, 3rd ed. (Oxford: Oxford University Press, 2012), 250.

[25] Shapiro (n. 22), 33.

[26] E.g., see J. d'Aspremont, *Formalism and the Sources of International Law: A Theory of the Ascertainment of Legal Rules* (Oxford: Oxford University Press, 2011), 157 (emphasis in original, footnote omitted):

> It is argued here that the criteria on the basis of which international legal rules are ascertained are not necessarily the same as those through which the *content* of law is determined. This means that the yardstick to distinguish between law and non-law may differ from that used, once a legal rule has been ascertained, to determine the scope of the legal obligation that the rule in question imposes.

positivism disagree about the role of morality as a condition for the existence of law, they nonetheless converge on its indispensability when it comes to adjudication and interpretation.[27] Indeed, the positivist view accepts that recourse to moral judgment may be necessary not only when there exists a gap in the applicable law but also when the applicable legal norms are simply vague or when multiple norms conflict and no clear guidance is offered for the resolution of the conflict.[28] In reaching outside the confines of the law in these cases, adjudicators are said to be acting under discretion and to be exercising a limited lawmaking function in identifying, interpreting, and applying the moral principles deemed necessary for the resolution of the case.[29]

Although rarely expressed in the same terms, in particular with respect to the quasi-legislative function of adjudicators,[30] the above position is

[27] E.g., see Hart (n. 13), 613–614 (confirming that in hard cases intelligent decisions are made not mechanically but in the light of 'aims, purposes, and policies, though not necessarily in the light of anything we would call moral principles' and also seeing the task of sentencing in criminal cases as a plain instance where the exercise of moral judgment is warranted); as well as Raz (n. 21), 49–50:

> [T]he law on a question is settled when legally binding sources provide its solution. In such cases judges are typically said to apply the law, and since it is source-based, its application involves technical, legal skills in reasoning from those sources and does not call for moral acumen. If a legal question is not answered by standards deriving from legal sources then it lacks a legal answer – the law on the question is unsettled. In deciding such cases courts inevitably break new (legal) ground and their decision develops the law (at least in precedent-based legal systems). Naturally, their decisions in such cases rely at least partly on moral and other extra-legal considerations.

J. Gardner, 'Legal Positivism: 5 1/2 Myths' (2001) 46 *American Journal of Jurisprudence* 199, 213, further argues that there exists complementarity between source-based and moral considerations, even within a positivist outlook of the law:

> At least sometimes, relying on source-based norms is warranted because it provides one way of resolving cases that cannot be completely resolved on their merits. . . . At least sometimes relying on some or all of the merits of a case is warranted because it provides a way of resolving cases that cannot be completely resolved according to the applicable source-based norms.

[28] Cf. Gardner (n. 27), 211ff.

[29] See Hart (n. 24), 272ff.

[30] However, cf. the views of Max Habicht who, as early as 1934, had argued that: '[L]a seule différence entre l'interprétation du droit et l'activité quasi législative du juge comblant les lacunes du droit positif, est une différence de degré. . . . S'il se présente une lacune, la Cour la comblera en "découvrant" ou en "créant" la règle nécessaire.' (M. Habicht, 'Le pouvoir du juge international de statuer "ex aequo et bono"' (1934) 49 *Recueil des cours* 277, 292 [footnote omitted]).

not foreign to international law. Several scholars have affirmed the power of international judges to fill gaps in international law, notably through the identification and deployment of general principles of law.[31] International courts and tribunals too have held that, in the absence of specific guidance from posited law or when coming across vague and ambiguous treaty standards, they enjoy a margin of bounded discretion to determine the appropriate rule or principle to be applied in the interest of achieving a just outcome.[32] One can see a prominent example of this

[31] Among a plethora of sources, see A. Verdross, 'Les principes généraux du droit dans la jurisprudence internationale' (1935) 52 *Recueil des cours* 195, 225; P. Weil, '"The Court Cannot Conclude Definitely . . ." *Non Liquet* Revisited' (1997) 36 *Columbia Journal of Transnational Law* 109, 110–112 (analogising general principles to reserve forces that are to be sent to the frontlines if necessary); G. Abi-Saab, 'Cours général de droit international public' (1987) 207 *Recueil des cours* 9, 188–189; M. Virally, 'The Sources of International Law', in M. Sørensen (ed.), *Manual of Public International Law* (London: MacMillan & Co, 1968) 116, 147–148; C. T. Kotuby Jr and L. Sobota, *General Principles of Law and International Due Process: Principles and Norms Applicable in Transnational Disputes* (New York: Oxford University Press, 2017), 30–31; Pellet and Müller (n. 10), 941 (paras 296–297) (describing the practice of the ICJ).

In the domain of international economic law in particular, see A. R. Ziegler and J. Baumgartner, 'Good Faith as a General Principle of (International) Law', in A. D. Mitchell, M. Sornarajah, and T. Voon (eds.), *Good Faith and International Economic Law* (Oxford: Oxford University Press, 2015) 9, 10, 14–15, 17; E. de Brabandere and I. van Damme, 'Good Faith in Treaty Interpretation', in ibid. 37, 41–42; T. Gazzini, 'General Principles of Law in the Field of Foreign Investment' (2009) 10 *Journal of World Investment and Trade* 103, 105, 108, 118–119; G. Hanessian, '"General Principles of Law" in the Iran-US Claims Tribunal' (1989) 27 *Columbia Journal of Transnational Law* 309, 324; C. Schreuer, L. Malintoppi, A. Reinisch, and A. Sinclair (eds.), *The ICSID Convention: A Commentary*, 2nd ed. (Cambridge: Cambridge University Press, 2009), 607–608 (para 178).

But cf. E. Voyiakis, 'Do General Principles Fill "Gaps" in International Law?' (2009) 14 *Austrian Review of International and European Law* 239, who argues convincingly that the role of general principles in international law is much more pervasive than simple gap-filling.

[32] E.g., see *Libyan American Oil Company (LIAMCO)* v. *Government of the Libyan Arab Republic*, Award, 12 April 1977, 62 *ILR* 140, 209 (using equity as a general principle of law, having first found that there were no applicable principles that were common to Libya's domestic law and to international law, as mandated by the applicable law clause of the concession agreement); *Responsabilité de l'Allemagne à raison des dommages causés dans les colonies portugaises du sud de l'Afrique (sentence sur le principe de la responsabilité) (Portugal* c. *Allemagne)*, Decision of 31 July 1928 (known as the *Naulilaa* arbitration), Vol II *RIAA* 1011, 1016 (footnote omitted):

> Enfin, à défaut de règles du droit des gens applicables aux faits litigieux, les arbitres estiment devoir combler la lacune, en statuant suivant les principes d'équité, tout en restant dans le sens du droit des gens, appliqué par analogie, et en tenant compte de son évolution;

judicial attitude also being at play in ISDS when tribunals allocate costs (administrative and legal fees) among the disputing parties. Given that the cost of litigating investor–state disputes can be substantial, awards on costs are important tools for restoring successful investors to the position they would be at but for the host state's breach, as well as for ensuring that states are not ultimately penalised for successfully defending government measures. However, most arbitral rules grant tribunals varying degrees of discretion to make determinations on cost allocation.[33] Thus, tribunals will often apply a variety of apportioning principles (e.g., 'bear your own costs', 'costs follow the event' (loser pays), or 'relative success') in a way that reflects what in the tribunal's mind is fair or just under the circumstances, considering factors such as the outcome of the dispute, the complexity or novelty of the issues raised, the relative merits of each party's case, or the parties' conduct during the proceedings.[34]

The Mavrommatis Palestine Concessions (Greece v. *Great Britain), Objection to the Jurisdiction of the Court*, Judgment of 30 August 1924, PCIJ Series A No 2 (1924) 5, 16:

> Neither the Statute nor the Rules of Court contain any rule regarding the procedure to be followed in the event of an objection being taken *in limine litis* to the Court's jurisdiction. The Court therefore is at liberty to adopt the principle which it considers best calculated to ensure the administration of justice, most suited to procedure before an international tribunal and most in conformity with the fundamental principles of international law.

[33] E.g., Article 61(2) ICSID Convention; Rule 62 ICSID Additional Facility Rules (2022); Article 42(1) UNCITRAL Rules (2013); Article 38(5) ICC Rules (2021); Article 49(6) SCC Rules (2017); Article 28 LCIA Rules (2020); Rules 33 and 35 SIAC Investment Arbitration Rules (2017). For an explicit confirmation of the existence of such bounded discretion, see *Piero Foresti, Laura de Carli & Others* v. *The Republic of South Africa*, ICSID Case No. ARB(AF)/07/01, Award, 4 August 2010, paras 104–105 (applying the 2006 ICSID Additional Facility Rules).

[34] E.g., see *Alasdair Ross Anderson et al* v. *Republic of Costa Rica*, ICSID Case No. ARB(AF)/07/3, Award, 19 May 2010, paras 62–64 (adopting the 'bear your own costs' principle as default presumption and finding that there were no special circumstances – e.g., procedural misconduct, a frivolous claim, an abuse of the BIT process or of the international investment protection regime – that could result in the reversal of this presumption); *Cementownia 'Nowa Huta' S.A.* v. *Republic of Turkey*, ICSID Case No. ARB(AF)/06/2, Award, 17 September 2009, paras 175–178 (adopting the 'loser pays' principle and thus ordering the investor to cover all of the state's arbitration costs and legal fees, in particular for having filed a fraudulent claim, failed on all its requests for relief, delayed the arbitration proceedings, not signed a custody agreement despite repeated requests, not complied with instructions regarding the deposit of advance payments to ICSID, abused nationality planning); *EnCana Corporation* v. *Republic of Ecuador*, LCIA Case No. UN3481, UNCITRAL Rules, Award, 3 February 2006, paras 201–204 (ordering the winning party to pay all the arbitration costs but not the other party's legal costs, based on what would be 'just and equitable' in light of the events giving rise to the arbitration); *ADF Group Inc.* v. *United States of America*, ICSID Case No. ARB(AF)/00/1, Award,

3.3.1.2 The Model of 'Double Coherence'

A consequence of the positivist position that regards a dispute as covered by the law whenever there exists a specific source-based rule expressly regulating it is that positivism sees two distinct stages in legal reasoning by courts. In the first stage, the judge uses only his or her technical, so-called legal skills to determine whether there exists a rule applicable to the case. If such a rule exists, then the case is regulated by law, the rule applies, and legal reasoning ends. If such a rule does not exist, then the case is unregulated by law and has no legal answer (there is a gap). This determination activates the second stage. In the second stage, the judge does not apply law but instead exercises a limited lawmaking function in an effort to discover the morally best solution given the available legal materials.[35]

Such an outlook on judicial reasoning, coupled with the identified need to ensure that the values of certainty and correctness are adhered to in the process, naturally leads to a double coherence model.[36] On this model, considerations of coherence can play a role at each of the two stages of legal reasoning. In the first stage, where the judge is thought to deploy only technical reasoning, coherence operates similarly to consistency albeit on a systemic scale. That is to say, the judge uses logic and the criteria of legal validity in the system (the system's doctrine of authoritative sources) to identify rules of law in a consistent manner, thus promoting certainty, predictability, and even-handedness. In the second stage, where the judge is thought to open himself or herself up to moral

9 January 2003, para 200 (ordering the parties each to bear its own costs, having regard to the nature and complexity of the questions raised); *Pantechniki S.A. Contractors & Engineers (Greece)* v. *The Republic of Albania*, ICSID Case No. ARB/07/21, Award, 30 July 2009, paras 103–104 (refusing Albania's request for the application of the 'loser pays' principle and instead adopting 'bear your own costs', for the reason that '[t]he claim [did] not fail for a lack of inherent validity[,] [but] rather falter[ed] because the Treaty [was] unavailable to the Claimant in the circumstances'); *International Thunderbird Gaming Corporation* v. *The United Mexican States*, UNCITRAL Rules, Award, 26 January 2006, paras 219–221 (adopting the 'relative success' principle and awarding administrative costs and legal fees in a 3/4–1/4 ratio in favour of Mexico, considering that Mexico prevailed on merits but not on jurisdiction/admissibility).

35 Hart (n. 24), 272–275; Raz (n. 21), 49–50, 96, 181.

36 The double coherence model is borrowed from M. A. Eisenberg, *The Nature of the Common Law* (Cambridge, MA: Harvard University Press, 1988), chapter 5. In outlining the model of double coherence, inspiration is drawn from Eisenberg's work, who usefully sketched it out as a possible model for common law adjudication, before rejecting it as unworkable in practice for not fully taking into account the common law doctrine of *stare decisis*.

considerations, coherence operates as an ideal of moral congruence. The judicial task in this stage involves exercising judgement, including a process of integrating together the system's various principles, values, and policies and an attempt to weave these elements together into a seamless pattern of conduct.

The upshot of the double coherence model, however, is that these two sides of coherence can never actually coexist or advance together as goals during legal reasoning. The reason for this being that, according to legal positivism, one is precluded from entering into the second stage of judicial reasoning if the dispute is already regulated by the first stage. Therefore, it is always the case in the double coherence model that one or the other of the two dimensions of coherence listed above will ultimately prevail, depending on the difficulty of the dispute presented before the court in every instance.

3.3.2 The Non-positivist Approach and the Model of 'Single Coherence'

Non-positivism takes a different view on the relationship between law and morality and, by extension, also takes a different view on the model of coherence in legal reasoning. Rather than separating the social and the moral in law, non-positivism regards them as intertwined and combined, both when determining the existence of law as well as when determining the law's content through interpretation. The particular non-positivist approach that this section explores in more detail is known as legal interpretivism. A key difference between positivism and interpretivism is a fundamentally different outlook on the kind of concept that law is. Recall from Chapter 1 that there are three kinds of concepts: criterial, natural-kind, and interpretative. Positivism regards law as a criterial concept, thus placing principal focus on a test of legality (i.e., the doctrine of sources) that must be met before a norm can be qualified as 'legal'. However, for legal interpretivism, law is an interpretative concept.[37] As described in Chapter 1, an interpretative concept is shared by people participating in a practice that seeks to identify instances of that concept by appealing to the purpose or value that this concept has or brings forward. When people disagree about the criteria or about the application of an interpretative concept, in reality they disagree about the value or

[37] See R. Dworkin, 'Hart's Postscript and the Character of Political Philosophy' (2004) 24 *Oxford Journal of Legal Studies* 1.

purpose of that concept and not about whether the concept itself actually applies.

Transposed to the domain of law, this means that questions about the existence and content of law are both interpretative questions and, as such, depend on factors that are social as well as moral. Moreover, such factors are intertwined. Consider, for example, the way in which interpretivism would make the case that institutional practice in a legal system (e.g., legislative acts, court decisions, and long-standing practices) is relevant in determining the law and its content. For interpretivism, the reason why institutional practice is relevant is not merely because of the fact that it happens to have a social pedigree. Such a line of reasoning would be circular.[38] Rather, the relevance of institutional practice is a normative conclusion based on moral (deontological or teleological) reasons that mandate that institutional practice ought to be authoritative because of its social pedigree.[39] Such reasons may, for instance, indicate that it would be contrary to our sense of fairness and dignity if the law's coercive force would be exercised against individuals when this could not

[38] Cf. N. Stavropoulos, 'Why Principles?', University of Oxford Faculty of Law Legal Studies Research Paper Series, Working Paper No 28/2007 (October 2007), available at https://papers.ssrn.com/sol3/papers.cfm?abstract_id=1023758 (pointing out at p. 10 that '[i]t is generally impossible for any descriptive facts of practice, alone, to determine their own normative significance, and therefore to determine a rule' [footnote omitted]).

[39] See MacCormick (n. 11), 19, usefully summarising a very similar point (emphases added):

> This omnipresence of authority reasons in legal argumentation is not, however, independent of substantive reasons. That which has authority is that which has a right to be obeyed; where there is authority exercised legitimately, disobedience is *prima facie* wrong. Notwithstanding theories of autopoiesis and self-referentiality, *the reasons on which authority claims are founded cannot all be themselves authority reasons.* Ultimately, *to make intelligible (not to say acceptable) any claim of authority, is to enter into either deontological reasoning or teleological reasoning, or both.* Authority has to be grounded in some way on the rightness of observing norms posed or evolved in a certain way, or on the values (peace and good order, perhaps) secured by such recognition. And the justification of norms posed by authorities must presumably be in terms of their rightness (justice) or the good they bring about. Even where the rightness of using authority reasons (or the value secured by respecting them) is deemed to exclude any further appeal to substantive reasons, that in itself indicates the ultimate dependency of reasons of authority upon reasons of substance, and shows how institutional argumentation has to be anchored in pure practical argumentation. Still, the law is a forum of institutional argumentation to the extent that it gives, and necessarily gives, a central place to 'authority reasons' in the form of statutes, precedents, doctrinal materials and the like.

be traced back in an appropriate way to some existing practice, rule, or principle.[40]

Interestingly, then, even when one follows interpretivism, one can still be a positivist, even an exclusive one. But this would be a normative kind of positivism, which must be argued for and defended on moral grounds.[41] This implies, further, that from the interpretivist point of view, positivism cannot be devoid of moral theory, since it is itself a moral theory. Indeed, the moral underpinnings of legal positivism in international law have been confirmed in an indirect yet clear manner by no less a positivist than Gerald Fitzmaurice, who once argued:

> The idealist is the most dangerous of all the enemies of the Rule of Law, and that for a simple but paradoxical reason, namely that his aim is to achieve 'justice', that is to say what he believes to be justice in relation to the particular issue confronting him. It may be at once asked what is wrong with that – is it not the aim of law to achieve justice? The answer is yes, in the ultimate and overall sense, it is certainly the aim of law to achieve the greatest general measure of justice over the whole field of the relations it has to deal with. But its *immediate* aim, or perhaps its method, is something rather different, namely order, system, regularity, certainty, precision; and last but not least, ascertainability. It is by achieving these things that law achieves justice in practice.[42] . . .
>
> [J]ustice is very seldom achieved by directly aiming at it: rather is it [*sic*] a by-product of the application of legal rules and principles, a

40 N. Stavropoulos, 'Legal Interpretivism', in E. N. Zalta (ed.), *The Stanford Encyclopedia of Philosophy* (Summer 2014), available at https://plato.stanford.edu/entries/law-interpretivist/.

41 E.g., see S. Hershovitz, 'The Model of Plans and the Prospects for Positivism' (2014) 125 *Ethics* 152, 163, 167, 170, 181; also, see R. Dworkin, *Justice for Hedgehogs* (Cambridge, MA: Harvard University Press, 2011), 403–404 (n. 6), pointing out that Jeremy Bentham, widely recognised as the most important of the early positivists, had based his version of legal positivism on the moral principle of utility, thus prompting Dworkin to describe him as a 'closet interpretivist'.

In the context of international law, Patrick Capps has argued that the legal theories of Lassa Oppenheim, Prosper Weil, Hersch Lauterpacht, and the New Haven School, are all examples of different interpretivist outlooks on international law. Capps sees the writings of Oppenheim and Weil in particular, as being instances of exactly the kind of normative legal positivism described above (P. Capps, 'Interpretivism', in J. d'Aspremont and S. Singh (eds.), *Concepts for International Law: Contributions to Disciplinary Thought* [Cheltenham: Edward Elgar, 2019] 566).

42 G. Fitzmaurice, 'The United Nations and the Rule of Law' (1952) 38 *Transactions of the Grotius* 135, 145 (emphasis in original). He adds further (ibid.) that the idealist's attitude to discard legal process in favour of 'look[ing] at the facts of each particular case', in situations where the strict application of law leads to some injustice or to less than ideal justice, is 'profoundly mistaken, and in the long run self defeating'.

> consequence of the general order, certainty and stability introduced into human and international relationships through the regular and systematic application of known legal rules and principles, even if these rules and principles are not always perfect and do not always achieve ideal results in every case.[43]

In short, interpretivism points out that there can be no process of identifying law that is separate and distinct from any process of interpreting law. Rather, identifying law is interpreting.[44] In the context of the decision-making practices of courts and tribunals, the upshot of an interpretivist outlook on law is that legal reasoning cannot be regarded as a bifurcated process, as positivism suggests, but rather as a single, unified process comprising both technical and moral arguments.[45] This would in turn give rise to a model of 'single coherence'. A single coherence model better fits with the analysis previously undertaken regarding the practical and deliberative nature of legal reasoning, on the one hand, and the simultaneous substantive and methodological dimensions of coherence, on the other hand.

Notwithstanding this affinity between our working understanding of coherence and the single coherence model of legal reasoning, Section 3.4 will engage in a more detailed assessment of the two models for coherence identified here before committing to the single model.

3.4 Assessing the Two Models for Coherence

It is argued that interpretivism and the model of single coherence better correspond to judicial practice. To see why this is the case, this section assesses the two models for coherence in two stages. In a first stage, the key assumption behind the bifurcated view of legal reasoning is critically examined. Recall that, according to positivism, mere technical reasoning is sufficient in easy cases whereas moral reasoning is required only in hard cases. This section argues that this dichotomy is false. If one scrutinises it, one can see that (i) the distinction between hard cases

43 Ibid., 147–148.

44 Taking a similar view in the context of the identification, interpretation, and application of norms of customary international law (although not doing so explicitly under the rubric of interpretivism), see O. Chasapis Tassinis, 'Customary International Law: Interpretation from Beginning to End' (2020) 31 *European Journal of International Law* 235.

45 See also J. Waldron, 'Judges as Moral Reasoners' (2009) 7 *International Journal of Constitutional Law* 2, 14.

and easy cases is itself an interpretative one and (ii) moral considerations abound in easy cases just like in hard cases. Following that, in a second stage, theoretical and practical pitfalls of adhering to the bifurcated view of legal reasoning are explored.

3.4.1 Easy and Hard Cases

A perception often seems to exist that the distinction between easy and hard cases is one of kind rather than degree. The description of easy and hard cases in legal theory may have at times contributed to this misunderstanding. Consider, for instance, the following descriptions of easy cases taken from the works of three influential legal theorists. Dworkin argued that a case is easy when it raises a very simple legal question, whose answer is completely obvious or can be reached in an almost unreflective manner.[46] In Dworkin's classic example, it is obvious that the speed limit in the State of California is 55 mph because it is obvious that any competent interpretation of Californian traffic law must yield that conclusion. Raz has expressed a similar view with his description of regulated and unregulated cases. He says:

> Regulated cases are those which fall under a common law or statutory rule which does not require judicial discretion for the determination of the dispute (rules referring to what is reasonable or just, etc., do require such discretion). A dispute is regulated if questions of the form: 'In this case should the court decide that p?' have a correct legal answer.[47]

Yet a third similar description has come from MacCormick. In *Legal Reasoning and Legal Theory*, MacCormick remarked that we are in the presence of an easy case when an applicable norm exists, that norm is clear, and there is no dispute about whether or not the case's facts fall under the norm's scope of application.[48]

These ways of describing easy cases can be misleading. They may be taken as suggesting that in easy cases there is no need for judgment, assessment, or interpretation when it comes to stating one's premises upon which one's legal syllogism would proceed. MacCormick's assertions, in particular, that in some cases it is possible for a decision to be

[46] R. Dworkin, *Law's Empire* (Cambridge, MA: Harvard University Press, 1986), 266, 353–354.

[47] Raz (n. 21), 181.

[48] N. MacCormick, *Legal Reasoning and Legal Theory* (Oxford: Clarendon Press, 1978), chapter II.

'legally justified by means of a purely deductive argument' or that 'the process of legal justification is sometimes purely deductive and logical in character',[49] make it seem like there are at least some legal outcomes that can be found to be correct by pure logic alone – that they are, in a way, determined already in advance of any process of legal reasoning having taken place and that it would be only in hard cases where the judge's intellect might be put to the test and his or her interpretative acumen be really engaged.

I hasten to clarify that this is, in fact, not the view shared by any of the above authors.[50] Rather, if we could recast it, the underlying idea behind such descriptions of easy cases seems to be not that these cases require a different, simpler, or less demanding style of reasoning but instead that in easy cases there appears to be widespread agreement regarding the content of the rules and principles that govern the outcome.[51] That being the case, two conclusions then follow: (i) the distinction between easy and hard cases is interpretative and therefore a matter of degree; and (ii) moral considerations abound in both easy and hard cases. The following thought experiment from the area of international human rights law showcases the validity of both conclusions.

Suppose one asks: 'Why has state A been condemned for the fact that its police forces used violence in interrogating prisoner B?' To answer the question competently, it suffices to point to the rule that prohibits states from torturing or subjecting individuals to inhuman and degrading treatment or punishment. The fact that there exists a rule against these

[49] Ibid., 19, 36–37, respectively.

[50] E.g., see Dworkin (n. 46), 266 (describing easy cases as special instances of hard cases), 354 (arguing that Hercules – Dworkin's imaginary super-judge – does not need separate methods for easy and hard cases, since his method is equally at work in both types of cases); Raz (n. 21), 182 (clarifying that there is nothing mechanical about regulated cases, that they can be complex and at times even more difficult to decide than unregulated cases); lastly, MacCormick (n. 48), 197, offers the clearest confirmation:

> Hitherto, it has been assumed without much argument that there is a relatively simple disjunction as between clear cases and hard cases. In the former, justification of decisions can be achieved by simple deduction from clear established rules. In the latter, since we face problems of 'interpretation' of 'classification' or 'relevancy', we have to have recourse to 'second-order justification'. Deduction comes in only after the interesting part of the argument, settling a ruling in law, has been carried through. But in truth there is no clear dividing line between clear cases and hard cases.

[51] Cf. C. R. Sunstein, *Legal Reasoning and Political Conflict*, 2nd ed. (New York: Oxford University Press, 2018), 216 ('Easy cases are easy only because of shared agreement on syntactic and substantive principles').

practices is enough of a reason for holding A accountable.[52] No additional justification needs to be offered because this reason holds good by virtue of the authority of its source (say, Article 3 of the ECHR). Suppose, however, that we are then asked a slightly different question: 'Why is it that we condemn states that engage in torture?' Pointing to the rule that prohibits torture is to no avail now, since doing so would only lead to a circular response. We may be able to plausibly justify the legal validity or binding character of a norm by pointing to its source of authority,[53] but we cannot justify the norm's existence in quite the same way. To answer this second question, we must rather seek moral reasons that justify having a rule against torture and, perhaps, even reasons justifying the practice of having an entire body of law known as human rights law.[54] Suppose we do so and we thus conclude that the reason why we protect human rights is out of respect for the dignity of human beings and that the reason we prohibit torture in particular is because torture is designed to inflict a particular kind of physical or mental pain or suffering that is an affront to human dignity.

Now suppose two cases come before us for judgment. In the first case, a prisoner has been beaten to within an inch of his or her life. We can quickly and clearly conclude that the prisoner has been tortured. The case is easy. In the second case, the prisoner was subjected to a series of less severe actions – such as prolonged standing, sitting in uncomfortable positions, loud noises, and sleep deprivation – which when seen separately and individually do not seem to rise to the level of torture. Faced with these facts, we may not be so certain whether the prisoner has been tortured or subjected to inhuman and degrading treatment. These were in a nutshell the facts in the 1978 *Ireland* v. *United Kingdom* case brought

[52] To clarify, several other questions are assumed under this simple reply. The answer to these other questions depends on separate sets of reasons that are here omitted (e.g., questions about the attribution of acts of police forces to the state are answered by reference to the rules on state responsibility). The omission is made here on purpose, to simplify the example, and does not affect the main point to be made.

[53] To recall, however, one could still not justify in a non-circular way that norms originating from certain types of sources carry authority and binding force, simply by pointing to the fact that these norms originate in such type of sources (as opposed to some other type), without offering any additional argument.

[54] On the difference between justifying a rule or practice and justifying particular actions falling under a rule or practice, see J. Rawls, 'Two Concepts of Rules' (1955) 64 *Philosophical Review* 3.

before the ECtHR.[55] The case was harder for the ECtHR to decide given its undeveloped jurisprudence at the time.

To determine whether the above actions – when practised systematically and in combination – indeed amount to torture, we will likely have to ask how our guiding principle of human dignity instructs us to decide. But if we think that an inquiry into the principle of human dignity will help us find the answer, then the question we are faced with is not unlike the question we are faced with when we were asked why we condemn torture in general.[56] In order to decide the case, we cannot but again ask what kind of infringements upon human dignity torture and inhuman and degrading treatment commit. This involves deciding what is so despicable about torture that violates human dignity, what degree of physical or mental pain or suffering is required for a finding of torture, and whether the challenged actions have crossed that threshold.[57]

Therefore, an assessment of the mandates of human dignity will not only help us in interpreting the prohibition of torture and inhuman and degrading treatment or punishment but will also help us in justifying any

[55] *Case of Ireland* v. *The United Kingdom*, Judgment, 18 January 1978, ECHR Series A, No 25.

[56] MacCormick makes essentially the same point in his analysis of the landmark common law case of *Donoghue* v. *Stevenson*, in N. MacCormick, *Practical Reason in Law and Morality* (Oxford: Oxford University Press, 2008), 187:

> Yet despite the technical legal quality of the reasoning, there is, particularly in the speech of Lord Atkin, a strong recognition that the legal issue runs in parallel with, and ought to be considered against the background of a moral question. That question concerns the moral basis of the law of torts – why ought one person ever to compensate another for harm suffered? An answer to that question can in [Lord Atkin's] view guide towards the correct legal answer, since the law must be presumed to have been developed by judges and legislators who are themselves moral agents. Hence, though it is necessary to 'aim off' to allow for the positive and highly institutionalized character of the law of England or Scotland, reflection on underlying moral principles will be essential.

For a similar position expressed in international law, see R. Higgins, *Problems and Process: International Law and How We Use It*, reprint (Oxford: Clarendon Press, 1995), 5 ('Reference to "the correct legal view" or "rules" can never avoid the element of choice (though it can seek to disguise it), nor can it provide guidance to the preferable decision. In making this choice one must inevitably have consideration for the humanitarian, moral, and social purposes of the law).

[57] Incidentally, the ECtHR in *Ireland* v. *United Kingdom* found that the interrogation techniques under challenge did not amount to torture but to inhuman and degrading treatment. This jurisprudence has since been reversed.

decision that we reach.[58] Crucially, however, it would be misleading to say that human dignity was only relevant in deciding the harder case but not the easy one. If the principle that all human beings partake of human dignity is the reason behind the prohibition of torture and inhuman and degrading treatment or punishment, then it is the principle that helped us to decide both cases. The difference is that the interpretation of the principle in the first case was generally accepted at the time the matter was brought to us for decision whereas in the second case it was not so, which is the reason why the principle's presence was felt more acutely there.

In short, the positivist view, according to which the adjudicator must open himself or herself up to moral reasoning only in hard cases, is not accurate because it puts the cart before the horse. It is not the difficulty of a case that makes resort to moral reasoning necessary. To the contrary, what makes a legal issue easier or harder to answer is the extent of our moral disagreement about the relevance to be accorded, and the interpretation to be given, to the various values or principles that justify our rules.[59]

[58] See C. McCrudden, 'Human Dignity and Judicial Interpretation of Human Rights' (2008) 19 *European Journal of International Law* 655, 724 (concluding that one significant use of human dignity is institutional in the sense that it 'provid[es] a language in which judges can appear to justify how they deal with issues such as the weight of rights, the domestication and contextualization of rights, and the generation of new or more extensive rights').

[59] For the same point made in more detail, see W. Lucy, 'Adjudication', in J. L. Coleman, K. E. Himma, and S. J. Shapiro (eds.), *The Oxford Handbook of Jurisprudence and Philosophy of Law* (Oxford: Oxford University Press, 2004) 206, 212:

> To be regarded as relevant, clear, and unambiguous, a proposition of law must be accepted as either beyond question or at least not worth challenging by (at a minimum) the members of the legal community. To be beyond question or unworthy of challenge, the proposition of law must be either regarded as in some sense normatively acceptable or unreflectively or habitually adhered to by, at a minimum, the legal community and, perhaps, segments of the wider community. When the proposition is challenged, either as a result of increased awareness of its effects or a greater appreciation of its normative shortcomings both within the legal community and beyond, it will no longer be regarded as obviously relevant, clear, and unambiguous. What was once accepted as an easy case and hence unworthy of argument – for example, that husbands cannot rape their wives in English criminal law – becomes harder, more controversial, and, perhaps, eventually overturned. Hence, the distinction between easy cases and hard cases is not absolute; it is a matter of degree.

3.4.2 The Pitfalls of the Bifurcated View

The above remarks cast doubt on the underlying assumption of the bifurcated view of legal reasoning that easier cases are decided by a different process or method than the more difficult cases. This alone gives us reason to distance ourselves from the bifurcated view and come closer to the unified view. To further buttress our reasons for committing to the unified view, this section addresses in greater detail the methodological pitfalls of following the bifurcated view of legal reasoning and its corollary model of double coherence. Three types of related pitfalls are identified: (i) infinite regress and the law's two dimensions, (ii) losing sight of the law's arguable character, and (iii) too readily assuming the existence of governing rules. The unified view, we shall see, does not face the same methodological pitfalls. This is not because it makes moral conflicts and disagreements disappear or easier to resolve but rather because it integrates moral disagreement within the concept of law itself.

3.4.2.1 Infinite Regress and the Two Dimensions of Law

The first series of methodological pitfalls of adhering to the bifurcated view can be described as the problem of infinite regress and the problem of the law's two dimensions. Both problems stem from the same source. It was said above that the bifurcated view of legal reasoning leads to a model of double coherence. It was also said that the result of such a model is that the two sides of coherence towards which the model points (i.e., systemic consistency and moral congruence) cannot coexist or advance together as goals during legal reasoning. The case rather is that one or the other side would ultimately prevail depending on the nature of the dispute presented before the court or tribunal in each case – that is to say, on whether the case is perceived by the judge as an easy or a hard one to resolve.

Therefore, under a double coherence model, we can experience situations where the requirements of systemic consistency and moral congruence themselves conflict if the case is hard enough. That would be the case, for example, when there exists an easily identifiable rule regulating the case, whose application however leads to an obviously unjust result under the circumstances. In those situations, the adjudicator may have to suppose a conflict-resolving meta-principle to break the deadlock. However, it is far from clear what such a meta-principle might be in international law or international investment law.[60] And even if we were to identify one such conflict-resolving meta-principle, the meta-principle would surely require interpretation so that, in the event of disagreement about its interpretation, another meta-principle might be needed, and so on and so forth ad infinitum. In other words, a meta-principle would do little to resolve our conundrum given the law's arguable character and the scope for moral disagreement in it.

Further to the above, the dual coherence model creates a dilemma that, either way we resolve it, may end up undermining our faith in law's two dimensions. If a judge openly admits that he or she has left the law aside because of the difficulty of the case and that his or her decision is based on moral, extra-legal considerations, we seem to be undermining the law's authority and planning function. Similarly, but in the opposite direction, if a judge admits that he or she must follow doctrine even if it leads to a morally subpar outcome, law also seems to lose one of its core assumptions, namely, the assumption of morally desirable and just solutions.

3.4.2.2 Losing Sight of the Law's Arguable Character

Adhering to the bifurcated view of legal reasoning also runs the risk of losing sight of the fact that law has an arguable character. We have said that the bifurcated view distinguishes between a first, technical stage of legal reasoning – where an applicable rule of law can be identified based on the legal system's doctrine of sources – and a second, moral stage that kicks in only in hard cases – where it is not possible to identify a clear rule during the first stage. But, given our above remarks regarding the pervasiveness of moral considerations throughout legal reasoning, this image is not entirely accurate considering the law's arguable character. We can see why this is so by looking into international law's assumption of just outcomes in particular.

International law uses the term 'equity' to refer to considerations of justice that international adjudicators take into account. Doctrine tends

[60] Cf. International Law Commission, 'Fragmentation of International Law: Difficulties Arising from the Diversification and Expansion of International Law – Report of the Study Group of the International Law Commission', UN Doc A/CN.4/L.682 (13 April 2006), 249 (para 493), describing the same problem in more general terms: '[T]he emergence of conflicting rules and overlapping legal regimes will undoubtedly create problems of coordination at the international level. But … *no homogenous, hierarchical meta-system is realistically available to do away with such problems*' (emphasis in original).

to distinguish between three types of equity as justice. There is equity *infra legem*, which is used to 'adapt the law to the facts of individual cases'.[61] There is equity *praeter legem*, which is used to fill gaps in the law.[62] And there is equity *contra legem*, which is used as a ground for not applying an unjust rule of law.[63] Attractive as this distinction of types of equity is in theory, it is unclear whether it can be always maintained as clear-cut in practice. Indeed, as Vaughan Lowe has shown, the three types seem to meld into each other in some cases.[64]

Equity *infra legem* is in reality a different way of saying that a judge must interpret the law before applying it and that, in so doing, he or she will have to exercise judgment and discretion. There is nothing exceptional in this statement of the judge's role. But suppose we think that the case before us is particularly hard and that the amount of judgment and discretion we must exercise is much greater than what is normally required. In this case, exercising equity *infra legem* may begin to look like gap-filling and therefore like an exercise of equity *praeter legem*. Something similar happens with equity *praeter legem* but in reverse. Equity *praeter legem* also depends on interpretation and is thus, to some extent, in the eye of the beholder. One can assume an essentially gap-less legal system through the residual application of general principles, the use of analogies, the invocation of controlling prior rulings, or the presumption of a closing rule of some kind (e.g., 'absent an expressed prohibition there exists a presumption of freedom'). In those situations, the gap is already filled by means of interpretation of the authoritative legal materials that are available to the judge (equity *infra legem*), perhaps even before its existence is noticed. Equity *contra legem* seems to follow a similar path. What counts as a *contra legem* exercise of equity may in some cases depend on how one interprets the law. Suppose we know that the morally just decision in our case is *x* but based on authoritative past practice the applicable rule seems to demand *y*. If we flatly decide *x* rather than *y*, we have exercised equity *contra legem*. Not so if we attempt to distinguish the available precedents from the instant case and interpret the rule as demanding *x* in the first place (equity *infra legem*) or if we

[61] M. Akehurst, 'Equity and General Principles of Law' (1976) 25 *International and Comparative Law Quarterly* 801, 801.
[62] Ibid.
[63] Ibid.
[64] V. Lowe, 'The Role of Equity in International Law' (1988–1989) 12 *Australian Yearbook of International Law* 54.

consider that the legal materials offer unclear guidance as between x and y (equity *praeter legem*).

An example may help to somewhat concretise the above rather abstract remarks. In *Santa Elena* v. *Costa Rica*, the investor's property had been expropriated by formal decree in 1978. Arbitral proceedings were not initiated until 1995, and a final award was not rendered until 2000. Twenty-two years had therefore passed between the unlawful act and the obligation to pay compensation for it. The dispute before the tribunal was not whether an expropriation had taken place but only with respect to determining the amount of compensation and interest owed. The tribunal quickly determined that compensation for expropriation must be prompt, adequate, and effective, based on the fair market value of the property taken.[65] The situation was more complex, however, with respect to the amount of interest owed. At the time of the *Santa Elena* decision, the prevailing position, as stated in the work of the ILC, was that simple rather than compound interest was the default norm in international law.[66] The prevailing view in ISDS seems to have been the same.[67]

[65] *Compañiá del Desarrollo de Santa Elena, S.A.* v. *The Republic of Costa Rica*, ICSID Case No. ARB/96/1, Final Award, 17 February 2000, paras 70–71.

[66] See Commentary to Article 38 of the Draft Articles on Responsibility of States for Internationally Wrongful Acts (adopted by the ILC at its 53rd session, 23 April–1 June and 2 July–10 August 2001) (2001) Vol II (Part Two) *Yearbook of the International Law Commission* 26, 108–109, concluding in para 9 that 'given the present state of international law, it cannot be said that an injured [s]tate has any entitlement to compound interest, in the absence of special circumstances which justify some element of compounding as an aspect of full reparation' (relying, inter alia, on *R.J. Reynolds Tobacco Company* v. *The Government of Iran, Iranian Tobacco Company*, Award No 145-35-3, 31 July 1984 (1984 – III) 7 *Iran-US CTR* 181, 191–192; and on *Affaire des biens britanniques au Maroc espagnol (Espagne* c. *Royaume-Uni)*, Award, 1 May 1925, Vol II *RIAA* 615, 650).

[67] See F. Grisel, 'The Sources of Foreign Investment Law', in Z. Douglas, J. Pauwelyn, and J. E. Viñuales (eds.), *The Foundations of International Investment Law: Bringing Theory into Practice* (Oxford: Oxford University Press, 2014) 213, 226. Grisel observes that, prior to 2000, the majority of investment tribunals granted simple interest to successful investors. He identifies only two tribunals – in *Atlantic Triton* and *SPP* – having awarded compound interest during that time. In both cases, however, the tribunals had considered themselves bound by applicable domestic laws that expressly allowed awarding compound interest (see *Atlantic Triton Company Limited* v. *People's Revolutionary Republic of Guinea*, ICSID Case No. ARB/84/1, Award, 21 April 1986 (1995) 3 ICSID Rep 13, 33; *Southern Pacific Properties (Middle East) Limited* v. *Arab Republic of Egypt*, ICSID Case No. ARB/84/3, Award, 20 May 1992 (1995) 3 ICSID Rep 189, paras 228–229).

The tribunal distinguished the dispute before it from previous cases by considering that much of the, then current, practice had arisen principally in relation to instances of injury or simple breach of contract. From this, the tribunal inferred that '[t]he same considerations [could] not apply to cases relating to the valuation of property or property rights'.[68] According to the tribunal, determining the amount of interest owed was 'a product of the exercise of judgment, taking into account all of the circumstances of the case at hand and especially *considerations of fairness which must form part of the law to be applied*'.[69] In determining what fairness demanded in the case before it, the tribunal remarked:

> [W]here an owner of property has at some earlier time lost the value of his asset but has not received the monetary equivalent that then became due to him, the amount of compensation should reflect, at least in part, the additional sum that his money would have earned, had it, and the income generated by it, been reinvested each year at generally prevailing rates of interest. It is not the purpose of compound interest to attribute blame to, or to punish, anybody for the delay in the payment made to the expropriated owner; it is a mechanism to ensure that the compensation awarded the Claimant is appropriate in the circumstances.[70]

The tribunal considered that simple interest could not be justified given the amount of time that had passed from the taking and the fact that during that time the claimant had been unable to use the property for the investment project for which it was originally intended. Yet full compound interest would not be just either, given that the claimant had technically remained in possession of the property and had thus been able to use and exploit it, even if to a limited extent. In the end, the tribunal concluded that the claimant was entitled to 'an award of compound interest adjusted to take account of all the relevant factors'.[71]

There are several prima facie plausible ways of describing what the tribunal did in this decision. One reading of the decision is that the moral principle of fairness was used to justify the awarding of compound interest in an exercise of equity *infra legem*. In particular, it may be said that the tribunal interpreted the international law norm that compensation should be 'prompt, adequate, and effective' and concluded that, in the circumstances of the case, simple interest would have resulted in

[68] *Santa Elena* v. *Costa Rica*, Award, para 97.
[69] Ibid., para 103 (emphasis added).
[70] Ibid., para 104.
[71] Ibid., para 106.

compensation falling short of that standard. That is certainly accurate but could not one also regard the use of fairness as an exercise in equity *praeter legem*, considering the tribunal's extensive examination of past practice? In other words, given that the tribunal found in its analysis of authorities that international law did not outright exclude compound interest in all situations, could we not also consider the deployment of fairness as an attempt to fill a legal gap in cases where there is no doubt that expropriation has in fact taken place and many years have passed without the payment of compensation? By a similar process of reasoning, one may even attempt to describe the decision as an exercise in equity *contra legem*. Though this may perhaps be a less plausible reading, it is nonetheless quite clear that the tribunal departed from what appeared to be prior consistent judicial practice both in general international law and in ISDS.

The *Santa Elena* example confirms the law's arguable character. Affixing a label on the type of equity performed by a court or tribunal therefore appears to be more a matter of interpretation than a straightforward analytical conclusion about the existence or absence of specific rules following examination of the system's sources. In that sense, the label itself seems to matter less when compared to the way the tribunal identified, assessed, and combined the various authoritative materials before it and to the reasons that the tribunal offered for these choices.

3.4.2.3 Too Readily Assuming the Existence of Governing Rules

The third type of pitfall is directly linked to the one above. By downplaying the law's arguable character, the bifurcated view of legal reasoning may too easily assume the existence of rules governing a case, simply because such rules are clothed in a particular authoritative form. This can have practical repercussions in ISDS, where it is routine practice for arbitrators to seek to determine the authoritative weight and relevance of prior judgments. Keeping with the example of simple and compound interest, following the *Santa Elena* decision several tribunals began awarding compound interest by relying solely or principally on the authoritativeness of *Santa Elena* as precedent for the rule that compound interest had become the prevailing international law standard.

In *MTD* v. *Chile*, for example, the tribunal took the view that compound interest was more in line with the reality of financial transactions and a closer approximation to the actual value lost by investors.[72] It offered no reason for this assertion except a direct quote from above-cited paragraph 104 of the *Santa Elena* award. In *Middle East Cement* v. *Egypt*, the tribunal relied, among others, on *Santa Elena* for the proposition that 'international jurisprudence and literature have recently, after detailed consideration, concluded that . . . compound (as opposed to simple) interest is at present deemed appropriate as the standard of international law in such expropriation cases'.[73] The tribunal considered that there was no reason to depart from this 'practice', taking instead the view that an award of compound interest was going to make the compensation due to the claimant in this case 'adequate and effective'.[74] In *Tecmed* v. *Mexico*, the tribunal awarded compound interest relying only on the exact same passage from the *Middle East Cement* award just quoted.[75] In a footnote, the *Tecmed* tribunal also referenced as additional authorities the awards that the *Middle East Cement* tribunal had relied upon, including *Santa Elena*.

All three of the above-mentioned decisions directly or indirectly relied on *Santa Elena*, but all arguably made too crude of a description of what the *Santa Elena* decision stands for. Recalling our analysis of it, the *Santa Elena* decision likely does not stand for the proposition that there exists a blanket, default rule for compound interest in ISDS. Rather, a better reading of the decision would cast it as authority for the more modest proposition that, depending on the circumstances of the case, compound interest may be awarded to ensure adequate compensation in cases of expropriation, in particular, when many years have passed without the payment of compensation. In other words, *Santa Elena* told subsequent tribunals to exercise judgment rather than to follow a blanket rule.

The bifurcated view of legal reasoning seems to facilitate the cursory treatment of past decisions just seen because, according to it, legal

[72] *MTD Equity Sdn. Bhd. and MTD Chile S.A.* v. *Republic of Chile*, ICSID Case No. ARB/01/7, Award, 25 May 2004, para 251.

[73] *Middle East Cement Shipping and Handling Co. S.A.* v. *Arab Republic of Egypt*, ICSID Case No. ARB/99/6, Award, 12 April 2002, para 174 (the other decisions the tribunal relied upon were: *Wena Hotels Ltd.* v. *Arab Republic of Egypt*, ICSID Case No. ARB/98/4, Award, 8 December 2000 (2002) 41 *International Legal Materials* 896; and *Metalclad Corporation* v. *The United Mexican States*, ICSID Case No. ARB(AF)/97/1, Award, 30 August 2000).

[74] *Middle East Cement* v. *Egypt*, Award, para 175.

[75] *Técnicas Medioambientales Tecmed, S.A.* v. *The United Mexican States*, ICSID Case No. ARB(AF)/00/2, Award, 29 May 2003, para 196.

reasoning is simply technical whenever it is possible to identify an applicable rule clothed in authoritative form (in this example, taking the form of an arbitral award). On this view, any consideration on the moral relevance of the identified rule for the case at hand is relegated to a subsequent stage that is activated only in the event of doubt or ambiguity. As previously argued in the examination of easy and hard cases, however, this mode of thinking is question-begging and circular. By contrast, the unified view of legal reasoning would invite tribunals to not so easily assume governing rules of the kind just described. Realising that legal reasoning is technical and moral throughout would encourage an overall inquisitorial and scrutinising attitude vis-à-vis the reasoning of prior awards.

For example, a principal consideration for subsequent tribunals to gauge the authority of the *Santa Elena* award would be the moral relevance of the fact that in *Santa Elena* a substantial amount of time had passed from the expropriatory act and the time when the investor was compensated for it. An additional consideration would be the fact that the existence of an expropriation was never in dispute in the *Santa Elena* case – only the amount of compensation was. In other words, Costa Rica knew that it had to compensate the investor but was unwilling to offer the amount that the investor believed the property was worth. That may render the imposition of compound interest inappropriate in cases of alleged indirect expropriation where the host state may have had a prima facie plausible police powers defence and therefore did not believe that it had violated its international obligations in the first place. Yet a third consideration would be the fact that *Santa Elena* was an expropriation case. Should other treaty breaches receive similar treatment with respect to awards of interest? Indeed, that could have been a subject of discussion in the *MTD* v. *Chile* case, where the tribunal did not find an expropriation of the investment but a violation of the FET standard.

3.5 Conclusion

Having already determined that coherence has a role to play in legal reasoning, the aim of this chapter was to determine the exact place within the process of reasoning where coherence operates. To answer that question, the discussion turned to theories about the nature and content of law. Two such theories were distinguished and examined – positivism and non-positivism/interpretivism. The two theories fundamentally disagree about how one should conceive the relationship between the law's two core values of certainty and correctness/justice. By extension, the two theories also fundamentally disagree about the process through which adjudicators seek to achieve the two values when discharging their duties.

With its strict separation between law and morality, positivism advocates in favour of a bifurcated view of legal reasoning that gives rise to what we here termed a model of 'double coherence'. According to this view, legal reasoning is mainly technical in easy cases and mainly moral in hard cases, meaning that coherence operates as systemic consistency in the former cases and as a standard of moral congruence in the latter cases. By contrast, the interpretivist view does not see a strict separation between law and morality but rather regards law as forming part of morality. Accordingly, interpretivism argues that legal reasoning is a single, unified process where technical and moral arguments are intertwined, thus giving rise to what we here termed a model of 'single coherence'.

The two models were then assessed, and it was concluded (i) that the core assumptions of the bifurcated view, regarding the different processes of reasoning allegedly at play in easy and hard cases, do not hold and (ii) that following the bifurcated view results in certain methodological pitfalls for adjudicators. Consequently, the chapter advocated for the interpretivist/single model view and for the conclusion that coherence, in its two dimensions, entirely pervades the process of legal reasoning at all times.

At this point we may take a bird's-eye view of our discussion so far. Chapters 1–3 formed part of a common thematic unit looking at the conceptual foundations of coherence and its relationship with legal reasoning. In the course of these chapters, we have seen that coherence (i) is an interpretative concept having links but also being different from consistency, correctness, and comprehensiveness in law; (ii) has a dual – substantive and methodological – role to play in legal reasoning, thus being relevant for interpretation and justification in law; and (iii) pervades the entire process of legal reasoning at all times. The task ahead of us now is to ascertain and clarify the ways through which these characteristics of coherence manifest in distinct aspects of interpretation and justification in ISDS. To that end, Chapters 4 and 5 principally address the domain of interpretation by looking into the rule of treaty interpretation in the VCLT and the widespread use of analogies in ISDS. Chapters 6 and 7 principally address the closely connected domain of justification by looking into the concepts of reflexive and morally responsible judicial deliberation.

4

Coherence and the Interpretation of Treaties

4.1 Introduction

A principal task of international courts and tribunals is to interpret and apply treaties. It is therefore appropriate that we begin our inquiry into the interpretative role of coherence by examining the role that coherence has to play in the interpretation of treaties. Rules of treaty interpretation are provided in Articles 31 and 32 of the VCLT.[1] The argument advanced in this chapter is that a role for coherence is necessarily assumed in the very structure of the VCLT's rule of interpretation. Absent considerations of coherence, application of the interpretative principles contained in the VCLT rule[2] risks falling into incompleteness or circularity.

Presented in more detail, this chapter's thesis is as follows. According to the analogy of the VCLT rule as a 'crucible', used by the ILC to describe its operation,[3] it is the combination of the interpretative principles contained in the rule that in each case yields the meaning of treaty provisions. Still, different interpretative principles may be assigned different weights in different cases, depending on the drafters' reconstructed intention that is followed by the adjudicator in each case. The underlying idea, therefore, is that all these interpretative principles must hang together well and that they must be combined in a way that makes sense in the context of each case. This is a sign that considerations of coherence are apposite, acting as reasons that justify the above combination in each

[1] There is also Article 33 of the VCLT, which addresses the interpretation of treaties authenticated in two or more languages. This article, however, will not feature in the analysis in this chapter.

[2] For an affirmation that, despite the general heading 'General *rule* of interpretation' being used in the VCLT, Articles 31 and 32 actually prescribe principles, see R. K. Gardiner, *Treaty Interpretation*, 2nd ed. (Oxford: Oxford University Press, 2015), 38–41 (and the authorities cited therein).

[3] Report of the International Law Commission on the Work of its Eighteenth Session (Geneva, 4 May–19 July 1966) (1967) Vol II *Yearbook of the International Law Commission* 172, 219–220 (para 8).

case and ultimately account for the outcome's persuasiveness. On this view of the operation of the VCLT rule, and in keeping with our remarks in Chapters 1–3, coherence acts both as a substantive principle offering reasons for or against an outcome and as a method for how adjudicators must go about addressing interpretative problems.[4]

Importantly, this should not be construed as an argument suggesting a peripheral role for the VCLT rule. No such argument is intended here. All that this chapter suggests is that properly applying the VCLT rule means constructing a coherent narrative of contextual/interpretative assumptions, supported by the relevant formal arguments provided by the VCLT, in order to reach and justify a normative outcome. In this sense, the VCLT rule plays an important legitimating function. By providing the participants of the international legal system with the rules of the interpretative game,[5] the VCLT ensures that the arguments each participant makes will be taken seriously by the rest and be given their due consideration, rather than be disregarded outright as irrelevant.[6]

Beyond its doctrinal importance, the chapter's thesis is also important for ISDS in a more practical sense. Shedding light on the mechanics of the VCLT rule through the lens of coherence could help to improve ISDS practice, since tribunals do not always integrate the VCLT into their reasoning in an appropriate manner. To the contrary, they often seem to misuse the VCLT rule by treating it as a way of merely stating a conclusion rather than as a way of reaching (and justifying) one.

The chapter proceeds as follows. Section 4.2 sets the stage for the examination by presenting the general *problématique* of the misapplication of the VCLT rule by investment tribunals. Section 4.3 presents the main theoretical argument regarding the necessary role for coherence in

[4] Cf. also a partial overlap between this conclusion and Georges Abi-Saab's tripartite characterisation of interpretation as 'savoir (ou processus d'appréhension)', 'vouloir (ou processus de décision)', and 'pouvoir (ou source de droits et d'obligations)'. See G. Abi-Saab, '"Interprétation" et "Auto-Interprétation": Quelques réflexions sur leur rôle dans la formation et la résolution du différend international', in U. Beyerlin, M. Bothe, R. Hofmann, and E.-U. Petersmann (eds.), *Recht zwischen Umbruch und Bewahrung: Festschrift für Rudolf Bernhardt* (Berlin: Springer, 1995) 9, 9–14.

[5] The metaphor of interpretation as a game is taken from A. Bianchi, 'The Game of Interpretation in International Law: The Players, the Cards, and Why the Game Is Worth the Candle', in A. Bianchi, D. Peat, and M. Windsor (eds.), *Interpretation in International Law* (Oxford: Oxford University Press, 2015) 34.

[6] See Report of the ILC on the Work of its Eighteenth Session (n. 3), 218–219 (para 5), hinting at such an understanding of the VCLT rule with its reference to 'admissible' means of interpretation.

the application of the VCLT rule of interpretation. It does so in two steps. Firstly, it describes interpretation as a broadly contextual enterprise and as an exercise in constructing coherent narratives among relevant interpretative contexts. Secondly, it tests this view for its fit within the structure of Articles 31 and 32 of the VCLT and the textualism/intentionalism debate that is prevalent therein. Section 4.4 turns attention to practice. It critically examines instances of judicial attempts at constructing coherent narratives for purposes of interpretation, taken from ISDS and other areas of international law. Section 4.5 summarises and concludes.

4.2 ISDS and the Problem of Interpretation and Justification under the VCLT Rule

Every application of a legal text requires some act of interpretation, since one must first form an understanding of what the text requires before applying it. Any act of apprehension of meaning, no matter how commonplace, intuitive, or unmediated, can thus be said to involve interpretation of some form or another.[7] This is a way of thinking about interpretation that we do not often see in law. Legal interpretation is often understood in a narrower sense, which is predicated upon the existence of doubt about the meaning or the proper application of a text, thus requiring the interpreter to resolve that doubt by forming a judgment on the matter.[8] For the purposes of this chapter, it is therefore important to keep in mind that interpretation is a process taking place irrespective of the existence of any normative ambiguity or disagreement.

The interpretation of international treaties is governed by a set of principles contained in the VCLT. These reflect customary international law and are thus binding on all states and with respect to all treaties, regardless of whether a treaty was concluded before or after the entry into

[7] N. MacCormick, 'Argumentation and Interpretation in Law' (1993) 6 *Ratio Juris* 16, 19–20. In the example used by MacCormick, putting out one's cigarette upon seeing a 'no smoking' sign is an instance of an interpretation of the sign prohibiting smoking.

[8] Ibid. But cf., in the ISDS context, *Windstream Energy LLC* v. *Government of Canada*, PCA Case No. 2013-22, Award, 27 September 2016, para 355 ('[T]here can be no "plain reading" of a treaty provision that would involve no interpretation at all; "plain meaning" [*sic*] is in itself a result of interpretation.').

force of the VCLT.[9] From a doctrinal point of view, it could be possible in theory for the content of the interpretative principles concerned to not always be exactly the same as between their treaty and their customary law form.[10] However, nothing in the present argument will hinge on this issue. Therefore, the term 'VCLT rule' is used here as an umbrella term to capture interpretative principles in both their treaty and customary law forms. By the same token, it is also supposed here that the customary law form of the principles of treaty interpretation has the same content as found in Articles 31 and 32 of the VCLT.[11]

4.2.1 The VCLT Rule

The general rule of interpretation in Article 31 of the VCLT places 'ordinary meaning' at the centre of the interpretative inquiry. It states:

> A treaty shall be interpreted in good faith in accordance with the ordinary meaning to be given to the terms of the treaty in their context and in the light of its object and purpose.[12]

The term 'context' is used in a rather narrow, textual sense comprising (i) the treaty as a whole, including its preamble and annexes; (ii) any

[9] See *Case Concerning Kasikili/Sedudu Island (Botswana/Namibia)*, Judgment of 13 December 1999, ICJ Rep (1999) 1045, para 18; *Case Concerning the Territorial Dispute (Libyan Arab Jamahiriya/Chad)*, Judgment of 3 February 1994, ICJ Rep (1994) 6, para 41; *Arbitration Regarding the Iron Rhine ("Ijzeren Rijn") Railway (Belgium/Netherlands)*, Award of the Arbitral Tribunal, 24 May 2005, Vol XXVII *RIAA* 35, para 45; *Aguas del Tunari, S.A.* v. *Republic of Bolivia*, ICSID Case No. ARB/02/3, Decision on Respondent's Objections to Jurisdiction, 21 October 2005, para 88; Appellate Body Report, *United States – Final Anti-Dumping Measures on Stainless Steel from Mexico*, WT/DS344/AB/R, 30 April 2008, para 76.

[10] Indeed, that the VCLT rule reflects customary international law does not preclude the theoretical possibility that the relevant interpretative principles might have a different content in each form or that their content (even if the same) might eventually diverge with the passage of time. This is doctrinally possible given the ICJ's assertion in the *Nicaragua* case that the act of codifying a customary norm in a treaty text does not in and of itself mean that the customary norm ceases to exist as a result. Rather, in these cases, 'customary international law continues to exist alongside treaty law' (*Case Concerning Military and Paramilitary Activities in and against Nicaragua [Nicaragua* v. *United States of America], Merits*, Judgment of 27 June 1986, ICJ Rep [1986] 14, para 176).

[11] In practice, international courts and tribunals seem to have consistently regarded the treaty and customary rules of interpretation as having the same content also. On this point, see P. Merkouris, *Article 31(3)(c) VCLT and the Principle of Systemic Integration: Normative Shadows in Plato's Cave* (Leiden: Brill/Nijhoff, 2015), 10–11.

[12] Article 31(1) VCLT.

agreement relating to the treaty that was made between all the parties in connection with the conclusion of the treaty; and (iii) any instrument that was made by one or more parties in connection with the conclusion of the treaty and accepted by the other parties as an instrument related to the treaty.[13] In addition, the interpreter must also take into account (i) any subsequent agreement between the parties regarding the interpretation of the treaty or the application of its provisions; (ii) any subsequent practice in the application of the treaty that establishes the parties' agreement regarding its interpretation; and (iii) any relevant rules of international law that are applicable in the relations between the parties.[14] Though all of the above elements must also be given their ordinary meaning, a special meaning must nevertheless be given to treaty terms if it can be established that the contracting parties so intended.[15]

With respect to the relationship and mode of interaction between these interpretative principles, it is generally accepted that their sequential enumeration in Article 31 was not meant to suggest the existence of a rigid hierarchy. The ILC's Commentary confirms this, stating explicitly that the intention of the VCLT drafters was for the application of the elements contained in Article 31 to take the form of a 'single combined operation', so that '[a]ll the various elements, as they were present in any given case, would be thrown into the crucible, and their interaction would give the legally relevant interpretation'.[16] Given that intention, the structure of Article 31 was chosen primarily for reasons of convenience.[17]

[13] Article 31(2) VCLT. But, cf. McRae who has argued for a broader understanding of 'context' in the VCLT rule to encompass 'the reality of international relations applicable to the matter in question' (D. McRae, 'Evolutionary Interpretation: The Relevance of Context', in G. Abi-Saab, K. Keith, G. Marceau, and C. Marquet [eds.], *Evolutionary Interpretation and International Law* [Oxford: Hart, 2019] 57, 60). The present chapter similarly adopts a broader and richer understanding of 'context' as seen in Sections 4.3 and 4.4.

[14] Article 31(3) VCLT.

[15] Article 31(4) VCLT.

[16] Report of the International Law Commission on the Work of its Eighteenth Session (n. 3), 219–220 (para 8).

[17] Gardiner (n. 2), 9–10; also cf. *Aguas del Tunari* v. *Bolivia*, Jurisdiction, para 91 ('Interpretation under Article 31 of the Vienna Convention is a process of progressive encirclement where the interpreter ... by cycling through this three step inquiry iteratively closes in upon the proper interpretation. In approaching this task, it is critical to observe ... [that] the Vienna Convention does not privilege any one of these three aspects of the interpretation method.').

Attached to the above primary means of interpretation are supplementary means contained in Article 32 of the VCLT. These may include an examination of the treaty's preparatory work or an appraisal of the circumstances of the treaty's conclusion. Recourse to them is allowed primarily in order to confirm the meaning reached in accordance with the general rule. The supplementary means cannot be used to determine meaning unless one is faced with a situation where following the general rule results in an interpretation that either leaves the meaning ambiguous or obscure or leads to a result that is manifestly absurd or unreasonable.[18]

4.2.2 *Misuse of the VCLT Rule in ISDS*

Studies by scholars indicate that although ISDS tribunals tend to make frequent references to the VCLT rule,[19] they rarely make proper use of it or take the care to justify the interpretative choices they make under it.[20]

However, this is a position apparently not shared in all judicial fora. For example, Abi-Saab famously criticised the WTO Appellate Body for perceiving the interpretative process 'as a rigid sequence of autonomous or discreet steps, each of which has to be explicitly addressed and "exhausted", before moving on to the next one' (G. Abi-Saab, 'The Appellate Body and Treaty Interpretation', in M. Fitzmaurice, O. Elias, and P. Merkouris [eds.], *Treaty Interpretation and the Vienna Convention on the Law of Treaties: 30 Years On* [Leiden: Martinus Nijhoff, 2010] 99, 104–105 [footnote omitted]).

18 Article 32 VCLT.

19 E.g., see J. Romesh Weeramantry, *Treaty Interpretation in Investment Arbitration* (Oxford: Oxford University Press, 2012), 205, noting an upward trend in the number of arbitral awards referring to the VCLT rule; O. K. Fauchald, 'The Legal Reasoning of ICSID Tribunals – An Empirical Analysis' (2008) 19 *European Journal of International Law* 301, 314, noting a similar trend but at the same time finding that a clear majority of tribunals limited their VCLT references for purposes of interpretation to Article 31 (1) only.

20 E.g., see A. R. Sureda, *Investment Treaty Arbitration: Judging under Uncertainty* (Cambridge: Cambridge University Press, 2012), 20 (footnotes omitted):

> Arbitral tribunals rarely justify their interpretative approach, instead, they start their task of interpreting investment treaties by referring to Articles 31 and 32 of the [VCLT], either because it is a treaty binding upon the host [s]tate and the [s]tate of which the investor is a national, or else because it is considered a manifestation of customary law . . .. However, reference to these articles does not necessarily illuminate the approach to interpretation chosen by the tribunal.

See also A. Saldarriaga, 'Investment Awards and the Rules of Interpretation of the Vienna Convention: Making Room for Improvement' (2013) 28 *ICSID Review – Foreign Investment Law Journal* 197, 213 ('Awards need to include clear explanations of the interpretative process and justifications for interpretative preferences.').

An empirical study on the reasoning of ISDS tribunals by Fauchald reaches some interesting conclusions in this respect. In a sample of ninety-eight decisions, Fauchald identified only twenty decisions having actively used the VCLT rule beyond a passing reference. Upon examining these cases in further detail, however, Fauchald ultimately concludes that '[o]nly in exceptional decisions did tribunals integrate the VCLT into their reasoning beyond general references'. Instead, in most decisions, application of the VCLT articles was in general very brief and were used only as general arguments in support of the tribunals' approaches.[21]

It is important to clarify at what this critique of the misuse of the VCLT rule is aiming. The critique cannot simply be about how many times ISDS tribunals do or do not explicitly mention the VCLT rule in their decisions. Certainly, few mentions to the VCLT rule may be a worrisome sign. But the answer cannot simply be that tribunals should make more frequent mentions to the VCLT rule. International investment law necessarily refers to the norms of general international law for everything that it does not itself regulate as *lex specialis*. And so, even if tribunals choose to not explicitly mention the VCLT rule, it does not mean that they should not be guided by it when they interpret investment treaties. Put differently, even if every ISDS decision made explicit mention to the VCLT rule, this would still be no guarantee of the rule's proper use.

Similarly, the critique cannot simply be about tribunals not taking care to always spell out in detail which aspect of the VCLT rule they are using in every instance of interpretation. In line with the broader and narrower senses of interpretation presented above, it follows that detailed demonstrations or explications may sometimes not be necessary because some meanings are widely considered to be clear and unambiguous. Indeed, as remarked by Gardiner:

> Consideration and application of the Vienna rules on interpretation tend to be incidental or occasional rather than systematic. This is in the sense that international courts and tribunals do not indicate at every step when interpreting a treaty which principle of the Vienna Convention they are applying. General references may make explicit that the court or tribunal intends to apply the rules, but particular references are more likely to be made only when some uncertainty arises whether a particular element of interpretation is admissible.[22]

[21] Fauchald (n. 19), 314 (footnote omitted).

[22] R. K. Gardiner, *International Law* (Harlow: Pearson Longman, 2003), 79. Accurate as this statement is from a practical standpoint, it does not refute the more general point to be

The critique of ISDS in connection to the VCLT rule must therefore run deeper. It should rather be regarded as a critique about the proper use (or misuse) of the mechanics of the VCLT rule, irrespective of whether the rule itself is or is not explicitly mentioned in an arbitral award. Thus, the conclusion that we should draw from Fauchald's study should be the following: there exists a general tendency in ISDS to take the text of Articles 31 and 32 of the VCLT as being the endpoint of the interpretative inquiry, as opposed to being its beginning. Seeing the text of the VCLT rule as the end of the interpretative discussion, and by extension as the ultimate source of justification for any outcome reached, risks obscuring the substantive choices actually made and the interpretative processes actually followed by ISDS tribunals.

Consider the award in *Tecmed* v. *Mexico* as a particularly egregious example of this risk. Called upon to assess Mexico's conduct against the FET standard of the Mexico-Spain BIT (1995), the tribunal proceeded to give FET an especially broad content including within it guarantees ranging from total transparency, consistency, and the protection of legitimate expectations, to even protection against uncompensated expropriations.[23] The only justification offered by the tribunal for assigning such a broad content is a general understanding of FET as 'an expression and part of the *bona fide* principle recognized in international law',[24] and the following passage:

> The Arbitral Tribunal understands that the scope of the undertaking of [FET] under Article 4(1) of the Agreement described above is that resulting from an autonomous interpretation, taking into account the text of Article 4(1) of the Agreement according to its ordinary meaning (Article 31(1) of the Vienna Convention), or from international law and the good faith principle, on the basis of which the scope of the obligation assumed under the Agreement and the actions related to compliance therewith are to be assessed.[25]

However, this is a far cry from a proper justification of the meaning to be given to a legal provision. The tribunal is not really telling us why this is the meaning that must be given to FET. As readers, we have no insight

established later in this chapter, namely, that what ought to count as the clear and unambiguous meaning of a text (as opposed to one surrounded by doubt) is itself a matter of interpretation and thus a conclusion in need of justification.

[23] *Técnicas Medioambientales Tecmed, S.A.* v. *The United Mexican States*, ICSID Case No. ARB(AF)/00/2, Award, 29 May 2003, para 154.

[24] Ibid., para 153 (footnote omitted).

[25] Ibid., para 155.

whatsoever into the tribunal's thinking behind its normative choices. At best, the above passage is a mere assurance by the tribunal that this is indeed the ordinary meaning of 'fair and equitable' in the context of the FET provision of the applicable BIT.[26]

4.3 The Role for Coherence in the VCLT Rule

Having set out the general *problématique*, this section now presents the theoretical underpinnings of the chapter's main argument that (i) coherence is necessarily assumed in the VCLT rule and (ii) absent considerations of coherence, application of the various interpretative principles of the VCLT rule risks producing interpretations that are incomplete or circular. The principal insight brought forward here is that applying the VCLT rule involves a task of constructing a coherent narrative of contextual/interpretative assumptions, supported by the relevant interpretative principles provided by the VCLT, in order to reach and justify a normative outcome. The treaty parties' constructed intentions are at the centre of this enterprise. Proposed interpretations or outcomes are thus tested for their degree of congruence with the parties' reconstructed intentions vis-à-vis linguistic conventions, aims, or values to be pursued by the treaty and the surrounding normative system (including the system's discernible norms, aims, or values). The degree of congruence thus achieved acts as a reason to assign normative weight to each of the VCLT-mandated, admissible interpretative arguments.

The argument proceeds in two steps. In a first step, the necessary link between interpretation and contextualisation will be established. This link forms the backbone of the argument as it points to the fact that an interpretation is one's 'reading' of a situation or practice, resulting from a coherent narrative formed out of a web of practice-relative presuppositions that constitute the necessary background context. In international law, these interpretative presuppositions are enshrined in the VCLT rule and give rise to four types of admissible arguments: linguistic, systemic, teleological/deontological, and arguments from intentions (transcategorical). In each case, such arguments must be moulded reasonably (i.e., 'in

[26] Cf. also the critique of this aspect of the *Tecmed* award in Z. Douglas, 'Nothing If Not Critical for Investment Treaty Arbitration: *Occidental, Eureko* and *Methanex*' (2006) 22 *Arbitration International* 27, 28 ('The *Tecmed* "standard" [of FET] is actually not a standard at all; it is rather a description of perfect public regulation in a perfect world, to which all states should aspire but very few [if any] will ever attain.').

good faith')[27] into a coherent narrative. In a second step, it will be demonstrated that the same view also holds true in the specific context of the VCLT rule. In particular, it is argued that attention must shift beyond the classic debate between textualism and intentionalism that has traditionally dominated discussions about the VCLT. This debate is more likely to lead to confusion or circular thinking rather than illumination. Thus, a reading of the VCLT rule is offered here whereby a treaty term's proposed ordinary meaning should be tested for its degree of congruence with the contracting parties' intentions, as these are (re-)constructed against the remaining elements of the VCLT rule (i.e., linguistic, systemic, and teleological/deontological).

4.3.1 *Interpretation and Contextualisation*

> 'Does your dog bite?', Inspector Jacques Clouseau asks the innkeeper while pointing to the small shaggy dog sitting on the floor in front of him. The innkeeper replies 'no', prompting Clouseau to kneel and attempt to pet the dog, who immediately chomps down on his glove.
> 'I thought you said your dog did not bite!', Clouseau exclaims startled.
> '*That* is not my dog', replies the innkeeper calmly.
>
> *The Pink Panther Strikes Again* (1976)

Consider for a moment the above dialogue between Clouseau and the innkeeper. Putting its comedic effect aside, the dialogue raises a few interesting questions about what is critical in interpreting a situation or a human interaction. The words that were exchanged between Clouseau and the innkeeper were clear and unambiguous. Clouseau asked the innkeeper a question about the dog that the latter owned and the innkeeper, whose sincerity and good faith are here assumed, complied by replying with reference to his own dog. We might safely say, then, that the two men exchanged words in their ordinary or plain meaning and that this was the meaning understood by both. If that is the case, what was then the cause of their misunderstanding? More importantly, were they both equally correct in their reading of the situation, or was one more correct than the other? And if so, who, and why?

[27] On the meaning of good faith as reasonableness in the context of the VCLT rule, see R. Jennings and A. Watts, *Oppenheim's International Law. Volume 1: Peace*, 9th ed. (Oxford: Oxford University Press, 2008), 1272 (n. 7); also, Gardiner (n. 2), 168, 176–177.

On one reading of the encounter, the innkeeper was totally within the right in the reply that he gave to Clouseau if we consider the plain meaning of the words exchanged. Clouseau's single question was in fact three distinct questions in disguise (i.e., 'do you have a dog?', 'is this small shaggy dog sitting on the floor in front of me your dog?', 'does your dog bite?'). On this reading, Clouseau should have asked all three questions instead of just the last one to get the correct answer. But on a different and more reasonable reading, the innkeeper completely misjudged the context of the encounter. The physical proximity of the dog to the innkeeper and the fact that the dog was left unguarded in a public establishment like a hotel meant that Clouseau was reasonable to assume an affirmative answer to the first two questions and thus only ask the third one. On this reading, Clouseau is entitled to be upset with the innkeeper for misinforming him. In other words, we may say that Clouseau's 'reading' (i.e., interpretation) of the context of his interaction with the innkeeper exhibited a greater degree of coherence than the innkeeper's 'reading' of the same.[28] This is why we take Clouseau's expectations in petting the dog without being bitten to be reasonable following the innkeeper's reply and why their complete subversion makes this interaction comedic.

The above example thus shows the importance that contextualisation through assumptions and presuppositions plays in interpreting everyday situations. We may express the same idea in different terms as follows: a set of facts cannot lead to a normative conclusion without an understanding of the appropriate context. Or, differently still: it is not the case that the literal meaning of a sentence determines a set of truth conditions but rather that the literal meaning of a sentence only determines a set of truth conditions, or other sorts of conditions of satisfaction, given a set of background practices and assumptions.[29] For instance, the description 'A

[28] Recall from Chapter 1, J. Raz, 'The Relevance of Coherence' (1992) 72 *Boston University Law Review* 273, 287 ('[W]e attribute beliefs, goals, and actions to people, not singly but in interdependent clumps. This interdependence means nothing other than a presumption of coherence.').

[29] See J. R. Searle, 'The Background of Meaning', in J. R. Searle, F. Kiefer, and M. Bierwisch (eds.), *Speech Act Theory and Pragmatics* (Dordrecht: D. Reidel, 1980) 221, 227, 231; also, J. R. Searle, *Expression and Meaning: Studies in the Theory of Speech Acts*, reprint 1996 (Cambridge: Cambridge University Press, 1979), 117ff. For similar positions, see A. Bianchi, 'Textual Interpretation and (International) Law Reading: The Myth of (In) Determinacy and the Genealogy of Meaning', in P. H. F Bekker, R. Dolzer, and M. Waibel (eds.), *Making Transnational Law Work in the Global Economy: Essays in Honour of Detlev Vagts* (Cambridge: Cambridge University Press, 2010) 34, 40 ('In fact, what makes

delivered to B a quarter of potatoes' leads to the conclusion that 'B owes A a sum of money equal to the value of potatoes received' in the context of a sales contract, but not in the context of a film set where A and B are actors merely pretending to engage in a commercial transaction.[30] Simply put, what we take as the ordinary or plain meaning of a situation or a sentence is a contextual matter depending on a set of background presuppositions.[31]

the meaning of a word "plain", "clear", or "unambiguous" is not any linguistic property the word may have but rather the context in which it is used and the code used for communication in a particular situation by a certain community.'); and J. D. Mortenson, 'The *Travaux* of *Travaux*: Is the Vienna Convention Hostile to Drafting History?' (2013) 107 *American Journal of International Law* 780, 785, reporting on a view generally expressed during the VCLT deliberations as follows: 'As participant after participant said during the drafting process [of the VCLT], it makes no sense to speak of marks on a page as if they possessed inherent substantive content without reference to social context.' Mortenson uses this statement to introduce his thesis about the non-subsidiary role of a treaty's *travaux*. Regardless, the point of principle expressed in the statement is also valid for the argument made here.

30 The example is adapted from G. E. M. Anscombe, 'On Brute Facts' (1958) 18 *Analysis* 69.

31 Part of the seminal debate between Herbert Hart and Lon Fuller on the pages of the *Harvard Law Review* also touches on this issue (see H. L. A. Hart, 'Positivism and the Separation of Law and Morals' [1958] 71 *Harvard Law Review* 593; and L. L. Fuller, 'Positivism and Fidelity to Law: A Reply to Professor Hart' [1958] 71 *Harvard Law Review* 630). Hart's famous example asks us to imagine a rule prohibiting vehicles from entering a public park. Plainly, the rule prohibits automobiles. But does it also prohibit bicycles, roller skates, or toy cars? An automobile clearly triggers the rule's prohibition because it is a standard instance of a 'vehicle' (falling under what Hart called the 'core' of the term 'vehicle'). But bicycles, roller skates, and toy cars are not standard instances of vehicles (falling under what Hart called the 'penumbra' of the term 'vehicle'), meaning that there cannot be instances where we apply the rule to them without at the same time having some doubt about the correctness of our interpretation. Hart thus argues that a judge faced with problems of the penumbra of the word 'vehicle' would inevitably have to consider context, i.e., other elements beyond the rule's text, such as the social purpose served by the promulgation of the rule prohibiting vehicles in parks.

Hart is certainly correct in his general analysis, but it would be a mistake to conclude from it that contextual elements, such as a norm's social purpose, are only relevant when we are faced with a penumbral or non-ordinary meaning of a word or phrase. The case is rather the opposite. The reason why we consider ourselves to be faced with a clear or penumbral interpretative problem is already because of our appreciation of the appropriate context. In his response to Hart, Fuller makes this point with the following counterexample. Imagine the same rule, but this time suppose that some local patriots wanted to mount on a pedestal in the park a World War II truck (in perfect working condition) as a memorial. Clearly, a truck falls under the core of the term 'vehicle'. However, should the rule's prohibition apply in this case? If we think that it should not, it is not because of any intrinsic linguistic properties of the word 'vehicle' but from other factors, such as our appreciation of the social purpose of rules prohibiting vehicles in parks. Put differently,

The kind of presuppositions one needs, as well as their number and individual weight, are relative to what one is doing or is seeking to do and to the practice one finds himself or herself in. For instance, legal interpretation tends to focus on such elements as a rule's language, its expressed purpose, or the social policy that motivated its promulgation. The presuppositions one must consider when interpreting a treaty under international law are provided by the VCLT. We may extrapolate four. Recall that, according to the VCLT rule, the interpreter's aim is to give the treaty's terms their ordinary meaning. This is not a task to be done in isolation. The text's ordinary meaning is immediately and intimately linked to all other elements prescribed by the rule, namely: (i) the linguistic (including 'context' in the narrow VCLT sense); (ii) the systemic (Article 31[3][c]); (iii) the teleological/deontological ('object and purpose' in Article 31[1]); and (iv) the intentional (in the particular sense of Article 32).[32] Each of these presuppositions thus constitutes relevant interpretative context giving rise to admissible interpretative arguments that can be advanced by the contracting parties to the treaty.

But, being presuppositions, these interpretative arguments should not be regarded as individually providing conclusive reasons justifying specific interpretations or decisions. The analogy of the crucible,[33] used by the ILC to describe interpretation under the VCLT as a single combined operation, indicates that even though all of the aforementioned contextual elements are relevant, it could be that not all of them are equally relevant in every case. Or, to put the same point differently, the meaning ascribed to a legal text in each case ought to take account of the whole context, even if in some instances not all of the contextual facets are made explicit, are directly problematised, or are given the same weight.[34] Such interdependence between contexts means that coherence has a role to play in constructing the appropriate contextual narrative in each instance of interpretation.

there cannot be a plain, clear, or ordinary meaning that would involve no interpretation at all, since any plain, clear, or ordinary meaning is itself the result of interpretation.

32 Similarly, Gardiner (n. 2), 181.

33 Recall the Report of the International Law Commission on the Work of its Eighteenth Session (n. 3), 219–220 (para 8): 'All the various elements, as they [are] present in any given case, would be thrown into the crucible, and their interaction would give the legally relevant interpretation.'

34 D. N. MacCormick and R. S. Summers (eds.), *Interpreting Statutes: A Comparative Study* (Dartmouth: Ashgate, 1991), 26.

The above remarks notwithstanding, further clarifications are necessary as to how constructing coherent contextual narratives might fit within the VCLT rule. The direction that the VCLT rule on its face appears to give to interpreters, in relation to the context of the contracting parties' intentions, seems to have a potentially disruptive effect that threatens to turn the construction of contextual narratives circular. An appreciation of the relationship between Articles 31 and 32 of the VCLT is therefore necessary.

4.3.2 *(Re-)Constructed Intentions, Formation of Narratives, and the VCLT Rule*

The VCLT rule makes the treaty parties' intentions relevant to the interpretative enterprise. But, according to conventional wisdom, their relevance is only secondary, meaning that their influence and weight in the contextual narrative described above would be very limited in most situations. Recall that, according to Article 32 of the VCLT, taking cognisance of the parties' intentions is allowed principally to confirm the meaning reached in accordance with Article 31. Parties' intentions may not be used to determine meaning except in situations where following Article 31 results in an interpretation that leaves the meaning ambiguous or obscure or leads to a result that is manifestly absurd or unreasonable. It is submitted that the direction given by Article 32 cannot cohere with the view that intentions are of secondary importance only. If we insist that intentions are strictly of secondary importance then interpretation turns circular, the two permissible uses of the parties' intentions in Article 32 cancel each other out, and ensuring a coherent interpretative reasoning is ultimately forfeit.

Take, for example, the second permissible use of the parties' intentions under Article 32. Saying that intentions are relevant to determine meaning only when a proposed meaning is ambiguous, obscure, absurd, or unreasonable is plainly question-begging. How can we know whether the proposed meaning is ambiguous, obscure, absurd, or unreasonable without some understanding or some assumptions in the first place about what the parties may have intended for that meaning to be? Moreover, this then renders the distinction between the first and the second permissible uses of the parties' intentions somewhat irrelevant.[35] This is

[35] Similarly, S. M. Schwebel, 'May Preparatory Work Be Used to Correct Rather than Confirm the "Clear" Meaning of a Treaty Provision?', in J. Makarczyk (ed.), *Theory of International Law at the Threshold of the 21st Century: Essays in Honour of Krzysztof Skubiszewski* (The Hague: Kluwer Law International, 1996), 541; P. Merkouris, '"Third

because it makes little sense to say that we should consider intentions in order to confirm meaning reached via other means, since we have found this meaning already by considering intentions in some shape or form. In short, the directives of Article 32 do not cohere with the view that a consideration of the parties' intentions is of secondary importance.

We must thus change tacks on how we regard the relationship between Articles 31 and 32 of the VCLT. The argument to be pursued here is that the danger of circular interpretation just described is averted if we regard interpretative arguments from intentions as being in reality 'transcategorical'.[36] That is to say, if we regard them not as constituting a fourth independent type of interpretative argument but rather as being necessarily included in the other three types of arguments (i.e., linguistic usage, teleological/deontological, and systemic).[37] If that is the case, then the context of the parties' intentions is not a separate element to be weighed against others for its relevance but is rather more like a base upon which a coherent contextual narrative will be built.[38] And if that is so, then perhaps a better view would be not to regard Article 32 of the VCLT as declaring the secondary importance of the parties' intentions but as offering direction on when recourse to certain sources of evidence of intentions may be admissible as part of a legal argument. Let us see below how such a conclusion may fit within the VCLT rule.

4.3.2.1 Recasting the Debate between Textualism and Intentionalism

On an initial reading of the VCLT rule, two mandates appear to be at odds in the search for a treaty's ordinary meaning. The first mandate is that the interpreter must always interpret the text of the treaty. The second mandate is that the interpreter must seek to ascertain the parties'

Party" Considerations and "Corrective Interpretation" in the Interpretative Use of *Travaux Préparatoires:* – Is It Fahrenheit 451 for Preparatory Work?', in Fitzmaurice and others (n. 17) 75.

36 The term is borrowed from MacCormick and Summers (n. 34), 27, 522–525.

37 In support of this view, see also E. Bjorge, 'Time Present and Time Past: The Intention of the Parties and the Evolutionary Interpretation of Treaties', in Abi-Saab and others (n. 13) 35; International Law Commission, 'Draft Conclusions on Subsequent Agreements and Subsequent Practice in Relation to the Interpretation of Treaties, with Commentaries', UN Doc A/73/10 (2018), Draft Conclusion 8 (incl. para 9 of commentary stating that: '[B]y using the phrase "presumed intention", [draft conclusion 8] refers to the intention of the parties as determined through the application of the various means of interpretation that are recognized in articles 31 and 32.').

38 Alluding to a similar view, see S. Fish, 'Intention Is All There Is: A Critical Analysis of Aharon Barak's Purposive Interpretation in Law' (2008) 29 *Cardozo Law Review* 1109, 1138 (incl. n. 98).

intentions. These are called, respectively, textualism and intentionalism. At their core, both are similar in the sense that they both seek to ascertain what has been consented to and agreed by the parties at any given time.[39] Nevertheless, textualism and intentionalism have been at odds throughout the pre-VCLT history of interpretation in international law.

In its strict sense, textualism stands for the view that the text of a treaty must always be interpreted as it stands with no reference to any extraneous factors.[40] More moderate textualist views argue that absent rare exceptions, the text of a treaty corresponds to the only and most recent expression of the common intentions of the parties.[41] Conversely, intentionalism argues against the primacy of the text in interpretation. It holds the view that the purpose of interpretation is to ascertain the so-called real intentions of the parties.[42] The entry into force of the VCLT

[39] Cf. A. Orakhelashvili, *The Interpretation of Acts and Rules in Public International Law* (Oxford: Oxford University Press, 2008), 286 ('Interpretation is linked to the structural profile of international law based on consent and agreement. All international acts embody [s]tate consent and agreement, expressed in one or another form. Therefore, interpretation methods must be those which deduce the meaning exactly of what has been consented to and agreed.').

[40] This is known as the 'Vattelian' sense of textualism, expressed in E. de Vattel, *The Law of Nations, or, Principles of the Law of Nature, Applied to the Conduct and Affairs of Nations and Sovereigns. From the French of Monsieur de Vattel*, A New Edition, Revised, Corrected and Enriched with Many Valuable Notes (London: Printed for G. G. and J. Robinson, Paternoster-Row, 1797), 245 (emphasis in original omitted):

> On every occasion when a person could and ought to have made known his intention, we assume for true against him what he has sufficiently declared. This is an incontestable principle, applied to treaties; for if they are not a vain play of words, the contracting parties ought to express themselves in them with truth, and according to their real intentions. If the intention which is sufficiently declared were not to be taken of course as the true intention of him who speaks and enters into engagements, it would be perfectly useless to form contracts or treaties.

[41] E.g., see Institut de Droit International, 'De l'interprétation des traités: Observations complémentaires et projet définitif de Résolutions, présentés par M. H. Lauterpacht' (1952 – I) 44 *Annuaire de l'Institute de Droit International* 197, 199 (Huber: 'Le texte signé est, sauf de rares exceptions, la seule et la plus récente expression de la volonté commune des parties.').

[42] E.g., see A. McNair, *The Law of Treaties* (Oxford: Clarendon Press, 1961), 366 ('The many maxims and phrases which have crystallized out and abound in the text-books and elsewhere are merely prima facie guides to the intention of the parties and must always give way to contrary evidence of the intention of the parties in a particular case.'); H. Lauterpacht, 'Restrictive Interpretation and the Principle of Effectiveness in the Interpretation of Treaties' (1949) 26 *British Yearbook of International Law* 48, 83 ('It is the intention of the authors of the legal rule in question – whether it be a contract, a treaty, or a statute – which is the starting-point and the goal of all interpretation.');

seemingly ended the conflict by granting a clear victory to the modest version of textualism, judging by the wording of Article 31. This is also in line with the views expressed in the ILC and with Special Rapporteur Waldock's frequent affirmations during the deliberations on the primacy of the so-called 'textual approach'.[43] The ILC's Commentary also stands in confirmation of this, stating that:

> [T]he text must be presumed to be the authentic expression of the intentions of the parties ... in consequence, the starting point of interpretation is the elucidation of the meaning of the text, not an investigation *ab initio* into the intentions of the parties.[44]

J. Westlake, *International Law*, 2nd ed. (Cambridge: Cambridge University Press, 1910), 293 ('The important point is to get at the real intention of the parties[.]').

43 E.g., see Summary Records of the Sixteenth Session (11 May–24 July 1964) (1965) Vol I *Yearbook of the International Law Commission*, 314 (para 71), expressing the ILC's 'strong predilection for textual interpretation, in the interests of stability and certainty of treaty relations'; Third Report on the Law of Treaties, by Sir Humphrey Waldock, Special Rapporteur (1965) Vol II *Yearbook of the International Law Commission* 5, 56 (para 13).

44 Report of the ILC on the Work of its Eighteenth Session (n. 3), 220 (para 11). For illustrative examples of the same view as expressed by international courts and tribunals, see:

Dispute Regarding Navigational and Related Rights (Costa Rica v. *Nicaragua)*, Judgment of 13 July 2009, ICJ Rep (2009) 213, para 48:

> A treaty provision which has the purpose of limiting the sovereign powers of a [s]tate must be interpreted like any other provision of a treaty, i.e. in accordance with the intentions of its authors as reflected by the text of the treaty and the other relevant factors in terms of interpretation;

Aegean Sea Continental Shelf Case (Greece v. *Turkey)*, Judgment of 19 December 1978, ICJ Rep (1978) 3, Dissenting Opinion of Judge de Castro, 62, para 4:

> It is a well-established principle that the purpose of interpretation is to ascertain the true will of the parties. The terms used in a declaration of intention must be regarded as the means ('traces', clues, *indicia*) to be used in order to reach a conclusion as to the intention of the authors of the declaration;

Appellate Body Report, *European Communities – Customs Classification of Certain Computer Equipment*, WT/DS62/AB/R, WT/DS67/AB/R, WT/DS68/AB/R, 5 June 1998, para 84 (emphases in original):

> The purpose of treaty interpretation under Article 31 of the *Vienna Convention* is to ascertain the *common* intentions of the parties. These *common* intentions cannot be ascertained on the basis of the subjective and unilaterally determined "expectations" of *one* of the parties to a treaty. ... [T]he only rules which may be applied in interpreting the meaning of a concession are the general rules of treaty interpretation set out in the *Vienna Convention*;

Does this mean, however, that, following textualism's confirmation, ascertaining the parties' intentions is now a wholly peripheral or unimportant endeavour in the interpretative process? Not so. Literary theorist Stanley Fish has sought to dispel what he regards as a confusion in the textualism/intentionalism debate. The confusion, according to Fish, lies in treating the debate as a competition between two different 'approaches' to, or 'theories' of, interpretation.[45] Describing textualism and intentionalism as approaches or theories implies that one is better than the other, that we can adduce arguments for or against each of them, and that in the end we have a choice in following one or the other. But no such choice exists. In fact, one cannot avoid circularity when thinking of textualism or intentionalism as general theories of interpretation capable of justifying the correctness of proposed interpretations.

The reason is this. The textualist who regards the text as the most recent evidence of the common intention of the parties has no choice but to again refer to the parties' so-called 'real' or 'actual' intentions in instances of uncertainty or textual ambiguity. And the intentionalist, whose principal task is to give effect to the 'real' or 'actual' intentions

Methanex Corporation v. *United States of America*, UNCITRAL Rules, Final Award on Jurisdiction and Merits, 3 August 2005 (2005) 44 *International Legal Materials* 1345, Part II, Chapter B, para 22 (footnote omitted):

> [T]he approach of the Vienna Convention is that the text of the treaty is deemed to be the authentic expression of the intentions of the parties; and its elucidation, rather than wide-ranging searches for the supposed intentions of the parties, is the proper object of interpretation;

Wintershall Aktiengesellschaft v. *Argentine Republic*, ICSID Case No. ARB/04/14, Award, 8 December 2008, para 88 (emphasis in original):

> [T]he Tribunal holds that, there is no room for any presumed intention of the Contracting Parties to a bilateral treaty, as an independent basis of interpretation; because this opens up the possibility of an interpreter (often, with the best of intentions) altering the text of the treaty in order to make it conform better with what he (or she) considers to be the treaty's 'true purpose'.

45 Fish (n. 38), 1109–1116. In a similar vein, cf. the views in C. R. Sunstein, *Legal Reasoning and Political Conflict*, 2nd ed. (New York: Oxford University Press, 2018), 189 ('[A]ny approach to interpretation requires a substantive justification of some kind – an argument, not a language lesson. That justification must be independent of any texts that are being interpreted. Any understanding of the "meaning" of texts depends on judgments and commitments that are independent of the texts themselves.'); and G. Letsas, 'Intentionalism and the Interpretation of the ECHR', in Fitzmaurice and others (n. 17) 257, 269 ('[A]ny theory of interpretation . . . must at some stage stand outside drafters' intentions and provide a normative justification based on values of political morality.').

of the parties, likewise has no choice but to refer again to intentions (more 'real' or 'actual' this time?) in cases of uncertainty or ambiguity. In the end, they both run into the same circular argument: 'It is not clear whether the parties intended for *x* or *y* to be the meaning of the text, so we must find out what the parties actually intended for the text to mean.' And, if asked why in the end they chose *x* over *y*, they both cannot but reply: 'Because that is what the parties intended.'[46]

Fish thus draws two main conclusions. First, intentionalism is really all there is to interpretation, for without intentionalism textualism cannot even begin to get off the ground.[47] Second, rather than being an approach or a theory, intentionalism is simply the answer to the question: 'What is the meaning of a text?'[48] Interpreting inevitably involves identifying a purposive author and seeking to understand what that author meant by the words, marks, sounds, and so on, used.[49] A consequence of the fact that intentionalism is not an interpretative approach or theory is that it cannot ultimately decide questions of interpretation, precisely because it has no methodology to offer on how such questions are to be answered.[50] Put differently, intentionalism tells interpreters what it is that they are

46 For a historical example of this kind of circular reasoning committed to paper, see *Georges Pinson (France)* v. *United Mexican States*, Decision No 1, 19 October 1928, French-Mexican Claims Commission, Vol V *RIAA* 327, 422 (para 50).

47 In particular, Fish (n. 38), 1111–1112 (incl. n. 15), argues that a text cannot be a text absent an author with the intention of transforming a series of shapes into something that has meaning.

48 Ibid., 1112–1113.

49 In this respect, consider the following exchange that reportedly took place during the VCLT deliberations at the ILC. As seen in Waldock's Third Report on the Law of Treaties (n. 43), 52, the initial draft proposal for what is now Article 31 VCLT said that: 'The terms of a treaty shall be interpreted in good faith in accordance with the *natural and ordinary* meaning to be given to each term' [emphasis added]. The reference to a 'natural' meaning was immediately challenged. For instance, Roberto Ago (speaking as Chairman) suggested the elimination of the word, which he would find difficult to accept, since 'the meaning of a term was a convention created by the human mind.' (see Summary Records of the Sixteenth Session [n. 43], 280–281 [para 80]). For the same view, also see Lauterpacht (n. 42), 83 ('Words have no absolute meaning in themselves. They are an expression of will.').

50 Fish (n. 38), 1114 (also n. 17):

> One of the unfortunate consequences of thinking of intentionalism as a method and a theory is to saddle it with expectations it could not meet and should not be asked to meet: the expectation, for example, that the intentionalist thesis – a text means what its author or authors intend – will direct you to the text's meaning, or rule in or out evidence of its meaning, or provide a set of directions for realizing its imperative.

doing, not how they should do it. The 'how', according to Fish, is 'just good old-fashioned empirical inquiry in the course of which you mine for evidence, put it together when found, and build it into an account of the author's intention and therefore of the meaning of his her or their text'.[51]

Reconstructing a narrative of intentions based on available evidence is an enterprise involving the exercise of judgment. Different interpreters might judge the evidence differently and come to different conclusions as a result. Thus, the key to a successful interpretative exercise lies in its persuasiveness. And, as alluded to in this book already, persuasiveness is linked to the concept of coherence.[52] Recall again the dialogue between Clouseau and the innkeeper. We were persuaded that Clouseau's actions were reasonable because they exhibited greater coherence with the facts of their interaction.

It is thus not a stretch to consider that the four interpretative contexts/arguments previously identified in the VCLT rule are in fact sources of evidence of the contracting parties' intentions. Indeed, as Fitzmaurice has clarified, the essence of the controversy between textualism and intentionalism in the pre-VCLT era lay not in the question of whether the intentions of the parties should prevail but in the question of where those intentions were to be found or where they were primarily to be looked for.[53] The VCLT opted to somewhat restrict recourse to sources not mentioned in Article 31, in particular the *travaux* and the circumstances of a treaty's conclusion. But placing restrictions on when the use of a source evincing intentions can be admissible in legal argumentation is not the same as relegating intentions to a secondary role.

This conclusion also finds support in the views expressed in the ILC. Separating the interpretative steps into two articles was not meant to prejudice the unity of the exercise.[54] The ILC's Commentary makes clear that '[t]he fact that [Article 32] admits recourse to the supplementary

[51] Ibid., 1141.

[52] See Chapters 1 and 2.

[53] G. Fitzmaurice, 'The Law and Procedure of the International Court of Justice: Treaty Interpretation and Certain Other Treaty Points' (1951) 28 *British Yearbook of International Law* 1, 4.

[54] E.g., ILC member Mustafa Yasseen objected to any attempts at rupturing such unity by saying that he could not accept 'an article which would impose a chronological order and which would permit reference to preparatory work only after it had been decided that the text was not clear, that decision itself being often influenced by the consultation of the same sources' (Summary Records of the Sixteenth Session [n. 43], 313 [para 56]).

means for the purpose of "confirming" the meaning resulting from the application of [Article 31] establishes a general link between the two articles and maintains the unity of the process of interpretation'.[55] In his examination of the VCLT's preparatory work, Julian Mortenson goes a step further still. He sees the separation of the interpretative exercise into two articles as an attempt to guard against Myres McDougal's views about interpretation and the role of the international judge.[56] Mortenson thus argues, contrary to conventional wisdom, that the VCLT's reference to a treaty's *travaux* as a supplementary means of interpretation should not be taken to imply a prejudice against their use or their relegation to a strictly subsidiary role of secondary importance. Rather, it should be understood as an attempt to limit the purposes for which the *travaux* could be invoked as a source of evidence.[57]

4.3.2.2 (Re-)Constructed Intentions at Play: *Qatar* v. *Bahrain*

Two decisions by the ICJ during the jurisdiction and admissibility phase of the *Qatar* v. *Bahrain* case offer a good illustration of all of the above elements being at play during interpretation. To recall, these elements are the immanence of intentions, the construction of narratives, and the variable forensic value of the various sources evincing intentions.

In its first decision on jurisdiction and admissibility, the ICJ had to determine whether the text of the Doha Minutes, which was signed by the foreign ministers of both countries, and in which they committed to submit their delimitation dispute to the Court, could be construed as a binding treaty granting the Court jurisdiction. Bahrain had objected to this on the ground that the Doha Minutes merely reflected a political understanding and that the two countries never intended for the Minutes

[55] Report of the ILC on the Work of its Eighteenth Session (n. 3), 220 (para 10).

[56] Mortenson (n. 29), 789–790. Mortenson sees the final VCLT compromise as 'a path-dependent function of the gradually evolving course of discussions, which were directed initially at accreting mechanisms designed to suppress McDougalism, and then at relaxing those same mechanisms so as to allow unfettered recourse to travaux for the right purpose'.

[57] Ibid., 798 (emphases in original):

> In short, despite a commonsense recognition that travaux could be abused or interpreted poorly, the ILC members understood their 1964 draft to eliminate threshold requirements for the consultation of travaux. The reason it specified particular avenues [for having recourse to travaux] was not to limit the occasions on which drafting history could be used but to limit the purposes for which it could be invoked.

to act as a binding international agreement.[58] The judgment even mentions a statement issued by the foreign minister of Bahrain in which he had declared: '[A]t no time did I consider that in signing the Minutes I was committing Bahrain to a legally binding agreement.'[59] The Court made short work of Bahrain's objection, summarily rejecting it in the following manner:

> The Court does not find it necessary to consider what might have been the intentions of the Foreign Minister of Bahrain or, for that matter, those of the Foreign Minister of Qatar. The two Ministers signed a text recording commitments accepted by their Governments, some of which were to be given immediate application. Having signed such a text, the Foreign Minister of Bahrain is not in a position subsequently to say that he intended to subscribe only to a 'statement recording a political understanding', and not to an international agreement.[60]

This passage is important not so much for what it says but for what it seems to imply. On one reading, it may be said that the decision is flawed for not devoting greater attention to Bahrain's objection and to the parties' intentions. This is a plausible concern since, in Bahrain's view, the Court is committing a grave infraction by assuming adjudicatory power over a country that allegedly never consented to such power being assumed over it. But consider this. In following what it perceived to be the text's ordinary meaning, the Court was not acting irrespective of the parties' intentions. It did follow an intention, albeit a constructed one. That is to say, it ascribed to the parties the intention that they meant their words. In choosing this avenue, the Court may have had in mind other, no less important, concerns than the ones Bahrain had raised.

One could imagine (and notice that in saying this we are also reconstructing an intention) that the Court wanted to tell states that they must always be ready to take responsibility for their words and actions. Adopting Bahrain's objection could lead to situations where commitments did not carry weight and where states would be able to escape their duties simply by pleading their contrary actual intentions. Such a state of affairs would surely bring the international legal system to complete disarray and would not be conducive to the maintenance of international

58 *Case Concerning Maritime Delimitation and Territorial Questions between Qatar and Bahrain (Qatar* v. *Bahrain), Jurisdiction and Admissibility*, Judgment of 1 July 1994, ICJ Rep (1994) 112, para 26.

59 Ibid.

60 Ibid., para 27.

peace and security, towards which the judicial function of the Court is after all directed. It is likely that considerations of this kind may have led the judges to place little forensic value to the foreign minister's statement of his actual intentions.

The second illustrative example comes from the Court's second decision on jurisdiction and admissibility in the same case. This time, a disagreement between Judge Valticos and the majority showcases once more the forensic aspect of interpretation and the interpretative force of narratives. A point of contention during that stage of the dispute was the Court's *seisin*. The Doha Minutes were drafted in Arabic and the key phrase used therein, '*al-tarafan*', was broad enough to mean, either that 'both parties together' must approach the Court, or that 'either party individually' could do so also. The Court began by engaging in a grammatical interpretation of the disputed phrase, taking into account its immediate textual context and the purpose of the Doha Minutes, and thus concluded that the phrase must be construed as allowing for unilateral *seisin* too.[61] Judge Valticos disagreed. At the heart of this disagreement lay a different appreciation of the evidence provided by the *travaux* of the Minutes. Two points had been raised by the disputing parties in that respect. First, an earlier draft of the Minutes clearly and unambiguously provided for the possibility of unilateral application to the Court. Second, the Minutes were signed during a meeting of the Cooperation Council of Arab States of the Gulf that was not convened to achieve a settlement between Qatar and Bahrain but rather to resolve the much more serious military conflict between Iraq and Kuwait at the time.

The Court's majority did not attach great weight to these facts. With respect to the presence of the earlier draft, the Court ultimately said that it was 'unable to see why the abandonment of a form of words corresponding to the interpretation given by Qatar to the Doha Minutes should imply that they must be interpreted in accordance with Bahrain's thesis'.[62] With respect to the circumstances of the meeting, the Court similarly declined to draw any normative conclusions. Instead, it simply acknowledged that these dire circumstances were probably the reason why the parties were unable to reach agreement on a clearer text.[63] For Judge Valticos, however, those same facts told a different story.

[61] *Qatar* v. *Bahrain, Jurisdiction and Admissibility*, Judgment of 15 February 1995, ICJ Rep (1995) 6, paras 30–40.

[62] Ibid., para 41.

[63] Ibid., para 42.

Regarding them as mutually reinforcing, he argued that the change in language between drafts 'would have been pointless if it meant the same thing as the initial draft' and that '[i]n the hectic atmosphere of the meeting, then overridingly concerned by the serious problems of Iraq and Kuwait, the previous text would not have been changed in favour of a text with the same meaning'.[64]

4.3.2.3 Coherence as Contextual Harmonisation

It is time to summarise a long discussion. An interpreter may not approach his or her intentionalist interpretative task with a blank slate but must do so with certain presuppositions in mind. The most obvious of these in international law, as mandated by the VCLT rule, is that the treaty parties have intended to use words in their conventionally understood meaning. Hence, considering that the interpreter must begin from somewhere and the language of the treaty text is the sensible place to do so, emphasis is placed on the so-called 'textual approach'. This presupposition moreover acts as a rather powerful presumption considering the inclusion of Article 31(4) on the special meaning of treaty terms.[65] That being said, this presupposition is but a starting point and one element to be considered in conjunction with others, and, therefore, cannot act as

[64] Ibid., Dissenting Opinion of Judge Valticos, para 13.

[65] Article 31(4) of the VCLT mandates that a special meaning must be given to a treaty term if it can be established that the parties so intended. It had been initially suggested during the ILC deliberations that such a provision could safely be omitted, since a 'special' meaning would simply be the ordinary meaning in the particular context in which the word was found (see United Nations Conference on the Law of Treaties, First Session [Vienna, 26 March–24 May 1968], *Official Records, Summary Records of the Plenary Meetings and of the Meetings of the Committee of the Whole*, A/CONF.39/11, 33rd Meeting, 184 [para 70] [Waldock]). The provision was ultimately included since it was believed that 'there was a certain utility in laying down a specific rule on the point, if only to emphasize that the burden of proof lies on the party invoking the special meaning of the term' (see Report of the ILC on the Work of its Eighteenth Session [n. 3], 222 [para 17]). In so deciding, the ILC referred for support to *Legal Status of Eastern Greenland*, Judgment of 5 April 1933, PCIJ Series A/B No 53 (1933) 21, 49, where the PCIJ had held that:

> The geographical meaning of the word 'Greenland', i.e. the name which is habitually used in the maps to denominate the whole island, must be regarded as the ordinary meaning of the word. If it is alleged by one of the Parties that some unusual or exceptional meaning is to be attributed to it, it lies on that Party to establish its contention.

the ultimate justification for deciding a case one way or another.[66] This was a point well-taken by the ILC during the drafting of the VCLT, with Special Rapporteur Waldock clarifying that 'nothing could have been further from the Commission's intention than to suggest that words had a "dictionary" or intrinsic meaning in themselves'.[67] Conventional linguistic usage is thus not the only presupposition in connection with the parties' intentions encouraged by the VCLT. Other such presuppositions include that the contracting parties acted purposively when entering into the treaty and that they did not intend for their treaty to be completely severed from the basic structures, norms, principles, and values of the international legal system.

These presuppositions may appear obvious and common-sensical. Still, spelling them out is important if we are to realise that the act of reconstructing intentions into narratives is central to the interpretative enterprise. And only if we do that may we appreciate that coherence has a necessary role to play in this exercise of narrative-formation, acting in the background to assign weight and relevance to the various interpretative arguments that the VCLT rule makes admissible. In conclusion, words can have many meanings and what may be an ordinary meaning according to one set of circumstances could be an extraordinary meaning according to another.[68] Therefore, a substantial part of one's interpretative task consists in identifying the context(s) or the area(s) of human

[66] Cf. J. Raz, *Between Authority and Interpretation: On the Theory of Law and Practical Reason* (Oxford: Oxford University Press, 2009), 229 (emphases in original):

> The existence of conventions of meaning in a certain population indicates that they all regard the same things as having the same meaning. Such conventions are necessary for communication, and indirectly they are necessary for anything to have meaning at all. But conventions are not grounds justifying one interpretation rather than another. Admittedly we can correctly say that 'sister' means female sibling, and add that everyone understands 'sister' to mean female sibling. That everyone so understands it *shows* that this is its right meaning but it is not *a reason* for it being the right meaning.

[67] Conference on the Law of Treaties, First Session (n. 65), 33rd Meeting, 184 (para 70) (Waldock). Similarly, see Appellate Body Report, *China – Measures Affecting Trading Rights and Distribution Services for Certain Publications and Audiovisual Entertainment Products*, WT/DS363/AB/R, 21 December 2009, para 348 (criticising the approach followed by earlier WTO Panels).

[68] See G. Schwarzenberger, 'Myths and Realities of Treaty Interpretation: Articles 27–29 of the Vienna Draft Convention on the Law of Treaties' (1968) 9 *Virginia Journal of International Law* 1, 13 (n. 42), quoting directly from a Note Verbale dated 10 October 1967 from the Permanent Representative of the United States at the United Nations.

endeavour that are relevant in each case and in harmonising them to the best degree possible. This is just another way of saying that coherence has an important role to play during interpretation. As Section 4.4 demonstrates through examples taken from international judicial practice, such role includes both substantive and methodological aspects.

4.4 Coherence as Contextual Harmonisation: Practical Examples

Up to this point, we have offered a mostly theoretical account of the chapter's main thesis regarding the necessary role of coherence in legal interpretation. In this section, we turn towards practice and critically assess a number of examples of attempts at constructing coherent narratives in the context of treaty interpretation. In particular, this section examines instances where international courts and tribunals have attempted to use linguistic arguments in their appropriate context, such context on occasion being peritextual and extra-textual (Section 4.4.1); systemic (Section 4.4.2); and teleological/deontological (Section 4.4.3).

The analysis undertaken below demonstrates that the coherency of an interpretation depends in large part on two closely linked processes, namely, (i) framing the central legal question in dispute and (ii) identifying the appropriate interpretative context against which that legal question will be answered (normative contextualisation). Like coherence, the acts of framing and normative contextualisation exhibit aspects that are at once substantive and methodological.

4.4.1 Linguistic Arguments, in Their Context: Metal-Tech *and* Jan de Nul

Words and phrases must be read in their context. The context that is most immediately relevant is often that of the treaty in which the word or phrase is found. Taking stock of the relationships and linkages between the various provisions of a treaty contributes towards a more coherent reading of the treaty as a whole. Yet, at the same time, the context in which words get their meaning is not limited to the four corners of a treaty text. Such context, rather, is broader and includes extra-textual elements as well.[69] Accordingly, taking care to create a coherent narrative between words and their textual and extra-textual context is a critical

[69] Given this, the so-called 'textualist' approach is an unfortunate label to describe the VCLT rule, especially when the label is used to describe a theory advocating strict

aspect of any interpretative exercise having a bearing on the persuasiveness of the outcome. Consider the decisions in two investment disputes, *Metal-Tech* v. *Uzbekistan* and *Jan de Nul* v. *Egypt*, both acting as cases in point.

4.4.1.1 *Metal-Tech* v. *Uzbekistan*

The tribunal in *Metal-Tech* v. *Uzbekistan* had to determine the temporal scope of the legality requirement found in Article 1(1) of the Israel-Uzbekistan BIT (1994). Article 1(1) provided that: 'The term "investments" shall comprise any kind of assets, *implemented* in accordance with the laws and regulations of the Contracting Party in whose territory the investment is made.'[70] Uzbekistan had raised a jurisdictional objection on the ground that the claimant in that case had engaged in unlawful, corrupt, and fraudulent practices both when establishing the investment as well as during the investment's operation. The critical question for the tribunal, therefore, was whether the word 'implemented' in Article 1(1) of the BIT meant 'established' or 'established and operated'.[71]

The tribunal was quick to realise that, seen in the abstract, the conventional meaning of the word was broad enough to support both outcomes.[72] In working towards the conclusion that 'implemented' meant only 'established', the tribunal sought to form a coherent narrative of supportive structures, both within Article 1(1) itself as well as between Article 1(1) and other provisions in the same treaty. The tribunal began by noting that the action 'implemented' in Article 1(1) was attached to the word 'assets' and not to the word 'investments', the latter being the broader concept encompassing the former (i.e., an investment being an economic project comprising assets).[73] Though not spelled out explicitly by the tribunal, the implication of this point seems to be the following.

interpretation with no recourse to extra-textual arguments whatsoever (see also Letsas [n. 45], 266).

[70] The emphasis is added.

[71] *Metal-Tech Ltd* v. *Republic of Uzbekistan*, ICSID Case No. ARB/10/3, Award, 4 October 2013, para 185.

[72] Ibid., para 187. In addition, the tribunal was quick to conclude that the Hebrew and Uzbek versions of Article 1(1) were also unhelpful as they gave rise to contradictory results (ibid., para 188). In particular, the Hebrew word translated to 'applied' (indicating an one-time action of establishment), whereas the Uzbek word translated to 'used' (indicating a continuous action analogous to 'operate').

[73] Ibid., para 186.

An asset may be acquired lawfully or unlawfully but cannot be acquired lawfully and maintained unlawfully all at the same time, at least not without some unlawful action committed by its owner in the meantime. In other words, if acquired lawfully, later unlawful conduct by the claimant during the operation of the investment would not affect the lawfulness of the initial acquisition of the asset and, therefore, would not in principle affect a tribunal's jurisdiction. This argument thus acts as a logical bar to the broad interpretation of 'implemented' in relation to an asset.

Further to this, the tribunal sought to offer a plausible reason for the choice of the word 'implemented' made by the contracting parties. It recalled that legality clauses in the definition of investment are a common feature in investment treaties and that most of these clauses tend to take the tautological form '*investment* includes any kind of asset *invested* in accordance with the law'. The tribunal opined that in choosing the word 'implemented' rather than the boilerplate 'invested' it was plausible that the contracting parties had intended to avoid a tautological definition of what should qualify as an investment under their BIT.[74] To support the plausibility of this inference, the tribunal also contrasted paragraphs 1 and 2 of Article 1. Paragraph 2 provided that a change in the form in which 'assets' are 'invested or reinvested' would not affect their character as an investment. From that comparison, the arbitrators then concluded that the parties may have intended for 'implemented' to be used as a synonym for 'invested', since both the word 'implemented' in paragraph 1 and the phrase 'invested or reinvested' in paragraph 2 attached to the word 'assets'.[75]

Lastly, seeing the BIT as a coherent unit, the tribunal also drew a comparison between Articles 1(1) and 6(1) of the treaty. The latter article provided that the contracting parties would guarantee investors 'all the rights and benefits regarding the unrestricted transfer of . . . investments and returns which were in force *on the day the current investment was implemented*'.[76] The tribunal remarked that the word 'implemented' in Article 6(1) clearly meant to indicate an 'one-time initial action of establishment',[77] thus lending further support to its interpretation.[78]

[74] Ibid.

[75] Ibid., para 189.

[76] The emphasis is added.

[77] *Metal-Tech* v. *Uzbekistan*, Award, para 189.

[78] For additional examples of investment tribunals attempting, to various degrees, to construct coherent narratives in a similar way, see *Beijing Urban Construction Group*

The *Metal-Tech* example thus shows that attempts at creating as many supporting structures as possible between the conventional meaning of words, the surrounding context, and the contracting parties' intentions cumulate. As a result, the tribunal's decision appears sufficiently well-justified and persuasive in the end. By contrast, the jurisdictional decision in *Jan de Nul* v. *Egypt* examined below is an example of the consequences that come about from a rift between the conventional meaning of words and their proper context.

4.4.1.2 *Jan de Nul* v. *Egypt*

The *Jan de Nul* dispute arose out of a contract for the widening and deepening of certain stretches of the Suez Canal concluded between the claimants and the Suez Canal Authority, an Egyptian public agency. Due to certain matters pertaining to the tribunal's temporal jurisdiction, the claimants brought proceedings against Egypt under two BITs – a 1977 BIT between the Belgium-Luxembourg Economic Union (BLEU) and Egypt and a subsequent 1999 BIT between the same parties. Thus, the tribunal had to determine whether it had jurisdiction under both treaties. Presently, the focus is on the tribunal's reasoning with respect to the existence of an investment under the 1977 BIT.

Co. Ltd. v. *Republic of Yemen*, ICSID Case No. ARB/14/30, Decision on Jurisdiction, 31 May 2017, para 87:

> Accordingly, the consideration of the disputed text in the context of the whole structure of Article 10 of the BIT leads this Tribunal to conclude that the Contracting Parties intended to confer a real choice, not an illusory choice, on investors from their respective countries, and that the words 'relating to the amount of compensation for expropriation' must, in context, be read to include disputes relating to whether or not an expropriation has occurred;

Adel A Hamadi Al Tamimi v. *Sultanate of Oman*, ICSID Case No. ARB/11/33, Award, 3 November 2015, para 388 (emphasis in original, footnote omitted):

> Moreover, chapter 17 of the US-Oman FTA entitled '*Environment*', although it does not fall directly within the Tribunal's jurisdiction, provides further relevant context in which the provisions of chapter 10 must be interpreted;

The Canadian Cattlemen for Fair Trade v. *United States of America (formerly Consolidated Canadian Claims* v. *United States of America)*, UNCITRAL Rules, Award on Jurisdiction, 28 January 2008, para 166:

> [I]t is clear to this Tribunal that NAFTA Chapter Eleven cannot be viewed in isolation but must be considered in light of its larger context – the NAFTA as a whole.

The 1977 BLEU-Egypt BIT contained a narrow definition of investment, limiting its protection to 'every direct or indirect contribution of capital and any other kind of assets, invested or reinvested in enterprises in the field of agriculture, industry, mining, forestry, communications and tourism'.[79] The matter in dispute was whether the claimants had made a contribution in one of the listed fields and in particular whether the dredging of the Suez Canal was related to the field of 'communications'. Egypt took the view that no such contribution had been made because the ordinary meaning of the word 'communications' was limited to the exchange of information only.[80] By contrast, the claimants pointed to several dictionary definitions of the word 'communication' that also included the meanings of 'any connective passage or channel', 'a system (as of telephones) for communicating', 'a system of routes for moving troops, supplies, and vehicles', 'access or means of access between two or more persons or places', 'passage', and 'passage or an opportunity or means of passage between places'.[81]

Armed with these definitions, the tribunal accepted the claimants' contention that the ordinary meaning of the term 'communications' encompasses instances of exchanges of information as well as instances of transportation of persons or goods. To Egypt's counter-argument that, at any rate, the claimants' business was in dredging and not in communications even if broadly understood in the sense of transportation of persons or goods, the tribunal replied:

> Of course, in the sense of 'economic productive units', the Claimants are companies that are active in the field of dredging (or, in the [Respondent's] words of 'travaux publics') and not in the field of communications. This does not mean that they did not invest in an enterprise in the field of communications in the sense of a 'project' in that field.[82]

The tribunal thus seems to have expressed the view that, even though the claimants' work did not directly relate to the field of communications

[79] Article III(1) BLEU-Egypt BIT (1977). By contrast, the definition of investment of the 1999 BIT was much more capacious, as it included 'any kind of assets and any direct or indirect contribution in cash, in kind or in services, invested or reinvested in any sector of economic activity in the territory of one Contracting Party in accordance with its laws and regulations by an investor of the other Contracting Party ...' (Article 1[1] BLEU-Egypt BIT [1999]).

[80] *Jan de Nul N.V. and Dredging International N.V.* v. *Arab Republic of Egypt*, ICSID Case No. ARB/04/13, Decision on Jurisdiction, 16 June 2006, para 99.

[81] Ibid., paras 99–100 (incl. n. 31).

[82] Ibid., para 102 (footnote omitted).

(broadly understood in the sense of transporting people or goods from one place to another through the Suez Canal), the dredging activities undertaken were nevertheless contributing to the possibility of such communications taking place.

This reasoning is flawed and lacks in coherence thus rendering the decision on this point unpersuasive. The sole focus on the dictionary definition of 'communications' falls short of justifying why the ordinary meaning assigned to the term by the tribunal was also the ordinary meaning envisaged by the 1977 BIT. This is especially the case considering that the word 'communications' has multiple ordinary (i.e., acceptable) meanings.[83] The textual ambiguity in *Jan de Nul* required additional investigation in order to be cleared, which is to say, it required the consideration of additional interpretative contexts going beyond the treaty's text.

For example, the tribunal could have referred to one or more sectoral classification lists regarding services. Had it done so, it would have likely concluded that, as a services sector, 'communications' does not include construction or engineering works like dredging and neither does the sector of 'transport', which is the sector that the tribunal used to justify its interpretation.[84] It is true that such a move would not necessarily provide the tribunal with a conclusive justification, as it would raise additional questions of inter-temporal law and, in particular, whether an evolutive meaning was intended by the treaty drafters in relation to the word 'communications'.[85] Still, doing so would at the very least give the tribunal cause to further question the interpretation favoured by the claimants, rather than accepting it as self-evident and with virtually no critical assessment.[86]

[83] In this respect, see Fish (n. 38), 1122–1123, putting the function of dictionaries into perspective (emphasis in original):

> A dictionary doesn't tell you what meanings go naturally with what sounds (that is the fantasy Plato has fun with in the *Cratylus*); it tells you what meanings are *more often than not* associated with what sounds (or marks). A dictionary is a statistical report, not a normative one; it tell[s] you about the usage most people employ (in ordinary situations), not the usage demanded by some linguistic essence.

[84] E.g., see the WTO Services Sectoral Classification List (MTN.GNS/W/120), 10 July 1991, available at www.wto.org/english/tratop_e/serv_e/serv_sectors_e.htm.

[85] Inter-temporal law questions would arise because, historically, sectoral classification lists for services emerged much later than the date the 1977 BIT was concluded.

[86] For additional examples of the use of extra-textual documents along the lines advocated here, e.g., see *Kasikili/Sedudu Island*, Judgment of 13 December 1999, paras 21–25 (where

4.4.2 *Linguistic and Systemic Arguments:* Oil Platforms

The range of extra-textual considerations that may be relevant for the interpretation of a treaty provision extends much farther than what Section 4.4.1 may seem to suggest. According to the principle of systemic integration, in Article 31(3)(c) of the VCLT, the various norms of the international legal system as a whole also form part of the relevant context. The basic idea behind the principle of systemic integration is that legal norms are not created in a vacuum and, therefore, their interpretation should not be undertaken in isolation of the normative environment within which they exist.[87] To that end, Article 31(3)(c) of the VCLT refers to other 'rules' of international law that must be 'taken into account' when interpreting a treaty. This reference is generally accepted to include norms emanating from a cognisable source of international law.[88]

the Court referred to a draft on fluvial navigation prepared by the *Institut de Droit International*, which was contemporaneous to the applicable boundary treaty in that case, in order to determine the meaning of the term 'thalweg' found in the latter); *Daimler Financial Services AG* v. *Argentine Republic*, ICSID Case No. ARB/05/1, Award, 22 August 2012, paras 221–224 (where the tribunal referred to certain World Bank Guidelines, that were contemporaneous to the applicable BIT, in order to reach a prima facie understanding of the substantive scope of the term 'treatment' found in the BIT's MFN clause; but cf. the dissenting opinion of Charles N. Brower in this case [paras 18–22] disagreeing with the majority's approach).

87 International Law Commission, 'Fragmentation of International Law: Difficulties Arising from the Diversification and Expansion of International Law – Report of the Study Group of the International Law Commission', UN Doc A/CN.4/L.682 (13 April 2006), 23 (para 33) (footnote omitted):

> It is often said that law is a 'system'. By this, no more need be meant than that the various decisions, rules and principles of which the law consists do not appear ... randomly related to each other. Although there may be disagreement among lawyers about just how the systemic relationship between the various decisions, rules and principles should be conceived, there is seldom disagreement that it is one of the tasks of legal reasoning to establish it.

88 From a plethora of sources, see M. E. Villiger, *Commentary on the 1969 Vienna Convention on the Law of Treaties* (Leiden: Martinus Nijhoff, 2009), 433; C. McLachlan, 'The Principle of Systemic Integration and Article 31(3)(c) of the Vienna Convention' (2005) 54 *International and Comparative Law Quarterly* 279, 290; J. Pauwelyn, *Conflict of Norms in Public International Law: How WTO Law Relates to Other Rules of International Law*, 5th reprint (Cambridge: Cambridge University Press, 2006), 254–256; ILC Report on Fragmentation of International Law (n. 87), 212 (para 422), 214–215 (para 426); Merkouris (n. 11), 19.

But, cf. I. Sinclair, *The Vienna Convention on the Law of Treaties*, 2nd ed. (Manchester: Manchester University Press, 1984), 139 (possibly excluding general principles);

The principle of systemic integration naturally introduces elements of normative fit and coherence into the interpretative exercise.[89] These derive from the instruction to interpreters, implied within Article 31(3)(c), to operate under the assumption that the parties to a treaty must not have intended for something inconsistent with generally recognised principles of international law or with previously assumed obligations.[90] Although not always referencing Article 31(3)(c) directly,[91] well-publicised

Schwarzenberger (n. 68), 14 (excluding treaties); and Gardiner (n. 2), 299–300 (noting the ambiguity of the term 'international law' used in Article 31[3][c] of the VCLT), 307 (leaving the door open for judicial decisions and the writings of publicists to be included also).

89 See ILC Report on Fragmentation of International Law (n. 87), 211 (para 419), reflecting on the need:

> [T]o carry out the interpretation so as to see the rules in view of some comprehensible and coherent objective, to prioritize concerns that are more important at the cost of less important objectives. This is all that article 31(3)(c) [VCLT] requires; the integration into the process of legal reasoning – including reasoning by courts and tribunals – of a sense of coherence and meaningfulness. Success [or] failure here is measured by how the legal world will view the outcome.

Cf. also *Vattenfall AB and others* v. *Federal Republic of Germany*, ICSID Case No. ARB/12/12, Decision on the *Achmea* Issue, 31 August 2018, paras 151–165 (where the tribunal rejected the EU's argument that, following Article 31[3][c] of the VCLT, EU law should be taken into account when interpreting Article 26 of the ECT, by pointing out instead that following the EU's position would result in fragmentation rather than coherence in the interpretation of the ECT).

90 Jennings and Watts (n. 27), 1274–1275. States are thus taken to have had due regard for the way in which new treaties would hang together within the international legal system seen as a whole. From a plethora of authorities in support of the latter position, see *Amoco International Finance Corporation* v. *The Government of the Islamic Republic of Iran, National Iranian Oil Company, National Petrochemical Company and Kharg Chemical Company Limited*, Partial Award No 310-56-3, 14 July 1987, (1988) 27 *International Legal Materials* 1314, para 112; *Case Concerning Right of Passage Over Indian Territory (Portugal* v. *India), Preliminary Objections*, Judgment of 26 November 1957, ICJ Rep (1957) 125, 142; *Asian Agricultural Products Ltd.* v. *Republic of Sri Lanka*, ICSID Case No. ARB/87/3, Final Award, 27 June 1990, (1991) 6 *ICSID Review – Foreign Investment Law Journal* 526, para 41; *Case of Golder* v. *The United Kingdom*, Judgment, 21 February 1975, ECHR Series A, No 18, para 35; Appellate Body Report, *United States – Import Prohibition of Certain Shrimp and Shrimp Products*, WT/DS58/AB/R, 12 October 1998, para 158; *Georges Pinson*, Decision No 1, 422 (para 50); H. Lauterpacht, 'The Sources of International Law', in E. Lauterpacht (ed.), *International Law: Being the Collected Papers of Hersch Lauterpacht: Volume I* (Cambridge: Cambridge University Press, 1970) 51, 53–54; McNair (n. 42), 466.

91 Indeed, in the context of ISDS in particular, commentators indicate that explicit mentions to, and discussions about, Article 31(3)(c) of the VCLT have been rather infrequent in practice (e.g., see Weeramantry (n. 19), 89, and references therein).

examples of systemic interpretations of this kind in international economic law include:

(i) The WTO Appellate Body's decision in *US – Shrimp* to refer to Appendix I of the CITES in deciding that sea turtles are an 'exhaustible' natural resource for purposes of Article XX of the GATT;[92]
(ii) Determinations made by the *Al-Warraq* v. *Indonesia* tribunal and the *Tulip Real Estate* v. *Turkey* annulment committee that international human rights conventions and instruments on the right to a fair trial are relevant when interpreting the FET standard (*Al-Warraq*) and Article 52(1)(d) of the ICSID Convention (*Tulip Real Estate*);[93]
(iii) The tribunal's decision in *Chemtura* v. *Canada* to consider the provisions of several international conventions (including the Aarhus Protocol on Persistent Organic Pollutants to the UNECE Convention on Long-Range Transboundary Air Pollution, the Stockholm Convention on Persistent Organic Pollutants, and the OSPAR Convention), in determining whether Canada's decision to launch a review on the chemical compound lindane, with the intent of banning its use, was in bad faith;[94] or
(iv) The tribunal's decision in *Philip Morris* v. *Uruguay* to consider the provisions of the WHO's Framework Convention on Tobacco Control as 'a point of reference on the basis of which to determine the reasonableness of [Uruguay's tobacco control measures]'.[95]

At the same time, Article 31(3)(c) of the VCLT makes clear that such other rules of international law must be 'relevant'.[96] The criterion of relevancy indicates that considerations of narrative construction are

[92] ABR, *US – Shrimp*, para 132.

[93] *Hesham T.M. Al Warraq* v. *Republic of Indonesia*, UNCITRAL Rules, Final Award, 15 December 2014, paras 556ff; *Tulip Real Estate and Development Netherlands B.V.* v. *Republic of Turkey*, ICSID Case No. ARB/11/28, Decision on Annulment, 30 December 2015, paras 86–92.

[94] *Chemtura Corporation (formerly Crompton Corporation)* v. *Government of Canada*, UNCITRAL Rules, Award, 2 August 2010, paras 133–143.

[95] *Philip Morris Brands Sàrl, Philip Morris Products S.A. and Abal Hermanos S.A.* v. *Oriental Republic of Uruguay (formerly FTR Holding S.A., Philip Morris Products S.A. and Abal Hermanos S.A.* v. *Oriental Republic of Uruguay)*, ICSID Case No. ARB/10/7, Award, 8 July 2016, para 401. See also, paras 404, 420 and 429–430 of the award.

[96] It is noted here that Article 31(3)(c) of the VCLT also contains one additional condition, namely, that these other relevant rules of international law must be 'applicable in the relations between the parties'. This is an element of Article 31(3)(c) that is not under examination in this chapter.

apposite in systemic interpretations. Put differently, the search for relevancy implies that, at its core, the systemic interpretative exercise is about identifying and harmonising the normative contexts one uses to characterise and frame the dispute one is called upon to resolve.[97] The *Oil Platforms* case, to which the discussion now turns, serves as a good illustration of the above remarks.

4.4.2.1 The Facts of the Case

The *Oil Platforms* case was set against the background of the Iraq-Iran war that broke out in 1980 and the attacks by both belligerents on commercial shipping in the Persian Gulf (the so-called 'Tanker War'). In response to an attack against a US-flagged commercial vessel and the mining of a US warship (both attributed by the United States to Iran), the United States destroyed four Iranian oil platform complexes, which were alleged to having been used for carrying out the attacks against the two vessels. The justification invoked by the United States for its actions was that the oil platforms posed a threat to the freedom of commerce, navigation, and neutral shipping in the Persian Gulf.

The case was brought before the ICJ for adjudication on the basis of a 1955 Treaty of Amity, Economic Relations, and Consular Rights between the United States and Iran. The 1955 Treaty presented the only legal instrument upon which Iran could base the Court's jurisdiction. Iran's main contention was that the US attack constituted a violation of Article X of the Treaty, which mandated that there would be 'freedom of commerce and navigation' between the contracting parties.[98] The US reply was that its actions did not violate Article X and that, in any event, they fell under Article XX of the same Treaty, which did not preclude the taking of measures that were 'necessary to fulfil the obligations of a High Contracting Party for the maintenance or restoration of international peace and security, or necessary to protect its essential security interests'.[99] In particular, the United States argued that its actions were legitimate acts of self-defence and therefore 'necessary' in the context of the 1955 Treaty to protect its essential security interests.[100]

[97] Generally on this point, see R. Higgins, 'A Babel of Judicial Voices? Ruminations from the Bench' (2006) 55 *International and Comparative Law Quarterly* 791.

[98] *Case Concerning Oil Platforms (Islamic Republic of Iran* v. *United States of America)*, Judgment of 6 November 2003, ICJ Rep (2003) 161, para 20.

[99] Ibid., paras 20, 32.

[100] Ibid., para 37.

4.4.2.2 The Majority Decision

The Court began with the examination of the Article XX exception first. Using Article 31(3)(c) of the VCLT, it held that Article XX could not be construed to exist independently of the international rules on the use of force and more specifically held that '[t]he *application* of the relevant rules of international law relating to [the use of force] thus forms an integral part of the task of *interpretation* entrusted to the Court'.[101] Methodologically, this statement may have been a step in the wrong direction as it did not pay regard to the distinction between, on the one hand, the interpretation of a treaty norm by reference to other norms of international law and, on the other hand, the direct application of those other norms.[102]

Eliding this distinction had important normative implications. Indeed, despite repeated mentions to the fact that its jurisdiction was limited to the application of Articles X and XX of the 1955 Treaty,[103] the Court nonetheless went on to say that 'the question whether the measures taken were "necessary" *overlaps* with the question of their validity as acts of self-defence' as well as that 'the criteria of necessity and proportionality must be observed if a measure is to be qualified as self-defence'.[104] Furthermore, at a later point in the judgment, while prefacing the examination of the evidence before it, the Court outright said that it

101 Ibid., para 41 (emphases added).

102 On such a distinction, generally, see A. Gourgourinis, 'The Distinction between Interpretation and Application of Norms in International Adjudication' (2011) 2 *Journal of International Dispute Settlement* 31. The distinction, though often subtle, is an important one. For example, the use that an ISDS tribunal makes of the customary norm of attribution, according to which the actions of a political subdivision are attributable to the central government (e.g., in *Compañiá de Aguas del Aconquija S.A. and Vivendi Universal S.A.* v. *Argentine Republic [formerly Compañía de Aguas del Aconquija, S.A. and Compagnie Générale des Eaux* v. *Argentine Republic]*, ICSID Case No. ARB/97/3, Award, 21 November 2000 [*Vivendi I*], para 49) is very different from the use of the 'customary international law notion' that 'a deprivation [of property] can be justified if it results from the exercise of regulatory actions aimed at the maintenance of public order' (e.g., in *Saluka Investments B.V.* v. *The Czech Republic*, UNCITRAL Rules, Partial Award, 17 March 2006, para 254). The former use is a direct application of the rules of attribution given the absence of relevant rules in the investment treaty, whereas the latter use is an interpretation of an investment treaty's expropriation clause in light of what the tribunal considers to be customary principles on the justifiability of measures taken by a state for the sake of public order. That is to say, in the latter case, it is the treaty-based expropriation clause that is being directly applied by the tribunal and not the customary principles themselves.

103 *Oil Platforms*, Judgment of 6 November 2003, paras 31, 40, 42.

104 Ibid., para 43 (emphasis added).

would first concentrate 'on the facts tending to show the validity or otherwise of the claim [of the United States] to exercise the right of self-defence'.[105] Ultimately, the Court declared that the United States could not benefit from the defence of Article XX because its actions were not legitimate instances of self-defence under the law on the use of force and therefore were not 'necessary'. Having rejected the US defence, the Court went on to examine Iran's main claim that the US attacks violated Article X of the Treaty, which it also rejected.

The judgment was met with a number of dissenting and separate opinions. Of relevance for our purposes are the separate opinions of Judges Buergenthal, Higgins, and Kooijmans.[106] All three judges took issue, first, with the majority's backward sequence in dealing with Articles X and XX and, second, with the majority's treatment of the relevance of the customary law on the use of force.

4.4.2.3 The Opinion of Judge Buergenthal

Judge Buergenthal's opinion is the strictest of the three when it comes to the relevance of the systemic context during interpretation. It is thus an interesting opinion to note here for its potential wide-ranging implications. In Judge Buergenthal's view, the fact that the Court only had jurisdiction to apply the 1955 Treaty meant that Article 31(3)(c) of the VCLT could never allow the Court to take into account norms falling outside its jurisdictional scope, period.[107] Simplified, Judge Buergenthal's view seems to be that a norm *x* may be interpreted in light of a norm *y*, if and only if a court or tribunal has jurisdiction to apply both norms *x* and *y*. The reason for this, in Judge Buergenthal's view, is the concern that interpreting norm *x* in light of norm *y* would require a prior determination on whether norm *y* has been violated.

105 Ibid., para 50.

106 It is however noted that remarks similar in spirit to the ones made by Judges Buergenthal, Higgins, and Kooijmans were also made in the separate opinions of Judges Owada and Parra-Aranguren.

107 *Oil Platforms*, Judgment of 6 November 2003, Separate Opinion of Judge Buergenthal, paras 20–24. In particular Judge Buergenthal says (ibid., para 24): 'It follows that the Court errs when it asserts that it may, on the basis of the general principle of treaty interpretation codified in Article 31, paragraph 3 *(c)*, of the Vienna Convention, interpret Article XX, paragraph 1 *(d)*, of the 1955 Treaty in light of international law on the use of force or any other international law rules with regard to which the United States has not accepted the Court's jurisdiction.'

However, this is only a concern if one does not pay due regard to the difference between, on the one hand, interpreting norm *x* in light of norm *y* and, on the other hand, directly applying norm *y*. Taking this difference into account, one could thus counteract Judge Buergenthal's concern by replying: true, interpreting *x* in light of *y* may result in a determination that *y* has not been complied with, but, in any event, a state's international responsibility would be triggered only if norm *x* is found to also have been violated as a result, because that is the only norm that the adjudicator had jurisdiction to apply in any case.[108]

The trouble with Judge Buergenthal's view for present purposes is that, by eliding the distinction between application and interpretation, it risks overtly constraining the interpretative function.[109] As stated at the outset, interpretation is a broadly contextual process. Taking Judge Buergenthal's approach to its logical conclusion risks characterising most attempts at interpretation as *ultra vires*. Such a counter-intuitive conclusion would not only apply in the above-mentioned cases of *US – Shrimp*, *Al Warraq* v. *Indonesia*, *Tulip Real Estate* v. *Turkey*, *Chemtura* v. *Canada*, and *Philip Morris* v. *Uruguay* but perhaps also in cases such as *Al Tamimi* v. *Oman*, where the tribunal, seeing the applicable FTA as a coherent whole, took into account that FTA's chapter on environment (over which it did not have jurisdiction) in its interpretation of the FET provision found in the FTA's investment chapter.[110]

4.4.2.4 The Opinions of Judges Higgins and Kooijmans

Judges Higgins and Kooijmans also criticised the majority decision for failing to discharge its interpretative function properly. Yet their reasons

[108] For support, see also ILC Report on Fragmentation of International Law (n. 87), 212–213 (para 423).

[109] For an indirect, yet clear statement in support, see *Certain Questions Relating to Settlers of German Origin in the Territory Ceded by Germany to Poland*, Advisory Opinion of 10 September 1923, PCIJ Series B No 6 (1923) 5, 25:

> Poland contends that her action as regards the settlers has been taken in the exercise of the rights conferred upon her by the Peace Treaty, and especially by Article 256, and that the interpretation of this treaty does not belong to the Council of the League of Nations when acting under the Minorities Treaty. The Court is unable to share this view. . . . It does not matter whether the rights the infraction of which is alleged are derived from a legislative, judicial or administrative act, or from an international engagement. If the Council ceased to be competent whenever the subject before it involved the interpretation of such an international engagement, the Minorities Treaty would to a great extent be deprived of value.

[110] *Al Tamimi* v. *Oman*, Award, paras 388ff.

for thinking so differ substantially from those of Judge Buergenthal. Rather, both separate opinions illustrate with clarity the practical importance of adequately framing the legal question at issue, identifying an appropriate context, and constructing an appropriate narrative during one's interpretative exercise.

Judge Higgins made three related points. Firstly, the majority incorporated the totality of the substantive international law on the use of force, without taking care to determine whether this was warranted in the context of the dispute that was actually brought before the Court. For Judge Higgins, the appropriate context was rather shaped by the fact that the dispute was brought under an economic and commercial treaty.[111] Secondly, this led the majority to displace the applicable law. Instead of applying the 1955 Treaty, the Court directly applied the law on the use of force under the guise of treaty interpretation.[112] Thirdly, and as an additional consequence, the Court had effectively narrowed down the potential scope and range of its inquiry.[113]

[111] *Oil Platforms*, Judgment of 6 November 2003, Separate Opinion of Judge Higgins, para 46:

> What is envisaged by Article 31, paragraph 3 *(c)* [of the Vienna Convention], is that a provision that requires interpretation in Article XX, paragraph 1 *(d)*, will be illuminated by recalling what type of a treaty this is and any other 'relevant rules' governing Iran-United States relations. It is not a provision that on the face of it envisages incorporating the entire substance of international law on a topic not mentioned in the clause – at least not without more explanation than the Court provides.

[112] Ibid., para 49:

> The Court has, however, not interpreted Article XX, paragraph 1 *(d)*, by reference to the rules on treaty interpretation. It has rather invoked the concept of treaty interpretation to displace the applicable law. It has replaced the terms of Article XX, paragraph 1 *(d)*, with those of international law on the use of force and all sight of the text of Article XX, paragraph 1 *(d)*, is lost. Emphasizing that 'originally' and 'in front of the Security Council' . . . the United States had stated that it had acted in self-defence, the Court essentially finds that 'the real case' is about the law of armed attack and self-defence. This is said to be the law by reference to which Article XX, paragraph 1 *(d)*, is to be interpreted, and the actual provisions of Article XX, paragraph 1 *(d)*, are put to one side and not in fact interpreted at all.

[113] Ibid., para 51:

> Further, in reformulating the matter as one of self-defence under international law rather than 'necessary' action for the 'protection of essential security interests' within the terms of the 1955 Treaty, the Court narrows the range of factual issues to be examined. Through this recasting of the United States case the Court reduces to nil the legal interest in what was

Judge Kooijmans' opinion is a reiteration of the points made by Judge Higgins, although he was in general more open to the relevance of the law on the use of force. According to Judge Kooijmans, '[i]t can be readily admitted that if these measures involve the use of force, the rules of general international law become relevant for the question whether these measures can qualify as being "necessary"'.[114] He, however, further clarified this statement by immediately pointing out that saying this is 'something completely different from putting these measures directly to the test of the general rules of law on the use of force'.[115] For Judge Kooijmans, the interpretative relevance of the law on the use of force is borne out of a combination of elements, namely that (i) the 1955 Treaty provided no guidance on how to determine whether measures taken for the protection of a party's essential security interests were indeed 'necessary' and (ii) the United States in fact chose the military route as opposed to the route of economic sanctions or any other diplomatic avenues.[116]

In essence, both judges criticised the majority for framing the dispute exclusively under a use of force lens. The two judges did not suggest that the law on the use of force, and the conditions for a legitimate exercise of self-defence found therein, were wholly irrelevant to the case. What the two judges did suggest, however, was that the law on the use of force was not necessarily as relevant as the majority made it out to be. It seems clear that the Court's majority wanted to frame *Oil Platforms* as a case about the unlawful use of force by the United States.[117] True, Judges Higgins

> happening to oil commerce generally during the 'Tanker War'. Instead it makes the sole question that of whether an attack on two vessels (*Sea Isle City* and USS *Samuel B. Roberts*) constituted an armed attack on the United States that warranted military action in self-defence.

114 *Oil Platforms*, Judgment of 6 November 2003, Separate Opinion of Judge Kooijmans, para 23.

115 Ibid.

116 Ibid., paras 48–49.

117 E.g., see ibid., Declaration of Vice-President Ranjeva, para 3:

> In the present case, the Court has not allowed itself to be obstructed by obstacles of a formalistic or formal nature. The terms in which the problem was posed have in fact been distorted by peripheral issues, on which the Parties focused to an unreasonable extent. The result has been a certain artificiality in the subject-matter of the dispute, in the claims presented by the Parties and in their overall forensic strategy, which has at times smacked of sophistry. In the face of these diversionary tactics, the Court has 'pierced the veil' of the dispute, relying directly on acts, conduct and statements contemporaneous with the events having given rise thereto. It has taken the view that it should begin by addressing the issue

and Kooijmans countered, the use of force was the issue between the disputing parties, but this was not the dispute that was brought before the Court.

One might react to this by saying that it all seems like hair-splitting. All said and done, the substantive outcome is what matters and, except for some genuine dissents on substantive points,[118] the majority of the judges in the *Oil Platforms* case (including Judges Buergenthal, Higgins, and Kooijmans) were in agreement that the United States could not rely on the defence of Article XX but neither did it violate Article X. But regarding the disagreement amongst the judges as peripheral in light of their agreement on the final outcome would be perilous and misleading. The way one gets to the outcome matters as much as the outcome itself. We can see, for instance, that the majority's approach has had some important implications.

Firstly, the Court's choice of interpretative context could have affected the outcome. What is a 'necessary' measure in the context of a commercial matter may not be the same as a 'necessary' measure of self-defence when facing an armed attack. The legal standards are not equivalent and neither are the relevant considerations in making a correct determination under each standard. This could have had substantive implications in the *Oil Platforms* case since the Court's approach gives the impression that only an armed attack would have allowed the United States to rely on Article XX of the 1955 Treaty. As the Court found that the United States had not suffered an armed attack, reliance on the Article XX defence was automatically precluded under the narrative frame of the law of self-defence. Conversely, under the narrative frame of a commercial dispute, the same conclusion would not have followed immediately, as it would likely require a more nuanced examination of the equities of the parties' case. That is, on the one hand, forms of force against the United States that were less grave and did not amount to an armed attack could still have been deemed prejudicial to the essential security interests of the United States. On the other hand, it is likely that the United States' commercial interests in the Gulf during the 'Tanker War' were broader than just an attack on two US vessels. Protecting such broader

of the lawfulness of use of force in light of the provisions of Article XX, paragraph 1 *(d)*, of the 1955 Treaty.

[118] E.g., see the dissenting opinions of Judges Al-Khasawneh and Elaraby (taking the opposite view on the interpretation of Article X), and the separate opinion of Judge Simma (taking the opposite view on the United States' counterclaim that Iran's actions during the Tanker War themselves violated Article X of the Treaty).

commercial interests by attacking the platforms could have been deemed excessive, especially when other approaches (e.g., economic sanctions or other diplomatic avenues) may had also been available to the United States.

Secondly, the Court's choice resulted in a methodologically odd sequencing of treating the US claims, namely, the backward treatment of Articles X and XX. The Court's sequencing seems artificial and does not add up to any payoff. One would expect of the Court, after rejecting the defence of Article XX, to find that the United States had violated Article X. But it did not, which raises the question of why then not follow the logical sequence: find no violation of Article X and stop the inquiry at that? The answer once again seems to be because the Court wanted to make a clear statement about the fact that the United States had not complied with the international law on the use of force.

Thirdly, the Court's choice resulted in two connected procedural improprieties: (i) reading Article 31(3)(c) of the VCLT as a type of 'incorporation by reference' provision[119] and (ii) violating its jurisdictional mandate in the process. As said, it had been clearly stated by the Court's majority that the law on the use of force was not among the applicable law to the dispute and that there was no jurisdiction to directly apply it against the United States. Yet this is precisely what the Court ended up doing in the end.

4.4.3 Linguistic and Teleological/Deontological Arguments: Navigational and Related Rights *and* The Volga

A third contextual aspect of treaty interpretation relates to the general purposes, principles, or policies that led the parties to conclude the treaty under interpretation. 'Object and purpose' are mentioned in Article 31(1) of the VCLT among the elements to be considered when determining the ordinary meaning of a treaty's terms. Establishing links between the text of the treaty and the purposive intentions of the contracting parties vis-à-vis the values, policies, or overall projects they wanted to advance is an

[119] The difference between, on the one hand, an 'incorporation by reference' (or 'referral') provision bringing extraneous norms within the basic treaty (and, hence, under a court's jurisdiction) and, on the other hand, the act of taking into account relevant rules of international law in the interpretation of the basic treaty (having no bearing on a court's jurisdictional scope) has been explicated by the ICJ in the *Case Concerning Pulp Mills on the River Uruguay (Argentina* v. *Uruguay)*, Judgment of 20 April 2010, ICJ Rep (2010) 14, paras 48–66.

important aspect of any interpretative exercise.[120] The interpreter must attempt to reconstruct the contracting parties' purposive intentions and, in so doing, he or she must regard the parties as actors who have accepted institutional roles and whose actions can be rationally understood in relation to those roles (e.g., states operating within a legal, historical, and political context; treaty drafters deliberating in the context of a negotiation).[121] Such reconstruction takes place through practical inference, which is to say, through an attempt to simulate the process of rational deliberation that an intentional, purposive, and institutionally situated agent would likely follow under the circumstances.

Take for instance *Navigational and Related Rights*, where the ICJ was asked to determine the extent of Costa Rica's right to free navigation on the San Juan River under an 1858 Treaty with Nicaragua. The river belongs to Nicaragua but the Treaty had granted Costa Rica a right to free navigation for the purposes of 'commerce'. The contentious issue was whether 'commerce' covered trade in goods and services or trade in goods only. Nicaragua's argument was that only trade in goods was covered because that was the meaning that the term 'commerce' had at the time of the Treaty's conclusion. In rejecting Nicaragua's argument, the Court put forward the following set of mutually reinforcing arguments. The Court first held that:

> [W]here the parties have used generic terms in a treaty, the parties necessarily having been aware that the meaning of the terms was likely to evolve over time, and where the treaty has been entered into for a very long period or is 'of continuing duration', *the parties must be presumed*, as a general rule, to have intended those terms to have an evolving meaning. … First, [the term 'comercio'] is a generic term, referring to a

120 In the same spirit, see *Interpretation of the Convention of 1919 Concerning Employment of Women during the Night*, Advisory Opinion of 15 November 1932, PCIJ Series A/B No 50 (1932) 364, Dissenting Opinion by M. Anzilotti, 383.

121 On this aspect of interpretation, see Fish (n. 38), 1131 (n. 80). As Fish argues, this aspect of interpretation is objectivised in the following manner (emphasis added):

> There is no need to examine or even speculate about [the actor's] mental landscape. If there is an actual legislator whose intentions are crucial, he or she is neither particularized independently of an institutional role nor idealized in the sense of being a fiction. He or she is a legislator, or in other institutional contexts, a parent or a teacher or a traffic cop or a checkout clerk. With respect to all of those actual persons, *we read their intentions in relation to the job they are performing*; and those are real intentions even though they have not been unearthed by brain surgery or psychoanalysis.

> class of activity. Second, the 1858 Treaty was entered into for an unlimited duration; from the outset it was intended to create a legal régime characterized by its perpetuity.[122]

Immediately following that remark, the Court added:

> This last observation is buttressed by the object itself of the Treaty, which was to achieve a permanent settlement between the parties of their territorial disputes. The territorial rules laid down in treaties of this type are, by nature, particularly marked in their permanence . . ..
>
> This is true as well of the right of free navigation guaranteed to Costa Rica by Article VI. This right, described as 'perpetual', is so closely linked with the territorial settlement defined by the Treaty – to such an extent that it can be considered an integral part of it – that it is characterized by the same permanence as the territorial régime *stricto sensu* itself.[123]

As this example demonstrates, reconstructing the purposive intentions of treaty parties can be objectivised by reference to an institutional role (in this case, political entities known as 'states' wishing to resolve a territorial dispute in perpetuity). Yet this is not a process that is free from the exercise of judgment on the interpreter's part. It follows that the interpreter's assessment cannot be taken as is but requires independent justification itself. As a case in point of that consider *The Volga*, an ITLOS prompt release case. A key issue there was whether a coastal state could impose as 'bond or other security' (as requirement for the release of an arrested foreign vessel and its crew under Article 73[2] of UNCLOS) conditions that were non-financial in nature. In that case, Australia had requested as additional conditions attached to the pecuniary bond for the Volga's release the disclosure of the vessel's beneficial owners and the installation of a vessel monitoring system to deter it from re-engaging in illicit fishing activities.

The majority of the Tribunal ruled against Australia. The principal reason put forward was that the phrase 'bond or other security' in Article 73(2) of UNCLOS should be interpreted in the context of other provisions of UNCLOS dealing with the arrest and release of vessels. The latter provisions used the more precise expression 'bond[-ing] or other [appropriate] financial security'.[124] Based on that, the majority concluded that

122 *Navigational and Related Rights*, Judgment of 13 July 2009, paras 66–67 (emphasis added).

123 Ibid., paras 68–69.

124 *The 'Volga' Case (Russian Federation* v. *Australia), Prompt Release*, Judgment of 23 December 2002, ITLOS Rep (2002) 10, para 77.

non-financial conditions could not be considered as components of a bond in relation to Article 73(2) of UNCLOS. The majority also added that its interpretation was consistent with the object and purpose of Article 73(2), which was 'to provide the flag [s]tate with a mechanism for obtaining the prompt release of a vessel and crew arrested for alleged fisheries violations *by posting a security of a financial nature* whose reasonableness can be assessed in financial terms'.[125]

A number of remarks can be offered in response. First, the majority assumes that reading Article 73(2) in the textual context of UNCLOS as a whole is a conclusive argument, as opposed to simply one argument to be weighed against other possible arguments. Second, and because of this, the force of the subsequent teleological argument is undermined. The teleological argument is not offered by the Tribunal as an independent inquiry to reinforce the textual argument. Its use, rather, contains a *petitio principii*, for it already assumes the correctness of the interpretation advanced by the textual argument. Furthermore, the object and purpose of Article 73(2) is simply stated by the majority, rather than being itself derived from an independent line of reasoning.

In this respect, consider the dissents of Judges Anderson and Shearer. Their reconstruction of the purposive intentions of the UNCLOS contracting parties appears to cohere better than the majority's, thus arguably making their dissents more persuasive. Judge Anderson began by saying that the word 'bond' had no fewer than twelve different ordinary meanings according to the dictionary.[126] Given this, it was critical to identify the background interpretative context for the term 'bond' that was the most relevant in the circumstances of the case. On this point, Judge Anderson clarified that:

> [T]he ordinary meaning of the word 'bond' depends upon its context. In article 73, paragraph 2, the context is clearly not the financial meaning of 'bond' as a simple deed. Rather, the context is legal and precisely that of release of an accused person against a bail bond which may, and often does, contain non-pecuniary conditions. Conditions may be temporal, financial or non-financial. All conditions form integral parts of a bail bond and are valid *prima facie*. No particular type of condition should be excluded *a priori*.[127]

[125] Ibid. (emphasis added).
[126] Ibid., Dissenting Opinion of Judge Anderson, para 9.
[127] Ibid., para 13.

In addition, Judge Anderson also questioned the majority's one-sided assessment of the purpose of Article 73(2). For Judge Anderson, it could not be the case that the purpose of the requirement to post a 'bond or other security' was only to serve the interests of flag states by ensuring the prompt release of vessels. Rather, the purpose must also have been to safeguard the interests of coastal states by ensuring that ongoing domestic legal proceedings against the owners and crew of violating vessels would not be prejudiced.[128] Seen in this light, a bond including, for example, the obligation to install a vessel monitoring system could not be ruled out as obviously unreasonable, especially considering that there were reasons to believe that the vessel concerned would likely reoffend once released.[129]

For his part, Judge Shearer accepted the core of Judge Anderson's analysis. To it he added one more substantive reason, namely, that the balance of interests between flag and coastal states in cases of illegal fishing was not something to be preserved exactly as it was conceived during the conclusion of UNCLOS. To the contrary, it should be allowed to evolve as the circumstances of the fishing industry change.[130] To that end, Judge Shearer noted that such changes in circumstances that were pertinent to the case included the catastrophic decline in the stocks of many fish species since the conclusion of UNCLOS, as well as the fact that most illegal fishing problems arose from privately owned rather than state-owned fishing fleets.

What makes the two dissenting opinions stronger and more persuasive than the majority decision essentially boils down to two things. Firstly, both dissenting judges formulated their views about the object and purpose of Article 73(2) of UNCLOS as an independent argument. That argument was in turn based on an attempt to reconstruct the purposive intentions of institutionally situated actors in addressing a

[128] Ibid., para 18. The majority's one-sided assessment of the purpose of Article 73(2) UNCLOS is indeed curious given that ITLOS itself had clearly stated in *Monte Confurco*, a prior prompt release case, the following: 'Article 73 identifies two interests, the interest of the coastal [s]tate to take appropriate measures as may be necessary to ensure compliance with the laws and regulations adopted by it on the one hand and the interest of the flag [s]tate in securing prompt release of its vessels and their crews from detention on the other. It strikes a fair balance between the two interests' (*The 'Monte Confurco' Case [Seychelles* v. *France], Prompt Release*, Judgment of 18 December 2000, ITLOS Rep [2000] 86, para 70).

[129] *The Volga*, Dissenting Opinion of Judge Anderson, paras 19–24.

[130] Ibid., Dissenting Opinion of Judge *Ad Hoc* Shearer, para 19.

moral and practical question, that is, the balance of interests between coastal and flag states vis-à-vis illegal fishing activities. Secondly, and because of this, the teleological argument in the two dissents informs and reinforces the textual argument in a non-circular way. In the end, the textual and teleological arguments appear to be mutually supporting, not just because of the absence of any vicious circularity but also because of the moral appeal of the presumed purposive intentions of the UNCLOS contracting parties offered by the two dissenting judges.

At this point, one may ask how ISDS tribunals fare in relation to the deployment of teleological interpretative arguments. ISDS tribunals often do not adopt an approach similar to the one advocated here. That is, often, they do not take care to establish the links between the object and purpose of an investment treaty, the language of the treaty's commitments, and the contracting parties' intentions in a manner that is adequate, coherent, or persuasive. To the contrary, on occasion tribunals have used the object and purpose of investment treaties in a way that is unreflective and opaque. One may consider the following telling examples.

In *MTD* v. *Chile*, the tribunal had to determine whether the state's failure to rezone a plot of land, which had the effect of rendering the investor's planned development project obsolete, amounted to unfair and inequitable treatment. After adopting a plain meaning view of the FET standard as requiring treatment that is 'just', 'even-handed', 'unbiased', and 'legitimate', the tribunal said:

> As regards the object and purpose of the BIT, the Tribunal refers to its Preamble where the parties state their desire 'to create favourable conditions for investments by investors of one Contracting Party in the territory of the other Contracting Party', and the recognition of 'the need to protect investments by investors of both Contracting Parties and to stimulate the flow of investments and individual business initiative with a view to the economic prosperity of both Contracting Parties'. Hence, in terms of the BIT, fair and equitable treatment should be understood to be treatment in an even-handed and just manner, conducive to fostering the promotion of foreign investment. Its terms are framed as a pro-active statement – 'to promote', 'to create', 'to stimulate' – rather than prescriptions for a passive behavior of the [s]tate or avoidance of prejudicial conduct to the investors.[131]

[131] *MTD Equity Sdn. Bhd. and MTD Chile S.A.* v. *Republic of Chile*, ICSID Case No. ARB/01/7, Award, 25 May 2004, para 113. For similar approaches, see also *Eco Oro Minerals Corp.* v. *Republic of Colombia*, ICSID Case No. ARB/16/41, Decision on Jurisdiction,

What is striking in the tribunal's reasoning is that such a pro-active nature was attributed to FET not as a result of a direct interpretation of the provision's actual text but in a much more indirect, and thus questionable, way. Specifically, the phrase '[i]ts terms are framed as a pro-active statement' in the above-quoted passage is in fact misleading since the requirements 'to promote', 'to create', and 'to stimulate' are nowhere to be found in the provision's actual text but were rather imported directly from the BIT's preamble and the title of the FET clause.

In *SGS* v. *Philippines*, resolving the dispute required a determination on the scope of the umbrella clause found in Article X(2) of the Philippines-Switzerland BIT (1997). Given the uncertainty surrounding the legal status of umbrella clauses in international investment law, the tribunal offered the following, rather blunt, statement:

> The object and purpose of the BIT supports an effective interpretation of Article X(2). The BIT is a treaty for the promotion and reciprocal protection of investments. According to the preamble it is intended 'to create and maintain favourable conditions for investments by investors of one Contracting Party in the territory of the other'. It is legitimate to resolve uncertainties in its interpretation so as to favour the protection of covered investments.[132]

No doubt, the object of an investment treaty is to protect investors. But surely this cannot mean that every uncertainty must be interpreted in favour of investor interests. States wishing to protect foreign investment may still choose to do this to a greater or lesser degree. There is thus no clear reason as to why an expansive or indeed a restrictive interpretation of a treaty's provisions should be preferred simply based on a generic statement of the treaty's aims.

In a similar vein, when called upon to determine the scope and possible self-judging character of the necessity exception in Article XI of the Argentina-United States BIT (1991), the tribunal in *Enron* v. *Argentina* held that:

Liability and Directions on Quantum, 9 September 2021, paras 747–751, 762; *National Grid plc* v. *The Argentine Republic*, UNCITRAL Rules, Award, 3 November 2008, para 170.

132 *SGS Société Générale de Surveillance S.A.* v. *Republic of the Philippines*, ICSID Case No. ARB/02/6, Decision on Jurisdiction, 29 January 2004, para 116. The passage was later quoted with approval, e.g., by the tribunal in *Tokios Tokelés* v. *Ukraine*, ICSID Case No. ARB/02/18, Decision on Jurisdiction, 29 April 2004, paras 31; and by the English Court of Appeal in the case of *The Republic of Ecuador* v. *Occidental Exploration & Production Co*, [2007] EWCA Civ 656, para 28.

> [T]he object and purpose of the Treaty is, as a general proposition, to apply in situations of economic difficulty and hardship that require the protection of the international guaranteed rights of its beneficiaries. To this extent, any interpretation resulting in an escape route from the obligations defined cannot be easily reconciled with that object and purpose. Accordingly, a restrictive interpretation of any such alternative is mandatory.
>
> While there is nothing that would prevent an interpretation allowing for the inclusion of economic emergency in the context of Article XI, to interpret that such a determination is self-judging would be *definitely inconsistent* with the object and purpose noted. In fact, the Treaty would be deprived of any substantive meaning.[133]

The tribunal seems to regard the BIT in question as a kind of insurance policy for the benefit of foreign investors. Yet, even if one accepts such a broad understanding of the BIT's aims, the conclusion that, because of this, the Article XI defence cannot be of a self-judging character does not necessarily follow. A self-judging clause would not be 'definitely inconsistent' with the investor-protective aims of the BIT, nor would it deprive the BIT of its meaning, because the tribunal could still review Argentina's conduct under the principle of good faith. The tribunal's reasoning becomes even more surprising considering that both it and Argentina conceded that point during the proceedings.[134] Thus, to be coherent, the conclusion that Article XI could not be of a self-judging character should have come from a different line of reasoning.[135]

As a last example, in assessing Argentina's argument that a FET violation may only be pronounced upon evidence of bad faith or malicious conduct from the part of the host state, the tribunal in *Azurix* v. *Argentina* said:

[133] *Enron Corporation and Ponderosa Assets, L.P.* v. *Argentine Republic (also known as: Enron Creditors Recovery Corp. and Ponderosa Assets, L.P.* v. *The Argentine Republic)*, ICSID Case No. ARB/01/3, Award, 22 May 2007, paras 331–332 (emphasis added). The exact same approach was later followed by the tribunal in *Sempra Energy International* v. *The Argentine Republic*, ICSID Case No. ARB/02/16, Award, 28 September 2007, paras 373–374.

[134] *Enron* v. *Argentina*, Award, paras 324, 339. Furthermore, at the time the *Enron* award was published, the availability of good faith review even in the presence of a self-judging necessity clause had already been affirmed in *LG&E Energy Corp., LG&E Capital Corp., and LG&E International, Inc.* v. *Argentine Republic*, ICSID Case No. ARB/02/1, Decision on Liability, 3 October 2006, para 214.

[135] The tribunal indeed follows a separate line of reasoning in paras 335–338 of its Award, yet it still seems that the primary line of reasoning for its decision remains the one based on the object and purpose of the BIT.

> The standards of conduct agreed by the parties to a BIT presuppose a favorable disposition towards foreign investment, in fact, a pro-active behavior of the [s]tate to encourage and protect it. To encourage and protect investment is the purpose of the BIT. It would be incoherent with such purpose and the expectations created by such a document to consider that a party to the BIT has breached the obligation of fair and equitable treatment only when it has acted in bad faith or its conduct can be qualified as outrageous or egregious.[136]

The tribunal may very well be correct in its remarks on the relationship between FET and bad faith, but its statements about the purpose of the BIT seem rather sweeping. Moreover, the conclusion that Argentina's interpretation would be 'incoherent' with the BIT's object and purpose does not necessarily follow. Rather, what appears to be a lack in coherence is the fact that no substantive reason was offered explaining how such an expansive view of the treaty's purpose may be justified.

The examples above showcase a misuse of the context of the contracting parties' purposive intentions. In the passages cited, tribunals have used teleological arguments in what appears to be a conclusory manner. The legal reasoning deployed tends to obscure the substantive arguments of policy or principle that seem to have actually motivated the conclusions reached (namely, the need to ensure certainty and predictability for foreign investors, and the concomitant stability of the regulatory framework). Rather than being subjected to independent scrutiny and inquiry, these substantive arguments are instead assumed as self-evident and are subsumed under the object and purpose of the investment treaty under interpretation.

4.5 Conclusion

This chapter has argued that coherence as described in Chapters 1–3 forms a necessary aspect of the interpretation of treaties. The argument offered has been based on insights drawn from the way in which considerations of coherence enter into interpretation in general, which were then transposed to the interpretation of international treaties in accordance with the rule of interpretation contained in Articles 31 and 32 of the VCLT. The conclusion thus drawn is that considerations of coherence are an integral component of the very structure of the VCLT rule of

[136] *Azurix Corp.* v. *The Argentine Republic*, ICSID Case No. ARB/01/12, Award, 14 July 2006, para 372.

interpretation. Absent considerations of coherence, judicial application of the various interpretative principles contained in the VCLT rule risks falling into incompleteness or circularity.

Reaching such a conclusion requires one to move beyond the classic debate between textualism and intentionalism that often dominates discussions about the VCLT rule. To the extent that textualism and intentionalism are treated as opposing theories or methods of interpretation, any debate between the two tends to mislead rather than provide clarity. Conversely, according to the position advanced in this chapter, any act of interpretation is by its very nature an inquiry into the intentions of a purposive agent. Transposing this to the VCLT context, it is the combination of the VCLT's interpretative principles that in each case provides adjudicators with reasons that both bring and justify the interpretation of individual treaty provisions. These must be made to hang together and be combined in a narrative of the interpretative context of each case. Still, different interpretative principles in the VCLT may be assigned different weights in different cases depending on the particular reconstruction of the contracting parties' intentions performed by the interpreter. This is a sign that considerations of coherence are apposite, acting as the reasons that justify the above combination and accounting for the outcome's persuasiveness.

It bears repeating that, in advancing this thesis, the intention has not been to argue or imply that the VCLT rule is unimportant or peripheral. All that the chapter seeks to suggest is that properly applying the VCLT rule means constructing an account of the contracting parties' intentions through a process of framing and normative contextualisation of the legal issue brought before the interpreter or law-applier. This, it is recalled, must be formally supported by the relevant interpretative principles provided by the VCLT, which in turn means that the VCLT rule plays an important legitimating function. By providing the participants of the international legal system with the canons of the interpretative game, the VCLT ensures that the arguments each participant makes will be taken seriously by the rest and be given their due consideration, rather than be disregarded outright as irrelevant.

Chapter 5 takes the lessons learnt here with respect to interpretation, including the processes of framing and normative contextualisation, as a starting point to examine how considerations of coherence manifest in yet another aspect of systemic interpretation routinely performed by investment tribunals – the use of analogies.

5

Coherence and Analogical Reasoning

5.1 Introduction

The domain of legal interpretation is not exhausted at the interpretation of texts or, in the case of international law, at the interpretation of treaties. A type of interpretative reasoning that is used frequently in adjudication is analogical reasoning. In its simplest form, a legal argument from analogy indicates that if one provision is significantly similar with some other provision, then the former provision may be interpreted so as to ensure similarity of sense with the latter (analogous) provision.[1] The use of analogies abounds in the legal field to such an extent that some scholars describe analogical reasoning as the most familiar form of legal reasoning.[2] Analogical reasoning is prevalent in ISDS too, often operating at various levels of abstraction.[3]

The present chapter thus examines how considerations of coherence manifest in the use of analogical reasoning by investment tribunals. It demonstrates through concrete examples and case studies that the persuasiveness and perceived correctness of a legal pronouncement based on analogical reasoning depends on the degree of its internal coherence. Coherence in an analogical inference once again manifests in the two interrelated senses that are familiar to us. Firstly, in a methodological sense, coherence manifests itself in the way the adjudicator frames the legal question at issue and in the degree to which the analogy that is drawn satisfies the elements of similarity, structural parallels, and

[1] D. N. MacCormick and R. S. Summers (eds.), *Interpreting Statutes: A Comparative Study* (Dartmouth: Ashgate, 1991), 513–514.

[2] C. R. Sunstein, 'On Analogical Reasoning' (1992–1993) 106 *Harvard Law Review* 741, 741.

[3] See, generally, V. Vadi, *Analogies in International Investment Law and Arbitration* (Cambridge: Cambridge University Press, 2016), distinguishing between 'micro-comparisons' (principally referring to reasoning from past arbitral awards and other types of cross-regime comparisons) and 'macro-comparisons' (principally referring to implied paradigm-setting).

purposiveness. Secondly, in a substantive sense, coherence manifests itself in the normative contextualisation of the legal question and in the moral appeal of the proposed interpretation, derived from the analogy, when examined against the legal system's guiding principles and professed ends, as well as against the adjudicator's understanding of his or her own institutional role in the system.

With respect to scope, the present chapter focuses primarily on the use of extraneous analogies in ISDS, which is to say, it focuses on comparisons that tribunals make between, on the one hand, international investment law and, on the other hand, general international law, other specialised branches of international law, or entire systems of legal ordering. Therefore, the chapter does not directly examine analogies taking place within international investment law, which most prominently take the form of reasoning from past arbitral decisions. Remarks on the latter kind of analogies are offered in the context of the discussion undertaken in Chapter 7.

Structurally, the chapter proceeds in the following manner. Section 5.2 outlines the basic format and contours of analogical inferences. In so doing, it draws from literature in cognitive sciences to identify the constitutive elements of analogical reasoning, namely, the mental processes of searching for similarities, drawing structural parallels, and devising a goal or purpose to guide the analogy. Taken together, these account for an analogy's overall coherence. Sections 5.3–5.5 then undertake detailed case studies that demonstrate how the interaction, use, or misuse of the above processes affect the perceived coherence of ISDS decisions in cases where tribunals have explicitly or implicitly relied on analogical reasoning. Section 5.6 summarises and concludes.

5.2 The Format of Analogical Inference

The term 'analogy' describes a cognitive process through which one attempts to learn about a new situation by comparing and relating it to a more familiar situation that can be regarded as parallel. An analogical inference, at its simplest, takes the following format: 'Because situation A is like situation B, what applies in B must also apply in A.' In the context of a legal argument, and given the law's arguable character, it is sometimes the case that at least two competing approaches or interpretations may be offered for how to characterise or treat a pending case. This means that a decision-maker may have multiple possible sources upon which to base his or her analogy. A legal argument from analogy would thus often take the following format: 'Because situation A is more like situation B than situation C, what applies in B must also apply in A.'

Notice, however, that in both the simple and the more complex format, the analogical argument is conclusory and not justificatory. It offers no reasons as to why A is like B or more like B than C. There is thus an evaluative step in the process that is not included in the above format but must be implied instead. Or, as Dworkin emphatically put it: '[A]nalogy without theory is blind.'[4] An analogy, says Dworkin, is a way of stating a conclusion, not a way of reaching one, meaning that theory must do the real work.[5] This first section seeks to demonstrate that the evaluative aspect of an analogical argument must be kept always in mind: it is that which ultimately accounts for the coherence of the analogical inference and therefore for the outcome's persuasiveness and perceived correctness.

One must thus ask two kinds of questions. How do substantive and evaluative elements enter into an analogy and what are the indicators of coherence in an analogical inference? According to Sunstein, for analogical reasoning to operate properly, we have to know that the situations we are comparing are 'relevantly similar' and that there are not 'relevant differences' between them.[6] The challenge, thus, is identifying when differences or similarities are relevant. As said, drawing an analogy essentially means comparing and relating situations together. Cognitive scientists Keith Holyoak and Paul Thagard have described this as a process of establishing a systematic set of correspondences – a 'mapping' – between the novel situation and a more familiar situation.[7] According to the two authors, solving a problem by analogy typically involves four steps: (i) selecting the source analogue (i.e., the familiar situation); (ii) mapping the source analogue to the target (i.e., the novel or problematic situation), thus generating inferences about the latter; (iii) evaluating these inferences by taking into account the unique characteristics of the target, thereby deciding whether the generated inferences need to be upheld, adapted, or rejected; and (iv) learning something more general from the success or failure of the analogy.[8]

[4] R. Dworkin, 'In Praise of Theory' (1997) 29 *Arizona State Law Journal* 353, 371.

[5] Ibid.

[6] Sunstein (n. 2), 745.

[7] K. J. Holyoak and P. Thagard, *Mental Leaps: Analogy in Creative Thought* (Cambridge, MA: MIT Press, 1995), 4.

[8] Ibid., 15.

From this four-step schema, Holyoak and Thagard extrapolate three kinds of mental operations, central to any analogical inference, that act as constraining and guiding forces throughout the analogical process.[9] These mental operations are (i) identifying similarities, (ii) drawing structural parallels, and (iii) purposiveness. They are examined in turn below alongside a preliminary exposition of how each process may be seen to relate to, and manifest in, ISDS.

5.2.1 *Similarities*

People naturally feel impelled to compare situations that are similar. Situations are similar when they exhibit one or several common elements, such as common objects, concepts, attributes, or relations. But similarities between two situations may not always be so obvious or direct. Sometimes they may be more abstract than literal. This is the case, for instance, when investment tribunals seek to give content to the legal concept of 'fair and equitable treatment' by implicitly mapping it onto the practice of promise-keeping. The upshot of such a mental link is that, if FET is metaphorically similar to promise-keeping, then an investor's legitimate expectations can be protected against detrimental reliance on prior specific commitments made by the host state towards that particular investor.[10]

Other times, similarities may be obvious and direct, but they may not be necessarily relevant to the problem one is facing.[11] Consider the following question: Is a petroleum company similar to a flower company, or a mining company, or a seafood company? The obvious answer seems to be yes. All of them are juridical persons, have a corporate structure of some kind, and are also engaged in some kind of business activity. Would it matter if the petroleum company was owned by foreign nationals while the rest were not? It depends. We may need more context before answering conclusively. Let us assume that the question arises in the

[9] Ibid., 5–6.

[10] E.g., see *Antaris Solar GmbH and Dr Michael Göde* v. *Czech Republic*, UNCITRAL Rules, PCA Case No. 2014-01, Award, 2 May 2018, para 360; *Parkerings-Compagniet AS* v. *Republic of Lithuania*, ICSID Case No. ARB/05/8, Award, 11 September 2007, para 331–334.

[11] Cf. L. C. Becker, 'Analogy in Legal Reasoning' (1973) 83 *Ethics* 248, 249 ('[I]t is not just the sheer *number* of similarities between the analogs which counts, but somehow the *significance* of their similarities. . . . It is *relevant* similarities and differences which are at stake.' [emphases in original]).

context of an investment claim. Investment treaties mandate that states take nationality as irrelevant in the way they treat investments in their territory. So, all companies are still similar and are thus entitled to the same treatment.

But now alter the question ever so slightly again but still within the context of an investment claim: Is the foreign petroleum company similar to the other domestic companies for the purposes of a VAT refund that is available to any exports made by the latter but not the former? All are companies and we have already concluded that nationality does not matter in this instance. But does it automatically follow that they are still similar enough so that they are entitled to the same treatment? Probably not. The element of the VAT refund has added to the question's context, so that, whereas nationality still does not matter, perhaps the business sector in which each company is engaged does. In this iteration of the question, we still know that a petroleum business is clearly as much of a company as a flower (or any other) business, but this does not tell us that this similarity ought to be material when seen against the aims of a domestic VAT refund policy or against the rationale of the national treatment protection afforded by international investment law.

Addressing the above question, however, the tribunal in the LCIA-administered *Occidental* v. *Ecuador* case rather controversially took the view that the companies compared were indeed similar and therefore entitled to the same treatment with respect to the VAT refund. Moreover, the tribunal did so despite the fact that Ecuador's state-owned petroleum company, Petroecuador, was also denied the VAT refund alongside the investor. The decision has been met with scepticism in literature.[12] The tribunal's primary reason for disregarding the business sector as a relevant comparator in this case was its assessment that 'the purpose of national treatment is to protect investors as compared to local producers, and this cannot be done by addressing exclusively the sector in which [a] particular activity is undertaken'.[13] But such reasoning is insufficient to justify the outcome. Even if we subscribe to the tribunal's position that the aim of national treatment indeed is to ensure a level playing field for

[12] E.g., see C. McLachlan, L. Shore, and M. Weiniger, *International Investment Arbitration: Substantive Principles*, 2nd ed. (Oxford: Oxford University Press, 2017), 339 (para 7.284); J. Kurtz, 'The Merits and Limits of Comparativism: National Treatment in International Investment Law and the WTO', in S.W. Schill (ed.), *International Investment Law and Comparative Public Law* (Oxford: Oxford University Press, 2010) 243, 255–258.

[13] *Occidental Exploration and Production Company* v. *The Republic of Ecuador*, LCIA Case No. UN 3467, Final Award, 1 July 2004, para 173.

foreign and domestic investors, the tribunal's understanding of the aim still seems too broad and the decision to disregard the business sector as a comparator does not necessarily follow. This conclusion is borne out if one considers, first, that no company directly competes with all other companies in a country and, second, that no two business sectors are exactly the same. In other words, a VAT refund that is available to flower exports does not put oil exports at a disadvantage. Therefore, and contrary to what the tribunal suggests, making the refund available to Occidental would not level the playing field for its oil exports vis-à-vis flower exports, because there is no such playing field to be levelled in the first place.[14] To the contrary, making the VAT refund available to Occidental's exports would make them more competitive when compared to Petroecuador's exports.

5.2.2 *Structural Parallels*

A second factor that guides and constrains an analogical inference is one's attempt at drawing structural parallels between the situations one is comparing. There exists a structural parallel between two situations when the similarities one has identified are between elements that tend to serve similar roles or purposes in both situations.[15] Ensuring that structural parallels can be drawn thus helps to ensure that the similarities identified are pertinent and relevant for the problem one is called upon to resolve. This kind of exercise is useful in law as well. Oftentimes an adjudicator will have to determine whether a particular fact-pattern or issue falls under a provision regulating one type of cases or under a provision regulating another type of cases.

Consider the ICJ's advisory opinion on *Reservations to the Genocide Convention*, where the Court was asked whether a state can be regarded

[14] Curiously, a mere two paragraphs following its general statement of the purpose of national treatment in para 173 of the award, the tribunal adopts a somewhat different purpose for the national treatment duties of host states. This new statement of purpose seems to undercut, if not contradict, the originally stated purpose and the consequent choice to disregard the business sector as a relevant comparator. In particular, in para 175 of the award, the tribunal says that: 'In fact, the purpose of national treatment in this dispute is . . . to avoid exporters being placed at a disadvantage in foreign markets because of the indirect taxes paid in the country of origin.' Following this new stated purpose of national treatment would likely result in a conclusion that is closer to the one advocated here, namely, that there was no breach of national treatment in this case.

[15] Holyoak and Thagard (n. 7), 5–6.

as being a party to the Genocide Convention while maintaining reservations to which some, but not all, of the other contracting parties object. The Court began by setting out the common position that analogises international agreements to contracts.[16] Under a contract analogy, a multilateral convention is an agreement freely concluded whose integrity must be preserved. Therefore, no contracting party would be entitled to unilaterally frustrate or impair the agreement's raison d'être, for instance, by way of lodging a reservation that is not accepted by all other contracting parties.[17] Immediately, however, the Court went on to clarify that the Genocide Convention presented certain special circumstances that mandated a more flexible application of this principle, among them being the fact that it was intended for the Genocide Convention to be of a universal character and to enjoy the widest possible degree of participation by states.[18] One could thus say that the contract analogy had proven inadequate here because it was not possible to establish structural parallels between a private law contract and a law-making multilateral convention of the kind and importance of the Genocide Convention. In the Court's view, the contract analogy could not balance appropriately the competing values of integrity and universality, which was the critical matter at issue in the opinion. Modelled after private law relationships, the contract analogy favoured exclusively the value of integrity.[19]

[16] *Reservations to the Convention on the Prevention and Punishment of the Crime of Genocide*, Advisory Opinion of 28 May 1951, ICJ Rep (1951) 15, 21.

[17] Ibid.

[18] Ibid.

[19] Ultimately, the Court gave a somewhat equivocal answer to the question. It concluded that it is the object and purpose of the Genocide Convention that limits a contracting party's freedom to make reservations and the other parties' freedom to object to these reservations and that, therefore, the appraisal of a reservation and of the effect of any objections to it would depend on the particular circumstances of each case (ibid., 24–26). The opinion was not without controversy. Several judges dissented, believing the object and purpose constraint to be unsatisfactory and ineffective. The dissenting judges instead gave a clear priority to the value of integrity over that of universality. Thus, a joint dissent by Judges Guerrero, McNair, Read, and Hsu Mo, argued that a reservation to the Genocide Convention could not be made unless all contracting parties consented to it (ibid., 46–47). Judge Alvarez appended an additional dissenting opinion taking an even harder stance in favour of integrity. He argued that, unless explicitly stated, no reservations whatsoever should in principle be admissible in the case of the Genocide Convention and that, even then, the exact scope of permissible reservations should be clearly defined at the outset, otherwise reservations should only be allowed to produce the minimum of legal results (ibid., 54–55).

ISDS is no stranger to these kinds of analogies or to the need to draw structural parallels, even though considerations of these aspects of a claim are often obscured in arbitral awards. Suppose, for example, that an investor is led to believe by state officials that a plot of land will soon be re-zoned to allow for its commercial exploitation and this convinces the investor to buy said land and commit significant sums to its development. Is the state's ultimate failure to re-zone the land, effectively rendering our investor's planned project useless, a possible FET violation and/or a potential indirect expropriation? In other words, is this case more like a direct and outright transfer of legal title to the state (expropriation) or more like the act of reneging on one's promises (FET)? To make matters simpler, suppose also that the investor did not have a concrete entitlement under the law of the host state that the re-zoning would in fact take place; and the investor still maintains full ownership of the property concerned.

There are similarities and parallels that can be drawn between the above set of facts and each of the provisions vying for application. For instance, an indirect expropriation fits the facts because it leaves the investor with formal title to its property but likely renders the latter valueless or useless. A broken promise also fits the facts as it frustrates the investor's plans, thus possibly also rendering the property valueless or useless in the process. The critical element in this fact-pattern seems to be the view that one takes as to the moral relevance of one's expectations borne out of the acts of state officials. The substantive question thus becomes: Do, or should, expectations borne out of the acts of state officials play the same role in a FET claim and an expropriation claim?

One may begin to answer this question by identifying the aims served by FET provisions and expropriation provisions. FET provisions are concerned with the regularity of a state's conduct vis-à-vis foreign investors, whereas expropriation provisions are concerned with the uncompensated taking of property rights that are created under the law of the host state and are vested to an investor.[20] If this is the case, then expectations created solely by the acts of state officials may be more relevant for an alleged FET breach but less so for an alleged expropriation, in particular if these expectations are not connected with a concrete right that has

[20] Z. Douglas, 'Property, Investment, and the Scope of Investment Protection Obligations', in Z. Douglas, J. Pauwelyn, and J. E. Viñuales (eds.), *The Foundations of International Investment Law: Bringing Theory into Practice* (Oxford: Oxford University Press, 2014) 363, 400–402.

been taken from the investor.[21] One may also consider that a contrary conclusion would result in an overly broad expansion of the scope of expropriation in international law that would not be deemed appropriate.[22] In short, given that the investor in the above example had no claim to expectation rights under the law of the host state that the rezoning would actually take place, but at best a claim that it was incited to invest under false pretences, then we seem to have a better reason to map our fact-pattern to a possible FET violation. Indeed, that was also the road taken by the tribunal in *MTD* v. *Chile*, which had to rule on a dispute bearing these facts.[23]

5.2.3 *Purposiveness*

Even after having taken care to identify similarities and draw parallels between the situations under comparison, one may still be faced with competing but plausible mappings. At this point, according to Holyoak

[21] See, e.g., *EnCana Corporation* v. *Republic of Ecuador*, LCIA Case No. UN3481, UNCITRAL Rules, Award, 3 February 2006, para 184 ('[F]or there to have been an expropriation of an investment or return (in a situation involving legal rights or claims as distinct from the seizure of physical assets) the rights affected must exist under the law which creates them, in this case, the law of Ecuador.').

[22] In this respect, compare *Metalclad Corporation* v. *The United Mexican States*, ICSID Case No. ARB(AF)/97/1, Award, 30 August 2000, para 103 (emphasis added):

> [E]xpropriation under NAFTA includes not only open, deliberate and acknowledged takings of property ... but also covert or incidental interference with the use of property which has the effect of depriving the owner, in whole or in significant part, of the use or *reasonably-to-be-expected economic benefit of property* even if not necessarily to the obvious benefit of the host [s]tate;

with *The United Mexican States* v. *Metalclad Corporation*, 2001 BCSC 644, (2002) 5 ICSID Rep 236, para 99:

> The [*Metalclad* v. *Mexico*] Tribunal gave an extremely broad definition of expropriation for the purposes of Article 1110. ... This definition is sufficiently broad to include a legitimate rezoning of property by a municipality or other zoning authority.

[23] *MTD Equity Sdn. Bhd. and MTD Chile S.A.* v. *Republic of Chile*, ICSID Case No. ARB/01/7, Award, 25 May 2004, para 214:

> The issue in this case is not of expropriation but unfair treatment by the [s]tate when it approved an investment against the policy of the [s]tate itself. The investor did not have the right to the amendment of the PMRS. It is not a permit that has been denied, but a change in a regulation. It was the policy of the Respondent and its right not to change it.

and Thagard, the purpose for considering the analogy in the first place becomes a determining factor guiding the analogy and helping to resolve ambiguities between different possible mappings.[24] The same ought to apply in the case of analogies deployed while resolving legal disputes, with the important caveat, however, that the goals that an adjudicator seeks to achieve are rather complex and at times even debated.

Broadly speaking, an adjudicator's role is not simply to resolve a dispute between two parties but also to do this in accordance with the principles and values promoted by the legal system or legal regime in which the adjudicator finds himself or herself. This implies the construction of an institutional role that is particular to adjudicators in each legal system or regime. As Chapter 7 will point out in greater detail, such introspection must take place in ISDS as well. In fact, it is particularly pronounced in this context given the system's hybrid foundations[25] and often takes the form of higher-order (or macro-level) comparisons seeking to draw analogies between ISDS and entire schools of thought or legal systems.[26] Such comparisons seek to improve one's understanding of international investment law and ISDS by comparing them to other systems of legal ordering in a process that can be described as 'paradigm-setting'.

Three kinds of such paradigm-setting analogies can be identified. The first begins from the understanding that international investment law is a creature and a specialised branch of public international law. Comparisons made through this lens seek to identify the various points of convergence and divergence between the investment treaty regime and general international law or other specialised branches of international law.[27] In contrast, the other two kinds of analogies look towards domestic law and the private/public divide one finds therein. Drawing parallels

[24] Holyoak and Thagard (n. 7), 34–37.

[25] See Z. Douglas, 'The Hybrid Foundations of Investment Treaty Arbitration' (2003) 74 *British Yearbook of International Law* 151.

[26] See Vadi (n. 3), chapter 5.

[27] By way of example, the question of the nature of investor rights has been addressed over time by comparing investment treaty law to the law on state responsibility, the law on diplomatic protection, the law of treaties, international trade law, and international human rights law. Generally, see A. Roberts, 'Clash of Paradigms: Actors and Analogies Shaping the Investment Treaty System' (2013) 107 *American Journal of International Law* 45, 69ff; M. Paparinskis, 'Analogies and Other Regimes of International Law', in Douglas and others (n. 20) 73; M. Paparinskis, 'Investment Treaty Arbitration and the (New) Law of State Responsibility' (2013) 24 *European Journal of International Law* 617; M. Paparinskis, 'Investment Arbitration and the Law

between international investment law and private or public law, or between ISDS and commercial or public law adjudication, is a normative rather than a purely descriptive exercise considering that the private/public divide cuts across several issues in international investment law.[28] Both of these domestic analogies begin by drawing structural parallels and by pointing out similarities of form between them and international investment law and ISDS.

For instance, the private/commercial law paradigm views states' investment treaty obligations towards foreign investors as akin to private contractual commitments and regards ISDS as an extension of ordinary commercial arbitration.[29] This paradigm draws its support from the fact that ISDS is modelled after international commercial arbitration, as well as from the fact that a majority of investment disputes concern contractual breaches to some extent.[30] By contrast, the public law paradigm regards ISDS as a form of international judicial review, akin to domestic administrative law adjudication.[31] This paradigm points to the fact that

of Countermeasures' (2008) 79 *British Yearbook of International Law* 264; Douglas (n. 25).

[28] See A. Mills, 'Antinomies of Public and Private at the Foundations of International Investment Law and Arbitration' (2011) 14 *Journal of International Economic Law* 469, who identifies the following issues:

- how we describe the object and purpose of investment treaties (e.g., are they more like inter-state contracts or more like international standardisation instruments and how much freedom do states enjoy when issuing binding interpretations of their investment treaty obligations?);
- how we interpret FET (i.e., is it an autonomous standard or not?);
- how we describe the role of arbitrators (i.e., do they only have a case-specific mandate or should they also be concerned with the systemic implications of their decisions?).

[29] J. A. Maupin, 'Public and Private in International Investment Law: An Integrated Systems Approach' (2013–2014) 54 *Virginia Journal of International Law* 367, 394. For views of ISDS through this lens, see C. N. Brower, 'W(h)ither International Commercial Arbitration?' (2008) 24 *Arbitration International* 181; B. Legum, 'Investment Treaty Arbitration's Contribution to International Commercial Arbitration' *Dispute Resolution Journal* (August/October 2005) 71.

[30] Maupin (n. 29), 394–395. There is also historical backing for this kind of argument. The original assumption, prior to the advent of investment treaties, was that foreign investors would enter the host state by way of an investment contract that would govern the particular investor–state relationship. This was also the prevailing thinking during the negotiations of the ICSID Convention as reported, for instance, by A. F. Lowenfeld, 'The ICSID Convention: Origins and Transformation' (2009–2010) 38 *Georgia Journal of International and Comparative Law* 47.

[31] E.g., see A. Kulick, *Global Public Interest in International Investment Law* (Cambridge: Cambridge University Press, 2012); S. W. Schill, 'Deference in Investment Treaty Arbitration: Re-conceptualizing the Standard of Review' (2012) 3 *Journal of International*

ISDS is conducted between parties that stand in a hierarchical relationship, whereby states can impose binding obligations on investors via regulation or legislation. Its proponents also note that the substantive law applied by tribunals is very often not found in individually negotiated contracts but in a web of similarly worded inter-state treaties. Lastly, the public law paradigm also shows that, in resolving many of the disputes in practice, arbitrators must often address questions about the scope of a state's regulatory powers.

It bears noting that the similarities of form drawn by each paradigm are in turn linked to a normative agenda about the investment arbitrator's institutional role. For example, the private/commercial law paradigm uses the formal structure of the commercial model of settling disputes not only to emphasise certain procedural principles (e.g., the autonomy and formal equality of the disputing parties) but also to influence the merits of decisions. That is to say, it uses the commercial model of dispute settlement as a reason for the arbitrator to uphold the commitments the disputing parties had made to each other or to refrain from exceeding the boundaries of the individual dispute between the parties.[32] Tribunals that are sensitive to this paradigm may thus regard

Dispute Settlement 577; S. W. Schill, 'Enhancing International Investment Law's Legitimacy: Conceptual and Methodological Foundations of a New Public Law Approach' (2011) 52 *Virginia Journal of International Law* 57; S. Montt, *State Liability in Investment Treaty Arbitration: Global Constitutional and Administrative Law in the BIT Generation* (Oxford: Hart, 2009); T. T. Landau, 'Reasons for Reasons: The Tribunal's Duty in Investor–State Arbitration', in A. J. van den Berg (ed.), *ICCA: 50 Years of the New York Convention* (Alphen aan den Rijn: Kluwer Law International, 2009) 187, 194; B. Kingsbury and S. W. Schill, 'Investor–State Arbitration as Governance: Fair and Equitable Treatment, Proportionality and the Emerging Global Administrative Law', NYU School of Law, Working Paper No 09-46 (September 2009); D. Schneiderman, *Constitutionalizing Economic Globalization: Investment Rules and Democracy's Promise* (New York: Cambridge University Press, 2008); G. van Harten, *Investment Treaty Arbitration and Public Law* (Oxford: Oxford University Press, 2007); comments by Thomas Wälde at L. Paradell, 'The BIT Experience of the Fair and Equitable Treatment Standard', in F. Ortino, L. Liberti, A. Sheppard, and H. Warner (eds.), *Investment Treaty Law: Current Issues II* (London: British Institute of International and Comparative Law, 2007) 117, 140–141; G. van Harten and M. Loughlin, 'Investment Treaty Arbitration as a Species of Global Administrative Law' (2006) 17 *European Journal of International Law* 121; T. W. Wälde, 'Investment Arbitration under the Energy Charter Treaty: An Overview of Selected Key Issues based on Recent Litigation Experience', in N. Horn and S. Kröll (eds.), *Arbitrating Foreign Investment Disputes: Procedural and Substantive Legal Aspects* (The Hague: Kluwer Law International, 2004) 193, 211.

32 T. W. Wälde, 'Procedural Challenges in Investment Arbitration under the Shadow of the Dual Role of the State: Asymmetries and Tribunals' Duty to Ensure, Pro-actively, the

the stability of the host state's regulatory framework as the principal value at issue in an investment claim[33] and may also be reluctant to make sweeping pronouncements on the content of the law in *obiter* or to otherwise be seen as going beyond the confines of the dispute before them.

Conversely, the public law paradigm uses the structural parallels it singles out as relevant in order to argue that ISDS should be concerned with more than just maximising the disputing parties' satisfaction or securing their expectations.[34] Instead, it advocates for the introduction into ISDS of more deferential standards of review that pay greater regard to states' margin of appreciation,[35] including the adoption of proportionality analysis or other public law standards of review to be identified following a comparative public law analysis.[36] Tribunals that are sensitive to this paradigm will generally be more careful before finding that a state has abused its powers to regulate[37] and may even go as far as adopting an *in dubio mitius* presumption in certain situations, which is to say, a presumption in favour of state sovereignty.[38]

Although certainly adding in complexity, the existence of multiple paradigms describing the ISDS process is not necessarily undesirable or a sign of investment law's irrevocable incoherence. Fixating on identifying the best macro-level analogy in an attempt to extract a single correct answer – one dominant paradigm – may be misleading. Analogies need

Equality of Arms' (2010) 26 *Arbitration International* 3, 5–6; Maupin (n. 29), 395; Roberts (n. 27), 61–62.

33 For possible examples, see *CMS Gas Transmission Company* v. *The Republic of Argentina*, ICSID Case No. ARB/01/8, Award, 12 May 2005, paras 274, 276, 284; *Occidental* v. *Ecuador* (LCIA case), Final Award, paras 183, 190–191.

34 E.g., T. W. Wälde, 'The Specific Nature of Investment Arbitration', in Centre for Studies and Research in International Law and International Relations, *New Aspects of International Investment Law* (Leiden: Brill/Nijhoff, 2007) 43, 87 ('The commercial arbitration community – international, competent, procedurally expert and entrepreneurial – has in fact taken over investment arbitration and runs it as a new form of commercial arbitration business, with little understanding that enforcing disciplines against [s]tates is quite different from holding mature and experienced international commercial players to their bargains.').

35 E.g., see the works by Schill (n. 31).

36 E.g., Kingsbury and Schill (n. 31); W. Burke-White and A. von Staden, 'The Need for Public Law Standards of Review in Investor–State Arbitrations', in Schill (n. 12) 689.

37 E.g., *Joseph Charles Lemire* v. *Ukraine*, ICSID Case No. ARB/06/18, Decision on Jurisdiction and Liability, 14 January 2010, para 283.

38 E.g., *SGS Société Générale de Surveillance S.A.* v. *Islamic Republic of Pakistan*, ICSID Case No. ARB/01/13, Decision of the Tribunal on Objections to Jurisdiction, 6 August 2003, paras 167–174.

not be taken as indivisible wholes and concentrating on a single analogue may lead one to focus on a narrow set of goals and a narrow course of action.[39] Indeed, all three paradigms identified – public international law, private/commercial law, domestic public law – offer to some extent relevant, accurate, and ultimately useful descriptions of critical aspects of the phenomenology of ISDS, which arbitrators must keep in mind. The public international law paradigm accounts for the system's creation and applicable law. The private/commercial law paradigm accounts for the structure and for many of the procedural aspects of the dispute settlement format used (including with respect to remedies and enforcement). The public law paradigm accounts for the type of legal controversies often presented before tribunals.

Thus, for example, between the private and public law paradigms the latter seems more sensitive to the realities of state regulation. Yet it is doubtful whether it actually does a better job in resolving all tensions between investor and state rights or whether treating it as the singular paradigm is appropriate. In the first place, not all investment disputes raise public interest concerns. Some disputes are essentially contractual, and it is not clear what would be gained by addressing such disputes under a public law lens.[40] In the second place, it should not necessarily follow from the fact that there are public law elements in international investment law that a presumption against restrictions on state sovereignty is warranted. There is reason to be wary of excessive deference towards state interests as much as there is reason to be wary of excessive deference towards investor interests, for either could result in a loss of legitimacy. Where an uncritical adherence to the private law paradigm may lead to a perception of tribunals as mere agents of investors, an uncritical adherence to the public law paradigm may lead to a perception of tribunals as susceptible to political pressures exerted by powerful states.[41]

39 Holyoak and Thagard (n. 7), 144, 146. As the authors argue (ibid., 146):

> A single analog can seldom provide a complete basis for a decision; but aspects of several analogs can often provide part of the basis for developing a coherent plan. Although analogy-based inferences never guarantee optimal decisions, they derive the strongest possible justification when multiple source analogs are mapped to the target at the system level, with the results of these mappings being used as part of an overall evaluation of decision coherence.

40 Maupin (n. 29), 400.

41 Wälde (n. 31), 211.

What is more, one should be cautious before imposing overarching, systemic values on ISDS without due regard to its public international law origins. For instance, the concept of judicial review – central to the public law paradigm – takes on multiple overlapping meanings and functions in different domestic jurisdictions, including:

- upholding the rule of law;
- protecting the individual;
- determining institutional relationships and the allocation of powers within the state;
- establishing general principles;
- representing the public interest and acting as an alternative forum for public discussion;
- structuring deliberative and administrative processes within the state (e.g., reason-giving obligations, duty to consult, etc);
- promoting core good governance values;
- elaborating and vindicating fundamental rights.[42]

Uncritically regarding the above as the ends to be pursued by international investment law and ISDS would lead to arbitral behaviour that would likely stretch our understanding of what international courts and tribunals have the authority or legitimacy to do under public international law.[43] It is a well-established position in international law, for example, that international courts and tribunals are not always well positioned to assess all possible issues pertaining to a state's discretion in exercising its regulatory powers.[44] ISDS tribunals are thus generally reluctant to act as domestic administrative review bodies or to substitute their judgment for that of national bodies and indeed often reiterate as a position of principle that ISDS is not meant to act as an appellate jurisdiction or as a continuation of domestic legislation at the international level.[45]

42 C. Harlow and R. Rawlings, *Law and Administration*, 3rd ed. (Cambridge: Cambridge University Press, 2009), 669–670.

43 Moreover, it is far from certain whether ISDS *actually* pursues any of these ends. For instance, see the sceptical view regarding two of the aforementioned functions that are often associated with ISDS – the protection of investors (from corrupt or biased domestic courts) and the promotion of fairness and the rule of law – expressed in G. van Harten, 'Five Justifications for Investment Treaties: A Critical Discussion' (2010) 2 *Trade Law and Development* 19.

44 E.g., V. Lowe, 'Regulation or Expropriation?' (2002) 55 *Current Legal Problems* 447, 463ff.

45 E.g., *Marfin Investment Group* v. *The Republic of Cyprus*, ICSID Case No. ARB/13/27, Award, 26 July 2018, paras 868–870, 895–900; *Fouad Alghanim & Sons Co. for General Trading & Contracting, W.L.L. and Fouad Mohammed Thunyan Alghanim* v. *Hashemite*

In conclusion, adopting a paradigm promotes different visions of the system, which in turn tend to privilege different actors and goals.[46] Yet it is unlikely that any one paradigm can exclusively account for the full picture of international investment law. In this sense, neither paradigm can be regarded as immediately or inevitably outcome-determinative. Rather than being a question of making a final choice, it is a combination of the different perspectives each paradigm brings that guides arbitrators in identifying their institutional role within the system and in discharging their dispute settlement function.[47]

5.2.4 *Summing up*

Taking a bird's-eye view, the above analysis has pointed towards two familiar key components of the analogical process as a whole, namely, the mental processes of framing and normative contextualisation. Framing takes place when we identify the problem case, its characteristics, and the question that needs answering. In so doing, we also identify our end-goal

Kingdom of Jordan, ICSID Case No. ARB/13/38, Award, 14 December 2017, paras 344–366; *Invesmart* v. *Czech Republic*, UNCITRAL Rules, Award, 26 June 2009, para 501; *Glamis Gold, Ltd.* v. *The United States of America*, UNCITRAL Rules, Award, 8 June 2009, paras 762, 779; *Saluka Investments B.V.* v. *The Czech Republic*, UNCITRAL Rules, Partial Award, 17 March 2006, paras 272–273; *Generation Ukraine, Inc.* v. *Ukraine*, ICSID Case No. ARB/00/9, Award, 16 September 2003, para 20.33; *S.D. Myers, Inc.* v. *Government of Canada*, UNCITRAL Rules, Partial Award, 13 November 2000, para 261; *Lemire* v. *Ukraine*, Jurisdiction & Liability, para 283.

46 In this sense, the paradigm is a framing device singling out what is relevant. It places issues against a normative context and an ordering framework. Indeed, as stated by T. S. Kuhn, *The Structure of Scientific Revolutions*, 2nd ed. (Chicago: University of Chicago Press, 1970), 15: 'In the absence of a paradigm or some candidate for paradigm, all of the facts that could possibly pertain to the development of a given science are likely to seem equally relevant.'

47 Cf. Roberts (n. 27); and also Mills (n. 28), 477:

> The argument is not that a public or private perspective has to be 'chosen', or that a decision has to be made as to which one is 'correct', but rather that international investment law inherently brings together apparently contradictory perspectives, and that it is the amalgamation of these oppositions, of these 'public-private' antinomies, which lies at its foundations.

In this direction, also see: *Wintershall Aktiengesellschaft* v. *Argentine Republic*, ICSID Case No. ARB/04/14, Award, 8 December 2008, para 160 ('The ICSID Convention, under which this arbitration case has been registered, combines a public law system of [s]tate liability with private arbitration' [emphasis in original omitted]); *Glamis* v. *United States of America*, Award, para 5 ('The reality is that Chapter 11 of the NAFTA contains a significant public system of private investment protection.').

and determine whether drawing an analogy can help us to achieve it satisfactorily. Normative contextualisation takes place when we seek to identify the most appropriate analogue(s) to the problem case, based on the similarities and structural parallels that can be drawn, as well as on our intended end goal. As previously seen in Chapter 4, framing and normative contextualisation go hand in hand as critical components of coherent interpretations.

The remaining sections in this chapter have two goals. Firstly, they seek to demonstrate the actual relevance in ISDS practice of the above-mentioned elements of similarities, structural parallels, and purposiveness. To that end, each one of the sections that follow undertakes a case study that illuminates one or more of these elements, their use, and misuse.[48] Secondly, and relatedly, the remaining sections also seek to reaffirm the importance of framing and normative contextualisation for the perceived coherence of ISDS arbitral decisions resulting from analogical reasoning.

5.3 Borrowing Meaning: The Defence of Necessity under Customary International Law

In the late 1990s and early 2000s, Argentina experienced a severe financial crisis that prompted the government to adopt certain emergency tariff measures that affected the operations of foreign investors in the country. A long series of investment claims against Argentina ensued most prominently, although not exclusively, brought by US investors. The question of the necessity of Argentina's measures was consistently raised and discussed in the course of these cases. This section examines six cases in particular: *Enron* v. *Argentina*; *CMS* v. *Argentina*; *Sempra* v. *Argentina*; *LG&E* v. *Argentina*; *El Paso* v. *Argentina*; and *Continental Casualty* v. *Argentina*. In each of these cases, Argentina sought to justify its emergency measures on the basis of the existence of a state of

[48] Although the case studies examined in this chapter could in theory also be examined under the rubric of Article 31(3)(c) of the VCLT, the situations addressed here are different from the ones addressed in Chapter 4. Chapter 4 principally addressed situations where ISDS tribunals have used Article 31(3)(c) of the VCLT to interpret an applicable treaty norm in light of another relevant norm that was applicable in the relations between the parties. In the situations addressed in this chapter, tribunals have done something that is at once similar and broader. They have looked towards general international law or other branches of international law to directly borrow and apply meaning, guiding principles, or methods to the dispute before them.

necessity. In so doing, it relied, among others,[49] on customary international law (Article 25 of the ILC Articles on State Responsibility) and on Article XI of the Argentina-United States BIT (1991) which provided that:

> This Treaty shall not preclude the application by either Party of measures necessary for the maintenance of public order, the fulfillment of its obligations with respect to the maintenance or restoration of international peace or security, or the protection of its own essential security interests.

A significant part of the judgment in all six cases touched on the meaning to be given to the word 'necessary' in Article XI and, in particular, on whether the customary law defence of necessity could be used as a helpful analogue to assist in the interpretation of that term. The result was three distinct methodological approaches that the above tribunals used in answering the question, which we may term 'confluence',[50] '*lex specialis*', and 'primary/secondary norms'.

As seen below, although all tribunals sought to produce systemically coherent decisions, most in fact failed to do so having relied on a mistaken use of analogy that did not take account of the fact that the treaty-based defence and the customary law defence were of a different nature, notwithstanding their apparent similarity (i.e., their common reference to necessity).

5.3.1 Confluence: CMS, Enron, *and* Sempra

The confluence approach was followed by the tribunals in *CMS*, *Enron*, and *Sempra*. All three tribunals began their analysis by examining Article 25 of the ILC Articles on State Responsibility first. It is only after finding that Argentina could not meet the high threshold required by the necessity defence of Article 25 that they went on to examine the necessity

[49] Argentina also relied on certain provisions of its Constitution, as well as on the compensation for losses provision of Article IV(3) of the Argentina-United States BIT (1991).

[50] The label 'confluence' is borrowed from J. Kurtz, 'Adjudging the Exceptional at International Investment Law: Security, Public Order and Financial Crisis' (2010) 59 *International and Comparative Law Quarterly* 325. The similar but less neutral label 'conflation' has been used by C. Binder, 'Changed Circumstances in Investment Law: Interfaces between the Law of Treaties and the Law of State Responsibility with a Special Focus on the Argentine Crisis', in C. Binder, U. Kriebaum, A. Reinisch, and S. Wittich (eds.), *International Investment Law for the 21st Century: Essays in Honour of Christoph Schreuer* (Oxford: Oxford University Press, 2009) 608, 613.

exception of Article XI of the BIT.[51] In interpreting the latter, and after finding that the BIT did not provide any guidance with respect to the legal elements needed for its successful invocation, these tribunals took the view that the meaning of the term 'necessary' found in Article XI must be the same as that found in Article 25 of the ILC Articles. The *Enron* and *Sempra* tribunals were more direct and explicit in equating the two standards,[52] as opposed to the *CMS* tribunal,[53] yet the practical result is the same in all three awards.

According to these tribunals, conflating the two defences is justified because international law is taken to be complete. In the absence of specific guidance in treaty law on a particular matter, there exists a gap that must be filled by the application of general principles or customary international law. That this was the probable reason at the core of these decisions is clear from the following passage taken from the *Sempra* award, in which the tribunal expresses its view on the interpretative approach to be followed with respect to Article XI of the BIT:

> Nor does the Tribunal believe that because Article XI did not make an express reference to customary law, this source of rights and obligations becomes inapplicable. International law is not a fragmented body of law as far as basic principles are concerned and necessity is no doubt one such basic principle.[54]

The confluence approach however suffers from important methodological flaws. There is considerable doubt whether the three tribunals adequately discharged their duty to engage in an independent interpretation of Article XI of the BIT. To the contrary, it rather seems that they merely assumed that Article XI is tautological to the necessity defence under customary international law. Indeed, the confluence approach

[51] It is certainly odd that the tribunals examined the customary law defence before the treaty-based one. However, this may be partly due to Argentina itself who chose to plead its defences in that order.

[52] *Enron Corporation and Ponderosa Assets, L.P.* v. *Argentine Republic*, ICSID Case No. ARB/01/3 (also known as: *Enron Creditors Recovery Corp. and Ponderosa Assets, L.P.* v. *The Argentine Republic*), Award, 22 May 2007, paras 333, 339; *Sempra Energy International* v. *The Argentine Republic*, ICSID Case No. ARB/02/16, Award, 28 September 2007, paras 375–378.

[53] *CMS* v. *Argentina*, Award, paras 315–331 (reviewing the defence of necessity under the ILC Articles), and 353–378 (reviewing Article XI of the Argentina-United States BIT), with the final analysis on the BIT drawing heavily from the elements of the customary law defence.

[54] *Sempra* v. *Argentina*, Award, para 378.

assumes with no argument that the defences of Articles XI and 25 are of the same nature just because they both contain the term 'necessary'. However, as it will be seen later on, this is not the case. Doctrinally, the two articles represent two different kinds of norms, each serving a different function. Consequently, it is not self-evident that Article 25 was at all relevant for the interpretation of Article XI. Furthermore, even if we were to assume that the Article 25 defence of necessity was relevant for the interpretation of Article XI, the tribunals of the confluence approach still did not do that but rather ended up directly applying Article 25 under the guise of interpretation. These flaws also give rise to a substantive challenge for the decisions that followed the confluence approach. An argument could be made that, by incorporating Article 25 into the BIT wholesale, these decisions imposed a particularly onerous standard of necessity under Article XI of the BIT, which a state will almost always fail to meet in situations of economic emergency (assuming that Article XI was intended to apply to such situations in the first place).

In short, although the tribunals of the confluence approach framed adequately the legal question that needed answering (i.e., what is the meaning of the term 'necessary' in Article XI of the BIT and does it encompass situations of economic emergency?), they failed to properly contextualise it. In particular, the tribunals attempted to use the customary international law on necessity as the proper interpretative context to address the question, yet stopped their reasoning at the apparent similarities between Articles XI and 25 (i.e., the use of the word 'necessary' in both and the fact that both were necessity defences). In so doing, they did not go on to test the validity of this analogy, for instance, by further examining whether structural parallels between the two defences could be plausibly drawn.

5.3.2 Lex specialis*:* LG&E *and* El Paso

The second approach to interpreting Article XI of the Argentina-United States BIT (1991) relies on the *lex specialis* principle and was adopted by the tribunals in *LG&E* v. *Argentina* and *El Paso* v. *Argentina*. Both tribunals began their analysis from the treaty provision, reserving for customary international law a residual role to the extent only that this was required.[55] That said, the awards in these two cases are not wholly

[55] *LG&E Energy Corp., LG&E Capital Corp., and LG&E International, Inc.* v. *Argentine Republic*, ICSID Case No. ARB/02/1, Decision on Liability, 3 October 2006, para 206; *El*

consistent with each other in relation to their respective understandings of the nature of Articles XI and 25.

Starting from the *LG&E* decision, the *lex specialis* approach used therein is subtle and the more consistently applied of the two. The *lex specialis* approach in *LG&E* can be extrapolated from the tribunal's general understanding of the nature of Article XI of the BIT as one going to the question of state liability as opposed to the wrongfulness of the acts challenged (although the tribunal does not seem to hold that view throughout the decision).[56] On this view, both Article XI of the BIT and Article 25 of the ILC Articles are provisions sharing the same nature and subject matter, albeit each with a different scope. Article XI is the more particular, whereas Article 25 is the more general. Testing the challenged measures under Article XI of the BIT, the *LG&E* tribunal concluded that Argentina was entitled to rely on the necessity defence, if only for a limited period of time.[57] As with the confluence approach, the key methodological flaw here is the contextualisation of the question that is to be answered, which is to say, the assumption that the Article XI and Article 25 defences are of the same nature and can thus be treated as analogues. Even then, the *LG&E* tribunal was not entirely consistent with its self-imposed *lex specialis* approach. Specifically, even though the tribunal declared that it would only use the ILC Articles in a residual capacity if this was warranted, it ended up doing differently by utilising Article 25 as a secondary legal basis supporting its finding that Argentina had no liability.[58] Even if one conceded to the tribunal's view that

Paso Energy International Company v. *The Argentine Republic*, ICSID Case No. ARB/03/15, Award, 31 October 2011, para 613.

[56] E.g., see *LG&E* v. *Argentina*, Decision on Liability, paras 205 ('[T]he Tribunal must determine whether the measures implemented by Argentina were necessary to maintain public order or to protect its essential security interests, *albeit in violation of the Treaty*.' [emphasis added]), 229 ('Thus, Argentina is excused under Article XI from *liability* for any breaches of the Treaty between 1 December 2001 and 26 April 2003.' [emphasis added]); but cf. ibid., para 261 ('Following this interpretation the Tribunal considers that Article XI establishes the state of necessity as a ground for *exclusion from wrongfulness of an act* of the [s]tate, and therefore, the [s]tate is exempted from liability.' [emphasis added]).

[57] Ibid., para 229.

[58] Ibid., paras 245ff. The most relevant passage, at para 245, reads (footnote omitted):

> The concept of excusing a [s]tate for the responsibility for violation of its international obligations during what is called a 'state of necessity' or 'state of emergency' also exists in international law. While the Tribunal considers that the protections afforded by Article XI have been triggered in this case, and are sufficient to excuse Argentina's liability, the Tribunal recognizes

Articles XI and 25 were of the same nature, this was an unnecessary step to take given that the tribunal had already fully interpreted and applied Article XI as *lex specialis*.

The *lex specialis* approach in the *El Paso* award is clearer but more inconsistently applied. The *El Paso* tribunal began by stating its interpretative methodology with respect to Article XI of the BIT in the following manner:

> Article XI has to be *interpreted* taking into account general principles of international law, some of those being embodied in Article 25 . . .. And only if Article XI is found by the Tribunal not to *apply* in the case would an analysis of Article 25 be performed. Article XI is the *lex specialis*, Article 25, the *lex generalis*. As the Tribunal will consider Article XI of the BIT to *apply* to the case, it can dispense to fully analyse and to *apply* as such Article 25 of the ILC Articles.[59]

This statement is somewhat unclear on its characterisation of the *lex specialis* principle. It seems to describe it both as a principle of interpretation and as a principle of norm-application. Yet it seems that only the latter would be correct.

Indeed, throughout its analysis of Article XI of the BIT, the *El Paso* tribunal purports to use the general rules and principles of customary international law as interpretative aids in determining what the term 'necessary' means.[60] At the same time, however, it also seems that under the guise of interpretation, the tribunal in actuality ended up directly applying a critical element from the customary law defence, namely, that the state invoking the defence must not have contributed to creating the situation of necessity in the first place.[61] This proved to be a decisive

> that satisfaction of the state of necessity standard as it exists in international law (reflected in Article 25 of the ILC's Draft Articles on State Responsibility) supports the Tribunal's conclusion.

Further, see Kurtz (n. 50), 355–356, also criticising this aspect of the decision.

59 *El Paso* v. *Argentina*, Award, para 552 (emphases added).

60 E.g., ibid., para 613 ('When *interpreted in light of the above principles*, the requirement under Article XI that the measures must be "necessary" presupposes that the [s]tate has not contributed, by acts or omissions, to creating the situation which it relies on when claiming the lawfulness of its measures.' [emphasis added]).

61 Ibid., paras 616ff. In particular, cf. paras 616–617 ('According to Article 31[3] [VCLT], the interpretation of treaty rules should take into account, *inter alia*, "any relevant rules of international law applicable in the relations between the Parties". . . . Surely one of those general rules of international law is that codified in Article 25[2] of the ILC's Articles on the Responsibility of States, which provides, in part, that: "In any case, necessity may not be invoked by a [s]tate as a ground for precluding wrongfulness if: . . . [b] The [s]tate has

move since, upon examining the evidence, the tribunal declared that Argentina could not rely on Article XI of the BIT because it had substantially contributed to its dire economic situation.[62]

One could point to the following flaws in the *El Paso* tribunal's reasoning. First, there exists an internal contradiction in the way the tribunal uses the *lex specialis* principle. Generally, there are two options when applying a *lex specialis*: either the general rule can still have some residual application even in the presence of the special rule or the general rule becomes completely displaced by the presence of the special rule.[63] The two would appear to be mutually exclusive, yet it seems that the tribunal is confident that it can perform both at the same time. As seen, the general approach taken initially by the tribunal seems to indicate that the relationship between Articles XI and 25 is an 'either-or' question.[64] In particular, the tribunal confirmed that because it would find Article XI applicable, it would not have to apply Article 25. Yet, as seen, under the guise of interpreting Article XI in a systemic manner the tribunal ended up directly applying a critical element of the Article 25 defence.

A second problem follows from the above. The tribunal incorporated the non-contribution requirement from Article 25 into Article XI in an exercise of systemic interpretation, without however offering a substantive argument for this move on the basis of Article XI. The absence of substantive argumentation on this point can be traced to the tribunal's

contributed to the situation of necessity."'), 620 ('The general applicability of the rule barring the invocation of necessity when the [s]tate concerned itself has created that necessity or has significantly contributed to it is also supported by other provisions of the ILC Articles dealing with the preclusion of wrongfulness.'), 621 ('So far, this Tribunal has limited itself to examining the question of whether the [non-contribution rule] is a rule of general international law, applicable between the Parties to the BIT and, hence, a rule which may be used to interpret Article XI of the latter. It has reached an affirmative conclusion on this point.').

Such a reading of the *El Paso* award is further supported by the fact that the tribunal (ibid., paras 621–624) took the extra step of establishing that there also exists a general principle of necessity, in the sense of Article 38(1)(c) of the ICJ Statute, which includes the non-contribution requirement.

62 Ibid., para 665. To note, arbitrator Brigitte Stern expressed her direct disagreement with that finding in the main text of the award. Her dissent (ibid., paras 666ff) was to the effect that the contribution of the Argentine authorities had not sufficiently been proven by strong and uncontroverted evidence.

63 International Law Commission, 'Fragmentation of International Law: Difficulties Arising from the Diversification and Expansion of International Law – Report of the Study Group of the International Law Commission', UN Doc A/CN.4/L.682 (13 April 2006), 49ff; also, Kurtz (n. 50), 352–355.

64 *El Paso* v. *Argentina*, Award, para 552.

view that the relationship between Articles XI and 25 is one between a *lex specialis* and a *lex generalis*, which in turn rests on the erroneous assumption that the two articles are of the same nature. But Articles XI and 25 are not of the same nature, which not only means that they do not share a general-particular relationship but also that Article 25 is not necessarily relevant for the interpretation of Article XI. This is not to say that it is impossible to read the non-contribution requirement into Article XI of the BIT. But, to do this, one has to offer a substantive argument for it that must come from a line of reasoning that does not draw exclusively or even principally from the Article 25 defence.

The above problems again arise out of the *El Paso* tribunal's reliance on the improper analogy from Article 25 of the ILC Articles on State Responsibility. Such reliance is all the more surprising considering that early in its analysis, the tribunal had taken full cognisance of the fact that the Article XI and Article 25 defences were indeed dissimilar and could not be regarded as parallels.[65] In spite of this, the tribunal proceeded on the assumption that Article 25 was a relevant general norm without offering an argument as to why or how this might be the case.

5.3.3 *Primary and Secondary Norms:* Continental Casualty *and the* CMS *and* Sempra *annulment decisions*

The primary/secondary norms approach was followed by the tribunal in *Continental Casualty* v. *Argentina*[66] and the two ad hoc committees formed to hear the annulment requests in the *Sempra* v. *Argentina* and *CMS* v. *Argentina* cases mentioned previously. Contrary to the confluence and *lex specialis* approaches, the primary/secondary norms approach correctly identifies that Article XI of the Argentina-United States BIT (1991) and Article 25 of the ILC Articles on State Responsibility serve fundamentally different functions, to the extent that

[65] Ibid., Award, para 553:

> Under Article XI, measures necessary 'for the maintenance of the public order' or for 'the protection of essential security interests' are not in breach of the relevant BIT . . .. On the contrary, if the rules of general international law regarding necessity apply, this is a ground for precluding the wrongfulness of an act not in conformity with an international obligation and thus implies that the acts be analysed first'.

[66] To note, the annulment committee in *Continental Casualty* upheld the original tribunal's approach on the relationship between Articles XI and 25. Therefore this decision is not examined here.

they cannot be treated as analogues. Such a conclusion rests on the doctrinal distinction between primary and secondary norms.[67]

The crux of this approach is as follows. Article XI of the BIT is a primary norm bearing on the scope of the rights and duties of the treaty parties. It specifies the conditions under which the BIT is applied. As such, and in the phrase used by the *CMS* committee, Article XI acts as a 'threshold requirement': if it applies, then no wrongful act has been committed by the host state.[68] By contrast, Article 25 of the ILC Articles is a secondary norm precluding state liability under certain strict conditions.[69] For Article 25 to apply, it must first be concluded that a state has flouted one or several of its (primary) international obligations.[70] In that case, Article 25 may be invoked by that state as an excuse precluding the international liability that would otherwise arise.[71] Put differently, under Article 25, the wrongfulness of the act is tolerated by the international community in light of the special circumstances, properties, or characteristics that are present on the actor of the wrongful act.[72]

The primary/secondary norms approach thus shows why it is not necessarily the case that the conditions of application of Articles XI

[67] H. L. A. Hart, *The Concept of Law*, 3rd ed. (Oxford: Oxford University Press, 2012), 81. According to Hart, primary norms prescribe or proscribe conduct and thus create legal rights and duties, whereas secondary norms stipulate the conditions or requirements under which primary norms may be introduced, modified or extinguished.

[68] *CMS* v. *Argentina*, Decision of the Ad Hoc Committee on the Application for Annulment of the Argentine Republic, 25 September 2007, para 129; similarly, *Continental Casualty Company* v. *The Argentine Republic*, ICSID Case No. ARB/03/9, Award, 5 September 2008, para 164.

[69] That the totality of the ILC Articles on State Responsibility are secondary norms is made clear in the ILC's Commentary. Moreover, with respect to the defence of necessity, in particular, the Commentary clearly states that 'the plea of necessity is not intended to cover conduct which is in principle regulated by the primary obligations' (see Draft Articles on Responsibility of States for Internationally Wrongful Acts [adopted by the ILC at its 53rd session, 23 April–1 June and 2 July–10 August 2001] [2001] Vol II [Part Two] *Yearbook of the International Law Commission* 26, 31 [para 1], 84 [para 21]).

[70] *Continental Casualty* v. *Argentina*, Award, para 166.

[71] *CMS* v. *Argentina*, Annulment, para 129.

[72] This being the case, the title 'circumstances precluding *wrongfulness*' used in Chapter V of the ILC Articles may be somewhat misleading. On the terminological question of describing necessity under Article 25 as a justification (i.e., precluding wrongfulness) or an excuse (i.e., precluding liability), see: F. Paddeu, *Justification and Excuse in International Law: Concept and Theory of General Defences* (Cambridge: Cambridge University Press, 2018), chapters 3 and 8; as well as V. Lowe, 'Precluding Wrongfulness or Responsibility: A Plea for Excuses' (1999) 10 *European Journal of International Law* 405.

and 25 are one and the same,[73] as, for example, the confluence approach readily assumes. It is a manifest error of law to assume with no argument that Articles XI and 25 are both of the same nature.[74] By the same token, the primary/secondary norms approach also demonstrates the shortcomings of the *lex specialis* approach. For the *lex specialis* approach to be validly used, the two articles must be of the same nature. They must both be interpreted as either primary or secondary norms. Whereas describing Article 25 as a primary norm would be impossible given the unequivocal nature of the entirety of the ILC Articles as secondary norms, it was still open to these tribunals to attempt an argument that Article XI of the BIT should itself be conceptualised as a secondary norm. As seen, this is not something that the tribunals of the *lex specialis* approach took care to clarify without equivocations.

In conclusion, the decisions that adopted the confluence and *lex specialis* approaches suffer from incoherence. Incoherence results from the significant discord in these decisions between the reasoning used and fundamental core mechanics of general international law. The discord can in turn be traced to the reliance by these tribunals on an incomplete, and ultimately mistaken, analogy between the necessity defence of Article XI of the Argentina-United States BIT (1991) and the necessity defence of Article 25 of the ILC Articles on State Responsibility.

5.4 Borrowing Guiding Principles: *UPS* v. *Canada* and the Principle of Equality of Competitive Opportunity under WTO Law

Beyond general international law, ISDS tribunals also look towards the other specialised branches of international law for guidance. International trade law figures prominently among these. On its face,

[73] *Continental Casualty* v. *Argentina*, Award, para 167; *CMS* v. *Argentina*, Annulment, paras 130–131.

[74] *Sempra* v. *Argentina*, Decision on the Argentine Republic's Application for Annulment of the Award, 29 June 2010, para 208. Note, however, that despite taking the same critical position against the confluence approach, the *CMS* and *Sempra* committees still rendered different decisions. Only the *Sempra* committee decided to annul because of a manifest excess of powers, whereas the *CMS* committee did not avail itself of this possibility recalling its limited mandate under the ICSID rules (*CMS* v. *Argentina*, Annulment, para 136). As far as the *Enron* case is concerned, the annulment committee there did not take issue with the tribunal's choice of equating Articles XI and 25. What it did take issue with, however, was the process of reasoning that led the *Enron* tribunal to rule that Argentina could not rely on Article 25. In the end, the committee annulled the award on the grounds of manifest excess of powers and failure to state reasons.

international trade law seems to be an appropriate comparator and source of analogies for international investment law. The fields of application of international trade and international investment law are partially overlapping. Both deal with trade in the domain of services through the establishment of a commercial presence in a foreign country.[75] Furthermore, there are certain types of provisions that are similar in both regimes, such as provisions on non-discrimination and general exceptions. Thus, analogies made between international investment law and international trade law tend to be text driven. This is to say that analogies between the two are used primarily to seek guidance on the interpretation of these similar provisions.[76]

As this section demonstrates, however, the similarities between international trade and international investment law are not enough to justify the drawing of analogies between the two regimes. Similarities notwithstanding, it may not always be possible to draw structural parallels or ensure convergence of purposes between international trade and international investment law. To illustrate the point, this section examines *UPS* v. *Canada*, a NAFTA case decided by a 2-1 majority at the core of which was a genuine disagreement on a point of principle based on an implied analogy drawing from WTO jurisprudence.

5.4.1 The Facts and the Majority's Decision

On 19 April 2000, US postal services company UPS filed a notice of arbitration against the government of Canada challenging a series of alleged anticompetitive measures and practices by the government, which, according to UPS, had the effect of favouring Canada's national postal services company (Canada Post) to the detriment of UPS' Canadian subsidiary (UPS Canada). Among the measures and practices challenged was Canada's Publications Assistance Program (PAP), which is the focus of the present case study. The PAP was a subsidy program for Canadian publications. Under the PAP, Canadian publishers were eligible to receive a subsidy to assist them in producing publications and in making these available throughout the country. Receipt of the subsidy was conditional on the publishers using Canada Post's mailing services.

[75] This is known as 'mode 3' supply of services in the WTO context, following Article I(2)(c) of the GATS.

[76] Vadi (n. 3), 148.

In UPS' view, the PAP violated the national treatment obligations of Canada under Article 1102 of the NAFTA because of UPS Canada's inability to compete with Canada Post for participation in the Program. Article 1102 of the NAFTA provided for the no less favourable treatment of foreign investors and investments when compared to treatment received by the host state's own investors and investments that are in 'like circumstances' to the foreign investor or investment. UPS' main argument was that it had consistently sought to compete alongside Canada Post in the provision of courier services to publishers that qualified for the PAP subsidy and that this fact showed that the two companies were in like circumstances in this respect.[77] Furthermore, according to UPS, the denial of the opportunity to compete for the distribution of PAP-eligible publications in violation of Article 1102 of the NAFTA had caused UPS Canada harm in the form of a loss of the profits that would have resulted from such distribution.[78]

Although the majority found that the PAP was covered by the cultural industries exception of NAFTA,[79] it nonetheless went on to consider whether UPS' national treatment claim could succeed in any event. On the latter question, the majority ruled that Canada Post and UPS Canada were not in like circumstances, thus rejecting the claim. For the majority, the appropriate comparator to UPS Canada was not Canada Post but other Canadian courier companies that were also unable to compete for participation in the PAP.[80] In coming to this conclusion, the majority did not explicitly address UPS' argument that a willingness to compete was in itself an indication of like circumstances. Rather, the majority's conclusion is the result of a consideration of several contextual factors, including, in particular:

- the PAP's public policy aims to provide easily accessible and affordable cultural products to all Canadians and to sustain and develop the Canadian publishing industry;
- the particularities of the Canadian market on publications, which was characterised by high numbers of home-delivery subscription sales as opposed to newsstand sales;

[77] *United Parcel Service of America Inc.* v. *Government of Canada*, UNCITRAL Rules, Award on the Merits, 24 May 2007, para 174.

[78] Ibid., Investor's Memorial (Merits Phase), 23 March 2005, para 603.

[79] Ibid., Award, paras 137ff.

[80] Ibid., para 177.

- Canada Post's statutory obligation to maintain a presence throughout the country;
- the unwillingness or inability of private courier companies (including UPS Canada) to deliver to all addresses in Canada, but instead only to densely populated areas, large retail customers and customers in shopping malls.[81]

According to the majority, given these factors, Canada was justified to exclusively use the services of Canada Post as the means through which to disperse the subsidy, since no other private courier company in the country was in like circumstances with Canada Post. In fact, UPS had never intended to fully substitute Canada Post in the PAP's operation. What is more, rather than claiming damages for the loss of a right vested to it under Canadian law, UPS was in reality claiming damages for the loss of a mere opportunity to compete on equal footing for the delivery of publications that were eligible for the PAP subsidy. Indeed, according to the majority's own assessment of UPS' claim:

> UPS is not truly asking that it be accorded the same treatment as Canada Post. Rather, it asks that the Program be re-designed for its benefit; specifically, that the choice of delivery mechanisms be left to each publisher to decide for itself. This is because UPS is interested in having UPS Canada compete for only a part of the PAP delivery business offered by Canada Post. It is not interested in having UPS Canada provide the same service or the same contribution as Canada Post under the Program – and in fact, it is not capable of doing so.[82]

5.4.2 The Dissent of Dean Ronald A. Cass

Arbitrator Ronald Cass took a different view with respect to the likeness of circumstances present between UPS Canada and Canada Post. His opinion on this question is structured differently than the majority's. Rather than examining the relevant contextual factors of the case in an attempt to assess whether these justify a finding of likeness between the two entities, Cass begins from the opposite direction. He first concludes that there exists prima facie likeness between UPS Canada and Canada Post and only then goes on to consider whether the differential treatment

[81] Ibid., paras 146–147, 155, 176–177.
[82] Ibid., para 178.

accorded could be justified on some ground or by taking into account any relevant contextual factors.

In detail, Cass' analysis begins by finding that UPS Canada and Canada Post were in competition with each other because both were active in the delivery of the kind of materials that could be covered by the PAP subsidy.[83] The existence of a competitive relationship was, in turn, a prima facie sign granting sufficient support to the conclusion that UPS Canada was in like circumstances with Canada Post vis-à-vis the PAP subsidy.[84] According to Cass, this being the case, the onus was on Canada to demonstrate that there were legitimate reasons for according differential treatment to the two companies.[85] Given that Canada's principal reason for the difference in treatment was the public policy aims of the PAP in conjunction with Canada Post's ability to perform nationwide delivery of the eligible publications, Cass thus proceeds to scrutinise this justification under three counter-arguments advanced by UPS.

In its first counter-argument, UPS claimed that UPS Canada had the capability of developing a delivery service that would cover the whole country, or nearly so. Upon reviewing the record, Cass determined that the available evidence could not bear that conclusion. The evidence did not show that UPS Canada could imminently perform nationwide deliveries or that it was even close to developing the necessary capacity to do so.[86]

Under its second counter-argument, UPS claimed that the design of the PAP was not reasonable because it did not allow for the possibility of two or more companies cooperating to ensure nationwide delivery.[87] In rejecting this ground, Cass' opinion echoes the views of the majority on the same point. He thus acknowledges that the NAFTA parties have a margin of discretion with respect to the way they choose to design domestic policies. In Cass' view, a contrary conclusion would not only severely constrain states' ability to regulate to pursue their own objectives but would also greatly and unduly expand the power of ISDS tribunals to evaluate the legitimacy of government objectives and the efficacy of the means chosen to implement those objectives.[88]

[83] Ibid., Separate Statement of Dean Ronald A. Cass, paras 94–95.
[84] Ibid., paras 96, 101.
[85] Ibid., paras 102–103.
[86] Ibid., paras 104–109.
[87] Ibid., paras 110–113.
[88] Ibid., paras 116–117.

According to the third counter-argument raised by UPS, the design of the PAP was not done in good faith because of Canada's failure to provide at the outset an opportunity for any other company to make a case that it was able to perform nationwide deliveries or that it would be willing to make the investment necessary to do so.[89] In Cass' view, this argument succeeded in countering Canada's public policy justification for the differential treatment between UPS Canada and Canada Post. In particular, Cass points out, Canada's justification was invoked for the first time during the NAFTA proceedings as an *ex post* rationalisation for the accorded treatment, when it should have been considered already at the setting-up phase of the PAP. In other words, Canada should have ascertained the 'likeness' of the services provided by Canada Post and UPS Canada already at the design phase of the PAP, for example, by openly and publicly announcing to all interested companies that their ability to perform nationwide delivery was a critical condition as well as the policy reasons for why that was the case.[90]

5.4.3 *Analysis*

It is submitted that the difference between the positions of the majority and the dissent essentially rests on the existence and relevance of a

[89] Ibid., paras 122, 124, 126.

[90] Cass' rationale is expressed in greater detail in the following two passages taken from paras 130 and 132 of his dissent:

> If Canada sought simply to assure that firms participating in the PAP meet legitimate conditions, it could have accomplished that readily with a public request for interested parties wanting to meet certain criteria to come forward. I am troubled that Canada instead used a procedure for constructing this aspect of the PAP that on its face seemed to ask only *how* to give PAP benefits to Canada Post, not *why* that was important to broader public policy goals [emphases in original];

and

> Accepting Canada's position on this issue would to a very substantial degree cede to Canada the right to decide on its own when investors will enjoy the protections of NAFTA's national treatment obligation. NAFTA Parties would not be required to articulate in advance a rationale for treating firms differently, but would be able to craft rationales during the course of a dispute that would be tailored to the legal issues arising in the proceeding. That would provide great flexibility for the NAFTA Parties but little protection for the investors (or investments) of other NAFTA Parties who were the intended beneficiaries of Article 1102's restrictions on state action.

principle of equality of competitive opportunity in international investment law. For the majority, such a principle has no import in international investment law, whereas for the dissent it is critical. Although not mentioned in the majority or the dissent, it is likely that the principle of equality of competitive opportunity came into the discussion by way of an implied analogy with international trade law and the jurisprudence of the WTO Appellate Body.

The implied import of the WTO analogy becomes apparent, in the first place, if one looks at the disputing parties' submissions. Recall that UPS had framed the harm suffered by its investment as the loss of the profits UPS Canada would have made had it been granted the opportunity to distribute publications subject to the PAP subsidy.[91] Further, one sees that in its Reply UPS makes multiple direct references to the principle of equality of competitive opportunity under WTO law, as well as to the case law of the WTO Appellate Body more generally, with the intention for them to be used by the tribunal as a source for guidance when determining the existence of 'like circumstances' under Article 1102 of the NAFTA.[92] Conversely, one sees in Canada's submissions a different framing of the case. For one, Canada alleges that UPS had failed to prove a fundamental aspect of ISDS claims, namely, that its investment had suffered any kind of actual damage or loss.[93] Furthermore, in its Rejoinder, Canada directly opposes the relevance of WTO law as a source of analogies for the case and of equality of competitive opportunity as a relevant guiding principle in this respect.[94]

The opposing views of Canada and UPS are reflected in the opinions of the majority and the dissent respectively. Siding with Canada, the majority's position of principle was that the purpose of the investment treaty regime is not to second-guess the way states choose to design their domestic policies in an attempt to make them more favourable to foreign investors. Rather, the purpose is to try and identify specific instances of harm done to specific foreign investors and to their rights. Therefore, the claim that UPS Canada was denied the opportunity to distribute publications subject to the PAP, which in turn caused it to lose the profits from such distribution, could not rise to the level of interference required for it to be sanctioned by international investment law.

[91] *UPS* v. *Canada*, Investor's Memorial (Merits), para 603.

[92] Ibid., Investor's Reply (Merits Phase), 15 August 2005, paras 500ff.

[93] Ibid., Canada's Counter-memorial (Merits Phase), 22 June 2005, paras 550–552.

[94] Ibid., Canada's Rejoinder (Merits Phase), 6 October 2005, paras 48ff, 68ff, 277.

On the flip side, Cass' position of principle was that international investment law is not only concerned with sanctioning specific instances of harm done to foreign investors but also with granting them equal opportunities of doing business in host states. It did not matter that UPS Canada was not deprived of any concrete right vested to it under Canadian law. It was instead sufficient that it was not extended an opportunity to compete with Canada Post. The influence of WTO jurisprudence in the dissent is evident not only because of the ultimate reason for vindicating UPS' claim but also because of the construction and sequencing of the national treatment test used. Recall that according to the dissent the most natural reading of NAFTA's Article 1102 gave weight to a showing of competition between foreign and national investors, the existence of a competitive relationship established a prima facie case of like circumstances, and this created a presumption of discrimination that was up to Canada to rebut. This way of addressing national treatment complaints is a characteristic of WTO law.[95]

However, the appropriateness of the implied WTO analogy used by the dissenting arbitrator can be questioned. The dissent presumably relied heavily on the apparent similarity between NAFTA and international trade law (i.e., the existence in both of national treatment provisions protecting investments and products/services in 'like circumstances') but did not take care to ensure that the equally important aspects of the existence of structural parallels and convergence of purpose were also met. One may thus offer the following remarks in response to the dissent.

The design of the national treatment test in WTO law is connected to the overall purpose of the WTO's non-discrimination obligations, which is to equalise the competitive opportunities afforded to foreign products or services when compared to each other and to domestic products or services. As a result, there is no requirement for the complaining country in WTO litigation to prove that actual harm has occurred in order for a national treatment claim to succeed.[96] The reason why the principle of

[95] E.g., see N. DiMascio and J. Pauwelyn, 'Nondiscrimination in Trade and Investment Treaties: Worlds Apart or Two Sides of the Same Coin?' (2008) 102 *American Journal of International Law* 48, 72.

[96] Ibid., 70:

> [T]rade law is about competitive opportunities, not actual trade flows. To win a national treatment claim, a WTO complaining country is not required to show that the challenged internal measure has actually

equality of competitive opportunity is central to the non-discrimination duties of WTO members is because non-discrimination is tied directly to the overall policy goals of the WTO to increase liberalisation of cross-border trade flows as well as market access for imported goods and services.[97] The WTO's overall systemic goals also explain why the principal remedy that is available to a successful complaining country is not for the losing country to pay retrospective compensation but for it to prospectively withdraw or modify the challenged measure.[98]

Yet the aims served by the arbitration of investment claims are not necessarily the same as those served by the adjudication of WTO complaints. The social purpose served by international investment law is the encouragement of cross-border investment for development. Investment protection is regarded as simply the means to encourage investment flows. ISDS is therefore primarily concerned with redressing injuries

> impeded specific trade flows; it is sufficient to point to a measure as it exists on the books and to explain how that measure affects competitive opportunities in favor of domestic products. . . . In investment law, it is more important to prove a measure's actual impact on, or harm to, a specific investor or investment.

97 Ibid., 61–62. In the context of the GATT, e.g., see Appellate Body Report, *Japan – Taxes on Alcoholic Beverages*, WT/DS8/AB/R, WT/DS10/AB/R, WT/DS11/AB/R, 4 October 1996, 16 ('Article III [national treatment under the GATT] protects expectations not of any particular trade volume but rather of the equal competitive relationship between imported and domestic products.' [footnote omitted]).

98 The primary and final remedy of a successful WTO litigation is described in Article 19(1), first sentence, of the DSU, which states: 'Where a panel or the Appellate Body concludes that a measure is inconsistent with a covered agreement, it shall recommend that the Member concerned bring the measure into conformity with that agreement.' Article 22 of the DSU also recognises two additional temporary remedies in the event of continuous non-compliance: compensation and the suspension of concessions or other obligations (retaliation). Upon closer inspection, however, the latter are not in reality remedies since they are not intended to have a directly corrective or even a punitive rationale. They rather seek to enforce compliance by putting pressure on the violating state. Thus, compensation, if agreed by the disputing parties, is only forward-looking. It only seeks to cover damages that will be suffered by the injured party due to the violating party's continued non-compliance. In the event that the parties cannot agree on an appropriate compensation, retaliation is then the injured party's last resort to put pressure on the violating party to comply, for instance, by drastically increasing customs duties on selected products of export interest to the latter.

The above notwithstanding, a controversial exception does exist with respect to prohibited subsidies. The Panel Report in *Australia – Subsidies Provided to Producers and Exporters of Automotive Leather (Article 21.5 – US)*, WT/DS126/RW, 21 January 2000, paras 6.46–6.49, ruled that in certain, very specific circumstances, the duty to 'withdraw' a prohibited subsidy may necessitate a repayment in full of the subsidy to the injured party.

suffered by individual investors and their investments. This also explains why the principal remedy in ISDS is retrospective compensation for the damage suffered by an investor due to the host state's conduct and not an order for the host state to prospectively bring itself into compliance, for instance, by amending the challenged measure. Indeed, arbitral practice suggests that a showing of actual damage sustained by the investment – as opposed to a mere loss of opportunity for the investment to be more profitable – is critical to the success of an ISDS claim.[99]

Given the above remarks, the coherence of the dissent is affected on two interconnected levels. On a first level, there appear to be missing premises in the dissent's reasoning. There exists no obvious reason why one should have constructed the non-discrimination obligations of NAFTA's Chapter 11 in the same way as they are constructed in the WTO context. The relevance of a WTO analogy cannot be merely assumed but must be argued. Yet the dissent imports by default the principle of equality of competitive opportunity and the full national treatment test exactly as they exist in WTO law, without a substantive argument or an examination of the ways in which these would have to be adapted to fit the ISDS context given the structural differences between the two regimes. On a second level, the WTO analogy leads the dissent towards a position of principle that stands in contrast to existing arbitral practice requiring actual harm to an investment or an investor as a necessary condition for the success of an ISDS claim. One should not disregard the relevance of this practice but rather put an argument forward on why moving beyond that practice would have been a morally superior course of action in the context of the *UPS* case.[100]

[99] E.g., *Philip Morris Brands Sàrl, Philip Morris Products S.A. and Abal Hermanos S.A.* v. *Oriental Republic of Uruguay (formerly FTR Holding S.A., Philip Morris Products S.A. and Abal Hermanos S.A.* v. *Oriental Republic of Uruguay)*, ICSID Case No. ARB/10/7, Award, 8 July 2016, paras 284–286 (rejecting the investor's argument that an expropriation took place since the investment would have been even more profitable had Uruguay not adopted the challenged measures).

[100] The closest to such an argument comes in para 132 of the dissent (see also, n. 90), where Cass argues that Canada's position would cede to host states the right to decide on their own when investors will enjoy the protections of NAFTA's national treatment obligation, since NAFTA parties would not be required to articulate in advance a rationale for treating investors differently. This argument seems insufficient to warrant a departure from the practice that proof of actual harm is required. This is for two reasons. Firstly, it is question-begging insofar as it appears to already assume the validity of the dissenting arbitrator's view of the NAFTA's national treatment obligation. In other words, the argument carries weight only if the WTO analogy and the principle of equality of competitive opportunity are valid in the context of ISDS. But, if the analogy is not a

5.5 Borrowing Methods: Proportionality and the Question of the Standard of Review

Investment tribunals look towards other branches of international law not only to borrow meaning and guiding principles but at times also to borrow methods that could assist in the resolution of investment disputes. One such commonly used method is proportionality. There is no uniform source analogue from which proportionality is imported into ISDS. For some tribunals, the source analogue is human rights law and, in particular, the jurisprudence of the ECtHR.[101] For other tribunals, proportionality (or at least a version of it) is imported by way of a comparison with WTO law.[102] For a third group of tribunals, proportionality is imported into their legal analysis by way of mere reference to the decisions of prior tribunals.[103] Reliance on past decisions is a form of analogy in itself, which is, however, beyond the scope of the present chapter as stated in the introductory section. Furthermore, as we have already addressed the pitfalls of an uncritical reliance on WTO jurisprudence as a source analogue for ISDS, the emphasis in this section will be

valid one and the principle is not applicable in the ISDS context, then the argument ought to carry no weight as the mere loss of an opportunity (absent perhaps a specific promise to the contrary by the state giving rise to a legitimate expectation) would not constitute a violation of an investor's right. Secondly, the argument is also insufficient because it seems to disregard the question of a tribunal's standard of review. Just because a host state can articulate a rationale for its measures at any point in time (even during an arbitration) does not mean that a tribunal may not adopt an inquisitive standard of review to test the veracity of the state's motivation (e.g., cf. the case of *Metalclad* v. *Mexico*, where the tribunal reviewed the local municipality's reasons for denying the construction permit to the investor's landfill project and thus concluded that the rejection was not motivated by the municipality's professed environmental concerns but more likely by mounting local opposition to the landfill).

[101] E.g., *Técnicas Medioambientales Tecmed, S.A.* v. *The United Mexican States*, ICSID Case No. ARB(AF)/00/2, Award, 29 May 2003, para 122 (expressly relying on *James and others* v. *UK* among other ECtHR cases); *Azurix Corp.* v. *The Argentine Republic*, ICSID Case No. ARB/01/12, Award, 14 July 2006, paras 311–312, (similarly relying on *James and others* v. *UK*).

[102] E.g., *SD Myers* v. *Canada*, Partial Award, paras 246, 252, 255 (implied reliance on WTO law for the use of proportionality); *Continental Casualty* v. *Argentina*, Award, paras 192–195 (relying on the 'least restrictive alternative' test used in the interpretation of GATT Article XX).

[103] E.g., *Cortec Mining Kenya Limited, Cortec (Pty) Limited and Stirling Capital Limited* v. *Republic of Kenya*, ICSID Case No. ARB/15/29, Award, 22 October 2018, paras 319–321, 343ff (citing to *Kim* v. *Uzbekistan*); *LG&E* v. *Argentina*, Decision on Liability, paras 194–195 (citing to *Tecmed* v. *Mexico*).

on the potential pitfalls of using human rights law – in particular, the jurisprudence of the ECtHR – in the same way.

The analysis proceeds in the following manner. Following an introduction into the content and blind spots of proportionality analysis, the section undertakes a critical appraisal of the use of proportionality analysis in two ISDS cases: *Philip Morris* v. *Uruguay* and *Kim* v. *Uzbekistan*.

5.5.1 *Proportionality Analysis and Some Unanswered Questions*

Investment tribunals have used the jurisprudence of the ECtHR as a source for guidance on a wide range of issues,[104] principal among them being the import of proportionality analysis. Yet the exact reasons why tribunals have considered that an analogy with the ECtHR is appropriate are not clear. Tribunals do not address this question in their decisions.[105] Still, one could perhaps extrapolate some similarities between the two regimes that may make such an analogy at least prima facie appropriate. Thus, according to Alvarez, the analogy may be based on the fact that both regimes seem to share at least two common design features: safeguarding individuals' access to justice and protecting some forms of property.[106] In particular, both regimes defend the right to compensation for certain violations of property rights, as well as the proposition that individuals are guaranteed certain rights that are not necessarily accorded to nationals of the host state.[107] From that, one could then attempt to draw the following structural parallel with respect to proportionality in particular: just like the ECtHR uses proportionality to determine the permissible scope of state regulation vis-à-vis an individual's property interests, so can ISDS tribunals use proportionality to determine the same vis-à-vis the foreign investors who are protected under an investment treaty.

[104] See J. E. Alvarez, *The Boundaries of Investment Arbitration: The Use of Trade and European Human Rights Law in Investor-State Disputes* (Huntington: Juris, 2018), 49–50.

[105] See ibid., 47ff; also, N. Jansen Calamita, 'The Principle of Proportionality and the Problem of Indeterminacy in International Investment Treaties', in A. K. Bjorklund (ed.), *Yearbook on International Investment Law & Policy 2013–2014* (New York: Oxford University Press, 2015) 157, 182ff.

[106] Alvarez (n. 104), 46.

[107] Ibid.

Similarly to the WTO analogy, however, the above analogical inference between international human rights and international investment law is not as straightforward as it may at first seem. The reason is this. As used by the ECtHR, proportionality acts both as method and as normative test. That is to say that proportionality in the ECtHR acts, firstly, as framework for the appropriate way to examine arguments about competing rights and interests and, secondly, as benchmark against which the state's conduct is to be judged. As seen in the discussion below, using proportionality thus presupposes answers to several fundamental legal questions relating to the relative weights to be assigned to competing rights, interests, or other considerations; institutional competence; and the standard of review.[108] These are key substantive issues that are not necessarily similar across legal regimes or systems. Therefore, even if one were to subscribe to the above-mentioned prima facie similarities between international investment and international human rights law, doing so would still not constitute sufficiently solid ground for importing the proportionality test from the ECtHR to the investment treaty regime.

5.5.1.1 Proportionality as Method

In the first place, the term 'proportionality' seeks to describe the method and the series of steps that an adjudicator must take in order to address arguments about a conflict of rights and interests between an individual and a state. In the sense of method, proportionality analysis as used by the ECtHR is a three-stage process, with each stage addressing a different question. In the first stage, the adjudicator examines the suitability of the state's conduct that is under challenge. The question to be answered here is whether the means chosen by the state to achieve the aim it wishes to pursue are reasonably likely to achieve it. In the second stage, the adjudicator examines the necessity of the state's conduct, that is to say, whether the means chosen are indispensable to achieve the aim pursued. Lastly, in the third stage, the adjudicator examines the so-called proportionality *stricto sensu* of the state's conduct. In this stage, the adjudicator asks the following question: Even if there are no less restrictive suitable means for the pursued aim, is it the case that the burden on the individual is still excessive relative to the benefits secured by the state's aim? This is the stage in the process where 'balancing' and 'weighing' are said to take place.

[108] Calamita (n. 105), 178.

Although an equal amount of importance is placed on each of the three stages, in practice, proportionality has become largely synonymous to the ideas of weighing and balancing.[109] The proportionality test will often not fail in the first two stages. State measures are rarely completely irrational, and it is therefore often possible to argue that a particular measure is suitable and necessary to accomplish a legitimate aim. This means that the proportionality of a measure frequently stands or falls on the third stage, during an examination of the relative intensity of the interference when compared to the importance of the aim pursued.

5.5.1.2 Proportionality as Test

In addition to describing a method to approach questions regarding a state's conduct vis-à-vis individual rights, proportionality is also intended to describe a test for judging the lawfulness of said conduct. It is here that the normative side of proportionality analysis comes into sharp focus. It is also here that a series of presumed answers to critical questions arise. As Calamita points out, using proportionality as a test requires answers to certain kinds of normative questions that proportionality itself does not, and indeed cannot, provide.[110] These questions involve matters such as what is being weighed, how the weighing is done, and who does (or should do) the weighing.

In the first place, the proportionality test does not specify whether it is moral rights and principles or mere interests and values that one is weighing. In other words, proportionality does not specify whether the intention is to safeguard the rights of the individual from their potential infringement by the state or whether the intention is instead to ensure the maximisation of both the individual's interests and the public interest, by achieving an appropriate compromise between them in cases of conflict. Looking at the way proportionality is used by the ECtHR, some scholars have pointed out that proportionality in actuality ends up performing the latter of the two aforementioned purposes irrespective of what the

[109] S. Tsakyrakis, 'Proportionality: An Assault on Human Rights?' (2009) 7 *International Journal of Constitutional Law* 468, 473–474.

[110] Calamita (n. 105), 175ff. As Calamita argues in particular (ibid., 178): 'Instead, it is left to the person applying the principle of proportionality to find answers to these questions in the normative socio-political values of the system in which the principle is being applied.' Similarly, see Tsakyrakis (n. 109), 470.

ECtHR purports to be doing.[111] That is to say, given its structure and the prevalence of the third stage of the test (proportionality *stricto sensu*), proportionality ends up reducing deontological arguments about right and wrong to a cost-benefit calculation of maximisation of interests and values.

This in turn results in situations where arguments based on rights enter into the proportionality analysis on a par with arguments based on interests and values.[112] In so doing, proportionality seems to assume a readily available and weighted scale on which the value of protecting individual rights and the value of protecting the public interest can be measured, compared, and balanced. Indeed, this also seems to be the way in which most ISDS tribunals approach the balancing exercise when they use proportionality analysis. For instance, in examining the investor's indirect expropriation claim, the tribunal in *Tecmed* v. *Mexico* declared that:

> After establishing that regulatory actions and measures will not be initially excluded from the definition of expropriatory acts, in addition to the negative financial impact of such actions or measures, the Arbitral Tribunal will consider, in order to determine if they are to be characterised as expropriatory, whether such actions or measures are proportional to the public interest presumably protected thereby and to the protection legally granted to investments, taking into account that the significance of such impact has a key role upon deciding the proportionality. . . . There must be a reasonable relationship of proportionality between the charge

[111] E.g., see D. Meyerson, 'Why Courts Should Not Balance Rights against the Public Interest' (2007) 31 *Melbourne University Law Review* 873, 881; Calamita (n. 105); Alvarez (n. 104), 107–108; Tsakyrakis (n. 109).

[112] Indeed, as explained by J. Habermas, *Between Facts and Norms: Contributions to a Discourse Theory of Law and Democracy*, trans. William Rehg, reprint 2009 (Cambridge, MA: Polity Press, 1996), 259 (emphases in original):

> As soon as rights are transformed into goods and values in any individual case, each must compete with the others at the same level of priority. Every value is inherently just as particular as every other, whereas norms owe their validity to a universalisation test. . . . This is one reason why Dworkin regards rights as 'trumps' that one can play against policy arguments in legal discourse. True, not every right will win out over every collective good in the justifications of concrete decisions. But a right will not prevail only when the priority of a collective good over a corresponding norm can itself be justified in light of higher norms or principles. Because norms and principles, in virtue of their deontological character, can claim to be *universally binding* and not just *specially preferred*, they possess a greater justificatory force than values.

> or weight imposed to the foreign investor and the aim sought to be realised by any expropriatory measure.[113]

The interest maximisation approach to proportionality was also evident in *Total* v. *Argentina*. Addressing allegations of a FET violation, the tribunal adopted the following position of principle with respect to how to resolve the conflict between the host state's right to regulate and the investor's expectations:

> [T]he host [s]tate's right to regulate domestic matters in the public interest has to be taken into consideration as well. The circumstances and reasons (importance and urgency of the public need pursued) for carrying out a change impacting negatively on a foreign investor's operations on the one hand, and the seriousness of the prejudice caused on the other hand, compared in the light of a standard of reasonableness and proportionality are relevant. The determination of a breach of the standard requires, therefore, 'a weighing of the Claimant's reasonable and legitimate expectations on the one hand and the Respondent's legitimate regulatory interest on the other'.[114]

More recently, the same approach has been followed by tribunals tasked with resolving disputes arising out of Spain's reforms of its renewable energy sector. In *SolEs* v. *Spain*, the tribunal incorporated the proportionality test in its analysis through the concept of legitimate expectations. For the tribunal, investors protected under the ECT have a legitimate expectation that the host state will not act in a manner that is unreasonable, contrary to the public interest, or disproportionate. Borrowing from *Charanne* v. *Spain*, the tribunal then took the view that proportionality in such a setting is ensured when modifications to the regulatory framework are not random or unnecessary or when they do not suddenly and unexpectedly remove the essential features of the regulatory framework that was in place at the time when the investment was made.[115] From this the tribunal concluded that the assessment of the investor's legitimate expectations claim required a weighing of the invest-

[113] *Tecmed* v. *Mexico*, Award, para 122 (footnotes omitted).

[114] *Total S.A.* v. *The Argentine Republic*, ICSID Case No. ARB/04/01, Decision on Liability, 27 December 2010, para 123 (footnotes omitted), citing to *Saluka* v. *Czech Republic*, Partial Award, paras 305–306.

[115] *SolEs Badajoz GmbH* v. *Kingdom of Spain*, ICSID Case No. ARB/15/38, Award, 31 July 2019, para 316 (citing to *Charanne B.V. and Construction Investments S.à.r.l.* v. *Spain*, SCC Case No. V 062/2012, Award, 21 January 2016, para 517).

or's expectations and the state's regulatory interests.[116] In the words of the tribunal:

> Both the legitimacy of the investor's expectations and the host [s]tate's scope to modify its regulatory regime without violating the FET obligation must be measured in light of any undertakings of stability that are contained in the laws, regulations and authoritative pronouncements of the host [s]tate, upon which the investor relied when it made its investment.[117]

In the above examples, tribunals have placed private and public interests initially on the same level of priority and have then used proportionality to balance them. Yet proportionality does not provide decision-makers with any appropriate common metric for such a balancing to be performed. As Calamita points out with a touch of irony, proportionality ends up being a scale without weights.[118] This brings into sharper focus the issue of incommensurability, which is to say, the fact that certain rights and interests cannot be compared by being brought under a common metric for balancing. For instance, how does one bring under

[116] Ibid., para 318 (citing to *Electrabel S.A.* v. *Republic of Hungary*, ICSID Case No. ARB/07/19, Award, 25 November 2015, para 165, and to *Saluka* v. *Czech Republic*, Partial Award, para 306).

[117] *SolEs* v. *Spain*, Award, para 318. Somewhat curiously, however, in a later part of the award (ibid., paras 327–328), the tribunal seems to distinguish between two possible approaches to determining the proportionality of a state measure (emphasis in original, footnotes omitted):

> As to Claimant's contention that the Disputed Measures are disproportionate, the Tribunal takes note of two ways in which disproportionality can be understood. The first of these is the formulation of the Tribunal in *Charanne*, cited earlier, which this Tribunal has adopted.
>
> The question of proportionality can also be addressed by weighing the legitimate policy interest pursued by the [s]tate against the impact of the measure on the investment or a class of investments to which the claim belongs. These competing considerations can be examined in light of the degree of stability in the regulatory regime in place at the time of an investment. As stated in *Electrabel*, the requirement that measures be reasonable and not arbitrary '*includes the requirement that the impact of the measure on the investor be proportional to the policy objective sought*'.

Although in paras 316–318 the tribunal seems to be suggesting that the *Electrabel* proportionality test is the way to operationalise the position of principle expressed in *Charanne*, in the above-quoted passages the tribunal seems to treat the two as separate. Ultimately, it seems that the *SolEs* award uses both in its review of Spain's measures. (e.g., see, ibid., paras 450–453, 462–463).

[118] Calamita (n. 105), 175.

a common metric an investor's interest in uninterrupted business activity and the state's interest in ensuring that the environment is protected or that social unrest is effectively addressed? And how does one determine whether the former or the latter of these two public interests ought to carry the greater weight when compared to the investor's interest?[119]

To clarify, incommensurability does not necessarily mean that rights and interests cannot be brought in relation with each other and prioritised in a rational manner.[120] What the incommensurability point seeks to show, rather, is that such prioritisation cannot take place in the way that proportionality seems to suggest, which is to say by pretending that no recourse to moral reasoning is required from the decision-maker.[121] Quite to the contrary, the balance to be struck, or the ordering of values to be imposed, is something towards which the decision-maker must argue rather than merely suppose as self-evident fact.[122]

[119] E.g., see the critique of the *Tecmed* decision along these lines by Calamita (n. 105), 187.

[120] Following J. Waldron, 'Fake Incommensurability: A Response to Professor Schauer' (1994) 45 *Hastings Law Journal* 813, 817, this is known as 'weak' incommensurability, which can be contrasted to 'strong' incommensurability. Waldron argues for the weak version of incommensurability and establishes the difference between the two versions as follows (emphasis in original):

> In a case of strong incommensurability, the competing values cannot even be brought into relation with one another: They are genuinely incomparable in the practical realm, leaving us paralysed in the face of their competition. In a case of weak incommensurability – and this is why I call it 'weak' – the values *can* be brought into relation with one another. We look at them both, we consider them, and we find an immediately discernible order. If free speech values trump prosperity values, then that is a fact about the relation between these values. Their lack of commensurability refers only to the absence of a common dimension of measurement that would allow trade-offs between them in either direction. But there is certainly a table or an order of priority, just as there is an order of suits in a bridge contract or an order of letters in an alphabet.

[121] Tsakyrakis (n. 109), 473–474 ('[I]n practice, the term "balancing" has become tantamount to the principle of proportionality, that is, a specific judicial test that pretends to balance values while avoiding any moral reasoning. In fact, the principle of proportionality, bypassing any discourse on priorities, pretends to resolve value conflicts by assessing the degree of their relative coexistence.').

[122] This is not to deny that there may be instances where the balance to be struck, or the ordering of values to be imposed, is so obvious and intuitive that offering a detailed argument for it may be redundant. One can think of the following example used by Waldron (n. 120), 818: 'Any reasonable person can see that saving an innocent child from a painful death is to have priority over the preservation of the statue that has fallen on top of her.' Yet, in keeping with the themes of this book, it is not the case that the decision to prioritise the right to life over the right to property in this example is reached

This leads us to yet another normative question that proportionality leaves unanswered: Who does (or should do) the weighing? Proportionality does not specify whether the most appropriate institutional actor to perform the balancing in every case is the adjudicator or rather the legislator. In other words, proportionality does not specify the adjudicator's standard of review over the state's conduct or the exact margin of appreciation that an international adjudicator ought to give to domestic authorities. This raises, once again, the question of purpose. As we have seen, the question of purpose is an overarching one and a key feature of coherent practical decision-making and analogical reasoning.[123] Surely, the purpose of arbitrating disputes in ISDS is to protect foreign investors and their investments from harm but protect them to what extent? Is the institutional role of the investment arbitrator to replicate and 'validate' the reasons put forward by the host state's officials,[124] to supervise and 'correct' them,[125] or perhaps to principally accord deference to them save for the most egregious instances?[126]

with no recourse to moral reasoning whatsoever. Rather, the case is that the interpretation and moral assessment of the life/property value-conflict in this example is so widespread and generally accepted that renders detailed explications unnecessary.

123 See Chapter 2 and Section 5.2.3.

124 E.g., see the narrow test for determining 'likeness' in the context of a national treatment claim, followed by the tribunal in *Methanex Corporation* v. *United States of America*, UNCITRAL Rules, Final Award on Jurisdiction and Merits, 3 August 2005, (2005) 44 *International Legal Materials* 1345, Part IV, Chapter B, paras 11–38. A critique of this approach expressed in literature (e.g., Kurtz [n. 12], 258–262), is that it tends to take the host state's reasons for differentiating in its treatment between domestic and foreign investors at face value. In so doing, it makes it unnecessary for the host state to present compelling and objective reasons for the different treatment and because of this it may end up validating paradigmatic cases of protectionism.

125 E.g., see *Occidental Petroleum Corporation and Occidental Exploration and Production Company* v. *The Republic of Ecuador*, ICSID Case No. ARB/06/11, Award, 5 October 2012, paras 415–417, 440–452, for the tribunal's de novo review of the decision of the Ecuadorian minister who, acting under statutory discretion, issued a *caducidad* decree terminating Occidental's rights under a Participation Contract with the state's national oil company, Petroecuador.

126 E.g., see *Glamis* v. *United States of America*, Award, paras 20–22, 598–618; *Cargill, Incorporated* v. *United Mexican States*, ICSID Case No. ARB(AF)/05/2, Award, 18 September 2009, para 286; *Alex Genin, Eastern Credit Limited, Inc. and A.S. Baltoil* v. *The Republic of Estonia*, ICSID Case No. ARB/99/2, Award, 25 June 2001, para 367, all of which have held that the content of the minimum standard of treatment of aliens under customary international law is encapsulated in the *Neer* standard of 'outrage, bad faith, wilful neglect of duty, or insufficiency of governmental action so far short of international standards that every reasonable and impartial man would readily recognise its insufficiency'.

The proportionality test does not provide answers to these questions. Answers must once again come from the decision-makers themselves.

Indeed, scholars writing in the context of regulatory takings of property have pointed out that the case law of the ECtHR is ultimately premised on the assumption of a particular institutional role that the Court has made for itself – namely, the role of protector of democracy in Europe.[127] Given this role, the ECtHR can then justify its jurisprudence of deference and of a wide margin of appreciation to domestic determinations regarding regulatory takings and its willingness at times to let individuals bear the risk of regulatory change.[128] ISDS tribunals are generally silent with respect to addressing any of the above issues in any explicit manner, a phenomenon that is exacerbated by a practice of heavy reliance on past arbitral awards. Absent such discussions, however, the use of proportionality in ISDS often leaves one with an almost 'impressionistic assessment of the relative weights of competing considerations, which does not lend itself to a rational reconstruction of the argumentative path that has led to a particular decision'.[129]

[127] E.g., see S. R. Ratner, 'Regulatory Takings in Institutional Context: Beyond the Fear of Fragmented International Law' (2008) 102 *American Journal of International Law* 475, 496–501; H. Mountfield, 'Regulatory Expropriations in Europe: The Approach of the European Court of Human Rights' (2002) 11 *New York University Environmental Law Journal* 136, 146–147; Calamita (n. 105), 178–182.

[128] See, for instance, the assessment of the ECtHR's assumed role by Mountfield (n. 127), 146–147:

> [The ECtHR] affords signatory states a wide margin of appreciation as to what is in the public interest and the extent to which compensation is required, leaving itself, in effect, an equitable jurisdiction to interfere where signatory states have manifestly applied an unfair or disproportionate balance between the general and the individual interest. … [The ECtHR], an institution that is dedicated to protecting democracy, is mindful of the fact that … a democratically elected government must be permitted to make and change policy without being, in effect, held to ransom by a small group of persons who have invested in reliance upon an earlier policy. … [T]he Court considers that an element of risk is inherent in any commercial decision. … If any regulatory change resulting in the significant devaluation of a business asset were to be considered a compensable expropriation, the government would, in effect, be the insurer of last resort for changes in public policy. No government would be permitted to change or improve regulatory standards unless it could afford to 'buy out' any private interest which would be adversely affected. The case law suggests that the [ECtHR], with its role as a supra-national protector of democracy in mind, regards that as an unacceptable proposition.

[129] Cf. Tsakyrakis (n. 109), 482.

The remainder of this section is devoted to two case studies demonstrating the practical implications of the above remarks. The *Philip Morris* v. *Uruguay* case is examined first. The disagreement between the majority and the dissent in this case clearly demonstrates the unanswered questions left open by the proportionality test, as well as the importance of answering these questions for the case's outcome. The section concludes with an examination of the pitfalls of an uncritical reliance on proportionality as demonstrated in the jurisdictional decision in *Kim* v. *Uzbekistan*.

5.5.2 *Proportionality's 'Black Box': The Margin of Appreciation Controversy in* Philip Morris *v.*. Uruguay

In February 2010, Swiss company Philip Morris, alongside its wholly owned Uruguayan subsidiary, Abal Hermanos, brought a complaint against Uruguay challenging two types of tobacco control measures known as the 'Single Presentation Requirement' (SPR) and the '80/80 Regulation'. The SPR precluded tobacco manufacturers from marketing more than one variant of cigarette per brand family, whereas the 80/80 Regulation increased the size of health warnings on cigarette packs to cover 80 per cent of the pack thus leaving only 20 per cent for trademark and other information. In its application, Philip Morris claimed that the challenged measures violated several provisions of the Switzerland-Uruguay BIT (1988), including the duty to accord FET, by adversely impacting the value of its local subsidiary and by wrongfully limiting its right to use its legally protected trademarks.[130]

The present analysis focuses on the tribunal's assessment of the investor's FET claim and the dissenting arbitrator's opposing views on the matter. The *Philip Morris* example demonstrates the minimal actual contribution of the proportionality test itself, used by both majority and dissent, towards the outcome of the case. To the contrary, it seems that considerations of a moral character were determinative of both the majority's and the dissent's views.

5.5.2.1 The Majority's Decision

The majority began by declaring that it would review each of the challenged measures while taking into account 'all relevant circumstances,

[130] *Philip Morris* v. *Uruguay*, Award, paras 10–11.

including the margin of appreciation enjoyed by national regulatory agencies when dealing with public policy determinations'.[131] The majority's analysis is structured under the examination of two questions in particular, as raised by the investor: (i) were Uruguay's measures arbitrary and (ii) did the investor have a legitimate expectation of regulatory stability?

The investor's allegation of arbitrariness was in essence a disproportionality argument in disguise. According to the investor, the challenged measures were arbitrary because they were adopted without any scientific evidence of their effectiveness, without due consideration by public officials, and with no reasonable connection between the objectives pursued and the utility of the chosen measures.[132] These charges closely mirror the suitability and necessity stages of proportionality analysis. In essence, Philip Morris was arguing that the SPR and the 80/80 Regulation were neither suitable (alleged lack of scientific evidence of their effectiveness) nor necessary (alleged absence of consideration by public officials attesting to their indispensability).

In response to the suitability charge, the majority considered that the measures were taken in accordance with the 'evidence-based' provisions and guidelines of the Framework Convention on Tobacco Control and that, therefore, Uruguay was not under an obligation to conduct additional studies or gather additional evidence before adopting these measures.[133] In response to the necessity charge, the majority referred to a state's margin of appreciation, a doctrine developed by the ECtHR. In so doing, the tribunal agreed with Uruguay that the margin of appreciation is not limited to the context of the ECHR but can also apply to claims under investment treaties, at least in contexts such as that of public health.[134] The majority's position of principle is summarised in the following statement:

> The responsibility for public health measures rests with the government and investment tribunals should pay great deference to governmental judgments of national needs in matters such as the protection of public health. In such cases respect is due to the 'discretionary exercise of sovereign power, not made irrationally and not exercised in bad faith ... involving many complex factors'. As held by another investment

[131] Ibid., para 388.
[132] Ibid., para 389.
[133] Ibid., para 396.
[134] Ibid., para 399.

> tribunal, '[t]he sole inquiry for the Tribunal . . . is whether or not there was a manifest lack of reasons for the legislation'.[135]

The tribunal also held more generally that the provisions of the Framework Convention on Tobacco Control acted as a point of reference against which one could determine the reasonableness of the challenged measures. After examining the SPR and the 80/80 Regulation under the above standard and the evidence available before it, the majority of the tribunal concluded that neither measure was unreasonable, arbitrary, grossly unfair, unjust, discriminatory, or disproportionate.[136]

With respect to the second limb of the investor's FET claim (i.e., legitimate expectations of regulatory stability), the tribunal said in a tone similar to the above:

> [C]hanges to general legislation (at least in the absence of a stabilization clause) are not prevented by the fair and equitable treatment standard if they do not exceed the exercise of the host state's normal regulatory power in the pursuance of a public interest and do not modify the regulatory framework relied upon by the investor at the time of its investment 'outside of the acceptable margin of change'.[137]

Following this position of principle, the tribunal concluded, first, that Philip Morris had no legitimate expectation of regulatory stability considering its line of work[138] and, second, that in any event the fact that the challenged measures were not arbitrary and did not modify the regulatory framework beyond an 'acceptable margin of change', militated against finding an FET violation.[139]

5.5.2.2 Arbitrator Gary Born's Partial Dissent

Arbitrator Gary Born appended a partial dissent taking issue, among other things,[140] with the majority's reliance on the margin of appreciation as applied to the finding that the SPR measure in particular did not violate the treaty's FET provision. The core of Born's dissent rests

135 Ibid. (footnotes in original omitted).

136 Ibid., paras 409–410, 420.

137 Ibid., para 423 (footnote in original omitted).

138 Ibid., paras 429–430.

139 Ibid., para 433. A key factor for the tribunal to conclude that the challenged measures did not modify the regulatory framework beyond 'an acceptable margin of change' was the limited economic impact that the measures had on the local subsidiary's business.

140 Born also parted ways with the majority on the denial of justice allegation raised by the investor and with the majority's reliance on ECtHR case law in deciding the denial of justice claim.

on his assessment that 'notwithstanding the deference that is due sovereign regulatory measures and judgments, [the single presentation] requirement does not bear a rational relationship to its stated legislative objective, yet disproportionately injures important investor rights'.[141]

Born largely agrees with the majority's construction of the FET clause in the Switzerland-Uruguay BIT (1988) as containing an autonomous standard protecting investors against irrational and arbitrary treatment and, in particular, against measures that are 'unrelated to any legitimate governmental objective, or which are gravely disproportionate to the achievement of such an objective'.[142] Born also shares the majority's view that the FET standard does not empower tribunals to second-guess legislative or regulatory judgments, which are instead entitled to a 'substantial measure of deference'.[143]

But Born parts ways with the majority with respect to the application of the margin of appreciation 'as developed in ECtHR jurisprudence'.[144] For Born, the appropriate degree of deference due to national authorities must be derived from the terms and context of the BIT itself, in accordance with the customary international law rules of treaty interpretation, and from decisions involving similar guarantees of FET. These sources, Born continues, 'mandate substantial deference to Uruguay's regulatory and legislative judgments, and forbid any second-guessing of such judgments, but nonetheless require a minimum level of rationality and proportionality between the state's measure and a legitimate governmental objective'.[145] By declaring that deference is the starting point rather than the ending point of evaluating FET claims, Born, like the majority, is in essence also describing the test of proportionality to determine how much deference is due in every case.[146]

Applying this test on Uruguay's SPR measure, Born concludes that the measure was arbitrary and disproportionate. A number of considerations were critical for this conclusion. First, prior to the adoption of the SPR, Uruguayan law already contained prohibitions against the misleading use

[141] *Philip Morris* v. *Uruguay*, Award, Concurring and Dissenting Opinion of Mr Gary Born, para 129.
[142] Ibid., paras 131–133.
[143] Ibid., para 137.
[144] Ibid., para 138.
[145] Ibid., para 139.
[146] E.g., see, ibid., para 142 ('Rather, a sensitive and nuanced consideration of the nature of the governmental measure, the character and context of the governmental judgment, the relationship between the measure and its stated purpose, and the measure's impact on protected investments is necessary.').

of packaging, labelling, and trademarks in tobacco products. Given such provisions, Born says, one must ask 'what additional purpose the [SPR] would serve in achieving the measure's only stated purpose – namely, to prevent misleading use of trademarks'.[147] Second, Born finds that there was a fundamental mismatch between the character and terms of the SPR, on the one hand, and its stated objective, on the other. In particular, he considers the SPR to be a blunt and sweeping measure that contained nothing that specifically focused on the deceptive use of trademarks. As a result, he finds that the SPR was over- and under-inclusive as it 'prohibit[ed] many uses of trademarks that [were] not misleading or false, while allowing even more uses of trademarks that [were] in fact misleading and deceptive'.[148] Third, Born finds that Uruguay offered no sufficient evidence that all possible presentations of the trademark of a tobacco product were misleading or deceptive. Rather, for Born, Uruguay only cited limited evidence that the use of some variations of colours in some trademark presentations could mislead consumers.[149] He thus concludes:

> Put simply, the [SPR] is inherently and inescapably unrelated to its only articulated objective – protecting consumers against deceptive uses of trademarks. There is simply no logical or empirical relationship between a blanket [SPR] and misleading advertisements or packaging. Instead, the [SPR's] only independent effects are to forbid a substantial range of uses of trademarks that are not deceptive and misleading, while allowing other uses of trademarks that plainly are deceptive and misleading.[150]

5.5.2.3 Analysis

The key point of contention between the majority and the partial dissent in the *Philip Morris* case boils down to Born's view that, as a result of its

[147] Ibid., para 155.

[148] Ibid., para 158.

[149] Ibid., para 160. In saying this, Born accepts that the SPR was not an arbitrary or disproportionate measure vis-à-vis variations in trademark presentations that are actually deceptive and misleading (ibid., para 161). Yet, in his view, this could hardly justify the blanket prohibition of the SPR measure in the absence of more concrete and comprehensive evidence (ibid., paras 162–163).

[150] Ibid., para 172. To further buttress this conclusion Born also made the following remark (ibid., para 174): 'If the [SPR] made serious regulatory sense, it would have been included in the FCTC's lengthy catalogue of regulatory measures or in the Guidelines' supplementation of those measures. Or, even if not, the measure would have been recommended in the extensive literature on anti-smoking regulations or, alternatively, would have been the product of study and deliberations counselling in favor of its adoption.'

reliance on the margin of appreciation doctrine formulated by the ECtHR, the majority did not adequately scrutinise the rational justification offered by Uruguay for the SPR measure. Looking towards the ECtHR was an inappropriate analogy, Born argues, because the margin of appreciation doctrine was developed in the particular historical and normative context of the ECHR (and of Article 1 of its Protocol 1 in particular) which is not the same as, and thus cannot be transposed to, the normative context of investment treaties.[151] In other words, according to Born, the majority erred because it failed to properly identify and apply the standard of review required under the terms and context of the BIT between Uruguay and Switzerland.

Born is certainly correct to point out that the margin of appreciation doctrine as applied by the ECtHR cannot be transposed wholesale to the investment treaty regime. He is also correct to point out that the standard of review of domestic measures adopted by an ISDS tribunal must be based on the specific terms of the applicable investment treaty and the normative context of the settlement of investment, as opposed to human rights, disputes. That notwithstanding, his critique of the majority for the use of the margin of appreciation may be somewhat missing the point. As noted by Alvarez, it is not clear that the majority actually paid much attention to how the ECtHR applies the margin of appreciation.[152] The term, Alvarez notes, was rather used in the majority decision simply to suggest the need for some level of deference owed to the legislative choices made by Uruguay.

What the above signify for present purposes is that the margin of appreciation doctrine and, by extension, the proportionality test to which the margin of appreciation is a corollary, and to which both the majority and the dissent to some extent relied, did very little to dictate the outcome in the *Philip Morris* case. In the end, the real point of substantive disagreement between the majority and the dissent was not whether the concept of a margin of appreciation was being properly transposed or applied. Rather, the disagreement was whether the standard of review required by the FET provision of the Switzerland-Uruguay BIT (1988) was closer to the more deferential standard of 'plausible legislation',

[151] Ibid., para 185.
[152] Alvarez (n. 104), 103.

adopted by the majority, or to the less deferential standard of 'objective rational justification', adopted by Born.[153]

Born and the majority both offered their own, divergent views on this question and in an implicit manner also offered their divergent views on the underlying question regarding the institutional role of arbitrators in the ISDS regime. In so doing, neither side made any obvious or clearly identifiable errors of law that could affect the validity of its reasoning. The case could thus be described as a genuinely hard one, at least on the question of the SPR measure. Of the two opinions, Born's seems to be articulated in a more explicit manner overall. His presuppositions and moral underpinnings seem to be more clearly laid out. Irrespective of what one may think about the merits of the opinion itself, such clarity and explicitness are commendable. In the absence of a convergence of opinion on moral questions of the kind raised in *Philip Morris* and in the absence of institutional mechanisms, be it legislative or judicial, designed to authoritatively settle such questions, 'a free and fair battle of ideas is the only way to achieve coherency in the law and the sustainability of the system'.[154]

5.5.3 *Proportionality Off-the-Rails?* Kim *v.* Uzbekistan

We conclude this section with a second case study and a critical reading of the jurisdictional decision in *Kim* v. *Uzbekistan*. This second case study showcases the dangers stemming from what appears to be an uncritical reliance on proportionality as an apparently complete test that can be determinative of a judicial outcome.

[153] See also, ibid., 104 (emphasis in original):

> Focusing on the suitability of exporting the ECHR's concept of margin of appreciation seems something of a red herring in the *Philip Morris* case. It is not clear that the ECHR's margin of appreciation, as jurisprudential principle *or* as malleable deference tool applying different levels of scrutiny depending on the right at stake, actually played a critical role for the majority. It is equally plausible to read the separate majority and Born opinions addressing FET in *Philip Morris* as expressing disagreements over whether, under the facts as presented, the challenged measures were truly irrational or arbitrary. If this is so, the disagreement between Born and the majority concerning the applicability of the margin of appreciation (and of ECHR law more generally) seems to be much ado about nothing.

[154] Paraphrased from Z. Douglas, *The International Law of Investment Claims* (Cambridge: Cambridge University Press, 2009), xxiv.

5.5.3.1 The Facts and the Tribunal's Reasoning

In *Kim* v. *Uzbekistan*, the Kazakh partners in a private equity investment group had acquired shares in two cement plants in Uzbekistan. During the hearing on jurisdiction, Uzbekistan, among other objections, challenged claimants' acquisition of the shares in the two plants as having been contrary to Uzbek law and as the result of fraud.[155] Article 12 of the Kazakhstan-Uzbekistan BIT (1997) contained a legality requirement providing that the treaty would only apply to investments 'made in compliance' with the law of the host state.[156]

The tribunal was quick to determine that the legality requirement was jurisdictional in nature and that, from a temporal point of view, it applied at the moment an investment is established (and thus did not act as a continuous requirement throughout the investment's life).[157] The tribunal was also quick to determine that the term 'legislation' comprised all normative acts described as 'legal' in the legal system of Uzbekistan.[158] More difficult to answer was the question of the legal test for measuring compliance with the law of the host state. For the tribunal, legality requirements were not without limits. In other words, not all acts of non-compliance with domestic legislation would have the effect of placing an investment outside the protection of the treaty. The tribunal thus became preoccupied with identifying the substantive scope of the legality requirement and with devising a test to ascertain what acts of non-compliance would be 'sufficiently serious' to justify a complete denial of treaty protection.[159]

Finding no specific guidance in the text of Article 12 with respect to the aforementioned limits, the tribunal resorted to context and to the object and purpose of the BIT. In so doing, it first observed that the consequences of a failure to satisfy the legality requirement in the BIT were quite severe, namely, the total exclusion of any treaty protection.[160]

[155] To note, the present analysis does not directly examine other related allegations raised by Uzbekistan, such as, for example, allegations of corruption.

[156] The exact wording of Article 12 of the BIT was: 'This Agreement shall apply to investments within the territory of one Contracting Party's State, made in compliance with its legislation by investors from the other Contracting Party's State, regardless of whether they were made before or after the entry into force of this Agreement.'

[157] *Vladislav Kim and others* v. *Republic of Uzbekistan*, ICSID Case No. ARB/13/6, Decision on Jurisdiction, 8 March 2017, paras 373–377.

[158] Ibid., paras 378–380.

[159] Ibid., para 381.

[160] Ibid., para 392 ('The legality requirement does not only remove access to arbitration but removes the obligations of the Host State *vis-à-vis* the investor and the investment in total.').

The tribunal then examined the preamble of the BIT, from which it distilled the promotion of greater economic cooperation as the treaty's object and purpose. Relying on these two propositions, it then formulated the following position of principle regarding the legality requirement:

> It is the combination of desiring to 'promote greater economic cooperation' and the fact that an act not in compliance with legislation under Article 12 excludes an investment from the scope of application of the BIT generally, that indicates the necessary substantive limits on the legality requirement. Given the aim of encouraging investment through the provision of some measure of security, it is not plausible that the drafters of the BIT intended to include minor acts of noncompliance as a basis for denying jurisdiction.
>
> The exclusion of acts of noncompliance that are minor or trivial, however, does not establish that the legality requirement is limited to violations of fundamental laws.
>
> In the Tribunal's view, a more principled approach is to be guided in the interpretive task by the principle of proportionality. The Tribunal must balance the object of promoting economic relations by providing a stable investment framework with the harsh consequence of denying the application of the BIT in total when the investment is not made in compliance with legislation. The denial of the protections of the BIT is a harsh consequence that is a proportional response only when its application is triggered by *noncompliance with a law that results in a compromise of a correspondingly significant interest of the Host State.*[161]

Putting the above abstract statement of the proportionality test into practice, the tribunal declared that it would follow a three-step process of analysis. It would (i) assess the significance of the obligation with which the investor has allegedly not complied, (ii) assess the seriousness of the investor's conduct, and (iii) evaluate whether the legal consequences attached to the alleged illegality under the law of Uzbekistan demonstrate a gravity to the investor's act of non-compliance that is proportional to the harshness of denying access to BIT protection.[162] In applying this test to each of the alleged illegalities and irregularities, the tribunal ultimately concluded that some were not proven on the facts, while others were proven but were not significant enough to warrant a decline of jurisdiction.[163]

161 Ibid., paras 394–396 (emphases in original).

162 Ibid., paras 405–409.

163 To note, this decision was not unanimous. One of the arbitrators, left unnamed in the decision, dissented on several of the illegality findings (ibid., paras 418ff).

5.5.3.2 Analysis

The use of a proportionality test in the above context is quite striking. Three aspects of the tribunal's analysis stand out in particular. The first is that no argument or explicit analogy was offered justifying the use of the proportionality test in this manner. Rather, the only source relied upon appears to be the prior decision in *Metalpar* v. *Argentina*, where the tribunal had ruled that denying access to ISDS would be a disproportionate response to the investor's failure to register a foreign company as required by Argentine law.[164]

A second noteworthy aspect is the content of the proportionality test itself. As described by the tribunal, the proportionality test used in essence amounts to the following proposition: denying jurisdiction is a proportional response only if the state interest that is affected by the investor's non-compliance with domestic law is more significant than the state's interest in promoting cross-border economic cooperation through the international protection that the BIT affords to foreign investors. This is not the traditional three-step proportionality test but rather a single-step one. It omits entirely the stages of suitability and necessity and moves directly into the third stage of balancing/proportionality *stricto sensu*.

The third aspect of the decision that warrants consideration is more complex and it essentially amounts to the following criticism: notwithstanding the tribunal's assertions to the contrary in the above-quoted passage, it is arguable that its use of proportionality resulted in an unprincipled interpretative approach. This is so, moreover, both with respect to how the tribunal approached the question of its jurisdiction and with respect to how the tribunal viewed its institutional role. To begin with, the tribunal frames the legal question that it seeks to answer in an ambiguous way. Its discussion frequently shifts between two kinds of legal questions, namely, whether the tribunal has jurisdiction over the dispute, on the one hand, and whether the BIT protections apply to the investment given the alleged illegalities, on the other hand.[165] However, although certainly related, these questions are not one and the same. That is to say, and contrary to what the tribunal seems to suggest, querying the

[164] *Metalpar S.A. and Buen Aire S.A.* v. *The Argentine Republic*, ICSID Case No. ARB/03/5, Decision on Jurisdiction, 27 April 2006, paras 83–84.

[165] E.g., see *Kim* v. *Uzbekistan*, Jurisdiction, paras 392, 394, 396, 404.

scope of application of the BIT's protections under Article 12 does not necessarily give rise to obstacles to the tribunal's jurisdiction.

As previously stated in Section 5.2.3, ISDS borrows some key structural elements from commercial arbitration. Among these elements is that an ISDS tribunal gets its power to adjudicate (i.e., its jurisdiction)[166] from the arbitration agreement that is formed when a foreign investor accepts the host state's standing offer to arbitrate, pursuant to the arbitration clause found in an investment treaty concluded between the host state and the investor's home state.[167] The treaty's arbitration clause may subject the state's consent to arbitrate on a number of conditions (e.g., mandatory cooling-off periods, prior recourse to domestic courts, so-called 'fork-in-the-road' provisions, waivers, etc.). A key condition that applies across the board, however, is that the investor's dispute with the host state must relate, in some way or another,[168] to an investment that the former has made in the territory of the latter. Indeed, the arbitration clause found in Article 10 of the Kazakhstan-Uzbekistan BIT (1997), applicable in the *Kim* case, stated rather broadly:

> Each Contracting Party hereby consents to the referral of any legal dispute between one Contracting Party and an investor from the other Contracting Party's State in respect of investments made by it within the territory of the former Contracting Party to one of the following institutions: . . ..[169]

As Article 10 stated no other condition, it follows that the tribunal in *Kim* had jurisdiction *ratione materiae* provided that the claimants had

[166] On the meaning of the term 'jurisdiction', see J. Paulsson, 'Jurisdiction and Admissibility', in G. Aksen, K.-H. Böckstiegel, M. J. Mustill, P. M. Patocchi, and A. Whitesell (eds.), *Global Reflections on International Law, Commerce and Dispute Resolution: Liber Amicorum in Honour of Robert Briner* (Paris: ICC, 2005) 601; *Abaclat and Others* v. *Argentine Republic (formerly Giovanna a Beccara and Others* v. *The Argentine Republic)*, ICSID Case No. ARB/07/5, Decision on Jurisdiction and Admissibility, 4 August 2011, Dissenting Opinion of G. Abi-Saab, paras 10–19.

[167] Douglas (n. 154), 35.

[168] Different investment treaties regulate this relation in different ways. Some treaties allow investors to submit before a tribunal 'any dispute' relating to an investment, i.e., including those based on contracts (e.g., Article 8 Argentina-France BIT [1991]). Some treaties list specific legal bases upon which an investment claim may rely (e.g., disputes arising out of an investment authorisation, investment agreement, or a breach of the treaty itself, as found in Article IX Albania-United States BIT [1995]). Yet other treaties limit a tribunal's jurisdiction to hearing investment claims arising out of a breach of the treaty only (e.g., Article 10 Azerbaijan-Greece BIT [2004]).

[169] *Kim* v. *Uzbekistan*, Jurisdiction, para 164.

acquired an investment in Uzbekistan – something that the tribunal concluded that they indeed had acquired.[170] Given this, an alleged illegality of the investment would not affect the tribunal's *ratione materiae* jurisdiction unless it could be shown that the illegality had resulted in the claimants' failure to acquire the assets that constitute the investment.

Following Douglas, such an outcome is consistent with the fundamental doctrines of the separability of the arbitration clause and *competence-competence* as these are applicable in ISDS.[171] The doctrine of separability distinguishes questions about the validity of the arbitration agreement (including about whether the foreign national has acquired the assets forming the investment) from questions about the validity of the underlying transaction resulting in the acquisition of the investment. This being so, only the former type of questions are jurisdictional, whereas the latter type of questions are questions of admissibility (if the alleged illegality is grave enough and violates international public policy) or the merits.[172] The doctrine of *competence-competence*, for its part, is activated when an objection is raised regarding the validity of the arbitration agreement itself. In these situations, the doctrine of *competence-competence* empowers the tribunal to decide for itself whether the objection is a valid one and decide accordingly.

Considering the above remarks, the legality requirement in Article 12 of the Kazakhstan-Uzbekistan BIT (1997) could have given rise to three types of objections:

- jurisdictional objections, if the claimant could not demonstrate that it had acquired the assets that constituted its investment in the host state;
- admissibility objections, if the illegality pertained to the underlying transaction resulting in the acquisition of the investment and if it was

[170] Ibid., paras 301–305 (finding that the claimants had proven their ownership of the shares in the two Uzbek companies at the relevant time), 357 (finding that the claimants had made an 'investment' in accordance with the terms of the ICSID Convention and the BIT).

[171] Z. Douglas, 'The Plea of Illegality in Investment Treaty Arbitration' (2014) 29 *ICSID Review – Foreign Investment Law Journal* 155, 161–163. Reference can also be made to the decisions in *Plama Consortium Limited* v. *Republic of Bulgaria*, ICSID Case No. ARB/03/24, Decision on Jurisdiction, 8 February 2005, paras 130, 229; and *Malicorp Limited* v. *The Arab Republic of Egypt*, ICSID Case No. ARB/08/18, Award, 7 February 2011, para 119, both of which make this point clear.

[172] Douglas (n. 171), 177ff.

grave enough and violated international public policy (e.g., corruption of government officials);

- merits objections, if the illegality pertained to the underlying transaction resulting in the acquisition of the investment and if it contravened the law of the host state but was not grave enough to violate international public policy or if an illegality of any kind and seriousness pertained to the subsequent use of the investment assets by the claimant following the investment's establishment.[173]

The upshot of this tripartite distinction is that, although the tribunal in *Kim* was certainly correct in saying that not every illegality would deprive it of jurisdiction,[174] it did not go on to clarify which of the alleged illegalities in that case actually took aim at its jurisdiction and which did not. Had the tribunal clearly and unambiguously distinguished the kind of legal objection raised by each alleged illegality, a more principled approach would have been the result. Consider, for example, the following.

If the matter at issue really was just jurisdictional, then the only pertinent question for the tribunal to answer would have been whether any of the alleged illegalities took aim at its power to decide the case by pointing to a defect in the arbitration agreement. Yet, under the guise of a jurisdictional discussion, the tribunal ended up answering a different question altogether, namely, whether the investors were worthy of BIT protection in spite of the illegalities alleged by Uzbekistan. Furthermore, treating proportionality as determinative of the answer to that question seems to have been the wrong way to go about the matter. The proportionality test developed by the tribunal arguably resulted in incoherence of roles between the (national) legislative and the (international) judicial function. Balancing a state's interest or necessity of upholding domestic laws with its interest or necessity of investment protection turns an ISDS tribunal into an arbiter of the interests of the host state. This could qualify as an encroachment by the tribunal upon a domain of policy decision-making that is reserved for domestic legislators.

Similarly, if the question was whether the investors were in principle worthy of BIT protection despite the alleged illegalities in the transaction leading up to the establishment of their investment, then it was open to the tribunal to treat this question as one of admissibility if the alleged

[173] Cf. ibid.

[174] *Kim v. Uzbekistan*, Jurisdiction, paras 389–390.

illegalities amounted to a violation of international public policy.[175] In so doing, the tribunal in essence would be saying that, although it recognised that it was vested with adjudicative power (jurisdiction), it would refuse to exercise this power further if the investor's claim was not morally worthy of protection.[176] To be clear, some form of balancing would still be required by the tribunal in making this determination. The difference would, however, be that, in so doing, the arbitrators would be

175 For the doctrinal rationale behind this choice, see Douglas (n. 171), 180:

> The justification for treating a violation of international public policy as a ground of inadmissibility is as follows. The concept of international public policy vests a tribunal with a particular responsibility to condemn any violation regardless of the law applicable to the particular issues in dispute and regardless of whether it is specifically raised by one of the parties. That condemnation must entail that a party that has engaged in a violation of international public policy is not assisted in any way by the arbitral process in the vindication of any rights that are asserted by that party under any law.

176 In this sense, cf. what appears to be the uniform view in literature and international judicial practice, that an objection to admissibility takes aim at the claim itself rather than at the international court's or tribunal's power to decide. Among a plethora of authorities, see, e.g., S. Rosenne, 'International Courts and Tribunals, Jurisdiction and Admissibility of Inter-State Applications', *Max Planck Encyclopedia of Public International Law* (March 2006), available at https://opil.ouplaw.com/home/MPIL (describing jurisdiction as addressing the question of whether the court *can* entertain the case, and admissibility as addressing the question of whether all things considered it *should* entertain the case); G. Fitzmaurice, 'The Law and Procedure of the International Court of Justice, 1951–4: Questions of Jurisdiction, Competence and Procedure' (1958) 34 *British Yearbook of International Law* 1, 12–13 (describing an admissibility plea as seeking to establish that the court should reject a claim on some ground other than its ultimate merits and a jurisdictional plea as seeking to establish that the court is incompetent to give any ruling at all); *Case Concerning Oil Platforms (Islamic Republic of Iran* v. *United States of America)*, Judgment of 6 November 2003, ICJ Rep (2003) 161, para 29 ('Objections to admissibility normally take the form of an assertion that, even if the Court has jurisdiction and the facts stated by the applicant [s]tate are assumed to be correct, nonetheless there are reasons why the Court should not proceed to an examination of the merits.'); *Nottebohm Case (Liechtenstein* v. *Guatemala), Preliminary Objection*, Judgment of 18 November 1953, ICJ Rep (1953) 111, 122 (distinguishing between the seizing of the Court and the administration of justice; saying that when the Court has been properly seized (i.e., has jurisdiction), then it must exercise its powers to administer justice in accordance with its Rules and the Statute; also saying that the Court must exercise its adjudicative power when normally seized, unless it is proven on some other ground that it lacks jurisdiction or that the claim is inadmissible); *Waste Management, Inc.* v. *United Mexican States*, ICSID Case No. ARB(AF)/98/2, Arbitral Award, 2 June 2000 (*Waste Management I*), Dissenting Opinion of Keith Highet, para 58 ('Jurisdiction is the power of the tribunal to hear the case; admissibility is whether the case itself is defective – whether it is appropriate for the tribunal to hear it.').

interpreting their own legal practice, as opposed to be stepping into the shoes of the host state.

Lastly, if the alleged illegalities in the transaction leading up to the establishment of the investment were not grave enough to be considered a violation of international public policy, then it was open to the *Kim* tribunal to reserve its judgment until a full hearing on the merits. Indeed, an additional unfortunate consequence of the tribunal's approach is that it prejudged certain substantive questions already at the jurisdictional stage of the case. However, a finding of jurisdiction should remain agnostic on the merits of the parties' positions and for good reason. By examining and rejecting all of Uzbekistan's illegality arguments as jurisdictional issues regardless of the nature and severity of each alleged illegality, the tribunal may have rendered these same arguments useless for Uzbekistan as potential defences during the later substantive stages of the dispute.

5.6 Conclusion

The chapter has outlined the basic format, contours, and constitutive elements of analogical reasoning. Analogy is a form of practical reasoning and practical deliberation aimed to resolve practical problems of the type described in Chapter 2. This is done by comparing a novel and unfamiliar situation with a familiar one, in an effort to draw useful guidance from the latter on the best way to approach the former. Making a successful analogy thus rests on three mental processes: identifying similarities, drawing structural parallels, and devising an appropriate goal or purpose for the use of the analogy. As seen in the chapter, the operation of these processes in practice shows that analogical inferences exhibit the same coherence-related features identified in Chapter 2, namely, a web-like structure, a dimension of fit and mutual supportiveness between the premises used, and a purposive dimension.

In the first place, identifying similarities, drawing structural parallels, and having an underlying goal are forces that guide but also constrain analogical inferences. In so doing, they do not operate like rigid rules of logical consequence dictating the correct interpretation or like separate and independent steps in the analogical process. To the contrary, they are highly interdependent elements that at times may pull at opposite directions pressing the decision-maker to achieve a satisfactory compromise between them. Their interaction in the outcome thus resembles more a web of mutually supportive premises (and of reasons justifying these premises) than a chain a demonstrative reasoning.

In the second place, the decision-maker's goals and the similarities and structural parallels that the decision-maker singles out to meet these goals, must themselves be linked through consistent (logical) or at least plausible (fitting) relations. The entire process is moreover replete with substantive, moral judgments. This is with respect to setting up the decision-maker's goals, evaluating whether relevant similarities and parallels have been drawn, and determining whether key aspects of the problem case and the analogous case have been obscured in the process.

The above conclusions also match our findings in Chapter 4. Chapter 4 pointed out that framing and contextualisation are key elements of coherent interpretations in law. Based on the present chapter's analysis, problem-solving by way of analogical reasoning is at its core also a way of framing and normatively contextualising legal problems for resolution. Framing identifies the contours of the problem to be addressed. It singles out the legal question to be answered and the goal to be achieved by the adjudicator. Normative contextualisation places the question within a larger context, considered to be similar in relevant respects, within which it will be addressed, and which will contribute to its answering. The background normative context includes not only the various norms and guiding principles found in the system in question but also the decision-maker's appreciation of the institutional role he or she has within that system.

Taking a bird's eye view of Chapters 4 and 5, one sees that both chapters have begun painting a picture of legal interpretation as an inherently reflexive exercise. Adjudicators must reflect on frames and normative contexts before they can provide coherent answers to the legal questions posed to them. Accordingly, if coherence has a necessary role to play in legal reasoning, if legal reasoning is interpretative, and if interpretation is reflexive, then one must also consider the link between coherence and reflexivity as general judicial attitude or practice. Chapters 6 and 7 undertake such an inquiry.

6

Coherence as Reflexivity

6.1 Introduction

A number of findings and conclusions have been established in the preceding chapters. It will be useful to briefly recall these before moving forward with the last thematic section of the book, which will span the present chapter as well as the one that follows. Chapters 1–3 made three key points. One key point is that coherence describes a state of axiological compatibility, that is to say, a situation where a series of propositions hang together by being rationally linked to the ordering values or principles that are thought to justify them. A second key point is that when looked at in a legal setting, coherence plays a dual role acting as a descriptor, both of the quality of the outcome and of the method used to achieve the outcome. A third key point is that considerations of coherence are an endemic and pervasive feature of (practical) legal argumentation. Moreover, the single coherence model adopted in this book means that legal reasoning is technical and moral throughout.

Coherence thus has a direct link to interpretation and justification in law.[1] Consequently, Chapters 4 and 5 examined the ways in which considerations of coherence manifest during interpretation in the ISDS context. The focus was placed on the mechanics of the VCLT rule of interpretation and the frequent use of analogical inferences by ISDS tribunals. In so doing, Chapters 4 and 5 not only confirmed that considerations of coherence are indeed necessarily assumed in legal interpretation but also further identified that the mental processes of framing the legal questions/issues in dispute and of contextualising these for the purposes of resolution are critical elements of coherence.

[1] It bears noting that interpretation and justification are related concepts also. A proposed interpretation of a legal provision is nothing more than an argument that the provision in question ought to have the proposed meaning. As such, a proposed interpretation is at the same time a proposed justification as to why the provision must possess the meaning it is argued to have.

The common thread that has been followed throughout the discussion so far is that legal reasoning is never a purely technical, legalistic, or doctrinal exercise. Rather, the picture of legal reasoning that has emerged is that of a reflective practice. Indeed, reconstructing the contracting parties' intentions into narratives, framing the contours of legal questions, contextualising, distinguishing relevant from irrelevant details, and pondering one's institutional role when deciding a dispute are all activities that imply reflection. Therefore, the aim in this chapter as well as Chapter 7 is to elaborate on the ideas of reflective practice and reflexivity in a judicial context and, in particular, in the context of ISDS. The present chapter begins such a discussion by unpacking the idea of reflexivity in judicial decision-making and its relationship with coherence. The chapter's thesis is that coherence in legal reasoning and a commitment to reflexivity are intrinsically related notions. Reflexivity in adjudication is conducive towards coherence and, by extension, the degree of a decision-maker's reflexivity can act as a useful indicator (though probably not as a determinant) of the decision's overall coherence.

The discussion proceeds in two steps. Firstly, Section 6.2 describes reflexivity as an overall desirable disposition for adjudicators to have. Drawing on the works of Dewey, Schön, and Rawls, the section identifies key components of reflexivity in practical decision-making, considers potential critiques, and establishes reflexivity as an indicator of coherence. Secondly, Section 6.3 then places the discussion in a practical context by way of a case study on the reflective thinking likely at play behind ISDS decisions addressing nationality planning activities by foreign investors. In so doing, Section 6.3 also reviews instances where an arguably inadequate process of reflection may have negatively affected the overall coherence of an arbitral decision. Section 6.4 summarises the chapter's key findings and concludes.

6.2 Components of Reflexivity

For present purposes, the term 'reflexivity' is used to describe a general attitude of self-awareness and self-examination, whereby one critically examines one's motivations and how they influence one's action. Reflexivity thus encompasses a particular way of thinking about a subject and a particular way of seeking to justify actions, both of which, it is hereby argued, bear a strong link to the concept of coherence in judicial decision-making as that concept has been described in this book. This section traces a dotted line connecting the works of three twentieth-century philosophers – Dewey, Schön, and Rawls – who addressed reflexivity and reflective thinking in the fields of epistemology, professional learning, and political philosophy.

6.2.1 Dewey on the Importance of Thinking Reflectively

For early twentieth-century philosopher John Dewey, thinking well means thinking reflectively. Dewey defines reflective thinking as the 'turning [of] a subject over in the mind and giving it serious and consecutive consideration'.[2] Reflective thinking, Dewey argues, comprises two stages.[3] The first stage is characterised by uncertainty, doubt, or hesitation. Reflective thinking thus begins when an actor finds himself or herself in a state of doubt and perplexity or when he or she faces a problem that requires resolution. The second stage of reflective thinking is characterised by inquiry. The actor engages in a series of acts of searching for evidence that will clear the doubt, resolve the perplexity, or determine a course of action to overcome the problem. One can immediately identify obvious parallels between reflective thinking and practical legal reasoning as outlined in Chapter 2. Such parallels can also be directly confirmed from Dewey's own writings, which identify the following characteristics of reflective thinking:

(i) Reflective thinking is consequential: Thinking is reflective when it does not involve a mere sequence of ideas but rather a consecutive ordering of mutually supporting ideas, so that 'each [idea] determines the next as its proper outcome, while each outcome in turn leans back on, or refers to, its predecessors'.[4]

(ii) Reflective thinking is purposive: Reflective thinking must have an end goal to be reached which in turn controls the sequence and the necessary degree of mutual supportiveness of ideas.[5] The end goal is directly linked to the original doubt, perplexity, or problem that initiated the reflection. In the words of Dewey: 'The nature of the

[2] J. Dewey, *How We Think: A Restatement of the Relation of Reflective Thinking to the Educative Process*, 2nd ed. (Lexington: DC Heath & Co., 1933), 3.

[3] Ibid., 12.

[4] Ibid., 4.

[5] Ibid., 5–6.

problem fixes the end of thought, and the end controls the process of thinking'.[6]

(iii) Reflective thinking is inquisitorial and rational: Reflective thinking involves an active mental endeavour, the search for evidence, the exercise of judgment, and the use of reasons to establish logical entailment and plausible connections between the evidence adduced and the conclusion that the evidence seeks to justify.[7]

Given these characteristics of reflective thinking, the whole is at stake in every step and in every partial move made towards a conclusion. A wrong move at a pivotal point can mean failure. For Dewey, thinking reflectively about a subject can thus serve as a useful method to safeguard one's inferences from falling into obvious errors.[8]

We can easily confirm Dewey's assessment by considering an example. A key jurisdictional question in ISDS is whether there exists an 'investment'. Determining the contours of a protected investment in each case is a problem-framing operation that determines the moves that must be made to resolve the legal question presented before the tribunal and can thus affect the case's outcome. Take the case of *Ampal* v. *Egypt*, where the claimants owned an Egyptian company called EMG. EMG had entered into a general sale and purchase agreement with Egypt's national petroleum and natural gas companies. EMG's business under this agreement was to purchase natural gas from Egypt to export to Israel, as well as to build and operate a pipeline from Egypt to Israel through which to export said natural gas.[9] EMG was established as a free-zone company, benefitting from special status under relevant Egyptian laws, and granted a

[6] Ibid., 15 (emphasis in original omitted).

[7] Ibid., 7–12.

[8] On the importance of method, see, ibid., 166:

> Method of a systematic sort is required in order to safeguard the operations by which we move from one to the other, from facts to ideas, and back again from ideas to the facts that will test them. Without adequate method a person grabs, as it were, at the first facts that offer themselves; he does not examine them to see whether they are truly facts or whether, even though they be real facts, they are relevant to the inference that needs to be made. On the other side, we are given to jumping at the first solution that occurs to us, accepting it as a conclusion without examination and test. We are given also to generalizing an idea far beyond support by evidence. We extend it to new cases without careful study to see whether these cases may not be so different as not to justify the generalization.

[9] *Ampal-American Israel Corporation and Others* v. *Arab Republic of Egypt*, ICSID Case No. ARB/12/11, Decision on Jurisdiction, 1 February 2016, para 5; *Ampal-American*

licence to operate tax-free. Among the measures complained of in the arbitration was a change in Egyptian law that resulted in EMG's tax-free licence to be revoked and which was alleged by the claimants to constitute an expropriation of their investment. The tribunal agreed with the claimants.

It is submitted that this aspect of the decision suffers from a lack of adequate reflection, failing in particular to meet the characteristic of consequence. Central to the tribunal's decision was the fact that the licence to operate tax-free was itself a discreet investment whose revocation amounted, in the tribunal's own words, to a 'direct and total taking' and therefore an unlawful expropriation given the lack of accompanying compensation.[10] In rendering this decision, the tribunal relied directly and exclusively on the asset-based definition of 'investment' in the Egypt-United States BIT (1986).[11] Following the tribunal's logic, this should have been the end of the matter. If the licence to operate tax-free was a distinct investment in its own right, then its revocation by the Egyptian authorities qualifies as direct expropriation for which compensation should have been paid.[12] It is thus interesting to see that, having taken

Israel Corporation and Others v. *Arab Republic of Egypt*, ICSID Case No. ARB/12/11, Decision on Liability and Heads of Loss, 21 February 2017, para 30.

[10] Ibid., Liability & Heads of Loss, paras 179–180.

[11] Ibid., paras 173–174. The exclusive reference to the BIT's definition of investment is also interesting to note here for the fact that the tribunal did not follow the so-called 'double-barrelled' jurisdictional test, despite this being an ICSID case. The double-barrelled test constitutes well-established and long-standing practice in ICSID arbitrations. The test indicates that an ICSID tribunal must ensure that it has jurisdiction over a dispute both under the applicable investment treaty rules and the ICSID Convention rules. This means, among others, that the tribunal must determine the existence of an 'investment' both under the relevant definition of the applicable investment treaty and under Article 25 of the ICSID Convention.

[12] To further emphasise this point about the directness of the taking, the *Ampal* tribunal (ibid., para 180) directly quoted as authority a statement from the *GAMI* v. *Mexico* award that: 'The taking of 50 acres of a farm is equally expropriatory whether that is the whole farm or just a fraction' (*GAMI Investments Inc.* v. *Mexico*, UNCITRAL Rules, Final Award, 15 November 2004, para 126). This quote, offered in *obiter* by the *GAMI* tribunal, is ultimately misleading as authority as it is taken out of context. The *GAMI* tribunal used this example to properly contextualise the key question to be asked in expropriation cases, namely: What is the property right or property interest alleged to have been affected by the host state's actions? In *GAMI*, the investor was a US company with a minority shareholding in a Mexican company named GAM. GAM owned five sugar mills in Mexico, all five of which had been expropriated by formal decree. Therefore, GAMI's investment in Mexico were not the mills themselves but its minority shareholding in GAM. Consequently, the tribunal held that GAMI could not substantiate a claim for expropriation unless it could demonstrate that its investment (i.e., the shareholding) had

the above route, the tribunal seems to fall into self-contradiction in subsequent parts of the decision. In particular, in countering Egypt's arguments that the revocation of the licence was a good faith exercise of public authority, the tribunal remarks that the incorporation of EMG as a special free-zone company and 'as the vehicle for the Claimants' *investment* was an integral part of the *investment*'.[13] The tribunal further goes on to argue:

> [T]he inclusion of EMG within the tax-free zone system in Egypt was a fundamental part of the economic structure of the *investment* ... which [Egypt] confirmed by the issue of the specific licence to EMG .... These facts take the consideration of a change in the tax regime applicable to Claimants' *investment in EMG* well outside the realm of the ordinary exercise of the [s]tate's regulatory power.
>
> In the case of this *investment*, the Respondent's decision to remove EMG's tax-free status took away a defined and valuable interest that had been validly conferred ... at the time that the *investment* was made and that had been guaranteed by the [s]tate for a defined period.[14]

It is difficult to reconcile these statements with the view that EMG's licence to operate as a free-zone company was in itself an investment. Not only are such statements unnecessary and inconsequential if the expropriation alleged is direct, but they also reveal logical contradictions in the tribunal's thinking process. Consider this. If the investment was the licence, then, based on the above statements by the tribunal, how can EMG be considered as a corporate vehicle for a licence, or how can the licence be considered as an integral part of itself or as a fundamental part of its own economic structure? The above-quoted statements rather seem to indicate, first, that claimants' investment was in fact much broader than a mere licence and in fact altogether different, that is, it also comprised claimants' shareholding in EMG[15] and, second, that the licence was nothing more than a valuable asset of the investment that

effectively been taken or its value had been destroyed because of Mexico's expropriation decree (*GAMI* v. *Mexico*, Final Award, paras 127–133).

13 *Ampal* v. *Egypt*, Liability & Heads of Loss, para 181 (emphases added).

14 Ibid., paras 182–183 (emphases added).

15 To note, 'a company or shares, stock, or other interests in a company or interests in the assets thereof' was mentioned in the definition of investment found in Article I(c)(ii) of the Egypt-United States BIT (1986). Treating the shareholding in EMG, rather than the licence itself, as the protected investment is the better view for the added reason that the licence was held by EMG and not by the entities that actually acted as claimants in *Ampal*.

was taken by the state. Ultimately, the tribunal indirectly confirms as much in its conclusion, where it finds that the revocation of the licence was 'tantamount' to expropriation (i.e., an indirect taking), which in turn necessarily presupposes that claimants' investment was broader than EMG's licence to operate tax-free.[16]

The above remarks are not meant to suggest that the tribunal was precluded as a matter of principle from finding that the revocation of the licence constituted an expropriation. Rather, the suggestion is that this would have been an inquiry of a different kind that would require different kinds of evidence. Indeed, the tribunal's remarks about the centrality of EMG's revoked free-zone status are among the kinds of elements one would need to consider in determining whether said revocation resulted in such dire consequences for the claimants' shareholding that could be seen to rise to the level of an indirect expropriation. Furthermore, in not framing properly the threshold question 'what is the protected investment?', the tribunal also failed to take into consideration and to scrutinise a significant concession made by the claimants that could act as evidence tipping the balance in Egypt's favour. This is the concession that a substantial part of EMG's business (namely, the pipeline project) had not been significantly affected or rendered impossible by the revocation of the licence.[17]

6.2.2 *Schön's 'Reflective Practitioner'*

The *Ampal* example usefully illustrates that there is scope for reflexivity not just in one's everyday thinking but in one's professional practice as well. The latter idea is associated with the work of Donald Schön, who argued that the iterative process of reflection also takes place in the line of

[16] See *Ampal* v. *Egypt*, Liability & Heads of Loss, paras 183, 187.

[17] See, ibid., para 179. In this respect one can contrast *Ampal* to the decision in *Philip Morris* v. *Uruguay*, where the claimant argued, similarly to the claimants in *Ampal*, that each one of the trademarks it owned constituted a protected investment in its own right. The *Philip Morris* tribunal disagreed, taking the view that the investment was much broader and comprised the claimant's business in Uruguay as a whole. Ultimately, the tribunal found that no indirect expropriation had taken place because not only had the value of the claimant's local subsidiary not been diminished as a result of the plain packaging measures that limited the use of these trademarks in the market but had in fact increased despite the measures (see *Philip Morris Brands Sàrl, Philip Morris Products S.A. and Abal Hermanos S.A.* v. *Oriental Republic of Uruguay (formerly FTR Holding S.A., Philip Morris Products S.A. and Abal Hermanos S.A.* v. *Oriental Republic of Uruguay)*, ICSID Case No. ARB/10/7, Award, 8 July 2016, paras 278, 280–286).

work of practitioners. His image of the 'reflective practitioner' may thus be regarded as an intellectual continuation of Dewey's views on reflective thinking in epistemology and learning. Schön builds his understanding of reflective practice around three processes, which he terms 'knowing-in-practice', 'reflection-on-practice', and 'reflection-in-practice'.

Knowing-in-practice indicates that one's know-how is often found in the course of acting.[18] Skilful practice, Schön argues, reveals a kind of knowing that cannot be said to stem from a prior intellectual operation[19] but rather seems to derive from one's 'gut feel' of the situation. Such knowing is often tacit, spontaneous, and developed over time during one's practice, at least in practices that are relatively stable.[20] In the practice of international law, knowing-in-practice may take various forms with each form exhibiting its own degree of normative pull and often acting as a launch pad for further reasoning and argumentation. Such forms include, for example, legal doctrine (e.g., territorial jurisdiction,[21] intertem-

[18] D. A. Schön, *The Reflective Practitioner: How Professionals Think in Action* (New York: Basic Books, 1983), 50.

[19] Ibid., 51.

[20] Ibid., 60:

> As a practitioner experiences many variations of a small number of types of cases, he is able to 'practice' his practice. He develops a repertoire of expectations, images, and techniques. He learns what to look for and how to respond to what he finds. As long as his practice is stable, in the sense that it brings him the same types of cases, he becomes less and less subject to surprise. His knowing-in-practice tends to become increasingly tacit, spontaneous, and automatic, thereby conferring upon him and his clients the benefits of specialization.

[21] E.g., *Vlastimir and Borka Banković, Živana Stojanović, Mirjana Stoimenovski, Dragana Joksimović and Dragan Suković* v. *Belgium, the Czech Republic, Denmark, France, Germany, Greece, Hungary, Iceland, Italy, Luxembourg, the Netherlands, Norway, Poland, Portugal, Spain, Turkey and the United Kingdom* (Admissibility), Decision, 12 December 2001, ECHR 2001-XII, paras 59, 61:

> [T]he Court is satisfied that, from the standpoint of public international law, the jurisdictional competence of a [s]tate is primarily territorial. While international law does not exclude a [s]tate's exercise of jurisdiction extra-territorially, the suggested bases of such jurisdiction ... are, as a general rule, defined and limited by the sovereign territorial rights of the other relevant [s]tates.
>
> The Court is of the view, therefore, that Article 1 of the Convention must be considered to reflect this ordinary and essentially territorial notion of jurisdiction, other bases of jurisdiction being exceptional and requiring special justification in the particular circumstances of each case[.]

poral law,[22] police powers);[23] logical maxims (e.g., *lex specialis derogat legi generali*)[24]; certain general principles (e.g., *pacta sunt servanda,*[25] no one may benefit from their own wrongdoing[26]); interpretative 'rules of thumb' (e.g., *ut res magis valeat quam pereat,*[27] *contra proferentem,*[28] *expressio unius*

[22] E.g., *Island of Palmas Case (Netherlands/United States of America)*, Award, 4 April 1928, Vol II *RIAA* 829, 845 (the intertemporal law doctrine states that (i) a juridical fact must be appreciated in the light of the law contemporary with it and not of the law in force at the time when a dispute in regard to it arises or falls to be settled; but (ii) the juridical fact's existence and continued manifestation must follow the conditions required by the evolution of law).

[23] E.g., *Chemtura Corporation (formerly Crompton Corporation)* v. *Government of Canada*, UNCITRAL Rules, Award, 2 August 2010, para 266; *Philip Morris* v. *Uruguay*, Award, para 307 (both standing for the proposition in principle that a measure adopted in the exercise of the state's police powers does not constitute an indirect expropriation).

[24] E.g., *Case Concerning Right of Passage Over Indian Territory (Portugal* v. *India), Merits*, Judgment of 12 April 1960, ICJ Rep (1960) 6, 39–44 (practice establishing localised customary law prevails over general rules or practice establishing general customary law).

[25] E.g., *Rudloff Case* (Interlocutory Decision), Mixed Claims Commission United States-Venezuela 1903–1905, Vol IX *RIAA* 244, 255:

> [E]ven admitting the facts as stated by the Government of Venezuela, this argument does not seem to go against the provisions of the protocol .... [I]t must be remembered that this protocol under what circumstances soever originated, is an agreement between two parties, and that the Commission, whose whole jurisdiction is only founded on this agreement, has certainly above all to apply the great rule, '*pacta servanda*', without which international as well as civil law would be a mere mockery[.]

[26] E.g., *Plama Consortium Limited* v. *Republic of Bulgaria*, ICSID Case No. ARB/03/24, Award, 27 August 2008, para 143; *Inceysa Vallisoletana S.L.* v. *Republic of El Salvador*, ICSID Case No. ARB/03/26, Award, 2 August 2006, paras 240–242 (in both cases the principle was applied in relation to deceitful conduct and false representations made by the investor in order to procure the investment).

[27] E.g., *Asian Agricultural Products Ltd.* v. *Republic of Sri Lanka*, ICSID Case No. ARB/87/3, Final Award, 27 June 1990, (1991) 6 *ICSID Review – Foreign Investment Law Journal* 526, paras 40, 52 (citing to the maxim to conclude that the BIT in question did not impose a strict liability standard vis-à-vis the duty to provide full protection and security, as this would render meaningless other provisions of the treaty).

[28] E.g., *International Thunderbird Gaming Corporation* v. *The United Mexican States*, UNCITRAL Rules, Award, 26 January 2006, Separate Opinion of Thomas Wälde, para 50 (used for the proposition that the risk of ambiguities in statutes and regulations should fall on the public authority that drafted them); *Ceskoslovenska Obchodni Banka, A.S.* v. *The Slovak Republic*, ICSID Case No. ARB/97/4, Decision of the Tribunal on Objections to Jurisdiction, 24 May 1999, (1999) 14 *ICSID Review – Foreign Investment Law Journal* 251, para 51 (used for the proposition that ambiguities should not be taken to count in favour of the party that requested the critical changes to the parties' agreement).

est exclusio alterius[29]); or, especially in the ISDS context and at least for some tribunals, consistent lines of past decisions showcasing a jurisprudential trend.[30]

When intuitive and spontaneous performance yields the expected results then we tend not to think about it. But practices are not without novel situations or perplexing problems. Sometimes, the intuitive and spontaneous performance of one's knowing-in-practice may yield results that are surprising, unwanted, or contrary to one's own intuitions. At this point, practitioners may begin a process of active reflection by focusing interactively on the outcomes of their action, the action itself, and the intuitive knowing that was implicit in their action.[31] Through reflection, practitioners can surface and critically assess the tacit understandings that have emerged out of the repetitive experiences of their practice.[32] In the process, they may modify these tacit understandings.[33] The objects of the practitioner's reflection, Schön points out, can be 'as varied as the

[29] E.g., *Petroleum Development (Trucial Coast) Ltd* v. *The Sheikh of Abu Dhabi*, (1952) 1 *International and Comparative Law Quarterly* 247, 251 (applying it as a principle 'rooted in the good sense and common practice of the generality of civilised nations').

[30] E.g., *Saipem S.p.A.* v. *The People's Republic of Bangladesh*, ICSID Case No. ARB/05/07, Decision on Jurisdiction and Recommendation on Provisional Measures, 21 March 2007, para 67 (footnotes omitted):

> The Tribunal considers that it is not bound by previous decisions. At the same time, it is of the opinion that it must pay due consideration to earlier decisions of international tribunals. It believes that, subject to compelling contrary grounds, it has a duty to adopt solutions established in a series of consistent cases. It also believes that, subject to the specifics of a given treaty and of the circumstances of the actual case, it has a duty to seek to contribute to the harmonious development of investment law and thereby to meet the legitimate expectations of the community of [s]tates and investors towards certainty of the rule of law.

[31] Schön (n. 18), 56.

[32] Ibid., 61.

[33] Consider for instance the following 'modifications' in international law:

- although jurisdiction in international law is principally territorial, international courts have held that there do exist instances where extra-territorial jurisdiction is acknowledged (e.g., *Case of Al-Skeini and others* v. *The United Kingdom*, Judgment, 7 July 2011, ECHR 2011-IV, paras 130–150);
- the *pacta sunt servanda* principle at times conflicts with the *rebus sic stantibus* principle (e.g., *Fisheries Jurisdiction Case (United Kingdom of Great Britain and Northern Ireland* v. *Iceland), Jurisdiction of the Court*, Judgment of 2 February 1973, ICJ Rep (1973) 3, paras 35–40; and for a historical source, see, *Case of the Free Zones of Upper Savoy and the District of Gex*, Judgment of 7 June 1932, PCIJ Series A/B No 46 (1932) 95, 155–157, where the PCIJ entertained – but did not accept or flesh out – a variation of *rebus sic stantibus* raised by France);

kinds of phenomena before him and the systems of knowing-in-practice which he brings to them'.[34] In other words:

> [The practitioner] may reflect on the tacit norms and appreciations which underlie a judgment, or on the strategies and theories implicit in a pattern of behavior. He may reflect on the feeling for a situation which has led him to adopt a particular course of action, on the way in which he has framed the problem he is trying to solve, or on the role he has constructed for himself within a larger institutional context.[35]

Reflection of this kind can take place at different time-horizons. It can take place retrospectively, after the action has been completed by the practitioner, in an effort to prepare himself or herself for future cases. Schön calls this 'reflection-*on*-practice', and it is, in essence, the same sort of operation as the critical examination of the *Ampal* v. *Egypt* decision undertaken in Section 6.2.1. But Schön's more innovative insight is that this kind of reflection also takes place live and 'in action'. That is to say, it takes place at the same time as the practitioner grapples with doubt, uncertainty, or a problematic and complex situation in his or her line of work. Schön calls this process of active, on-the-spot problem-solving 'reflection-*in*-practice'.

When a practitioner reflects in practice, then he or she becomes a 'researcher in the practice context'.[36] The practitioner's disposition must be curious and inquisitive, welcoming uncertainty and puzzlement as new and challenging situations emerge, and standing ready to re-evaluate aspects of his or her knowing-in-practice if so required.[37] Reflective

- although some investment arbitrators believe that a consistent line of past decisions constitutes a weighty *de facto* precedent, there are other arbitrators who view their institutional role differently (e.g., *Quiborax S.A., Non Metallic Minerals S.A. and Allan Fosk Kaplún* v. *Plurinational State of Bolivia*, ICSID Case No. ARB/06/2, Decision on Jurisdiction, 27 September 2012, para 46);
- the police powers doctrine will not safeguard a state against a finding of indirect expropriation, if the measure in question has been applied disproportionately or if it is seen as a disguised attempt to discriminate against, or otherwise harm, the investment (e.g., *LG&E Energy Corp., LG&E Capital Corp., and LG&E International, Inc.* v. *Argentine Republic*, ICSID Case No. ARB/02/1, Decision on Liability, 3 October 2006, para 195; *Methanex Corporation* v. *United States of America*, UNCITRAL Rules, Final Award on Jurisdiction and Merits, 3 August 2005, (2005) 44 *International Legal Materials* 1345, Part IV, Chapter D, para 7).

[34] Schön (n. 18), 62.
[35] Ibid.
[36] Ibid., 68.
[37] Ibid., 164 (emphasis in original; footnote omitted):

> At the same time that the inquirer tries to shape the situation to his frame, he must hold himself open to the situation's back-talk. He must be willing

practical inquiry is thus not limited to a deliberation purely about suitable means to achieve clearly defined and previously agreed upon ends. Means and ends are not kept separate. They are defined interactively as the practitioner frames the problematic situation that he or she must address.[38]

6.2.3 *A Search for Equilibrium*

A question arises at this point. When reflecting-*on*-practice, one can attempt to reconstruct or reverse engineer one's own prior process of acting in order to critically assess it. But how does one proceed with reflecting-*in*-practice without the benefit of hindsight? Put differently, how can one proceed in one's live engagement with a practical problem so as to ensure reflexivity? And when does one stop the inquiry? John Rawls' idea of the reflective equilibrium technique can serve as a useful point of reference in this regard.[39]

6.2.3.1 Rawls on Reflective Equilibrium

In Rawls' theory of justice, reflective equilibrium is a technique of justification. It serves as one of the conditions that the participants in

> to enter into new confusions and uncertainties. Hence, he must adopt a kind of double vision. He must act in accordance with the view he has adopted, but he must recognize that he can always break it open later, indeed, *must* break it open later in order to make new sense of his transaction with the situation. This becomes more difficult to do as the process continues. His choices become more committing; his moves, more nearly irreversible. As the risk of uncertainty increases, so does the temptation to treat the view as the reality. Nevertheless, if the inquirer maintains his double vision, even while deepening his commitment to a chosen frame, he increases his chances of arriving at a deeper and broader coherence of artifact and idea.

[38] See, ibid., 68. Schön continues further: '[The practitioner] does not separate thinking from doing, ratiocinating his way to a decision which he must later convert to action. Because his experimenting is a kind of action, implementation is built into his inquiry. Thus reflection-in-action can proceed, even in situations of uncertainty or uniqueness . . . .'

[39] See J. Rawls, *A Theory of Justice*, rev. ed. (Cambridge, MA: Harvard University Press, 1999), 15–19; also J. Rawls, *Justice as Fairness: A Restatement*, edited by E. Kelly (Cambridge, MA: Harvard University Press, 2001), 29–32; and for a concise summary, see N. Daniels, 'Reflective Equilibrium', in E. N. Zalta (ed.), *The Stanford Encyclopedia of Philosophy* (Summer 2020), available at https://plato.stanford.edu/archives/sum2020/entries/reflective-equilibrium/.

the original position[40] must fulfil when choosing the principles of justice that will govern their common life. Roughly put, the idea behind reflective equilibrium in justifying moral inferences is that we must work back and forth between our considered judgments about particular instances or cases, the principles that we believe underpin those judgments, and the theoretical considerations that we believe bear on accepting our considered judgments and principles, revising any of these elements whenever necessary in order to achieve an acceptable level of convergence among them.[41] An acceptable level of convergence, according to Rawls, is 'wide' as opposed to 'narrow'. That is to say, the convergence we should strive towards is not only that our considered judgments be consistent with each other but also that some of them provide support or the best explanation for the others.[42] In the course of this process of reflection, we may modify our prior judgments or add new ones. The ultimate goal is to

[40] By the term 'original position', Rawls, ibid. (1999), 11, describes a hypothetical state of nature where individual human beings exist and operate under a veil of ignorance: no one knows his or her place in society, class, social status, fortune in the distribution of natural assets and abilities, intelligence, or strengths. The veil of ignorance ensures that none of the participants is advantaged or disadvantaged during their deliberation about the principles of justice that will govern their common life, since no one will be able to push for principles of justice that will favour his or her particular condition. Rawls argues that the fundamental principles of justice agreed upon in the original position will be fair to all.

[41] Rawls (n. 39) (1999), 18, himself describes this process as follows (footnote omitted):

> In searching for the most favored description of [the initial] situation we work from both ends. We begin by describing it so that it represents generally shared and preferably weak conditions. We then see if these conditions are strong enough to yield a significant set of principles. If not, we look for further premises equally reasonable. But if so, and these principles match our considered convictions of justice, then so far well and good. But presumably there will be discrepancies. In this case we have a choice. We can either modify the account of the initial situation or we can revise our existing judgments, for even the judgments we take provisionally as fixed points are liable to revision. By going back and forth, sometimes altering the conditions of the contractual circumstances, at others withdrawing our judgments and conforming them to principle, I assume that eventually we shall find a description of the initial situation that both expresses reasonable conditions and yields principles which match our considered judgments duly pruned and adjusted. This state of affairs I refer to as reflective equilibrium. It is equilibrium because at last our principles and judgments coincide; and it is reflective since we know to what principles our judgments conform and the premises of their derivation.

[42] Rawls (n. 39) (1999), 42–43; also, Rawls (n. 39) (2001), 30–31.

reach an equilibrium that is 'optimal' before stopping the inquiry. We arrive at an optimal equilibrium when the component judgments, principles, and theories are such that we are not inclined to revise any further because, taken together, they have the highest degree of acceptability or credibility.[43] Echoing the discussion in Chapter 2, optimal equilibrium thus implies a commitment to a statement of reasons that is ideally compelling or at least genuine and adequate in character.[44]

Three key characteristics of reflective equilibrium may be drawn from the above description. The first characteristic is that to be able to even get off the ground, the process requires certain so-called 'fixed points'. These are judgments that we would not expect to withdraw or alter during the process of reflection.[45] Some of the judgments irrespective of their level of abstraction must therefore be judgments of this kind, although this does not mean that even these judgments would be necessarily immune from revision in the future.[46] A second, related characteristic of reflective equilibrium is that our judgments are relevant regardless of their level of generality or abstraction. At no one level, say that of abstract principle or that of the particular situation, are judgments to be regarded as foundational or as enjoying an axiomatic higher credibility than the rest.[47] The third characteristic then follows logically from the first two. The point of optimal equilibrium cannot be pre-determined by the existence of an advanced test. Rather, it is our sense of the degree of mutual supportiveness of all judgments that are brought to bear on the outcome that dictates whether the inquiry should stop or keep going.[48]

[43] Daniels (n. 39).

[44] Such a process of justification may appear viciously circular, since it indicates that practical inferences about the concrete case, about guiding principles, and about governing abstract theories in the end justify each other. But the circularity is virtuous rather than vicious. Competing judgments about principles, theories, and the concrete case are held, in the first place, provisionally. Each judgment then acts as the necessary interpretative framework for the rest, expanding or narrowing the scope and context of the reflective inquiry in the process. In this manner, the image of optimal reflective equilibrium that emerges is not strictly speaking circular but, rather, spiral.

[45] Rawls (n. 39) (2001), 29.

[46] See Rawls (n. 39) (1999), 18: 'At the moment everything is in order. But this equilibrium is not necessarily stable. It is liable to be upset by further examination of the conditions which should be imposed on the contractual situation and by particular cases which may lead us to revise our judgments.'

[47] Rawls (n. 39) (2001), 30.

[48] Cf. R. Dworkin, 'In Praise of Theory' (1997) 29 *Arizona State Law Journal* 353, 372: 'Lawyers (like other people) discover the scope of reflection they need to pursue in the course of inquiry, by finding where inquiry leads before a responsible resting place is

6.2.3.2 A Critique: Cass Sunstein's Complete versus Incomplete Theorisation

In *Legal Reasoning and Political Conflict*, Cass Sunstein advances a thought-provoking thesis based on what he terms 'incompletely theorised agreements', which he argues can be used as an alternative to reflective equilibrium in a legal context. Sunstein shares with the reflective equilibrium technique a common epistemic goal, namely, the desire to devise a strategy for producing stability and agreement in the midst of social disagreement and pluralism.[49] He also shares with reflective equilibrium the realisation that people tend to reason at various levels of abstraction.

On any given subject or issue, Sunstein argues, it is possible for people to be in agreement on any one level of abstraction but likely not on all of them at the same time – hence their agreement being 'incompletely theorised'. Put differently, on any given subject or issue, people may agree on what the correct answer ought to be when that subject or issue is examined at one level of abstraction but may still disagree when the same subject or issue is examined at a different level of abstraction.[50] Thus, Sunstein points out, people may agree on an abstract principle but disagree on what the principle entails in particular cases (e.g., we all believe in the sanctity of life, but we disagree on abortion); people may agree on a mid-level principle but disagree on both general theory and particular outcomes (e.g., we can all agree that racial discrimination is impermissible, without sharing a common theory of equality and also without agreeing on the permissibility of affirmative action policies); and people may agree on a narrow or low-level principle without always agreeing on the particular outcomes this principle gives rise to (e.g., we may agree that a finding of discriminatory treatment necessarily implies the existence of situations that are similar or 'like', but we may disagree about how to determine similarity or 'likeness' in each case).[51]

Sunstein does not intend for these remarks to be taken as merely descriptive in character. Rather, his core normative claim is that incompletely theorised agreements are not simply well-suited to a moral

reached. They do not – cannot – accept a methodology that stipulates in advance where they must stop no matter how inconclusive or unsatisfying their reflection to that point.'

49 C. R. Sunstein, *Legal Reasoning and Political Conflict*, 2nd ed. (New York: Oxford University Press, 2018), 3–7.

50 Ibid.

51 Ibid., 35–38.

universe that is diverse and pluralistic but that they are also the best option available to adjudicators. This claim rests on several arguments. Sunstein argues, for example, that incompletely theorised agreements reduce the political costs of enduring disagreements (i.e., the losers lose a decision but their convictions remain intact and thus capable of carrying the day at the next instance), make easier the evolution of the law over time, and take cognisance of the limited time and capacities of judges as well as of the different roles fulfilled by the legislative and the judicial function.[52] The upshot, according to Sunstein, is that the 'distinctly legal solution to the problem of pluralism is to strive to produce agreement on particulars'.[53] Adjudicators should therefore actively avoid general theorising and should instead base their decisions on what Sunstein calls 'low-level principles'.[54]

A problem with the incompletely theorised agreements thesis, however, is that one cannot hold it coherently, at least not without putting in place caveats that severely undermine its expressed normative aspirations. Indeed, Sunstein inserts throughout his analysis important clarifications attesting to the value and even indispensability of general theorising for sound decision-making.[55] Indeed, as it will be shown in

[52] Ibid., 41–47.

[53] Ibid., 47.

[54] For Sunstein (ibid., 37), the term 'low-level principles' includes 'most of the ordinary material of legal "doctrine" – the general class of principles and justifications that are not said to derive from any large theories of the right or the good, that have ambiguous relations to large theories, and that are compatible with more than one such theory'.

[55] E.g., see the following passages from, ibid., 43–44, 48–49, 54, 56–57, 59 (emphases in original):

> None of these points suggests that incompletely theorized agreements always deserve celebration. Some incompletely theorized agreements are unjust. . . . [F]uller theorization – in the form of wider and deeper inquiry into the grounds for judgment – may be valuable or even necessary to prevent inconsistency, bias, or self-interest. If judges on a panel have actually agreed on a general theory, and if they are really committed to it, they should say so. Judges and the general community will learn much more if they are able to discuss the true motivating grounds for outcomes.
>
> Of course some background abstractions, connected with liberty and equality, should limit the permissible set of incompletely theorized agreements. Otherwise there is no assurance that an incompletely theorized agreement is just . . .. If we want to . . . ensure that [incompletely theorized agreements] are defensible, we will have to make some movement in Rawls's direction, or at least toward more ambitious ways of thinking.
>
> [S]ome cases cannot be decided *at all* without introducing a fair amount in the way of theory. Moreover, some cases cannot be decided *well* without

the examination of the *Phoenix* v. *Czech Republic* award in Section 6.3.5, agreement on particulars is in and of itself no guarantee of sound or coherent decision-making. What is more, arguing against general theorising may be seen as ironic considering that the 'incompletely theorised agreements' thesis is in itself a general theory based on abstract values and principles. It comprises a theory of just institutions in a democratic system, it makes a claim that fundamental principles are best developed politically and not judicially, and its success depends upon its general acceptance by adjudicators.[56]

An additional reason to be sceptical towards Sunstein's thesis for present purposes is particular to international law. Sunstein regards incompletely theorised agreements as suitable for, and well-adapted to, legal systems where judges must take precedents as fixed points of reference.[57] Indeed, Sunstein's reason for being sceptical towards the reflective equilibrium technique is that, even though it too grounds deliberation on fixed points, it still leaves considerable room that these points may be amended in the process. That is a fair point for Sunstein to make. Still, the close relationship between incompletely theorised agreements and precedents should not carry as much weight for present purposes since there exists no strict doctrine of precedent in international law or international investment law. What we can expect in the latter is, at best, a practice of *jurisprudence constante* where past decisions carry weight as strong presumptions rather than as a mandatory rule.

A full assessment of Sunstein's thesis is beyond the scope of the inquiry here.[58] The brief remarks offered should however suffice to cast doubt on the main normative claim against general theorising during judicial

> introducing more ambitious theory, in the form of greater depth. If a good theory is available and if judges can be persuaded that the theory is good, there should be no taboo on its judicial acceptance. The claims on behalf of incompletely theorized agreements are presumptive rather than conclusive.
>
> I am thus declining to endorse . . . a claim that incompletely theorized agreements are always the appropriate approach to law and that general theory is always illegitimate in law. . . . Judges should adopt a presumption rather than a taboo against high-level theorization.
>
> It would be foolish to say that no general theory can produce agreement, even more foolish to deny that some general theories deserve general support, and most foolish of all to say that incompletely theorized agreements warrant respect whatever their content.

56 Sunstein, ibid., 59–60, concedes this point as well.

57 See, ibid., 43, 52.

58 For comprehensive and critical assessments in this respect (in relation, however, to the first edition of Sunstein's book), see A. Kaufman, 'Incompletely Theorized Agreement:

reasoning. That notwithstanding, Sunstein's thesis is not without merit or practical usefulness. But rather than being an epistemic theory about what is necessary to ensure the objectivity of judgments in the face of moral disagreement or a theory about the inappropriateness of the reflective equilibrium technique for judicial decision-making, perhaps the thesis may be better described as a theory about managing judicial discretion and judicial moral responsibility.[59]

For instance, Sunstein seems to be correct when he says that using as a legal basis for a decision a highly abstract value, principle, or theory about the right and the good may be disrespectful to the losers' convictions, could risk ossifying the law by pre-determining a host of future controversies, and may even encroach upon the domain of legislators. If that is the case, then it may indeed be more prudent for a court to put forward a more readily acceptable, lower-level principle as a legal basis for its decision. In short, judicial decisions may seem incompletely theorised and, following Sunstein's insights, at times there may be practical usefulness in having them seem so. Yet saying this does not prove that theories (both general and narrow), or principles (both high and low), or values (both abstract and concrete), are not or should not be in the mind of a court deliberating about what the law demands in a particular situation. By way of example, one may look at the separate opinion of Judge ad hoc Shearer in the *Southern Bluefin Tuna* provisional measures order. After noting the prevalent doctrinal and practical difficulties in directly applying the precautionary principle, Judge Shearer clarified: 'The Tribunal has not found it necessary to enter into a discussion of the precautionary principle/approach. However, I believe that the

A Plausible Ideal for Legal Reasoning?' (1996) 85 *Georgetown Law Journal* 395; Dworkin (n. 48), 367–374.

59 In this respect, cf. a salient point made by Dworkin (n. 48), 360:

> [A] theory-embedded view . . . is an account of legal reasoning – of how we properly argue toward claims about what the law is. It is also an account of what truth in such claims consists in. It is not automatically an argument about the responsibilities of judges in ordinary cases or even in constitutional cases. . . . [S]o many people have resisted the embedded view on the ground that it licences judges to engage in, as they often put it, vast 'excursions' of theory. . . . It is a serious confusion to disguise your dislike of judges having great power, which can be remedied, in theory, by changing their jurisdictional power, as a false theory of legal reasoning.

measures ordered by the Tribunal are rightly based upon considerations deriving from a precautionary approach'.[60]

6.2.4 Coherence as Reflexivity

At this point, three principal conclusions may be drawn from the foregoing analysis. Firstly, there are clear parallels between reflective equilibrium as technique and the ideas of reflective thinking and reflection-in-practice. The constant, iterative process of moving from abstract to particular (and vice-versa), described by Rawls, is essentially the same as turning a subject over in the mind giving it serious and consecutive consideration, described by Dewey. Rawls' remarks on the necessity of 'fixed points' corresponds to Schön's idea of knowing-in-practice, which is to say the practitioner's implicit and intuitive knowing developed over years of practice. Further, Rawls' non-foundationalism with respect to the relative weight of one's judgments at all levels of abstraction finds correspondence in Schön's views about the reflective practitioner's propensity to embrace uncertainty and critical thinking.[61]

Secondly, reflective equilibrium as technique bears strong similarities with the content of coherence as interdependence, mutual supportiveness, and a web of propositions coming under a common set of ordering values or principles. In his description of reflective equilibrium, Rawls makes clear the interdependence of one's judgments expressed at any level of abstraction. Furthermore, the iterative 'back-and-forth' process that he describes seeks to ensure that one's judgments converge by being mutually supportive and able to stand together as a unit.

Thirdly, it thus follows that reflexivity and coherence are conceptually linked notions. Reflexivity in one's practice is conducive towards a coherent process of reasoning and argumentation, which, in turn, is conducive towards a well-justified outcome. The same conceptual link must carry over to the legal field. As previous chapters have argued, considerations of coherence are necessarily assumed in interpretation in ISDS, including, for instance, in the operation of the VCLT rule of

[60] *Southern Bluefin Tuna (New Zealand* v. *Japan; Australia* v. *Japan), Provisional Measures*, Order of 27 August 1999, ITLOS Rep (1999) 280, Separate Opinion of Judge *Ad Hoc* Shearer, 327. In a similar vein, see *The MOX Plant Case (Ireland* v. *United Kingdom), Provisional Measures*, Order of 3 December 2001, ITLOS Rep (2001) 95, Separate Opinion of Judge *Ad Hoc* Székely, paras 22–24.

[61] E.g., notice the parallels between Schön's quote from n. 37, and Rawls' quotes from nn. 41 and 46.

interpretation and in the use of analogies. Moreover, an act of interpretation of a legal norm is in essence a legal argument justifying why the norm in question possesses the content it is argued to possess. Therefore, it should follow that reflexivity – taking the form of reflection-in-practice and of a search for equilibrium – has relevance in the legal context too. Put differently, reflexivity in judicial reasoning by courts and tribunals is conducive to, and can act as an indicator of, coherence in the same. Section 6.3 seeks precisely to showcase the relevance and indeed importance of reflexivity for the coherence of ISDS decisions. This is done by way of a case study of arbitral awards reviewing nationality planning activities by foreign investors.

A caveat must however be made before continuing. The examination below is by necessity indirect, taking the form of a retrospective reflection-on-practice. This is because the principal source of evidence used are arbitral decisions. A judicial decision is in some respects a performative act by the adjudicator, who constructs it in such a way so as to persuade his or her audience that the decision's premises are well-chosen and that the outcome follows logically from the chosen premises.[62] There is an inherent difficulty in examining reflection-in-practice in judicial

[62] E.g., see E. Jouannet, 'La motivation ou le mystère de la boite noire', in H. Ruiz Fabri and J.-M. Sorel (eds.), *La motivation des décisions des juridictions internationales* (Paris: Pedone, 2008) 251, 267 (footnote omitted):

> [L]e syllogisme est maintenu par le juge mais ce n'est pas un procédé normatif de découverte de la solution comme le juge voudrait le faire croire, mais un procédé de justification de cette solution afin de la présenter comme évidente et parfaitement objective.

In a similar vein, and from a broader epistemological perspective, cf. Dewey (n. 2), 128–129 (emphases in original; footnote omitted):

> The method that is employed in discovery, in reflective inquiry, cannot possibly be identified with the method that emerges *after* the discovery is made. In the genuine operation of inference, the mind is in the attitude of *search*, of *hunting*, of *projection*, of *trying this and that*; when the conclusion is reached, the search is at an end. ... After we have reached the conclusion, a reconsideration of the steps of the process to see what is helpful, what is harmful, what is merely useless, assists in dealing more promptly and efficaciously with analogous problems in the future.
>
> As a matter of fact, the gradual, largely unconscious, development of *logical attitude and habit* comes first. A conscious setting forth of the method logically adapted for reaching an end is possible only after the result has first been reached by unconscious and tentative methods.

reasoning from that point of view.[63] The attempt is thus made below to reconstruct the reflective thinking likely at play behind the decisions examined in the case study, rather than to identify conclusively the actual process of reflection-in-practice exhibited by the arbitrators in these cases. Yet, although it is not possible to observe the live 'back-and-forth' in the adjudicator's mind, it is nonetheless still possible to identify instances where attempts at an equilibrium have been made by arbitrators, as well as to critically review instances where an arguably inadequate process of reflection may have affected the overall coherence of a decision.

6.3 Reflexivity at Play: Dissecting Nationality Planning Jurisprudence

As Schreuer observes, nationality plays somewhat of a paradoxical role in ISDS.[64] Nationality is regarded both as very important and as inconsequential, depending on the stage in the life cycle of an investment one is looking at. Nationality is very important when it comes to being granted the benefit of treaty protection, as investment treaties will only protect investors originating from the states that are parties to them. But once an investment is established in the host state, nationality is treated as inconsequential. A host state may then not discriminate among investors because of their nationality. Since nationality serves as investors' entry point to the investment protection regime and grants tribunals one aspect of their decision-making power (i.e., their *ratione personae* jurisdiction),[65] it comes as no surprise to see prospective investors engaging

[63] An empirical, qualitative method would be required to examine reflexivity in practice. However, such an inquiry is beyond the scope and aims of the present book.

[64] C. Schreuer, 'Nationality Planning', in A. W. Rovine (ed.), *Contemporary Issues in International Arbitration and Mediation: The Fordham Papers 2012* (Leiden: Martinus Nijhoff, 2013) 17, 17.

[65] This can be contrasted to the situation under the rules on diplomatic protection, where the question of nationality is one of admissibility rather than jurisdiction. In *Nottebohm*, Liechtenstein claimed against Guatemala restitution and compensation on behalf of Friedrich Nottebohm, on the ground that Guatemala had acted towards him in a manner contrary to international law. The case was split in two stages. During the preliminary objections stage, the ICJ addressed the question of its jurisdiction. The Court found that it possessed jurisdiction since both states had issued a valid declaration under the optional clause (see *Nottebohm Case [Liechtenstein* v. *Guatemala], Preliminary Objection*, Judgment of 18 November 1953, ICJ Rep [1953] 111, 122–123). The question of Nottebohm's nationality came up only during the second stage, as the factor that confers upon a state the right to exercise diplomatic protection. There, the ICJ used the criterion of real and effective nationality and ruled that Nottebohm had no real bond of

in nationality planning activities, structuring their businesses in ways that overcome any limitations owed to nationality, in an effort to benefit from the coverage of international investment agreements.

At the same time, however, the practice of nationality planning raises concerns of potential abuse of the system by investors engaging in treaty- and forum-shopping. Nationality planning thus leads to conflicts between investors' general economic freedom to structure their business at will and conceptions of fairness vis-à-vis the host state. Yet, in examining cases where tribunals have dealt with nationality planning, one primarily sees rather technical analyses on the import of legal doctrines, such as jurisdiction, admissibility, non-retroactivity, and abuse of rights.

The argument that is pursued here is that these doctrinal discussions are a manifestation of reflective thinking. Doctrine serves to concretise and contextualise the legal problem presented before the arbitrators, by framing it within long held and accepted practices and mechanics of the system. In so doing, doctrine effectively assists arbitrators to strike the balance in the rather abstract conflict between investors' economic freedom and a sense of fairness towards the host state. Thus, we do indeed observe a situation that comes close to Sunstein's views when these are recast as the occasional practical benefits of seeming incomplete theorisation. At the same time, however, we will also observe during the discussion that higher-level theorising in light of a surprising or counter-intuitive outcome (see the *Tokios Tokelés* v. *Ukraine* example below) and a commitment to the search for equilibrium (see the *Phoenix* v. *Czech Republic* example below) are indispensable aspects of coherent judicial decision-making.

6.3.1 *The General Principle of Economic Freedom, Permitting Nationality Planning*

As a matter of basic economic freedom and general legal principle there exists a presumption of freedom of nationality planning. As Schreuer observes: 'It is neither illegal nor improper for an investor of one nationality to establish a new entity in a jurisdiction perceived to provide a beneficial regulatory and legal environment, including the availability

attachment with Liechtenstein, thus rendering the latter's claims inadmissible (see *Nottebohm Case [Liechtenstein* v. *Guatemala], Preliminary Objection, Second Phase*, Judgment of 6 April 1955, ICJ Rep [1955] 4, 25–26).

of an investment treaty.'[66] The point of departure for most tribunals faced with a nationality planning challenge, therefore, is to reiterate this general principle. In *HICEE* v. *Slovakia*, for example, the tribunal said the following with respect to the claimant's 'structured investment':

> This is not unusual, nor is there anything in the least reprehensible about it; structured investments are commonplace. The purpose is to secure advantages from incorporation or operation in a particular jurisdiction . . .. The advantages anticipated often include the protection of particular bilateral (or other) treaties covering foreign investment.[67]

In *Aguas del Tunari* v. *Bolivia*, the tribunal said similarly:

> [I]t is not uncommon in practice, and – absent a particular limitation – not illegal to locate one's operations in a jurisdiction perceived to provide a beneficial regulatory and legal environment in terms, [for example], of taxation or the substantive law of the jurisdiction, including the availability of a BIT.[68]

Similar in spirit statements have been made by several other tribunals also, including those in *Levy and Gremcitel* v. *Peru*, *Tidewater* v. *Venezuela*, and *Venezuela Holdings* v. *Venezuela*.[69] This abstract in-principle freedom of nationality planning is further buttressed by the fact that nationality planning is implicitly encouraged by many investment treaties, considering that the test most often used to determine a corporate investor's nationality is that of incorporation.[70] Corporate entities are

[66] Schreuer (n. 64), 19; similarly, J. Baumgartner, *Treaty Shopping in International Investment Law* (Oxford: Oxford University Press, 2016), 10–12, 65; R. Dolzer and C. Schreuer, *Principles of International Investment Law*, 2nd ed. (Oxford: Oxford University Press, 2012), 52; and Z. Douglas, *The International Law of Investment Claims* (Cambridge: Cambridge University Press, 2009), 297–298.

[67] *HICEE B.V.* v. *The Slovak Republic*, UNCITRAL Rules, PCA Case No. 2009-11, Partial Award, 23 May 2011, para 103.

[68] *Aguas del Tunari, S.A.* v. *Republic of Bolivia*, ICSID Case No. ARB/02/3, Decision on Respondent's Objections to Jurisdiction, 21 October 2005, para 330.

[69] See *Renée Rose Levy and Gremcitel S.A.* v. *Republic of Peru*, ICSID Case No. ARB/11/17, Award, 9 January 2015, para 184; *Tidewater Inc., Tidewater Investment SRL, Tidewater Caribe, C.A., et al.* v. *The Bolivarian Republic of Venezuela*, ICSID Case No. ARB/10/5, Decision on Jurisdiction, 8 February 2013, para 184; *Venezuela Holdings, B.V., et al (case formerly known as Mobil Corporation, Venezuela Holdings, B.V., et al.)* v. *Bolivarian Republic of Venezuela*, ICSID Case No. ARB/07/27, Decision on Jurisdiction, 10 June 2010, para 204.

[70] See *Aguas del Tunari* v. *Bolivia*, Jurisdiction, para 332 ('The language of the definition of national in many BITs evidences that such national routing of investment is entirely in keeping with the purpose of the instruments and the motivations of the state parties.').

thus protected as 'foreign investors' insofar as they are incorporated in one of the contracting parties to the treaty in question.

While the general principle of economic freedom acts as a fixed point and a launch pad for discussion, it is also well-recognised that the incorporation approach has the capacity to significantly expand an investment treaty's coverage. Complex beneficial ownership structures may result in host states finding themselves in litigation against investors whose nationality hails from non-contracting parties or even from the host state itself. This raises concerns about fairness and potential abuse of the arbitral process. One way states have sought to address these concerns has been to introduce treaty mechanisms placing limits on a putative investor's nationality planning. Some of these mechanisms may take aim at a tribunal's jurisdiction,[71] while others may leave jurisdiction intact and instead seek to render investor claims inadmissible if certain conditions are met.[72] The remainder of the case study focuses

[71] Mechanisms taking aim at a tribunal's jurisdiction tend to provide for certain characteristics that corporations must exhibit in order to qualify for treaty coverage, such as (i) being directly or indirectly owned or controlled by nationals of a contracting party irrespective of their place of incorporation (e.g., Article 1[b][iii] Argentina-Netherlands BIT [1992]) or (ii) having substantial or real economic activities in the territory of the contracting party whose nationality they claim (e.g., Article 8.1 Canada-EU CETA [2016]). Other mechanisms taking aim at jurisdiction may go a step beyond and further clarify when a company may be considered as being 'owned or controlled' by nationals of the other contracting party (e.g., Article 1[c] Japan-Kenya BIT [2016]).

These being jurisdictional limitations, their examination must take priority over any parallel questions about the good or bad faith of the corporate restructuring or about a possible abuse of process by the investor. For instance, in *Alps Finance and Trade AG* v. *The Slovak Republic*, UNCITRAL Rules, Award (redacted version), 5 March 2011, there were allegations made by Slovakia that the claimant had not brought the arbitration proceedings in good faith. Specifically, Slovakia argued that the claimant had established a commercial presence in Switzerland for the sole purpose of benefitting from the Slovakia-Switzerland BIT (1990), by creating an international jurisdiction vis-à-vis a foreseeable dispute where none such jurisdiction existed previously. This was a challenge of inadmissibility of the investor's claim. The tribunal instead chose to decline jurisdiction on *ratione personae* grounds. The reason was that the claimant could not demonstrate real economic activities in Switzerland as per the BIT's definition of 'investor' (ibid., paras 215–227). This finding in turn rendered any question regarding the claimant's bad faith or abuse of process beside the point (ibid., para 247).

[72] Denial of benefits clauses fit this description. Such clauses allow the host state to deny the benefits of treaty protection to certain types of investors, such as, e.g., to companies directly or indirectly owned or controlled by nationals of a non-contracting party or of the host state itself, or to so-called 'mailbox' companies lacking substantial business activities in the territory of the state whose nationality they claim (e.g., Article 22 Morocco-Nigeria BIT [2016]).

not on these limiting mechanisms but, rather, on the interpretative principles that tribunals have used in the absence of such mechanisms. Arbitral jurisprudence indicates that in these cases the dimension of time is important. In reviewing attempts at nationality planning under the dimension of time, tribunals follow a process of reasoning that is structured around principles that are both abstract and more concrete, including the principles of non-retroactivity, good faith, and abuse of rights/process.[73]

6.3.2 *Intertemporal Law, Non-retroactivity, and the Doctrine of Jurisdiction in ISDS*

Although in principle permitted, an investor's corporate restructuring must still be done consistently with the system's procedural rules and core mechanics. It is thus possible for nationality planning to raise, in the first place, issues relating to a tribunal's jurisdiction *ratione temporis*.[74] The legal norm that accounts for this possibility is the general principle that laws apply prospectively. This principle has the status of customary international law and is moreover codified in at least two international documents. With respect to treaties, the principle is codified in Article 28 of the VCLT.[75] With respect to the law of state responsibility, it is codified in Article 13 of the ILC's Articles.[76] The principle of the non-retroactive application of legal norms is a manifestation in practice of a fundamental principle of intertemporal law, according to which 'a juridical fact must be appreciated in the light of the law contemporary with it,

[73] For present purposes, the terms 'abuse of rights' and 'abuse of process' are used interchangeably. The abuse of process doctrine is generally regarded as a subset of the abuse of rights doctrine, which in turn hails from the more general principle of good faith (see A. D. Mitchell and T. Malone, 'Abuse of Process in Inter-State Dispute Resolution', *Max Planck Encyclopedia of Public International Law* (December 2018), available at https://opil.ouplaw.com/home/MPIL). That said, nothing in the present analysis will bear on any differences existing between abuse of process and abuse of rights.

[74] The necessary assumption is being made here that the restructuring has resulted in something that can be legally characterised as an 'investment', thus raising no issues of jurisdiction *ratione materiae*.

[75] Article 28 of the VCLT states: 'Unless a different intention appears from the treaty or is otherwise established, its provisions do not bind a party in relation to any act or fact which took place or any situation which ceased to exist before the date of the entry into force of the treaty with respect to that party.'

[76] Article 13 of the ILC Articles on State Responsibility states: 'An act of a [s]tate does not constitute a breach of an international obligation unless the [s]tate is bound by the obligation in question at the time the act occurs.'

and not of the law in force at the time when a dispute in regard to it arises or falls to be settled'.[77] The intertemporal principle itself rests on the fundamental moral imperative that one cannot be asked to abide by a rule that does not exist at the time one acts.

Viewed in the context of ISDS, the principle of non-retroactivity requires both that the investment treaty must be in force at the time the investor–state dispute arises (e.g., when the measures under challenge were adopted by the state) and that the investor had made the investment before the dispute with the state arose.[78] This dual requirement follows from the fact that the investment treaty also serves a dual function. The investment treaty is at once (i) the instrument that creates the substantive obligations that form the basis of the investor's claim (meaning that the state cannot be held liable for an international obligation that did not exist when the challenged measures were taken) and (ii) the instrument that confers jurisdiction on the tribunal (meaning that a tribunal cannot review measures taken against claimants whose business at the time could not qualify as a covered 'investment'). In other words, any corporate restructuring leading to ownership or control of an 'investment' (jurisdiction *ratione materiae*) must be completed before the point in time when the dispute between the parties is deemed to have arisen.[79]

[77] *Island of Palmas*, Award, 845. To note, this principle of intertemporal law is with no prejudice to the principles of treaty interpretation. As the ILC's Commentary to Article 13 confirms:

> [T]he intertemporal principle does not entail that treaty provisions are to be interpreted as if frozen in time. The evolutionary interpretation of treaty provisions is permissible in certain cases, but this has nothing to do with the principle that a [s]tate can only be held responsible for breach of an obligation which was in force for that [s]tate at the time of its conduct.

(Draft Articles on Responsibility of States for Internationally Wrongful Acts (adopted by the ILC at its 53rd session, 23 April–1 June and 2 July–10 August 2001) (2001) Vol II (Part Two) *Yearbook of the International Law Commission* 26, 59 (para 9) [footnote omitted]).

[78] E.g., *Lao Holdings N.V.* v. *Lao People's Democratic Republic*, ICSID Case No. ARB(AF)/12/6, Decision on Jurisdiction, 21 February 2014, paras 68ff; *Pac Rim Cayman LLC* v. *Republic of El Salvador*, ICSID Case No. ARB/09/12, Decision on the Respondent's Jurisdictional Objections, 1 June 2012, paras 2.96ff; *Levy and Gremcitel* v. *Peru*, Award, paras 146–147.

[79] *Levy and Gremcitel* v. *Peru*, Award, paras 146–147. In determining the critical date, the tribunal (ibid., para 149) said:

> In the Tribunal's view, the critical date is the one on which the [s]tate adopts the disputed measure, even when the measure represents the culmination of a process or sequence of events which may have started years

Failure to fulfil this condition will inevitably deprive a tribunal of jurisdiction on *ratione temporis* grounds.

In conclusion, by working iteratively through the various aspects of the doctrine of jurisdiction in international law – from the more abstract doctrine of intertemporal law to the more concrete jurisdictional mechanics of investment treaties and ISDS – arbitrators do not have to directly confront the original moral dilemma between investors' economic freedom, on the one hand, and fairness towards the host state, on the other. The answer to the dilemma is in this instance provided by legal doctrine itself.

6.3.3 *Good Faith, Non-abuse of Rights, and the Doctrine of Admissibility in ISDS*

Even if investors are duly covered jurisdictionally, concerns could still arise about the potential abuse of their right to structure their business at will. As observed by Hersch Lauterpacht, the doctrine of abuse of rights indicates that '[t]here is no legal right, however well established, which could not, in some circumstances, be refused recognition on the ground that it has been abused'.[80] The doctrine of abuse of rights rests on the fairly abstract principle of good faith and on the fundamental moral imperative that society should not permit the unchecked use of rights, which is to say, the use of rights with no due regard paid to the social consequences arising out of their exercise. The social consequences at issue in cases of nationality planning pertain to investors' attempts to use the procedural right to initiate ISDS so as to obtain an unfair or illegitimate advantage over the host state.[81] Unfairness in this case results from

> earlier. It is not uncommon that divergences or disagreements develop over a period of time before they finally 'crystallize' in an actual measure affecting the investor's treaty rights.

For a similar approach, see *Venezuela Holdings* v. *Venezuela*, Jurisdiction, para 203:

> At that time [i.e., time of corporate restructuring], there were already pending disputes relating to royalties and income tax. However, nationalisation measures were taken by the Venezuelan authorities only from January 2007 on. Thus, the dispute over such nationalisation measures can only be deemed to have arisen after the measures were taken.

[80] H. Lauterpacht, *The Development of International Law by the International Court*, rev. ed. (London: Stevens & Sons, 1958), 164.

[81] Cf. similar statements in R. Kolb, 'General Principles of Procedural Law', in A. Zimmermann, C. J. Tams, and others (eds.), *The Statute of the International Court of Justice: A Commentary*, 3rd ed. (Oxford: Oxford University Press, 2019) 963, 998–999;

the fact that certain nationality planning and corporate restructuring activities may end up endowing the investor with international rights and protection to which it would not be entitled in the normal course of events.

The dimension of time is once again important to tribunals determining whether abuse is involved. Arbitral jurisprudence suggests that the right to structure one's investment at will is not abused when the dispute giving rise to the arbitration had not yet arisen at the time when the corporate restructuring took place. In *Venezuela Holdings* v. *Venezuela*, and well within its investment in the host state, the US investor (Delaware-incorporated Mobil Corporation) decided to alter the original corporate structure by introducing in the chain of ownership a Dutch company called Venezuela Holdings. The claimant admitted that this was done to protect Mobil's investment by gaining access to ICSID arbitration via the Netherlands-Venezuela BIT (1991). The tribunal found this to be 'a perfectly legitimate goal *as far as it concerned future disputes*'.[82] In a similar vein, the tribunal in *Transglobal* v. *Panama* had little trouble rejecting the investor's claim after concluding that the partnership and share transfer agreement between the Panamanian company La Mina and the US company Transglobal was signed with the sole aim to explore ways of legal redress via international arbitration in connection with a pre-existing contractual dispute between La Mina and the government of Panama.[83]

At the same time, tribunals have also made clear that corporate restructuring that took place at a point in time when a full-fledged legal dispute, although not yet arisen, was nonetheless a veritable certainty,[84]

International Law Association, Committee on International Commercial Arbitration, 'Interim Report: "*Res Judicata*" and Arbitration' (2004), 8.

[82] *Venezuela Holdings* v. *Venezuela*, Jurisdiction, para 204 (emphasis added).

[83] *Transglobal Green Energy, LLC and Transglobal Green Energy de Panama, S.A.* v. *The Republic of Panama*, ICSID Case No. ARB/13/28, Award, 2 June 2016. In particular, the aim of the partnership and share transfer agreement was to seek ways to execute and enforce via arbitration a decision of the Panamanian courts that was favourable to La Mina and related to the latter's pre-existing contractual dispute with the government (see, ibid., paras 116–118).

[84] E.g., *Lao Holdings* v. *Lao*, Jurisdiction, para 70:

> The Tribunal considers that it is clearly an abuse for an investor to manipulate the nationality of a company subsidiary to gain jurisdiction under an international treaty at a time when the investor is aware that events have occurred that negatively affect its investment and may lead to arbitration. In particular, abuse of process must preclude unacceptable

or even highly probable or foreseeable,[85] would still be contrary to the principle of good faith and thus amount to an abuse of the investor's freedom to structure its corporate nationality at will.[86]

It thus becomes apparent that tribunals in such cases address the original moral dilemma between safeguarding investors' economic freedom and ensuring fairness towards the host state in a more direct manner. This is done through the deployment of the rather abstract, yet widely held and accepted in international law, principle of good faith as concretised in the doctrine of abuse of rights/process.

A point of further reflection that tribunals must perform pertains to the doctrinal outcome to which the above cases give rise. Given that the investor would have formally complied with applicable nationality requirements, a successful abuse of process plea would typically result in a finding of inadmissibility as opposed to one of lack of jurisdiction. In *Pac Rim* v. *El Salvador*, for example, the tribunal stated that 'the Respondent's jurisdictional objection based on Abuse of Process by the Claimant does not, in legal theory, operate as a bar to the *existence* of

> manipulations by a claimant acting in bad faith who is fully aware prior to the change in nationality of the 'legal dispute'.

85 E.g., *Philip Morris Asia Limited* v. *The Commonwealth of Australia*, UNCITRAL Rules, PCA Case No. 2012-12, Award on Jurisdiction and Admissibility, 17 December 2015, para 545:

> [I]t may amount to an abuse of process to restructure an investment to obtain BIT benefits in respect of a foreseeable dispute;

Pac Rim v. *El Salvador*, Jurisdiction, para 2.99:

> In the Tribunal's view, the dividing-line occurs when the relevant party can see an actual dispute or can foresee a specific future dispute as a very high probability and not merely as a possible controversy. In the Tribunal's view, before that dividing-line is reached, there will be ordinarily no abuse of process; but after that dividing-line is passed, there ordinarily will be;

Levy and Gremcitel v. *Peru*, Award, para 185 (footnote omitted):

> [A] restructuring carried out with the intention to invoke the treaty's protections at a time when the dispute is foreseeable may constitute an abuse of process depending on the circumstances.

86 To note, the element of 'foreseeability' is used as an objective test to overcome the inherent limitations of proving the investor's subjective motives, or even bad faith, in having engaged in corporate restructuring. Fulfilling the element of 'foreseeability' thus creates a rebuttable presumption of abusive nationality planning. According to the tribunal in *Philip Morris* v. *Australia*, the presumption can be rebutted if the investor can demonstrate that legitimate reasons existed for the restructuring independently of the possibility of bringing a treaty claim against the host state (see *Philip Morris* v. *Australia*, Jurisdiction & Admissibility, paras 570ff).

the Tribunal's jurisdiction; but, rather, as a bar to the *exercise* of that jurisdiction, necessarily assuming jurisdiction to exist'.[87] Using substantially similar language, the tribunal in *Transglobal* v. *Panama* examined allegations of abusive nationality planning at a priority as 'a threshold issue that would bar the *exercise* of the Tribunal's jurisdiction even if jurisdiction *existed*'.[88] Although not stating it explicitly, these examples leave little doubt that an objection of abusive nationality planning takes aim at the admissibility of the investor's claims rather than at the tribunal's power to definitively rule on the abusive character of these claims.[89]

6.3.4 *Systemic Considerations, the Object and Purpose of the ICSID Convention, and the Disagreement in* Tokios Tokelės *v.* Ukraine

More controversially, nationality planning irrespective of its timing could potentially raise *ratione personae* jurisdictional impediments in ICSID arbitrations, as a consequence of the objective limitations imposed by the ICSID Convention on ICSID tribunals. According to this view, which does not seem to hold wide support in practice, a *ratione personae* jurisdictional bar may be possible in ICSID arbitrations even if nationality planning had occurred before the dispute and even if the dispute was not reasonably foreseeable to the investor at the time of corporate restructuring. This point was debated in the *Tokios Tokelės* v. *Ukraine* case. The case was brought by a Lithuanian company against Ukraine challenging measures taken by the latter against the former's wholly owned Ukrainian subsidiary. A key point of contention between the

[87] *Pac Rim* v. *El Salvador*, Jurisdiction, para 2.10 (and similarly, ibid., para 2.107) (emphases added).

[88] *Transglobal* v. *Panama*, Award, para 100 (emphases added).

[89] For additional examples of the same position expressed at various degrees of clarity, e.g., see *Philip Morris* v. *Australia*, Jurisdiction & Admissibility, para 588; *Levy and Gremcitel* v. *Peru*, Award, para 195; *Tidewater* v. *Venezuela*, Jurisdiction, paras 197–198; *Lao Holdings* v. *Lao*, Jurisdiction, paras 68–83; *Cementownia 'Nowa Huta' S.A.* v. *Republic of Turkey*, ICSID Case No. ARB(AF)/06/2, Award, 17 September 2009, paras 156–159. In a somewhat different context, see also *Banro American Resources, Inc. and Société Aurifère du Kivu et du Maniema S.A.R.L.* v. *Democratic Republic of the Congo*, ICSID Case No. ARB/98/7, Award (excerpts), 1 September 2000, (2002) 17 *ICSID Review – Foreign Investment Law Journal* 382, 383–391 (for a statement of the facts in *Banro*, see E. Obadia, '*Banro American Resources, Inc. and Société Aurifère du Kivu et du Maniema S.A.R.L.* v. *Democratic Republic of the Congo* [ICSID Case No. ARB/98/7]: Introductory Note' [2002] 17 *ICSID Review – Foreign Investment Law Journal* 380).

parties was whether Tokios Tokelés could be truly thought of as a 'foreign investor' in Ukraine given that Ukrainian nationals owned 99 per cent of its shares and comprised two-thirds of its management. No allegations were made and no evidence was adduced regarding fraud or purposeful corporate structuring to gain access to international arbitration in light of a foreseeable dispute.

The majority of the tribunal upheld jurisdiction. In so doing, it reasoned that because Article 25(2)(b) of the ICSID Convention does not specify the method for determining a corporation's nationality, deference must be extended to the contracting parties' chosen method as found in the definition of 'investor' of their investment treaty.[90] Presiding arbitrator Prosper Weil took a different view. Urging realism, he argued that what ought to have been decisive in that case was 'the simple, straightforward, objective fact that the dispute … [was] not between the Ukrainian [s]tate and a foreign investor but between the Ukrainian [s]tate and an Ukrainian investor'.[91] Weil argued further that, in deciding otherwise, the majority's decision was acting contrary to the object and purpose of the ICSID Convention, which was designed to facilitate the settlement of investment disputes that were 'foreign' vis-à-vis the host state.[92] In Weil's view, the majority decision had the effect of eroding the 'integrity' of the ICSID Convention and of the ICSID system.[93]

The dissent in *Tokios Tokelés* must be placed in its proper context to safeguard against unwarranted outcomes. Firstly, the dissent is meant as an argument against a finding of jurisdiction on *ratione personae* grounds, in ICSID arbitrations, and in cases where a company that is

90 *Tokios Tokelés* v. *Ukraine*, ICSID Case No. ARB/02/18, Decision on Jurisdiction, 29 April 2004, paras 24–52.

91 Ibid., Dissenting Opinion of P. Weil, para 21.

92 Ibid., paras 19–21. In making this claim, Weil relied on the widely held view that the ICSID Convention provides the outer limits of an ICSID tribunal's jurisdiction, beyond which state consent to ICSID arbitration is invalid. See ibid., para 16:

> While it is true that no definition of the nationality of corporations is to be found in the [ICSID] Convention, it cannot be the case that this definition is left to the discretion of the Parties, because it is not for the Parties to extend the jurisdiction of ICSID beyond what the Convention provides for. It is the Convention which determines the jurisdiction of ICSID, and it is within the limits of the ICSID jurisdiction as determined by the Convention that the Parties may in their BIT define the disputes they agree to submit to an ICSID arbitration.

93 Ibid., para 25.

incorporated in one of the contracting parties to an investment treaty is in fact ultimately owned or controlled by nationals of the host state. As such, any insights drawn from Weil's dissent should not be generalised to cover other instances of ultimate or beneficial ownership of a company by third country nationals, unless the investment treaty in question makes it clear that such companies are excluded from protection. Secondly, Weil's dissent is an argument about the interpretation of Article 25(2)(b) of the ICSID Convention, which provides the outer limits of an ICSID tribunal's *ratione personae* jurisdiction with respect to corporations.[94] It is thus not an argument about the interpretation of the nationality conditions of the investment treaty under which a dispute is brought.[95] Nevertheless, Weil's dissent has been controversial and not generally embraced by subsequent tribunals or scholars.[96] The majority

[94] See A. Broches, 'The Convention on the Settlement of Investment Disputes between States and Nationals of Other States' (1972) 136 *Recueil des cours* 331, 360–361.

[95] In this respect, cf. the decision in *The Rompetrol Group N.V.* v. *Romania*, ICSID Case No. ARB/06/3, Decision on Respondent's Preliminary Objections on Jurisdiction and Admissibility, 18 April 2008, paras 80–85, where the tribunal says in para 85 that 'Prof. Weil differed sharply from his co-arbitrators in [*Tokios Tokelés*], taking the view that economic reality should prevail over formal legal structure when it comes to the interpretation of both the ICSID Convention and the specific provisions of BITs for the purposes of ascertaining the nationality of corporate investors.' This statement does not appear to be entirely accurate. Weil's dissent addressed exclusively the interpretation of Article 25 of the ICSID Convention, and nowhere did it mention that economic reality should prevail in the interpretation of the nationality requirements of an investment treaty. It is therefore conceivable that were he presiding over a tribunal constituted under the UNCITRAL rules, as opposed to the ICSID rules, Weil would have had no issues in upholding jurisdiction over the *Tokios Tokelés* case following the provisions of the applicable BIT.

[96] For summaries of the generally negative reactions to the dissent, see C. McLachlan, L. Shore, and M. Weiniger, *International Investment Arbitration: Substantive Principles*, 2nd ed. (Oxford: Oxford University Press, 2017), 189–194 (esp. paras 5.121–5.125); C. Schreuer, L. Malintoppi, A. Reinisch, and A. Sinclair (eds.), *The ICSID Convention: A Commentary*, 2nd ed. (Cambridge: Cambridge University Press, 2009), 290; Baumgartner (n. 66), 105ff. For scholars in support of Weil's dissent, see E. C. Schlemmer, 'Investment, Investor, Nationality, and Shareholders', in P. Muchlinski, F. Ortino, and C. Schreuer (eds.), *The Oxford Handbook of International Investment Law* (Oxford: Oxford University Press, 2008) 49, 79–81; M. Burgstaller, 'Nationality of Corporate Investors and International Claims against the Investor's Own State' (2006) 7 *Journal of World Investment and Trade* 857. For an example of support in the case law, see *Venoklim Holding B.V.* v. *Bolivarian Republic of Venezuela*, ICSID Case No. ARB/12/22, Award, 3 April 2015, para 156 (to note, however, that the *Venoklim* award was not unanimous, with one of the arbitrators dissenting on this point precisely).

of tribunals have instead followed the ICJ's ruling in *Barcelona Traction*[97] in support of the position that incorporation is the dominant criterion of corporate nationality and that in-depth inquiries into a claimant's corporate structure are reserved only for instances of abuse of corporate form, including fraud or other attempts at avoiding liability.[98]

In *Tokios Tokelés*, the original moral dilemma between safeguarding investors' economic freedom and ensuring fairness towards the host state is laid bare. The tribunal's majority seems to have brought a singular context and framework to the resolution of the dispute – namely, the mechanics of jurisdiction under investment treaties – which provided a ready-made and inescapable answer to the moral dilemma. Weil, by contrast, introduced an additional relevant context and framework to the problem, which led him to insert an additional line of inquiry before rendering a decision. In his view, given the surprising and counter-intuitive practical consequences of the majority's approach, more reflection was required on the degree to which the mechanics of jurisdiction in

[97] *Case Concerning the Barcelona Traction, Light and Power Company, Limited (New Application: 1962, Belgium* v. *Spain), Second Phase*, Judgment of 5 February 1970, ICJ Rep (1970) 3, paras 56, 70. The use of *Barcelona Traction* as the guiding rule may be queried considering Aron Broches' contrary views on the matter. Widely regarded as the architect of the ICSID Convention, Broches pointed out that the *Barcelona Traction* case should have limited import in ICSID arbitrations and further clarified that, although Article 25 of the ICSID Convention implicitly assumes incorporation as a criterion of nationality, it does not indicate it as the only relevant criterion. On that note, it is moreover arguable that Weil's dissent in *Tokios Tokelés* may find some support in the spirit of the ICSID Convention. In particular, an indication supporting Weil's view may be gleaned by way of analogy from Broches' views on the permissibility of companies not incorporated in an ICSID contracting party to become a disputing party in ICSID proceedings. Broches argued that if a company and an ICSID country have agreed that the former be considered a national of an ICSID country despite its incorporation in a non-ICSID country, a tribunal should not hesitate to verify the company's nationality by 'taking into account not only formal criteria such as incorporation . . . but [by] adopting a broader approach which would give effect to economic realities such as ownership and control'. Broches also argued that if, nevertheless, a challenge to nationality is lodged in such a case, the tribunal should generally seek to uphold the parties' agreement, unless doing so 'would permit parties to use the Convention for purposes for which it was clearly not intended' (see Broches [n. 94], 360–361).

[98] E.g., *KT Asia Investment Group B.V.* v. *Republic of Kazakhstan*, ICSID Case No. ARB/09/8, Award, 17 October 2013, paras 111–139; *Rumeli Telekom A.S. and Telsim Mobil Telekomunikasyon Hizmetleri A.S.* v. *Republic of Kazakhstan*, ICSID Case No. ARB/05/16, Award, 29 July 2008, paras 202–206; *ADC Affiliate Limited and ADC & ADMC Management Limited* v. *The Republic of Hungary*, ICSID Case No. ARB/03/16, Award of the Tribunal, 2 October 2006, para 358.

investment treaties may be influenced and affected by the object and purpose of the ICSID Convention.

6.3.5 *(Dis-)Equilibrium, (In-)Coherence, and Just Outcomes:* Phoenix *v.* Czech Republic

The disagreement between the majority and the dissent in *Tokios Tokelés* raises an interesting question about the scope of the adjudicator's reflection. It was previously said that, in practice, the exact point when optimal reflective equilibrium is achieved cannot be identified by an advance test or in the abstract. Still, how can one begin to determine when such a point is being reached? Further, is it possible that a failure to pursue one's reflection until such a point is reached could still result in overall incoherence, despite the final outcome's correctness or moral appeal? The decision in *Phoenix* v. *Czech Republic* offers an illuminating example and some preliminary answers.

6.3.5.1 The Facts and the Tribunal's Reasoning

The dispute in *Phoenix* involved two Czech companies (Benet Praha and Benet Group) that were wholly owned by the Israeli company Phoenix Action. Phoenix Action had been created by the owner of the two Czech companies (himself a Czech citizen) for the sole purpose of buying Benet Praha and Benet Group after the actions complained about during the arbitration had been taken against them by the Czech Republic. It was thus clear from the evidence on the record that the incorporation of Phoenix Action in Israel was 'simply a rearrangement of assets within a family, to gain access to ICSID jurisdiction to which the initial investor was not entitled'.[99] At the same time, there were no allegations made or evidence adduced that the purchase of the shares had been done in any way illegally or in contravention to the laws of the Czech Republic – a point also confirmed by the tribunal.[100] The tribunal ultimately concluded that it did not enjoy jurisdiction *ratione materiae* over the dispute, in effect dismissing the case due to the absence of a protected investment. It is interesting to query how it arrived at this conclusion.

In its analysis, the tribunal was quick to determine that it had jurisdiction *ratione personae* (Phoenix being a national of Israel) and jurisdiction

[99] *Phoenix Action, Ltd.* v. *The Czech Republic*, ICSID Case No. ARB/06/5, Award, 15 April 2009, para 140.

[100] Ibid., para 134.

ratione voluntatis (both the Czech Republic and the investor having consented to the arbitration).[101] It also held that it lacked jurisdiction *ratione temporis* for any claims arising out of disputes between Benet Praha, Benet Group, and the Czech Republic that pre-dated the acquisition of those companies by Phoenix, or post-dated Phoenix's eventual sale of its interests in them to an unrelated third company.[102] Left only with determining the question of jurisdiction *ratione materiae*, the tribunal began by examining the concept of a protected 'investment' under the ICSID Convention. In so doing, the tribunal clarified that it would be interpreting the ICSID Convention in light of its object and purpose and according to the general principles of international law.[103]

Starting with the object and purpose of the ICSID Convention, the tribunal concluded that this was to 'encourage and protect international investment made for the purpose of contributing to the economy of the host [s]tate'.[104] From this general statement of purpose, the tribunal then extrapolated two conditions that a purported investment must fulfil in order to be subject to the protection of the ICSID Convention: first, it must be foreign vis-à-vis the host state (i.e., it cannot be used to camouflage a domestic claim as an international one); second, it must be undertaken with an economic activity in mind, and not for the sole purpose of pursuing an ICSID claim against the host state. Transactions that do not fulfil either of these two conditions are abusive of the ICSID system and thus would not be protected as 'investments' under it.[105]

The tribunal then moved to the applicable BIT's definition of investment but, rather than engaging with it directly, it took a side-step into principle, and in particular, the principle of good faith a component of which is the prohibition of abusing one's right.[106] Good faith is the cornerstone of the *Phoenix* decision, as it is against this principle that the terms of the ICSID Convention and the applicable BIT are viewed. The tribunal's general position on the role of good faith is summarised in the following two statements:

[101] Ibid., paras 65–66.
[102] Ibid., paras 67–71.
[103] Ibid., para 80.
[104] Ibid., para 87 (emphasis in original omitted).
[105] Ibid., paras 88–95.
[106] The tribunal's related inquiry into the legality of Phoenix's investment under Czech law is here omitted. As mentioned, there was no evidence of any illegality in this case.

> The purpose of the international mechanism of protection of investment through ICSID arbitration cannot be to protect investments made in violation of the laws of the host [s]tate or investments not made in good faith, obtained for example through misrepresentations, concealments or corruption, or amounting to an abuse of the international ICSID arbitration system. In other words, the purpose of international protection is to protect legal and *bona fide* investments;[107]

and

> States cannot be deemed to offer access to the ICSID dispute settlement mechanism to investments not made in good faith. The protection of international investment arbitration cannot be granted if such protection would run contrary to the general principles of international law, among which the principle of good faith is of utmost importance.[108]

As to the consequences of violating the principle of good faith, the tribunal relied on the *Inceysa* v. *El Salvador* and *Plama* v. *Bulgaria* decisions for the proposition that a breach of good faith is synonymous to a breach of both national and international law.[109] Having found no violation of the principle at the national level, the tribunal instead focused on 'the international principle of good faith as applied to the international arbitration mechanism of ICSID'.[110] This allowed the tribunal to re-evaluate its legal test for determining the existence of an investment in the form of an expanded *Salini* test, which now included a contribution in money or other assets, a certain duration, the element of risk, an operation made in order to develop an economic activity in the host state, assets invested in accordance with the laws of the host state, and assets invested *bona fide*.[111]

In applying this test, the tribunal held, unsurprisingly, that Phoenix's operations in the Czech Republic satisfied all elements but *bona fides*. All the facts surrounding Phoenix's case indeed led to the unavoidable conclusion that '[t]he unique goal of the "investment" was to transform

[107] *Phoenix* v. *Czech Republic*, Award, para 100 (footnote omitted).

[108] Ibid., para 106.

[109] Ibid., paras 111–112.

[110] Ibid., para 113 (emphasis in original omitted). The tribunal (ibid.) further clarified that its task was to 'prevent an abuse of the system of international investment protection under the ICSID Convention, in ensuring that only investments that are made in compliance with the international principle of good faith and do not attempt to misuse the system are protected'.

[111] Ibid., paras 114ff.

a pre-existing domestic dispute into an international dispute subject to ICSID arbitration under a bilateral investment treaty'.[112]

6.3.5.2 Analysis

It should be stated at the outset that the decision in its final outcome is correct to have dismissed the case. Yet the tribunal's approach in doing so is criticisable for arguably lacking in adequate reflection and thus resulting in incoherence, both internally in the award itself as well as systemically in the broader context of international investment law and ISDS. The following points may be raised against the tribunal's reasoning in particular.

First, the tribunal seems to contradict itself in its examination of its *ratione temporis* jurisdiction. The tribunal begins by declining jurisdiction for treaty claims linked to domestic law disputes that pre-dated Phoenix's acquisition of the two Czech companies. This implies that there exists a legal question that is properly brought before the tribunal timewise. But later, in examining the abuse of process argument, the tribunal finds that the sole purpose of the investment was to bring a pre-existing domestic dispute at the international level. This means that there was never a legitimate dispute from a temporal standpoint. One thus wonders, if the tribunal had all the evidence to make that assertion available to it already at the jurisdictional stage, why it did not decline jurisdiction *ratione temporis* in the first place. A plausible answer could have been that perhaps the alleged breaches were continuous in nature and ended up affecting Phoenix's investment (i.e., its shareholding in the two Czech companies), so that a prima facie plausible case could be said to exist jurisdictionally. But based on the decision's scant discussion of these issues, it seems that the tribunal did not believe this to be the case.[113]

Second, a similar contradiction seems to have taken place also with respect to the tribunal's *ratione personae* jurisdiction. The contradiction here is more implicit. Recall that the tribunal first asserted jurisdiction *ratione personae* given Phoenix's incorporation in Israel and later went to deny jurisdiction *ratione materiae* for lack of an investment. The reasons offered for the denial were, first, that Phoenix intentionally engaged in

[112] Ibid., para 142.

[113] E.g., see ibid., para 136 ('[A]ll the damages claimed by Phoenix had already *occurred* and were *inflicted* on the two Czech companies, when the alleged investment was made.' [emphases added]).

abusive nationality planning by trying to bring an essentially domestic dispute to the international plane and, second, that the ICSID regime was not designed to protect such activities.[114] These reasons echo somewhat the disagreement in the *Tokios Tokelés* v. *Ukraine* case examined previously, which the *Phoenix* tribunal briefly discusses in paragraph 94 of its decision siding itself with the position of the majority. In particular, the *Phoenix* tribunal seems to use the *Tokios Tokelés* majority decision for the proposition that a national of the host state may not structure his or her investment so as to get the advantages of ICSID arbitration against that state after the acts alleged to have caused damage to the investment had been committed.[115]

However, this is a mischaracterisation of the *Tokios Tokelés* decision. Recall that the controversy there was about the interpretation to be given to Article 25(2)(b) of the ICSID Convention on the nationality of corporations (i.e., a *ratione personae* question). In particular, the disagreement was whether incorporation is the only relevant criterion for determining corporate nationality *in the absence* of proof that the claimant had abused its legal personality to gain access to arbitration. The majority in *Tokios Tokelés* replied 'yes' to this question and Weil disagreed. Not only is this a fundamentally different legal question than the one at issue in *Phoenix*, but it also gives rise to the following contradiction in the latter arising from the reliance on *Tokios Tokelés* as authority. By treating its case and the *Tokios Tokelés* case as analogues vis-à-vis the jurisdictional relevance of the claimant's abusive intentions, the *Phoenix* tribunal may be rendering its own discussion on *ratione materiae* jurisdiction beside the point and unnecessary. Since all the evidence were available to the tribunal to determine the claimant's abusive intentions in *Phoenix*, following the tribunal's thinking would mean that it could had already declared itself without jurisdiction *ratione personae* despite its earlier conclusion to the contrary (which, recall, relied on the fact that Phoenix was a national of Israel).

Third, the decision's overall coherence is also affected by the tribunal's overstatement of the role of good faith, particularly through the latter's inclusion as a jurisdictional element under Article 25(1) of the ICSID Convention. Coherence is here affected in related ways. Even though there seem to exist several conceptions of good faith in international

[114] Ibid., para 144.
[115] Ibid., para 94.

law,[116] the decision does not specify in what capacity it uses the principle. The silence has far-reaching implications, not only because it introduces a great deal of uncertainty at the jurisdictional stage but also because it seems to affect international lawyers' collective understanding of the doctrine of adjudicative jurisdiction.

Let us begin with the tribunal's silence on the conception of good faith it means to use. Perhaps the tribunal meant to use good faith in a subjective sense as a way to describe the psychological state of the 'morally-worthy-of-protection investor'. But violating some directive or some piece of legislation does not automatically imply the violator's lack of subjective good faith.[117] Mistakes can be made unknowingly and in good faith. Consequently, if a tribunal is concerned with protecting the integrity of the ICSID system from abuses, as the *Phoenix* tribunal indeed seems to be, should it really matter whether the claimant knew that what he or she was doing when structuring the investment may had been forbidden or frowned upon?

But perhaps the tribunal meant to use good faith in an objective, normative capacity. Indeed, this seems more likely. However, other issues arise yet again because it is not entirely clear in doctrine whether good faith can be an autonomous source of legal obligation or, even if it can be such a source, whether it is always so. For instance, the ICJ seems to have treated good faith as an autonomous source of legal obligation in *Nuclear Tests*, having found that a series of public statements by French

[116] E.g., see R. Kolb, 'Principles as Sources of International Law (With Special Reference to Good Faith)' (2006) 53 *Netherlands International Law Review* 1, 13–20, who distinguishes between three conceptions of good faith as follows. The first is a subjective and psychological conception, referring to some sort of inner knowledge and moral correctness. In its subjective sense, good faith has no normativity and its application in international law is limited. The second conception of good faith takes the form of an open-ended legal standard. As a legal standard, good faith may be ancillary to a general principle or a specific legal norm thus aiding to their better application (i.e., good faith as reasonableness) or it may be autonomous, in which case good faith is simply a *renvoi* to the discretion of the adjudicator to act *ex aequo et bono* and according to universal principles of law. The third conception of good faith is good faith as a general principle of law. In this third conception, good faith has an objective character and can create legal rights and duties for international actors.

[117] E.g., see Appellate Body Report, *United States – Continued Dumping and Subsidy Offset Act of 2000*, WT/DS217AB/R, WT/DS234/AB/R, 16 January 2003, para 298 ('Nothing, however, in the covered agreements supports the conclusion that simply because a WTO Member is found to have violated a substantive treaty provision, it has therefore not acted in good faith. In our view, it would be necessary to prove more than mere violation to support such a conclusion.').

government officials, including the French President, that no further atmospheric nuclear tests would be conducted in the future, created a binding legal obligation upon France.[118] But in subsequent cases, the Court nuanced this position by saying that good faith cannot be a source of obligation where none would otherwise exist,[119] thus making good faith look more like an ancillary standard (i.e., good faith as reasonableness).

More critically, irrespective of whether good faith in *Phoenix* was seen as an autonomous source of obligation or as a standard of reasonableness, the principle creates considerable uncertainty (over- and under-inclusiveness) going beyond the problem of abusive nationality planning. With respect to good faith as a source, it is not clear exactly what kind of legal obligations good faith can create beyond the obvious ones regarding corruption, fraud, or a manifest abuse of rights. For instance, does structuring one's business in a way that ensures that the minimum amount of tax (or indeed no tax at all) is paid to the host state count as an investment not made in good faith vis-à-vis that state?[120] The

[118] *Nuclear Tests Case (Australia* v. *France)*, Judgment of 20 December 1974, ICJ Rep (1974) 253, para 46; *Nuclear Tests Case (New Zealand* v. *France)*, Judgment of 20 December 1974, ICJ Rep (1974) 457, para 49. The Court said in particular (emphasis added):

> One of the basic principles governing the *creation and performance* of legal obligations, whatever their source, is the principle of good faith. Trust and confidence are inherent in international co-operation, in particular in an age when this co-operation in many fields is becoming increasingly essential. Just as the very rule of *pacta sunt servanda* in the law of treaties is based on good faith, so also is the binding character of an international obligation assumed by unilateral declaration. Thus interested [s]tates may take cognizance of unilateral declarations and place confidence in them, and are entitled to require that the obligation thus created be respected.

[119] E.g., *Case Concerning Border and Transborder Armed Actions (Nicaragua* v. *Honduras), Jurisdiction and Admissibility*, Judgment of 20 December 1988, ICJ Rep (1988) 69, para 94; and later in, *Case Concerning the Land and Maritime Boundary between Cameroon and Nigeria (Cameroon* v. *Nigeria), Preliminary Objections*, Judgment of 11 June 1998, ICJ Rep (1998) 275, para 39.

[120] In this respect, cf. the reaction to the *Phoenix* approach by the tribunal in *Saba Fakes* v. *Republic of Turkey*, ICSID Case No. ARB/07/20, Award, 14 July 2010, para 112 (footnote omitted):

> [T]he principles of good faith and legality cannot be incorporated into the definition of Article 25(1) of the ICSID Convention without doing violence to the language of the ICSID Convention: an investment might be 'legal' or 'illegal', made in 'good faith' or not, it nonetheless remains an investment. The expressions 'legal investment' or 'investment made in

situation is similar with respect to good faith as a standard. What does it mean to say that the ICSID Convention ought to recognise as investments only economic projects that were made 'reasonably'? Reasonably with respect to what and according to whose test? Suppose, for instance, that a foreign claimant has controlling interest in local companies owning mining licences in the host state. Suppose also that these licences are fake and that the claimant had shown a striking lack of due diligence in this respect.[121] The claimant may well be unreasonable to believe that the mining project is lawful, but does this automatically mean that a tribunal does not have jurisdiction *ratione materiae* over a potential dispute? If yes, what about the fact that the claimant had lawfully acquired the shares in the local companies in question, which, according to most investment treaties, is recognised as a protected investment in its own right?

The more general point to be made is that principles, such as good faith, do not immediately offer ready-made and concrete solutions in individual cases. Rather, they offer arguments in support of a general direction that must be weighed against competing arguments, which themselves are based on competing principles or rules.[122] The absence of good faith may thus give a tribunal reason to find a violation of international law but cannot necessitate such an outcome in each and every case where good faith becomes relevant as a general principle. Indeed, in the two awards – *Inceysa* v. *El Salvador* and *Plama* v. *Bulgaria* – relied in *Phoenix* for support for the use of the principle of good faith, the tribunals did not just have the claimants' lack of good faith to rely on but also the fact that the claimants in those cases had committed fraud or had engaged in corrupt practices in direct contravention of domestic laws.

Seen in a broader context, there are two systemic dangers in following the *Phoenix* approach to jurisdiction. Firstly, the exact content of good faith being an elusive and highly contextual one, there is the risk of

good faith' are not pleonasms, and the expressions 'illegal investment' or 'investment made in bad faith' are not oxymorons.

121 These are, in a nutshell, the critical facts in the consolidated case *Churchill Mining Plc and Planet Mining Pty Ltd* v. *Republic of Indonesia*, ICSID Case No. ARB/12/14 and 12/40, Decision on Jurisdiction, 24 February 2014; and *Churchill Mining Plc and Planet Mining Pty Ltd* v. *Republic of Indonesia*, ICSID Case No. ARB/12/14 and 12/40, Award, 6 December 2016.

122 R. Dworkin, *Taking Rights Seriously* (Cambridge, MA: Harvard University Press, 1977), 26.

allowing ISDS tribunals a considerable margin of discretion in determining whether they should entertain a case or not. Secondly, and relatedly, the *Phoenix* approach risks changing the nature of the doctrine of adjudicative jurisdiction by modifying our understanding of what the doctrine is for. Traditionally, a determination of jurisdiction is only concerned with the narrow question of whether a court or tribunal is properly vested with adjudicatory power. Given this, a jurisdictional challenge should only take aim at the tribunal and its power to decide. It should not, however, concern the question of whether the claimant deserves the protection of the international arbitration system or whether it deserves a remedy. As pointed out in Chapter 5, such questions should rather be addressed by the doctrine of admissibility of claims, if the defects alleged are severe enough (i.e., if they violate international public policy) or should be otherwise addressed as a merits issue. If considerations of desert are treated as jurisdictional, the doctrines of jurisdiction and admissibility risk collapsing into each other. Keeping the two doctrines may add in complexity. Yet, as also seen in Chapter 5, doing so is conducive towards more coherent reasoning and more principled solutions. Eliding the distinction may lead to undesirable consequences with respect to the interests of the disputing parties,[123] our sense of justice,[124] or indeed the integrity of the ICSID system on the whole.[125]

[123] For example, in the context of sanctioning fraud and corruption, Douglas has argued that making such determinations may require evidence that might not be available to the tribunal during the initial stages of a dispute or may require a detailed examination of the equities arising out of both disputing parties' conduct under the domestic law of the host state (see Z. Douglas, 'The Plea of Illegality in Investment Treaty Arbitration' [2014] 29 *ICSID Review – Foreign Investment Law Journal* 155, 162, 176, 183–184, 185).

[124] E.g., see *Copper Mesa Mining Corporation* v. *Republic of Ecuador*, PCA No. 2012-2, Award, 15 March 2016, paras 5.54–5.56; *Fraport AG Frankfurt Airport Services Worldwide* v. *The Republic of the Philippines*, ICSID Case No. ARB/03/25, Award, 16 August 2007, Dissenting Opinion of Mr Bernardo M. Cremades, paras 36–41.

[125] E.g., cf. *Niko Resources (Bangladesh) Ltd.* v. *People's Republic of Bangladesh, Bangladesh Petroleum Exploration & Production Company Limited ('Bapex') and Bangladesh Oil Gas and Mineral Corporation ('Petrobangla')*, ICSID Case Nos. ARB/10/11 and ARB/10/18, Decision on Jurisdiction, 19 August 2013, para 474:

> The Tribunal is mindful of the importance of the ICSID dispute settlement mechanism and its integrity. In the Tribunal's view, such integrity is promoted, and not violated, by the adjudication of disputes submitted to the Centre under a valid consent to arbitrate. Faced with a binding arbitration agreement and subject to the specific requirements under the ICSID Convention ... the Tribunal must address the substance of the dispute. In so doing, the integrity of the system is protected by the

In conclusion, while seeking to address the systemic problem of abusive nationality planning and to promote coherence in the law by appeal to higher principle, the tribunal in *Phoenix* may have achieved the opposite result by not adequately reflecting upon the consequences of its own reasoning. The overall coherence of the *Phoenix* decision thus suffers, not only because it contains important internal contradictions but also because of the statements of principle used to justify the outcome. One may still understand what the tribunal sought to do yet may feel puzzled or even apprehensive with respect to the steps it took to do so, since its reflection was stopped before a point of optimal equilibrium could be achieved. More reflection on the desirability of each of the argumentative steps in terms of their conformity to the normative background, their consistency with the implications created by earlier argumentative steps, as well as their practical consequences (whether desirable or problematic),[126] would have likely yielded a more appropriate resting place with respect to the identified legal grounds for the decision. Transposing this to the context of the *Phoenix* case, more reflection would have instructed the tribunal, for instance, to take heed of the nuances between the different facets of adjudicative jurisdiction and the relation between adjudicative jurisdiction and related doctrines, to further scrutinise past awards cited as governing authorities, and to take into account the systemic implications that would follow from using good faith as a jurisdictional criterion. Stopping the reflective exercise short ultimately resulted in the final outcome being legally questionable despite its compelling moral correctness.

6.4 Conclusion

The chapter's thesis has been that coherence and a commitment to reflexivity are intrinsically connected concepts in judicial reasoning. Reflexivity is conducive towards coherent reasoning and, consequently, the degree of a decision-maker's reflexivity can act as an indicator of the decision's overall coherence. As used in this chapter, reflexivity refers to a general disposition of self-awareness and self-examination, whereby one examines one's motivations and how these motivations influence one's

resolution of the contentions made (including allegations of violation of public policy) rather than by avoiding them.

126 For this threefold process of reflection/evaluation, see the analysis in Schön (n. 18), 93–102.

action. Reflexivity encompasses a particular way of thinking about a subject and a particular way of seeking to justify actions, both of which, it has been argued, bear a strong link to coherence in adjudication and judicial decision-making. Three key conclusions may thus be drawn out of the present chapter's discussion on coherence as reflexivity.

Firstly, being reflective during adjudication means being attune to the consequential, purposive, and inquisitorial/rational dimensions of judicial decision-making. A reflective investment arbitrator thus recognises the importance that framing, contextualisation, chosen ends, and background assumptions play in the judicial process and stands ready to evaluate these if required by the circumstances of the case. A reflective arbitrator works iteratively, making judgments about the instant case and about the general theories, values, or principles that motivate his or her judgments. The arbitrator recognises that these are indispensable elements of the reasoning process, even though it is often the case in practice that general theories, values, and abstract principles remain hidden and implicit in the final decision.

Secondly, in approaching his or her work in the manner just described, the reflective arbitrator aims towards optimal reflective equilibrium before committing to an outcome. Optimal reflective equilibrium describes the point where the various component judgments, principles, and theories are ones we are not inclined to revise any further because, taken together, they have the highest degree of acceptability or credibility. Reflective evaluation takes place within a threefold framework. The desirability of each argumentative step is assessed in terms of its conformity to the prevailing normative background, its consistency with the implications created by earlier steps, and the consequences (whether desirable or problematic) that it will likely create. Taken together, these assessments help the arbitrator to identify an appropriate resting place for the judicial inquiry and to identify legal grounds for the decision.

Thirdly, it follows from the above that reflexivity also implies moral responsibility on the part of the decision-maker. This is to say that reflexivity implies certain desirable dispositions, or virtues, according to which the entire process of reasoning should be conducted. Moral responsibility becomes even more important in the judicial context, given the latter's authoritative power to alter the legal positions of the disputing parties and the fact that the judicial function is discharged through collegial bodies where substantive disagreement among the decision-makers often occurs. Indeed, it is possible for one adjudicator's individual process of reflection to coincide with, or differ from, another's on the same bench or panel. When this happens, common ground must be found. Chapter 7 thus concludes this book's examination of coherence by exploring in more detail the notion of moral responsibility in the particular collegial context of ISDS.

7

Coherence as Moral Responsibility

7.1 Introduction

Chapter 6 argued that the search for coherence requires an overall judicial attitude of reflexivity. Reflexivity was defined as self-awareness and self-examination whereby an arbitrator examines his or her motivations and how these may influence his or her reasoning and decisions. However, in practice, arbitrators do not work individually or in isolation. Barring the rare instance of sole arbitrator appointments,[1] arbitrators typically come together to deliberate collectively in groups. In such a setting, an individual arbitrator's process of reflection may coincide with, or differ from, another's on the same panel. This is by no means unique to ISDS. Adjudicators frequently agree on certain aspects of a case but disagree on others. For instance, they may agree on the outcome of the case but disagree on what would be the better way to achieve it.[2] When substantive disagreement occurs, common ground must be found.

This is now the challenge before us. How can reflexivity be promoted in the collective context of ISDS, so as to help bridge individually held views that often come into competition or conflict? The response that this chapter offers is that collective reflexivity can be promoted by acknowledging the presence of moral responsibility in arbitrators and

[1] Sole arbitrator appointments are indeed rare in ISDS. According to UNCTAD's ISDS Navigator database, sole arbitrator appointments have been made in a mere 10 treaty-based ISDS cases to date (out of a total of 1,190 treaty-based ISDS cases recorded as of the end of 2021). UNCTAD's ISDS Navigator database can be accessed at https://investmentpolicy.unctad.org/investment-dispute-settlement.

[2] E.g., cf. J. Shi, 'Speech by H.E. Judge Shi Jiuyong, President of the International Court of Justice, to the Sixth Committee of the General Assembly of the United Nations: The Internal Working Practice of the International Court of Justice' (28 October 2005), available at www.icj-cij.org/en/statements-by-the-president, 6 ('In order to fully understand the difficulty of the task of the [ICJ] drafting committee, it is important to note that even when Members of the Court agree on an outcome, they frequently disagree on the manner of reaching that outcome.').

by committing to five distinct judicial virtues, namely: faith, humility, acquiescence, integrity, and candour. In putting this argument forward, it is important to make clear at the outset that this is not a formula or an equation for the courtroom. Judicial virtues are habits and mental dispositions. As such, they are meant to be taken as a framework offering guidelines and a roadmap to develop better deliberative practices in ISDS. In that sense, the aim of the argument advanced here is a modest one. At the same time, the aim of the discussion in this chapter is also to serve as a synthesis of the arguments made throughout the book on the role of coherence in legal reasoning.

The discussion proceeds as follows. Section 7.2 begins by introducing the challenge of collective reflexivity in judicial decision-making. It argues that this challenge is linked to two general features of adjudication, namely, its collegial nature and the frequent substantive disagreements around its institutional aims. Section 7.3 then establishes a link between collective reflexivity as a goal and judicial moral responsibility as a method of work for arbitrators in ISDS. The section first identifies a series of factors unique to ISDS that make collective reflexivity harder to sustain in that context, before shedding light on the importance of arbitrators exercising individual moral responsibility. The same section also examines in greater detail the concept of individual moral responsibility as this applies in a judicial setting, as well as its relationship with five distinct judicial virtues called faith, humility, acquiescence, integrity, and candour. Sections 7.4–7.7 then use each of the identified judicial virtues to assess aspects of observable arbitral behaviour in ISDS. Section 7.8 summarises and concludes.

7.2 The Challenge of Collective Reflexivity

To make the case that a commitment to moral responsibility and to a series of judicial virtues can help arbitrators meet the challenge of collective reflexivity in ISDS, one must first examine two features of adjudication that are fundamental to the relationship between adjudicating disputes, on the one hand, and judicial moral responsibility, on the other. The two features in question are adjudication's collegial setting (Section 7.2.1) and institutional aims (Section 7.2.2). Clarifying what each of them entails naturally leads one to the notion of judicial moral responsibility. The latter will be elaborated further in Section 7.3 and in the remainder of the chapter.

7.2.1 *Adjudication's Collegial Setting*

A collective enterprise, broadly speaking, exists when individuals join in a coordinated effort and in pursuit of a common goal.[3] Evidently, courts and tribunals are collective bodies in this sense and, consequently, adjudication is a collective enterprise overall. What is perhaps less evident is an understanding of what such a characterisation of adjudication means. Lewis Kornhauser and Lawrence Sager usefully distinguish four types of collective enterprises, which they call 'distributed', 'team', 'redundant', and 'collegial'.[4] Each type is distinguished from the others by two kinds of variables, which are (i) the identification of the principal agent(s) of performance and (ii) the resultant modalities of internal coordination among the enterprises' participants. Distributed and team enterprises seek to amplify individual performance and reshape it into the group's performance.[5] On the opposite end, redundant and collegial enterprises seek to represent the group's effort as if it were the output of a single individual.[6] When international courts and tribunals deliver decisions, they invariably speak with one voice. That is to say, it is not the individual adjudicators who are projected outward as the authors of decisions, nor is it the court's or tribunal's 'majority' in cases where there exists a dissent.[7] This means that, in terms of the principal agent of performance,

[3] L. A. Kornhauser and L. G. Sager, 'The One and the Many: Adjudication in Collegial Courts' (1993) 81 *California Law Review* 1, 3.

[4] Ibid.

[5] However, in so doing, distributed and team enterprises adopt different approaches to internal coordination. According to Kornhauser and Sager (ibid., 3–4), distributed enterprises primarily aim towards efficiency, for instance, by amplifying effort or multiplying production given a common goal. Such enterprises can be simple, when all participants have identical tasks (e.g., workers painting a house), or more complex, when each participant is assigned a different task (e.g., workers on an assembly line). Even though participants in distributed enterprises typically act in isolation, the prior structuring of their tasks assures the necessary coordination effort. In team enterprises, by contrast, participants must actively work to coordinate their actions. As each participant performs, he or she must also consider, and react to, the performance of the other participants (e.g., team sports). Team enterprises thus primarily aim to transform the collective performance into something that only the group could have produced. Interaction among the participants in team enterprises is therefore valued intrinsically, which is to say, not just for its efficiency but also for its own sake and for the outcome it produces.

[6] Kornhauser and Sager, ibid., 4.

[7] Indeed, ICJ decisions are delivered by 'the Court', ITLOS and arbitral decisions (including in ISDS) are delivered by 'the Tribunal' in each case, decisions by the WTO DSU are delivered by 'the Panel' or 'the Appellate Body', decisions by the International Criminal Court are delivered by 'the Chamber' or 'the Appeals Chamber', and so on and so forth.

adjudication does not track the models of distributed or team enterprises. It also means that the models of redundant and collegial enterprises are both prima facie suitable templates for describing the collective nature of adjudication.

One must therefore consider the modalities of internal coordination between collegial and redundant enterprises. Indeed, this is where the critical difference between the two models lies. Redundant enterprises rely on multiple independent efforts that are aggregated into a single collective outcome (e.g., judges grading athletic events).[8] As a result, participants in such enterprises tend to be independent and their performances are often linked together by procedural rules rather than by internal collaboration or deliberation.[9] By contrast, in collegial enterprises, participants do not act independently from each other. Internal collaboration and deliberation are critical elements in collegial enterprises, as each participant must take into account the performance of his or her fellow participants (e.g., co-authors writing a novel).[10]

To be sure, there exist certain aspects of the adjudicative process that resemble a redundant enterprise.[11] For example, adjudicators at times work independently of their colleagues, reasoning about the just outcome for the case before them as if each was deciding the case alone on the court's or tribunal's behalf. The practice of the ICJ is a good example.[12] Following the closure of oral hearings and the so-called 'Article 3 Deliberation' phase (where judges come together to identify the legal issues that must be addressed in the decision) comes the 'Judges' Written Notes' phase under Article 4 of the Court's Internal Practice Resolution. During this phase, each judge individually commits to paper his or her tentative opinion on the answers that should be given to the questions of law presented before the Court and on the correct disposal of the case. In

8 Kornhauser and Sager (n. 3), 4.

9 Ibid.

10 Ibid., 4–5.

11 Indeed, as Kornhauser and Sager (ibid., 5) clarify, collective enterprises need not come in ideal types in practice. Some collective enterprises may be hybrids and may thus exhibit features of multiple ideal types to a greater or lesser extent.

12 The deliberative practice of the ICJ is outlined in the Resolution Concerning the Internal Judicial Practice of the Court (Internal Practice Resolution), available at www.icj-cij.org/en/other-texts/resolution-concerning-judicial-practice. An insider's perspective of the Court's deliberative practice can also be found in Shi (n. 2); and B. Simma and J. Ortgies, 'Deliberation and Drafting: International Court of Justice (ICJ)', *Max Planck Encyclopedia of Public International Law* (January 2019), available at https://opil.ouplaw.com/home/MPIL.

that sense, during the written notes phase, the deliberative practice of the ICJ resembles a redundant enterprise insofar as each judge solves the case individually as if he or she was deciding alone on the Court's behalf.

However, on the whole, adjudication tracks closer to the template of a collegial enterprise, especially during times of actual deliberation or during the drafting of a decision. Continuing with the example of the ICJ, following the written notes phase the so-called 'Article 5 Deliberation' phase takes place. This brings all judges together to collectively exchange views about the disposal of the case. A drafting committee is elected among the judges of the majority to write a preliminary draft judgment, which is subsequently circulated for comments and debated over two rounds of readings by all judges sitting together.[13] It thus follows that adjudicating a dispute is not simply about aggregating and tallying individually held opinions. Rather, it is about finding common ground through deliberation and projecting a unified view.[14] Indeed, such a view seems to better match lawyers' common understanding and expectations of adjudication as a practice as well.[15]

[13] Articles 6 and 7 of the Internal Practice Resolution.

[14] In this respect, also cf. Shi (n. 2), 6:

> Having taken part in many deliberations and drafting committees, I can guarantee you that the drafting of a Court's judgment is a complicated, arduous and very meticulous exercise. . . . [T]he drafting committee has to put into writing the majority view emerging from the deliberations. In the best case scenario, when all judges agree on the outcome of the case, that means turning 15 or more individual voices into one coherent decision. In the worst case, that means setting down the views of the majority while at the same time trying to accommodate the views of the minority on the less contentious points.

[15] E.g., see E. Jouannet, 'La motivation ou le mystère de la boite noire', in H. Ruiz Fabri and J.-M. Sorel (eds.), *La motivation des décisions des juridictions internationales* (Paris: Pedone, 2008) 251, 270–271 (describing judicial deliberation in a similar manner, i.e., as a process seeking to achieve compromise among divergent opinions). As clarified in n. 11, it may still be possible for redundant elements to exist in an otherwise collegial enterprise without necessarily altering the latter's character as such. This is not to say, however, that the presence of any redundant elements may not at times work against the overall collegial character of the enterprise. In this respect, cf. a critique, expressed by Richard B. Lillich and G. Edward White as far back as 1976, that the 'Judges' Written Notes' phase of the ICJ's deliberative practice may indeed have such an effect. Having interviewed acting members of the Court at the time, Lillich and White find that: 'Of all the steps of the Court's deliberative process, the notes received severest and most widespread criticism. . . . [A]ll judges acknowledged that notewriting [*sic*] tends to harden one's views, making subsequent oral discussion of the merits of a case less fruitful' (see R. B. Lillich and G. E. White, 'The Deliberative Process of the International Court of

Two conclusions thus follow from committing to an understanding of adjudication as a collegial enterprise. Firstly, one notices a transformation in institutional roles as one moves from a paradigm of a redundant enterprise to a paradigm of a collegial enterprise, which in the case of adjudication means the following. Whereas the principal agent of performance in an understanding of adjudication as a redundant enterprise would be the 'adjudicators', in adjudication as a collegial enterprise, the principal institutional agent of performance is the 'court' or the 'tribunal' itself rather than the individuals as 'adjudicators'.[16] Secondly, the collective nature of the enterprise places primacy on deliberation and the search for common ground. In other words, even though we acknowledge that individual adjudicators may come to deliberate each with views that are to some degree already formed, we also expect that they will still deliberate with an open mind – ready to persuade but also to be persuaded – in an attempt to reach common ground collectively as a 'court' or 'tribunal'.

7.2.2 Adjudication's Institutional Aims

As said, collective enterprises in general are formed to pursue certain aims. Therefore, a second feature of the judicial function that is of relevance for the present discussion pertains to the aim or aims of settling disputes via judicial means. Given our conclusions above, these must be institutional aims of the judicial function itself, considering the latter's collective nature and not any personal aims pursued by the individuals who act as adjudicators.

It is perhaps a truism to say that the principal institutional object and aim of the judicial settlement of disputes is the promotion of the satisfaction of the parties to the instant dispute and the restoration of the peace between them by way of resolving their disagreement.[17] This is a view that enjoys considerable support in practice, including in the practice of international arbitration where it is sometimes referred to by commentators as the 'peace treaty' view of arbitration's institutional

Justice: A Preliminary Critique and Some Possible Reforms' (1976) 70 *American Journal of International Law* 28, 34 [footnote omitted]).

16 Kornhauser and Sager (n. 3), 6–8.

17 See T. Schultz, 'The Three Pursuits of Dispute Settlement' (2010) 1 *Czech & Central European Yearbook of Arbitration* 227, 235ff (drawing on O. M. Fiss, 'Against Settlement' [1984] 93 *Yale Law Journal* 1073).

role.[18] Surely, restoring peace and satisfying the disputing parties are key goals of judicial dispute settlement. However, problems arise if we treat these goals as being exclusively pertinent. Consider the following remarks.

Exclusive preoccupation with satisfying the disputing parties and with moving cases along tends to give sole institutional primacy to values like efficiency and finality.[19] This may in turn imply a disinterestedness for the way in which efficiency and finality are achieved and especially for how well decisions fit within their larger context or for the consequences that a particular way of resolving a dispute may have in other disputes. However, it is not the case that we only expect adjudicators to resolve disputes efficiently and finally. We also expect them to do so accurately.[20] Indeed, it was argued in Chapter 3 that law has two simultaneous and interconnected dimensions, which we termed as the factual/social and the ideal. The former is represented in elements such as authoritative issuance and efficacy, whereas the latter is represented in a claim to the moral correctness of outcomes. We can therefore regard accuracy in the interpretation and application of the law during the judicial process as a function of the interaction of these two legal dimensions.

The above remarks point towards two additional aims served by the judicial settlement of disputes, which, following Schultz, we may call the promotion of the rule of law and the promotion of substantive societal values.[21] Promoting the rule of law refers to the adjudicator's task of

[18] E.g., see W. W. Park, 'Arbitrators and Accuracy' (2010) 1 *Journal of International Dispute Settlement* 25, 31, describing the 'peace treaty' view as follows (footnotes omitted):

> One camp of commentators posits that commercial litigants seek principally an end to hostilities so they can get on with their business. A recent listing of arbitral virtues omits any mention of correct awards, while other commentaries seem to down-play the need for arbitrator access to information. The story runs that the parties want not so much an accurate decision, but simply a decision, full stop, made by someone who dictates a peace treaty rather than pronounces the true state of the world.

[19] Schultz (n. 17), 237.

[20] In the context of international arbitration in particular, see Park (n. 18), 27 ('An arbitrator's main duty lies not in dictating a peace treaty, but in delivery of an accurate award that rests on a reasonable view of what happened and what the law says.'); and 33 ('Any account of international arbitration remains inadequate if it denigrates the aspiration to accuracy, or shifts an arbitrator's aim from a correct award to splitting the baby or dictating quick peace treaties.').

[21] Schultz (n. 17), 235.

giving expression to the law's formal legality in his or her decisions.[22] Formal legality is concerned with achieving so-called 'procedural' justice, namely, legal certainty understood as one's ability to rationally and reasonably predict the legal consequences of one's actions.[23] With respect to the aim of promoting substantive societal values, the adjudicator's task here is to 'explicate and give force to the values embodied in authoritative texts . . .: to interpret those values and to bring reality into accord with them'.[24] In other words, adjudicators must strive to treat everyone according to the agreed allocation of legal entitlements in the legal system. In so doing, often adjudicators must also determine how the law ought to allocate legal entitlements, especially in cases where parties claim entitlements that do not yet find clear expression in positive law.[25] Both of these additional aims of the judicial function are sensitive to the systemic implications that follow from resolving a case in one way rather than another.

In summation, restoring the peace between disputing parties by way of judicial resolution of their disagreement must be done in the appropriate way, which is to say, by adhering to the equally important aims of procedural and substantive justice. Furthermore, following the discussion in Chapter 3, neither procedural nor substantive justice has any a priori primacy over the other. Taken in isolation, both are largely agnostic towards a significant part of the law's value. Without substantive justice, procedural justice (as formal legality) may be used to perpetuate outcomes or solutions that are obviously unjust. Without procedural justice, substantive justice risks making judicial decisions look more like the subjective moral choices of adjudicators. In short, the three aims of dispute settlement just presented must be regarded as complementary and interconnected. None is distinct, separate, or independent from the others. By the same token, adjudicators collectively should not seek to achieve any one of them individually at any one point in time but rather should strive to achieve all of them, at all times.

Admittedly, this is a rather abstract statement of the aims of the judicial function. Regardless, it is adequate for present purposes. Since this book examines law as an interpretative concept it must follow that

22 Ibid., 239–240 (referring in particular to Lon Fuller's seminal exposition of the eight principles of legality).

23 Cf. ibid., summing up this goal as one of 'providing dependable guideposts'.

24 Fiss (n. 17), 1085.

25 Schultz (n. 17), 242.

adjudication's institutional aims are also of an interpretative character. People can meaningfully debate about them even when they disagree about their exact content and scope. An abstract statement of the aims of the judicial function can thus form a basis for discussion, since most lawyers can subscribe to its truthfulness even though they may reasonably disagree about how the three institutional aims should be conceptualised precisely or balanced out in practice. Borrowing from John Rawls, we may say that lawyers can achieve an overlapping consensus around the above list of institutional aims.[26] The abstractness and generality of the list renders these three aims 'modules' that can fit into any number of worldviews and interpretations that different adjudicators may have about their own institutional role. This enables meaningful debate to he had around specific points of disagreement, without however losing track of what the debate is actually about.

7.3 Towards Judicial Moral Responsibility in ISDS

Two propositions have so far been established to guide us forward and it may be good to restate them one more time. The first proposition is that adjudicating disputes is at its core a collegial enterprise. This means that adjudicators must come together as 'court' or 'tribunal' rather than as individuals and must deliberate towards a common solution even though their individual views may diverge. The second proposition is that resolving disputes judicially is not simply about moving cases along by pronouncing an outcome but also about doing so accurately. Adjudication does not seek to promote finality or efficiency with no regard given to the moral appeal of the outcomes it produces. Moral appeal is judged by the degree of legal certainty that these outcomes produce and by the final allocation of competing legal entitlements to which these outcomes give rise.

Given these propositions, it naturally follows that overall coherence in judicial decision-making depends not only on each adjudicator forming his or her own views in a coherent manner but also on all the adjudicators on a panel sharing a common understanding of the requirements of coherence in a judicial setting.[27] To the extent that coherence implies

[26] On the idea of overlapping consensus, see J. Rawls, *Political Liberalism* (New York: Columbia University Press, 1993), 133ff.

[27] For a similar view, see L. A. Kornhauser and L. G. Sager, 'Unpacking the Court' (1986) 96 *Yale Law Journal* 82, 111, 113, 116–117.

reflexivity, we must now supplement and clarify the analysis in Chapter 6 by pointing out that it is also collective reflexivity (rather than merely individual reflexivity) that is at stake. In other words, coherence requires both that the adjudicators form their views about the outcome of a case in a manner that is individually reflective and that the court or tribunal as a group arrives at its conclusion in a manner that is collectively reflective.

Moreover, with accuracy being a desirable aim and an attribute of judicial decision-making, a link could be established between collective reflexivity, as a means to achieve accuracy, and judicial moral responsibility, as a method of work towards collective reflexivity. The aim of this section is to propose a way to establish such a link in the particular context of ISDS. To that end, the discussion below begins by identifying a series of factors that make collective reflexivity harder to sustain in ISDS, thus shedding light on the importance of moral responsibility by arbitrators (Section 7.3.1). Following this, the concept of moral responsibility in a judicial setting is examined and its close relationship with five distinct judicial virtues – called faith, humility, acquiescence, integrity, and candour – is established (Section 7.3.2).

7.3.1 Collective Reflexivity and ISDS

Collective reflexivity may not be easy to achieve in adjudication, yet it is arguably even harder to sustain when it comes to the resolution of investment disputes. This is due to a series of related factors associated with ISDS covering virtually every aspect of the ISDS practice. For instance, one such factor is substantive as it relates to the hybrid foundations of international investment law. ISDS relies heavily on public international law doctrine but is often asked to resolve disputes of the type one comes across in domestic public law, and to do so it uses a style of dispute resolution which one typically finds in the resolution of private commercial disputes in international commercial arbitration. As seen in Chapter 5, this creates competition between ordering paradigms vying for relevance to describe the institutional aims of ISDS and investment arbitrators, which is still very much alive and ongoing.

A second factor is structural. In its current form, ISDS is an entirely ad hoc process. Contrary to what would often be the case for permanent bodies, there exists no firm historical track record of institutional rationality in ISDS that could help guide present-day arbitrators when they collectively act as a 'tribunal'.[28] This is not to say that there exists no collective rational point of view from which arbitrators deliberate in ISDS. To the contrary, the existence of such a collective rational point of view is necessarily presupposed every time we praise or criticise an arbitral award.[29] However, what is meant here by an absence of a historical record of institutional rationality in ISDS, is that there is little in the existing system that can anchor the views of present-day arbitrators with respect to what may constitute a collectively reflexive outcome. In other words, to some extent the rational point of view must be found and rediscovered by each tribunal in the context of each individual investment dispute.

A third factor is also structural in nature as it relates to the practice of party-appointed arbitrators. In a system that is ad hoc and without tenure for its decision-makers, the practice of party appointments gives strong incentives to arbitrators to become partisan – systematically favouring investors or states – in the hope of securing a steady stream of future appointments.[30] This creates a community of investment arbitrators that is ideologically polarised to a significant extent.[31] When seen

[28] For instance, among several examples of the ICJ using its own historical jurisprudence to justify normative choices, see *Maritime Delimitation in the Black Sea (Romania v. Ukraine)*, Judgment of 3 February 2009, ICJ Rep (2009) 61, paras 115–122.

[29] E.g., cf. D. Tollefsen, 'Organizations as True Believers' (2002) 33 *Journal of Social Philosophy* 395, 401:

> [A] rational point of view is a perspective from which deliberation takes place. When individuals deliberate in an organizational setting, they adopt the rational point of view of the organization. It is from the point of view of the organization, rather than their own personal point of view, that deliberation ought to take place. In fact, one explanation of the failure of individuals to act jointly and the failure of group decision making is that individuals are deliberating from their own rational points of view rather than adopting and sharing the perspective of the organization.

In a similar vein, see also D. P. Tollefsen, 'Collective Intentionality and the Social Sciences' (2002) 32 *Philosophy of the Social Sciences* 25, 34.

[30] This much is acknowledged by arbitrators themselves as reported, e.g., by T. Tucker, 'Inside the Black Box: Collegial Patterns on Investment Tribunals' (2016) 7 *Journal of International Dispute Settlement* 183, 194:

> While partisanship goes against the supposed need for neutrality in arbitration, my interviewees admitted that it is a rational approach to take, as you are guaranteed a steady stream of appointments (so long as you are at least somewhat effective at influencing your peers).

[31] J. Pauwelyn, 'The Rule of Law without the Rule of Lawyers? Why Investment Arbitrators Are from Mars, Trade Adjudicators from Venus' (2015) 109 *American Journal of*

together with the above-mentioned absence of an institutional anchor point of rationality for a tribunal's reasoning, partisanship can result in critical disruptions during internal deliberations.[32]

Lastly, a fourth and potentially exacerbating factor is procedural. Contrary to what the case may be in international courts or tribunals with more permanent structures, there are currently no firm rules, guidelines, or practices dictating how internal deliberations should be held, managed, and conducted by ISDS tribunals. Rather, the style and format of deliberations followed in each case largely depend on the individual who is appointed as tribunal president.[33] Therefore, it is

International Law 761, 781–783, contrasting in this respect the community of ISDS arbitrators to the relatively non-partisan community of WTO panellists.

[32] E.g., see Tucker (n. 30), 194–195 (quoting, in the relevant part, an interviewee arbitrator):

> A potential drawback to being seen as a frequent dissenter or partisan is that chairs know (or think they know) exactly how you will vote before you walk in the door. If they agree with your position, there is no problem for the partisan wingman (and in fact, this may reduce the influence of the other wingman, who is no longer needed for a majority). If the chair does not agree with the wing's presumptive position, they discount what the partisan wing says and may tilt towards the other side. When serving on a tribunal with people like them, 'the deliberation then is not a normal deliberation, because it is not three people with open minds who are just dealing with the instant case. It is a battle of competing portfolios'.

[33] E.g., see R. M. Mosk, 'Deliberations of Arbitrators', in D. D. Caron, S. W. Schill, A. C. Smutny, and E. E. Triantafilou (eds.), *Practising Virtue: Inside International Arbitration* (Oxford: Oxford University Press, 2015) 486, 488–489; also see A. J. van den Berg, 'Dissenting Opinions by Party-Appointed Arbitrators in Investment Arbitration', in M. H. Arsanjani, J. K. Cogan, R. D. Sloane, and S. Wiessner (eds.), *Looking to the Future: Essays on International Law in Honor of W. Michael Reisman* (Leiden: Martinus Nijhoff, 2011) 821, 830:

> A number of presiding arbitrators (myself included) attempt to convene with their colleagues after the hearing every day for some 20 to 30 minutes, usually addressing one question only: 'What did we learn today?' While some initially react 'Nothing!', the ensuing exchange of views assists in seeing where the arbitrators are in their thinking about the case, what needs further study and reflection, and what questions they may wish to explore with the parties. Some presiding arbitrators do not follow this kind of interactive deliberative process. They deliberate by asking each party-appointed arbitrator to write a note on the case and, having received notes from both arbitrators, the presiding arbitrator writes back that he or she prefers the views expressed in one of the notes. There is little or no exchange of views in person. It is therefore unsurprising that the arbitrator whose note is not chosen feels left out and later converts that note into a dissent.

perhaps unsurprising that often arbitrators anecdotally report having experienced internal deliberations of varying quality in their careers.[34]

Given the above characteristics of the ISDS regime and the general absence of institutional mechanisms designed to encourage collective reflexivity over time, we must now take a step back and focus on the investment arbitrators themselves as the actors who are principally responsible for how deliberations are conducted and for ensuring that arbitral awards are collectively reflexive.[35] The reference to arbitrators being 'responsible' is key. We need to examine the kind of responsibility that this is and what it entails in a judicial setting. This is the focus of Section 7.3.2, which argues that judicial responsibility is responsibility of the moral kind pointing to a series of judicial virtues.

7.3.2 *Arbitrator Moral Responsibility and Judicial Virtues*

There are two senses in which one can understand the term 'responsibility': the relational sense and the virtue sense.[36] In the relational sense, responsibility describes relations between people and events. Relational

[34] Indeed, in his study of the collegial practices of investment arbitrators, Tucker (n. 30), 187–191, identifies four ideal types of tribunal presidents, which he terms 'the socialite', 'the managerial', 'the dictatorial', and 'the weak'. 'Socialite' presidents seek to create a sense of camaraderie among the members of the tribunal and make significant efforts to achieve a consensus among their views, yet at the same time they tend to be highly averse to dissents. 'Managerial' presidents tend to be more preoccupied with ensuring a smooth and efficient arbitral process. They follow a strict agenda, avoid any appearances of favouritism between the other two arbitrators and, if possible, seek to sidestep points of significant disagreement by exercising judicial economy. They will seek unanimous awards, but they may not go to great lengths to avoid a dissent. So-called dictatorial presidents operate under the assumption that, whichever side of the dispute they favour, there will be at least one co-arbitrator who would vote with them. They thus tend not to give much room for compromise. They might announce their views on the merits, or even circulate draft awards, without always having engaged in any meaningful deliberation with their co-arbitrators. Lastly, presidents are often described as 'weak' when they move slowly, especially with procedural decisions, or give too much leeway to the disputing parties or their co-arbitrators in guiding the proceedings.

[35] More generally on the link between law and individual responsibility, see P. Allott, *The Health of Nations: Society and Law beyond the State* (Cambridge: Cambridge University Press, 2002), 293 (emphasis in original):

> Law is purposive human activity, a particular species of willing and acting, so that it is necessarily action of moral significance, action which is subject to moral duty and gives rise to moral responsibility. Moral duty – the duty to do good and avoid evil – attaches to the participation of *individual human beings* in law-making, law-applying, law-enforcing and law-abiding.

[36] R. Dworkin, *Justice for Hedgehogs* (Cambridge, MA: Harvard University Press, 2011), 102.

responsibility can have various sub-types. For example, person A will be causally responsible for an event occurring if A's actions or omissions caused that event to happen. And if that event further caused damage to another person B, then A may also bear liability responsibility to provide reparation to B. State responsibility in international law may for instance be understood as responsibility in the relational sense. By contrast, responsibility in the virtue sense acts as a qualifier of one's own behaviour. One can distinguish between different sub-types of responsibility in the virtue sense too. In particular, one may distinguish the intellectual, practical, ethical, and moral sub-types of it.[37] For the reasons stated below, the responsibility to which we are referring when we speak of the responsibility of arbitrators is responsibility understood in the virtue sense and, more precisely, it is responsibility of the moral sub-type.

According to Dworkin, moral responsibility attaches to one's expressed convictions and reasons for thinking or behaving in one way rather than another.[38] But moral responsibility is not necessarily, or even principally, concerned with the accuracy of one's expressed convictions or reasons.[39] Rather, it is about verifying that these convictions or reasons are genuinely held by the person who is advancing them. Recalling the discussion in Chapter 1, we may therefore say that moral responsibility is principally linked to epistemic as opposed to ontological objectivity. Transposed to the collegial context of adjudication, judicial moral responsibility thus describes a method of work if collective reflexivity and accuracy are desirable attributes of judicial decision-making. This is where its value lies. Approaching the collegial enterprise of adjudication in a morally responsible manner may not be able to guarantee that accuracy will actually be achieved in each and every case, yet, doing so may nevertheless facilitate agreement among individuals with divergent points of view.[40] Two

[37] For the content assigned to each of these sub-types, see, ibid., 102–103:

> A scientist who does not check his calculations lacks intellectual responsibility; a writer who does not back up his files lacks practical responsibility; someone who lives aimlessly lacks ethical responsibility; a voter who votes for a vice presidential candidate because he finds her sexy lacks moral responsibility. A political leader who sends a nation to war on plainly inadequate intelligence is irresponsible in all four ways.

[38] Ibid., 104ff.

[39] Cf. ibid., 113. ('Morally responsible people may not achieve truth, but they seek it.')

[40] E.g., cf. ibid., 100 (emphasis in original):

> [I]f I am faced with someone who holds moral opinions radically different from my own, I cannot count on finding anything in my set of reasons and arguments that he would be irrational not to accept. I cannot *demonstrate*

arbitrators who both reason in a responsible manner may still reach different conclusions on what would be a right or wrong outcome to a case. But, in reasoning responsibly, they will at least 'share the belief that there is a getting it right and a getting it wrong about what is right and wrong'.[41]

Thus understood, judicial moral responsibility is a necessary component of an entire arbitral panel's search for collective reflexivity,[42] and consequently, it is also closely related with this book's overall thesis on the dual role that coherence plays in legal reasoning.[43] Being morally responsible is therefore a type of work that is always in progress and which involves a significant amount of individual effort and commitment by arbitrators. Furthermore, judicial moral responsibility can never be outside the institutional purview of arbitrators considering that the question of trust in the arbitral process is paramount – trust both by the disputing parties (as the primary beneficiaries of the arbitral function) and by the community at large.[44] Having said this, it is possible to still ask further: What does judicial moral responsibility imply in more concrete terms for the way investment arbitrators should individually approach their collective enterprise? The answer, it is argued, is that it implies the same sort of thing identified by Jan Klabbers – virtue.

> to him that my opinions are true and his false. But I can hope to convince him – and myself – of something else that is often more important: that I have acted responsibly in reaching my opinions and acting on them. . . . I may be right about affirmative action when I flip a coin and wrong when I reflect carefully, but I am irresponsible in the first case and responsible in the second.

[41] Ibid., 121.

[42] In the same vein, see Jouannet (n. 15), 283:

> Le juge est un personnage politique de la scène internationale et sa motivation exerce une influence politique. Même s'il ne l'avoue pas, ce que l'on peut parfaitement comprendre, il trahit dans sa motivation ses préférences idéologiques et son système de valeurs éthiques. La question n'est dès lors plus celle de son pouvoir mais des responsabilités qui lui incombent en raison de l'exercice de ce pouvoir.

[43] On the link between coherence in law and standards of epistemic responsibility, see also A. Amaya, *The Tapestry of Reason: An Inquiry into the Nature of Coherence and Its Role in Legal Argument* (Oxford: Hart, 2015), 547–548.

[44] Indeed, see the opening sentence of the very first chapter in J. Paulsson, *The Idea of Arbitration* (Oxford: Oxford University Press, 2013), 1 ('The idea of arbitration is that of binding resolution of disputes accepted with serenity by those who bear its consequences because of their special trust in chosen decision-makers.').

For Klabbers, there exists ample scope for a virtuous approach to the way adjudicators engage in judicial reasoning and this is precisely because judging is an activity that taps directly into one's individual obligations as a moral actor.[45] In saying this, Klabbers in turn draws on the work of American constitutional theorist Haywood Jefferson Powell who identified the following five, distinct, yet closely related, judicial virtues: (i) faith, (ii) humility, (iii) acquiescence, (iv) integrity, and (v) candour.[46] According to Jefferson Powell, the term 'virtue' in this context denotes a habit or a disposition of mind or will.[47] Judicial virtues are thus habits and mental dispositions that should inform adjudicators when they deliberate and when they render judgments. As such, they are meant to be taken as offering guidelines and a framework for critical analysis and not as prescribing a precise formula or an equation for the courtroom.

The remainder of this chapter follows Klabbers' intuition on the importance of virtue in judicial decision-making. Sections 7.4–7.7 thus proceed by offering a preliminary and tentative sketch of what each of the five virtues identified may imply for arbitrators' deliberations in ISDS. The discussion draws from Jefferson Powell's exposition of these virtues and their content. The latter are used to assess aspects of observable arbitral behaviour as found in arbitral awards and as reported by scholars and commentators.

7.4 The Virtue of Faith

As described by Jefferson Powell, the judicial virtue of faith is an intellectual and a practical activity.[48] As intellectual activity, faith describes a professional commitment to the law's intelligibility. As practical activity, faith describes a professional commitment and an undertaking to conduct oneself in accordance with the law's intelligible meaning. Put differently, faith comprises, first, a belief in the power of legal language as this is organised within the legal profession and, second, a commitment to the importance of this language as the discipline through which the law's

45 J. Klabbers, 'Virtuous Interpretation', in M. Fitzmaurice, O. Elias, and P. Merkouris (eds.), *Treaty Interpretation and the Vienna Convention on the Law of Treaties: 30 Years On* (Leiden: Martinus Nijhoff, 2010) 17, 35–36.

46 H. Jefferson Powell, *Constitutional Conscience: The Moral Dimension of Judicial Decision* (Chicago: University of Chicago Press, 2008).

47 Ibid., 83.

48 Ibid., 85.

project is unfolded.[49] Thus understood, the virtue of faith is the cornerstone of law and the judicial function being collective enterprises. Without faith, law and the judicial function cannot exist as common enterprises collectively pursued among individuals.

In the more concrete context of ISDS, one can identify two sides of the arbitrator's faith in the intelligibility of international investment law. In the first place, faith makes it possible for arbitrators to address questions of legal interpretation as collaborative problems, which is to say, as problems that are resolvable by them working together despite the different perspectives that each arbitrator will bring to the table. To be sure, having faith in the collaborative nature of legal interpretation does not extinguish disagreement – even radical disagreement – among arbitrators. But faith can enable the possibility of conducting principled dialogue by placing disagreement in its proper context. Such is the context of seeking to identify the best approach to carrying out a judicial task about which arbitrators can share a common understanding in the deeper sense described in Section 7.2.2.[50]

Thus understood, faith in international investment law's intelligibility is a judicial attitude that is both reasonable and necessary if we are to have meaningful discussions about international investment law and ISDS. Indeed, in the alternative, a large part of the so-called 'legitimacy crisis' discourse about international investment law would not exist, concerns regarding consistency and coherence would not be raised with the same vigour, and certain types of arguments would not be made as often (e.g., on the normative significance of past arbitral awards). We would also not be asking certain questions, such as, for example, how international investment law on the whole relates to international environmental or international human rights law.[51] Rather, our questions would instead only be about how a particular bilateral or multilateral

[49] See L. Bonadiman, 'Faith', in J. d'Aspremont and S. Singh (eds.), *Concepts for International Law: Contributions to Disciplinary Thought* (Cheltenham: Edward Elgar, 2019) 294, 296.

[50] See Jefferson Powell (n. 46), 86–87; see also, Dworkin (n. 36), 136 ('Law is also collaborative: a judge takes himself to aim at the same goal – justice – as the statesmen who made the laws he interprets. Even when he sees his role as entirely subordinate to theirs, the subordination is, in his view, itself justified by the overall goal of justice he shares with them.').

[51] For instance, see L. Wandahl Mouyal, *International Investment Law and the Right to Regulate: A Human Rights Perspective* (New York: Routledge, 2016); J. E. Viñuales, *Foreign Investment and the Environment in International Law* (Cambridge: Cambridge University Press, 2012).

investment agreement relates to other kinds of international legal norms.[52]

It thus follows that, in the second place, faith in international investment law's intelligibility implies that dispute resolution within it does not take place in a legal vacuum. An intelligible body of law is more than a mere agglomeration of posited norms. By the same token, an intelligible international investment law is more properly construed as a specialised regime of international law, rather than as a mere agglomeration of individual investment treaties. Importantly, this is not the same as saying that each investment agreement must be interpreted in light of any other investment agreement.[53] However, it does suggest that as a specialised regime international investment law is more than the sum of its constituent parts. It is still a creature of general public international law but with its own particular norms, institutions, practices, values, and teleology, around which the expectations of investors and states converge over time in relation to the rights and obligations that each of them has.[54] The belief that the above constituent elements of international investment law should exhibit a degree of congruence in principle thus persists, even after taking into account the textual peculiarities of each individual investment agreement.[55]

[52] S. W. Schill, 'System-Building in Investment Treaty Arbitration and Lawmaking', in A. von Bogdandy and I. Venzke (eds.), *International Judicial Lawmaking: On Public Authority and Democratic Legitimation in Global Governance* (Heidelberg: Springer, 2012) 133, 140–141 (incl. n. 26).

[53] For arguments on the impermissibility of interpreting international investment agreements in light of each other, see J. D. Mortenson, 'International Investment Law', in M. J. Bowman and D. Kritsiotis (eds.), *Conceptual and Contextual Perspectives on the Modern Law of Treaties* (Cambridge: Cambridge University Press, 2018) 653, 669–675; A. D. Mitchell and J. Munro, 'Someone Else's Deal: Interpreting International Investment Agreements in the Light of Third-Party Agreements' (2017) 28 *European Journal of International Law* 669.

[54] J. W. Salacuse, 'The Emerging Global Regime for Investment' (2010) 51 *Harvard International Law Journal* 427, 431ff.

[55] For a historical analogue, one could look at the protection of minorities during the interwar period. Although not as expansive, the protection of minorities was in important respects a regime like that of modern investment protection. The minorities protection regime was composed of a series of treaties and declarations. Although not entirely identical, these still shared several common features and provisions that were modelled after the 1919 Minorities Treaty between the Principal Allied and Associated Powers and Poland (see P. Alston and R. Goodman, *International Human Rights* [Oxford: Oxford University Press, 2013], 102–105). Indeed, it was precisely this regime aspect that prompted the PCIJ in its 1935 advisory opinion to not interpret the provisions of an Albanian declaration protecting minorities in isolation but rather to do so against the

What do the above remarks mean for ISDS tribunals in more practical terms? Considering the high volume and frequency of ISDS cases, the relatively abstract formulation of core norms of international investment protection, and the generally slow process of international law-making by states, the above remarks paint an image of investment tribunals as de facto system-builders. As such, investment tribunals contribute to the gradual development of international investment law over time and have considerable influence over its intelligibility.[56] In more practical terms, therefore, the virtue of faith would instruct arbitrators to be cognisant of the fact that their interpretations and statements of legal principle cannot be purely ad hoc solutions that are suitable only for the case at hand but they must also be capable of being universalised.

Universalisation is not the same as saying that arbitrators have a duty to contribute to the harmonious development of a common law of international investment protection, as if compelled by a preordained plan about how international investment law should develop in the future.[57] What universalisation means, rather, is that a tribunal's

background of the minority protection regime as a whole (see *Minority Schools in Albania*, Advisory Opinion of 6 April 1935, PCIJ Series A/B No 64 (1935) 3, 15–17).

[56] See Schill (n. 52), 140, 155:

> [I]n deciding cases investment treaty tribunals contribute to a growing body of case law that concretizes the principles of investment protection contained in investment treaties and further develops them. ... [I]nvestment treaty tribunals generate coherence rather than divergence in arbitral jurisprudence, and forge one treaty-overarching body of international investment law that affects the behavior of [s]tates and investors and restricts [s]tates in their decision- and policy-making ....
>
> An even more important factor for the multilateralization of international investment treaties, however, is the activity of investment treaty tribunals. They generate, with some exceptions, largely coherent decisions even across different investment treaties, above all as regards the interpretation of the substantive principles of investment protection.

[57] Sometimes thought to come close to expressing such a view is the following passage from *Saipem S.p.A.* v. *The People's Republic of Bangladesh*, ICSID Case No. ARB/05/07, Decision on Jurisdiction and Recommendation on Provisional Measures, 21 March 2007, para 67 (footnotes omitted):

> The Tribunal considers that it is not bound by previous decisions. At the same time, it is of the opinion that it must pay due consideration to earlier decisions of international tribunals. It believes that, subject to compelling contrary grounds, it has a duty to adopt solutions established in a series of consistent cases. It also believes that, subject to the specifics of a given treaty and of the circumstances of the actual case, it has a duty to seek to contribute to the harmonious development of investment law and thereby

interpretations and statements of legal principle must be capable of being generalised beyond the instant case, so that they may themselves be able to act as guideposts for future similar cases without leading to absurd results.[58] As MacCormick put it, there can be no such thing as a good reason for deciding any single case that is not at the same time a good generic reason for deciding cases of that particular type.[59] The example of the *Phoenix* v. *Czech Republic* decision analysed in Chapter 6 is indeed useful to recall in the present context too.[60]

> to meet the legitimate expectations of the community of [s]tates and investors towards certainty of the rule of law.

This passage has been further reproduced verbatim in *Saipem* v. *Bangladesh*, Award, 30 June 2009, para 90; *Austrian Airlines* v. *The Slovak Republic*, UNCITRAL Rules, Final Award, 9 October 2009, para 84; *Quiborax S.A., Non Metallic Minerals S.A. and Allan Fosk Kaplún* v. *Plurinational State of Bolivia*, ICSID Case No. ARB/06/2, Decision on Jurisdiction, 27 September 2012, para 46; *Mesa Power Group, LLC* v. *Government of Canada*, UNCITRAL Rules, PCA Case No. 2012-17, Award, 24 March 2016, para 222.

58 Paulsson (n. 44), 8–9, seems to describe a substantially similar imperative when he speaks of the arbitral virtue of 'attentiveness to consequences':

> Arbitrators on occasion profess that they decide every case as though it is their last one – i.e.[,] without glances over their shoulders – but this is not always either realistic or appropriate. The archetype's authority is valuable to the community, and in particular to future disputants. The community perceives the archetype as such; and the archetype arbitrator perceives the community as it observes him or her. Observation affects comportment. This creates a tension with the ideal of an individualized approach to the dispute. How could it be otherwise?

59 See N. MacCormick, *Legal Reasoning and Legal Theory* (Oxford: Clarendon Press, 1978), 75, 79, 81, 97–99.

60 For another possible example in ISDS, see the critique partly on similar grounds of the test adopted by the *Abaclat* and *Ambiente Ufficio* tribunals for considering sovereign debt instruments as 'investments', offered by Z. Douglas, 'Property, Investment, and the Scope of Investment Protection Obligations', in Z. Douglas, J. Pauwelyn, and J. E. Viñuales (eds.), *The Foundations of International Investment Law: Bringing Theory into Practice* (Oxford: Oxford University Press, 2014) 363, 384–385:

> [T]he test devised is idiosyncratic and was clearly formulated to generate a particular result. Its weakness is exposed by the fact that it cannot possibly be generalized without leading to absurd results. If the test for establishing the territorial link for an investment is 'the benefit of whom the funds are ultimately used', then the purchase of Argentine beef from an Argentine state-owned distributor in Italy would be capable of constituting an investment in Argentina, as would the purchase of a visa to travel to Argentina at its consulate in Rome, as would the purchase of a ticket to fly from Rome to Buenos Aires on Aerolíneas Argentinas – the national airline of Argentina. It is not satisfactory to devise a test that is uniquely plausible for security interests in sovereign bonds and not for anything else.

It follows, therefore, that the judicial virtue of faith would likely disapprove of arbitral predispositions that are similar to the kind expressed, for instance, in *Romak* v. *Uzbekistan* where the tribunal took the view that:

> [T]he Arbitral Tribunal has not been entrusted, by the Parties or otherwise, with a mission to ensure the coherence or development of 'arbitral jurisprudence'. The Arbitral Tribunal's mission is more mundane, but no less important: to resolve the present dispute between the Parties in a reasoned and persuasive manner, *irrespective of the unintended consequences that this Arbitral Tribunal's analysis might have on future disputes in general.*[61]

The above cannot be endorsed as a statement of principle because it denies any practical and moral relevance to the widely known fact, known even at the time of *Romak*, that reasoning by reference to past decisions is an extremely common and indeed a principal mode of judicial reasoning in ISDS. Party pleadings are replete with references to prior arbitral awards, which are then routinely cited by tribunals as authorities to justify their interpretative choices.[62] The prevalence of such a mode of reasoning in ISDS must be thought to create a particular moral responsibility for arbitrators to be cognisant of the imperative of universalisability. In other words, considering the very high likelihood that the *Romak* decision would itself be cited by subsequent tribunals as authority,[63] the above statement arguably demonstrates a disregard by the

[61] *Romak S.A. (Switzerland)* v. *The Republic of Uzbekistan*, UNCITRAL Rules, PCA Case No. AA280, Award, 26 November 2009, para 171 (emphasis added).

[62] E.g., see J. P. Commission, 'Precedent in Investment Treaty Arbitration: A Citation Analysis of a Developing Jurisprudence' (2007) 24 *Journal of International Arbitration* 129, 148–153 (noting already at that time an exponential increase of citations to past awards and a decrease in reliance on other sources of law); see also a more recent study by N. Ridi and T. Schultz, 'Empirically Mapping Investment Arbitration Scholarship: Networks, Authorities, and the Research Front', in K. Fach Gómez (ed.), *Private Actors in International Investment Law* (Cham: Springer, 2021) 209, 229–230 (finding that citations to arbitral precedent keeps outpacing the number of arbitral decisions issued each year).

[63] History proves this. A citation analysis using the Investor–State Law Guide database shows that, as of the time of writing, the *Romak* decision has been cited by at least thirty-seven different, subsequent tribunals. By far the most cited passage from the decision is its paragraph 207 (twenty unique references), where the tribunal holds the position that the term 'investment' has an inherent meaning that is applicable irrespective of whether the investor has resorted to ICSID or UNCITRAL arbitration, so that 'if an asset does not correspond to the inherent definition of "investment", the fact that it falls within one of the categories listed in [the investment treaty] does not transform it into an

tribunal for international investment law's intelligibility over time and hence for the judicial virtue of faith.

7.5 The Virtue of Humility

Jefferson Powell defines the judicial virtue of humility in a particular way. His starting point is that the law is an arena where essentially political and moral arguments are being discussed in a different form.[64] The idea behind judicial humility is that adjudicators should recognise this as a fundamental feature of their practice and, by extension, that they should be cognisant of the limitations of their institutional role and of the fact that the law may not always provide clear-cut answers to all questions raised.[65] At the same time, humility is not an excuse to curtail judicial debate of contested legal issues. To the contrary, according to Jefferson Powell, a judicial virtue of humility is perfectly consistent with 'a strong and even passionate commitment to one's views on contested matters of ... interpretation'.[66] Although Jefferson Powell's focus is constitutional interpretation in the United States, his fundamental insight behind humility applies equally to all fields of law, including international investment law.

Judicial humility in the ISDS context would, in the first place, instruct arbitrators to be cognisant of the fact that they decide matters that bear directly on the allocation of power and authority, both within the host state as well as between the host state and the tribunal itself.[67] In virtually all ISDS disputes to date, arbitrators have been called upon to provide an answer to a question with clear political and moral underpinnings, namely, whether a host state has exercised its coercive powers against an investor in a legitimate manner and in accordance with the constraints put forward by international law. On its face, this question may seem to point towards a corrective outcome only (i.e., if found liable, the host state must provide the investor with reparation). Yet, in answering

"investment"'. This is a significant statement from a doctrinal standpoint. Not only does it confirm the validity of the so-called 'objective' approach to the meaning of investment but also expands it beyond the context of ICSID-administered disputes where it was previously thought to be confined.

64 Jefferson Powell (n. 46), 93–94.

65 Cf. a similar in spirit view expressed by V. Lowe, 'The Limits of the Law – Inaugural Lecture' (2016) 379 *Recueil des cours* 9, 34.

66 Jefferson Powell (n. 46), 94.

67 See V. Lowe, 'Regulation or Expropriation?' (2002) 55 *Current Legal Problems* 447, 466.

this question, arbitrators cannot avoid making normative choices having wider distributive consequences of the sort just described. Such choices may be, for example, with respect to the appropriate standard of review to be adopted by the tribunal or with respect to the level of diligence that the state must pursue in its treatment of foreign investors.[68] The distributive question comes about by reframing and recontextualising the original legal problem at a higher level of abstraction, in keeping with the virtue of faith. Thus, the legal question to be answered is not simply 'should investor A win this particular case?' but rather 'should investors as a class of persons or entities have a legal right to win cases that are similar to this one?'.

The way arbitrators view their institutional role individually can have an impact on their ability to practise humility. Indeed, according to Todd Tucker, different investment arbitrators view their role in the regime in substantially different ways, with two broad categories emerging.[69] For the so-called 'law appliers', arbitrating investment disputes is akin to science. The job is to take account of the facts and to interpret the treaty, not to worry about justice in the moral sense.[70] For these arbitrators, there is a right answer and a wrong answer to the legal problem posed. Getting the facts and the rules right will give the correct answer with very limited room for discretion. Tucker thus concludes that for the 'law appliers' ISDS can be described as a clerical exercise, consisting of the careful assembly of factual chronologies and dictionary entries to get to the plain meaning of words.[71] The second broad category includes the so-called 'law creators'. Arbitrators in this group see themselves as being

[68] Indeed, a strand of literature suggests that distributive choices abound even in areas of law, such as tort law, where the principal focus is securing corrective justice between those who have done and those who have suffered a wrong (e.g., see J. Gardner, 'What Is Tort Law For? Part 1. The Place of Corrective Justice' [2011] 30 *Law and Philosophy* 1; J. Gardner, 'What Is Tort Law For? Part 2. The Place of Distributive Justice', in J. Oberdiek [ed.], *Philosophical Foundations of the Law of Torts* [Oxford: Oxford University Press, 2014] 335; P. Cane, 'Distributive Justice and Tort Law' [2001] Issue 4 *New Zealand Law Review* 401).

[69] T. N. Tucker, *Judge Knot: Politics and Development in International Investment Law* (London: Anthem Press, 2018), 126–132.

[70] Ibid., 127, reporting the views of a 'law-applier' interviewee:

> The likelihood is that most of [the awards] are correct. Correct in the sense that they are rendered in accordance with the law. Whether they are correct in a more philosophical sense of justice being done and all that, is obviously to some extent a different story.

[71] Ibid.

to various degrees developers of a still underdeveloped and 'gappy' body of law, which often calls for creative legal thinking and for exercising discretion.[72] Arbitrators in this group may act on their moral assessment of the facts of the case and on their 'gut feeling' on whether the state's conduct was appropriate.[73]

To be sure, the above descriptions largely represent archetypes of arbitral behaviour. Reality likely falls somewhere in the middle. Still, keeping the archetypes in mind is useful for our purposes. Arbitral behaviour falling under either of these two categories is at risk of not exhibiting the judicial virtue of humility, as this concept is here understood. In both cases, there exists a particular risk of obscuring the fact that investment arbitrators make substantive, moral choices that have distributive consequences for the legal entitlements of states and investors alike. On the one hand, taking the view that arbitrating investment disputes is exclusively about applying law to facts begs the question of what the law demands in the first place. Indeed, as seen in Chapters 1–3, law has an arguable character and legal reasoning is practical rather than theoretical. Moreover, while arbitrators' instinct to establish the veracity of alleged facts is correct, facts tell us nothing by themselves. As seen in Chapter 4, facts only lead to normative conclusions when put in a normative context. On the other hand, while it is a common feature of experienced practitioners' 'knowing-in-practice' according to Chapter 6, judging by 'gut feel' or by one's personal moral assessment of the circumstances of a dispute may still render one oblivious to the systemic consequences of one's decisions if this is done unreflectively. An adjudicator's 'knowing-in-practice' includes such elements as doctrines, maxims, general principles, and interpretative 'rules of thumb', which often act as mental short-cuts in one's analysis of a case, but which also have clear distributive consequences for the disputing parties' legal entitlements.[74] In short, strict adherence to either view has the potential

[72] Ibid., 128 ('While some arbitrators claimed a modest role, they gave countless examples where they or their colleagues improvised solutions to legal problems.').

[73] Ibid., 129.

[74] By way of example, consider the two doctrines associated with claims of indirect expropriation. For the sole effects doctrine, a finding of indirect expropriation is warranted if the effect of government measures is one of substantial and lasting deprivation of the use, enjoyment, or disposal of the investor's property. By extension, the state's intent behind the measures is ultimately not decisive. Conversely, the police powers doctrine indicates that there are certain domains of state regulation (e.g., taxation, public order and morality, and the protection of human health and the environment) where states are

to lead to the same unwanted conclusion. It would risk obscuring the much more complex picture of reflexive judicial reasoning painted throughout this book.[75]

It thus follows that, in the second place, practising humility would also not be compatible with a reluctance to discuss contested legal questions in hard cases, for instance, by removing such questions from the debate altogether or by hiding their difficulty and contested nature behind mere technical argumentation.[76] In that sense, humility advances together with other virtues such as integrity and candour in the way legal reasoning is used and arguments are presented. Integrity and candour are examined in more detail below. For the moment, a few remarks can be offered about a particular aspect of the judicial practice that could over time enhance the practice of arbitral humility – dissenting opinions.

At first blush, focusing on dissenting opinions in a discussion about the importance of collective reflexivity in ISDS may appear somewhat odd. If anything, one could argue, the presence of a dissent means that the tribunal's attempts at collective reflexivity have failed or, at best, were

justified in taking measures, even if doing so would result in harm to the investor's property rights. It follows, then, that the state's intent is critical (as manifested, e.g., in the expressed purpose, form, or application of a measure or in any prior commitments made to the investor).

The general point made here is that an arbitrator should not choose to apply any of these two doctrines simply on 'gut feel' or habit alone, and without reflection on the distributive consequences following from this choice. This is mainly for two reasons. Firstly, each doctrine points to a different allocation of the risk of economic injury relating to property rights: by default, the sole effects doctrine allocates this risk against the state whereas the police powers doctrine allocates it against the investor. Secondly, each doctrine also argues for a different allocation of an ISDS tribunal's adjudicative authority. The police powers doctrine, in particular, indicates that it is in principle inappropriate for tribunals to exercise their powers in certain domains of regulation given their remoteness from local communities.

[75] E.g., cf. the following telling statements, expressing substantially the same point, and offered, respectively, by a 'law applier' and a 'law creator' interviewee in Tucker (n. 69), 127, 129 (emphasis in original):

> When I asked how another arbitrator 'put meat on the bones' of the fair [and] equitable treatment standard, he said, 'I am not sure I even thought about that too much. I was just applying the treaty as I thought *it had to be understood*.' . . .
>
> On the merits, said another [arbitrator], the rulings usually go by the facts of the case, and how offensive they are to you, you know, what has happened. So that then from that, you bridge it to fair and equitable [treatment]. Most people have a sense of their belief [in] what it should be. On damages, we are totally free to do whatever we think is reasonable.

[76] See Jefferson Powell (n. 46), 96.

only partially successful if, for example, the dissent takes the gentler form of a concurring opinion. Furthermore, there is indeed truth to the statement that, all things being equal, unanimous decisions tend to carry greater persuasive force and authority.[77] In that sense, there is nothing worrisome about arbitrators making an honest effort to find a compromise solution in the event of disagreement. At the same time, however, one must also query how far such an effort can go. Should unanimity be sought after at any cost? If persuasiveness and authority are attributes that we wish arbitral decisions to have, do we still achieve these goals if arbitrators, for example, reduce the strength or clarity of their decision in the search for unanimity?[78] The answer must be that we do not. Authority and persuasiveness are not attributes associated exclusively with unanimous decisions. Giving the outward impression that the decision could not have gone any other way does not invariably lead to greater legitimacy.[79] Rather, as seen throughout this book, the quality of the reasoning offered matters a great deal also.

Dissenting opinions may have a useful role to play in this respect,[80] provided that they are not motivated by partisanship or self-serving interests of the arbitrator. As the late David Caron had pointed out, by making transparent to the outside world the dissenter's contrary views, dissenting opinions allow the public testing of the strength of the majority's reasoning,[81] which is, after all, the one that carries the binding force. And so, even though they are not an ideal outcome, dissenting opinions still have the potential to foster the exercise of judicial humility over time precisely because law has an arguable character with scope for reasonable disagreement. In other words, dissenting opinions allow us to have a

[77] E.g., see van den Berg (n. 33), 828.

[78] See Tucker (n. 30), 188 (reporting that one of the strategies of highly dissent-averse presiding arbitrators can be to 'reduce the strength of an award until both wingmen sign on, with the risk that the end product will be unclear or "anodyne"').

[79] See ibid. (reporting on the contrary views expressed by a dissent-averse arbitrator).

[80] See R. M. Mosk and T. Ginsburg, 'Dissenting Opinions in International Arbitration', in M. Tupamäki (ed.), *Liber Amicorum Bengt Broms* (Helsinki: International Law Association, 1999) 259, 271, 283. However, see the contrary view of Albert Jan van den Berg (n. 33), 831, who argues strongly against dissenting opinions in ISDS save only for two occasions: (i) when something has gone fundamentally wrong in the arbitral process (e.g., a very serious violation of due process) or (ii) when the arbitrator has been threatened that, absent a dissent, he or she will be in physical danger upon returning to his or her state of nationality or residence.

[81] D. D. Caron, 'Regulating Opacity: Shaping How Tribunals Think', in Caron and others (n. 33) 379, 393.

public debate about important and sometimes contested issues surrounding the exercise of public authority by investment tribunals.

In this respect, consider again the majority decision and Gary Born's partial dissent in *Philip Morris* v. *Uruguay*, which were previously examined in Chapter 5. This is arguably an instance where a dissenting opinion has fulfilled the role just described and has served the virtue of humility. Recall from the discussion in Chapter 5 that the point of substantive disagreement between Born and the majority was not really about the application of the doctrinal test of proportionality. Instead, somewhat hidden behind the technical arguments, the real disagreement was about the better understanding of the arbitrator's institutional role, and in particular, about the arbitrator's scope and margin of review of domestic regulatory actions. The majority opted for a deferential standard of 'plausible legislation' in these cases, whereas Born argued for a less deferential standard of 'objective rational justification'. This is an important moral question about the allocation of power and authority in ISDS, which, however, does not always get the attention and debate it deserves in arbitral awards. Born's dissenting opinion is thus important for shedding light on this question and for putting the majority decision in a critical context. By juxtaposing the two, one can confirm the correctness of the majority decision or find it lacking given the dissent. Ultimately, the dissenting opinion shows us that the tribunal was collectively alive to the importance of this question. While it is unfortunate that an agreement could not be reached among the arbitrators, their debate surely cannot but be instructive for all.[82]

7.6 The Virtue of Acquiescence

Considering the above remarks on the distributive consequences of judicial decision-making, one may now pose the following question: Why not make present-day adjudicators follow a distribution of entitlements, power, and authority that is similar to that which has been done in the past? Indeed, several reasons can be offered for why adjudicators should do precisely that. One reason may be that referring to past

[82] For an additional example of a case where dissenting opinions may be said to have played the same role, see *Eco Oro Minerals Corp.* v. *Republic of Colombia*, ICSID Case No. ARB/16/41, Decision on Jurisdiction, Liability and Directions on Quantum, 9 September 2021. *Eco Oro* is moreover a rather unique example considering the two partial dissenting opinions appended to a majority decision issued by a three-member tribunal.

pronouncements would give present-day adjudicators an anchor-point of rationality upon which to rely and build when rendering their decisions. In turn, doing so would likely limit the range of contentious issues that would need to be reargued as we move forward. A second reason may be the certainty and predictability that would follow from allowing the past to inform present-day decisions. Yet a third reason may be that, in addition to producing certainty and predictability, wisdom that has accumulated and has been followed over a long period of time is, presumptively at least, more likely to also be correct in its substance.

We must grant all these reasons persuasive force and, in doing so, arrive at the virtue that Jefferson Powell calls acquiescence. In broad terms, acquiescence implies a moral commitment to the wisdom that has been accumulated up to the point in time one is called upon to rule on a particular legal problem.[83] In this sense, acquiescence is similar to the virtue of faith insofar as both instruct adjudicators to approach legal interpretation as a collaborative effort and legal problems as collaborative problems that can be solved by way of all participants – past, present, and future – working together. In more concrete terms, acquiescence instructs adjudicators to accept the premises of existing decisions even when they are not their own and, by extension, to also accept the fact that a settled legal position can be taken as a starting point for further thought rather than as an opportunity for endless re-argument.[84]

Given the absence of a formal doctrine of *stare decisis* in international law, acquiescence in ISDS is often thought to translate into a commitment to give serious consideration to any *jurisprudence constante* that has been accumulated over time around concrete legal issues.[85] In practice, this principally takes the form of examining arbitral awards that have dealt with similar issues in the past.[86] However, there is no reason in principle why practising acquiescence should be limited only to seeking

[83] Jefferson Powell (n. 46), 96–100.

[84] Ibid., 99.

[85] As explained by G. Kaufmann-Kohler, 'Arbitral Precedent: Dream, Necessity or Excuse?' (2007) 23 *Arbitration International* 357, 360 (n. 16): 'One speaks of *jurisprudence constante* where there is a series of cases that resolve a particular issue in a certain way, which then acts as a guide in the future in resolving the same issue. In Switzerland, the more constant and older the precedent is, the more reluctant the judge will be to reverse it.'

[86] E.g., see A. K. Bjorklund, 'Investment Treaty Arbitral Decisions as *Jurisprudence Constante*', in C. B. Picker, I. D. Bunn, and D. W. Arner (eds.), *International Economic Law: The State and Future of the Discipline* (Oxford: Hart, 2008) 265.

guidance from other arbitral awards. Some scholars have pointed out, for instance, that the accumulated history of the customary international law minimum standard of treatment of aliens could likewise serve as useful interpretative context offering insights into how certain treaty provisions, in particular FET, should be construed by present-day tribunals.[87]

To be sure, there is nothing surprising in arbitrators seeking guidance from the past on how to address a legal problem in the present. Bringing past experience to bear on a new situation is not only a common approach to practical reasoning by human beings,[88] it is also a mode of reasoning that is of particular usefulness in the legal field. As Ridi points out, citing precedents (and especially 'highly citable' ones) in international adjudication can be useful in two respects: (i) epistemically, precedents are useful because they contain information that can be reused, almost as a short-cut, to quickly dispose of recurring issues; (ii) functionally, precedents can be relied upon by adjudicators when the actual or perceived legitimacy of their decisions is at stake.[89]

Practising acquiescence in ISDS can thus be expected to help deliberating arbitrators to be more efficient, to secure intersubjective agreement around specific legal issues, or at least to achieve overlapping consensus around controversial issues thus breaking potential deadlocks. Put differently, acquiescence can help an arbitrator to accept a decision as being the tribunal's legitimate collective output, given the path that the regime on the whole has taken up to that point in time, even though he or she may not fully agree with it. In so doing, acquiescence can thus be expected to help arbitrators partially overcome some of the limitations

[87] E.g., see C. Giannakopoulos and M. Monga, 'History as Interpretative Context in the Evolutionary Interpretation of FET in International Investment Law', in G. Abi-Saab, K. Keith, G. Marceau, and C. Marquet (eds.), *Evolutionary Interpretation and International Law* (Oxford: Hart, 2019) 297; C. McLachlan, L. Shore, and M. Weiniger, *International Investment Arbitration: Substantive Principles*, 2nd ed. (Oxford: Oxford University Press, 2017), 270–273 (paras 7.09–7.17); M. Paparinskis, *The International Minimum Standard and Fair and Equitable Treatment* (Oxford: Oxford University Press, 2013), 166–167.

[88] Indeed, see Tucker (n. 69), 130, reporting on the views of an interviewee arbitrator: '[For] human beings, it is natural for us to look around, and say, "How was this done before? Who has decided it?"' In the same vein, see D. A. Schön, *The Reflective Practitioner: How Professionals Think in Action* (New York: Basic Books, 1983), 137–140 (pointing out that past experience helps practitioners build a repertoire of examples, images, understandings and actions, which they can then bring to bear on a novel situation by way of analogy).

[89] N. Ridi, 'The Shape and Structure of the "Usable Past": An Empirical Analysis of the Use of Precedent in International Adjudication' (2019) 10 *Journal of International Dispute Settlement* 200, 246.

resulting from the absence of a firm track record of institutional rationality in ISDS identified in Section 7.3.1.

Notwithstanding the general importance of acquiescence, care should nevertheless be taken to further clarify its scope, realise its complexity, and, in the process, also somewhat temper expectations of its overall practical effectiveness in ISDS. The focus in what follows is placed on the use of past arbitral awards by present-day tribunals. Three remarks are offered as caveats putting the practical effectiveness of the virtue of acquiescence in ISDS into perspective. The first caveat is general to law and to the character of legal reasoning. The other two caveats are particular to the unique context of ISDS.

The first caveat to offer is that the normative pull of precedent always exists on a sliding scale.[90] Being in effect a past event connected to present action, a precedent is a reason to presently act in a certain way that is introduced in legal reasoning through the medium of analogy.[91] To follow a precedent is to draw an explicit or implicit analogy between one instance (the past case) and another (the present case). As seen in Chapter 5, analogical reasoning comprises the mental processes of identifying similarities, drawing structural parallels, and devising a goal or purpose to guide the analogy. These processes contribute to adjudicators' interpretative function by way of framing and contextualising the legal issues they seek to resolve. Therefore, an analogy between two cases can be assessed as being persuasively or unpersuasively drawn out, which can then render the precedent itself persuasive or unpersuasive, which will ultimately result in it being characterised as a strong or a weak reason to guide present conduct.

It follows that a precedent's authority is itself a matter of interpretation. Precedential authority may well depend on more factors than the mere fact that the precedent in question is followed consistently in a series of past decisions. Put differently, the presence of any *jurisprudence constante* in ISDS is but one contextual factor for arbitrators to consider

[90] See N. Duxbury, *The Nature and Authority of Precedent* (Cambridge: Cambridge University Press, 2008), 23 (footnote omitted):

> [T]he reality is that precedents, unlike statutes, do not bind judges in an all-or-nothing fashion, that the binding force of a precedent is best explained not in terms of its validity (this being a non-scalar concept) but in terms of its authority (of which there can be degrees).

[91] See ibid., 2, 59.

in assessing the authority of a precedent. As stated by the tribunal in *Daimler* v. *Argentina*:

> [T]he Tribunal acknowledges that it is a fundamental principle of the rule of law that '"like cases should be decided alike," unless a strong reason exists to distinguish the current case from previous ones.' This latter consideration will weigh more or less heavily depending upon: a) how 'like' the prior and present cases are, having regard to all relevant considerations; b) the degree to which a clear *jurisprudence constante* has emerged in respect of a particular legal issue; and c) the Tribunal's independent estimation of the persuasiveness of prior tribunals' reasoning.[92]

Thus, the virtue of acquiescence is not served by a mechanical recitation of precedents without regard paid to their context, persuasiveness of reasoning, or indeed similarity to the case the tribunal is presently facing.[93] Chapter 3's examination of the decision in *Santa Elena* v. *Costa Rica*, and the imposition by subsequent tribunals of a default rule of compound interest in ISDS, is useful to recall at this juncture as an example of such mechanical recitation.[94]

The second caveat to offer follows logically from the first. Any commitment to consider and follow strands of *jurisprudence constante* while practising acquiescence in ISDS cannot but be a moral commitment. Absent some kind of judicial hierarchy or a formally pronounced doctrine of *stare decisis*, a tribunal is under no legal obligation to actually follow solutions prescribed by any one precedent. To the contrary, in fact, because of the flat and diffuse nature of the system, investment tribunals retain an air of 'sovereignty' and are free to disagree with each

[92] *Daimler Financial Services AG* v. *Argentine Republic*, ICSID Case No. ARB/05/1, Award, 22 August 2012, para 52 (partially quoting from *Suez, Sociedad General de Aguas de Barcelona, S.A. and Vivendi Universal, S.A.* v. *The Argentine Republic*, ICSID Case No. ARB/03/19, Decision on Liability, 30 July 2010, para 189) (footnote omitted).

[93] Similarly, see *Fraport AG Frankfurt Airport Services Worldwide* v. *The Republic of the Philippines*, ICSID Case No. ARB/03/25, Award, 16 August 2007, Dissenting Opinion of Mr Bernardo M. Cremades, para 40 (criticising the 'practice of the casual use of citations from other awards without regard to their original contexts' and pointing out that in the instant case '[a]wards [had] been cited as if they were authorities or precedents on, for example, the significance of illegal conduct by the investor that [bore] no similarity to the case at issue').

[94] Indeed, mechanical recitation of precedents seems to be a widespread practice in ISDS, as seen, e.g., in Tucker (n. 69), 130–131.

other.[95] As a result, a number of issues in international investment law are still subject to jurisprudential debate with no clearly discernible pattern of final resolution emerging.[96] Such issues include, for example, the admissibility of shareholders' claims for reflective loss, the scope of application of umbrella clauses, the substantive scope of application of MFN clauses, the standard of review of domestic regulatory conduct, or the exact import and relevance of the investor's expectations in cases of alleged indirect expropriation. On the flip side, wide support and agreement often seem to be garnered around fairly abstract statements of principle, such as the host state's inherent right to regulate or the police powers doctrine, which do very little to offer concrete solutions to concrete legal issues or to ensure predictability vis-à-vis the outcomes of cases.

Also following from the flat and diffuse nature of the system is the third caveat we must offer. The normative pull of past experience in ISDS is to a significant degree sociological. That is to say, the authority of past awards in ISDS depends not only on the quality of the reasoning used but also on the identity of the arbitrators who sat on the tribunal.[97] Offering this observation as a caveat does not mean to suggest that the sociological element precludes a particular decision from acting as a firm guide for

[95] See *AES Corporation* v. *The Argentine Republic*, ICSID Case No. ARB/02/17, Decision on Jurisdiction, 26 April 2005, para 30:

> An identity of the basis of jurisdiction of [earlier] tribunals, even when it meets with very similar if not even identical facts at the origin of the disputes, does not suffice to apply systematically to the present case positions or solutions already adopted in these cases. Each tribunal remains sovereign and may retain, as it is confirmed by ICSID practice, a different solution for resolving the same problem; but decisions on jurisdiction dealing with the same or very similar issues may at least indicate some lines of reasoning of real interest; this Tribunal may consider them in order to compare its own position with those already adopted by its predecessors and, if it shares the views already expressed by one or more of these tribunals on a specific point of law, it is free to adopt the same solution.

Also, see Tucker (n. 69), 129 ('As one interviewee said, "Because we have a flat legal system with no appellate review and each arbitral tribunal is sovereign, we are free to disagree with each other."').

[96] E.g., see Z. Douglas, 'Can a Doctrine of Precedent Be Justified in Investment Treaty Arbitration?' (2010) 25 *ICSID Review – Foreign Investment Law Journal* 104, 107–108.

[97] Indeed, see Tucker (n. 69), 130:

> As one interviewee said: 'Always look at the names. "Gabrielle Kaufmann Kohler, 10 out of 10. Mr. X, do not bother to read it." The name is very important. I think it reflects the quality of the reasoning.' . . .

future tribunals and even from acting as something akin to a binding precedent of sorts. A case in point, albeit a rare one, is the impact that the annulment committee's decision in *CMS* v. *Argentina* had on subsequent tribunals addressing the relationship between the defence of necessity under Article 25 of the ILC's Articles on State Responsibility, on the one hand, and state defences based on necessity found in investment treaties, on the other.[98] It seems virtually inconceivable that investors can plausibly put forward arguments conflating the two kinds of defences after the *CMS* annulment decision. It is evident that the *CMS* committee managed this not merely because of its well-reasoned decision but also by dint of its composition. The committee comprised two former ICJ Judges (Judges Gilbert Guillaume and Nabil Elaraby) and the late Judge James Crawford (at the time professor and the Special Rapporteur who had delivered the ILC's Articles on State Responsibility).

Nevertheless, the prominent sociological aspect of the authority of ISDS awards is offered as a caveat here to emphasise its arguably volatile nature. It could mean, for example, that decisions delivered by an arbitrator of high esteem will naturally seem more authoritative. But it could also mean that a series of 'bad performances' of inadequate or unpersuasive reasoning may render an arbitrator's present and past decisions less authoritative over time. These effects would be compounded if the arbitrator in question frequently acts as tribunal president, considering the central role that tribunal presidents play in managing deliberations and drafting awards. Conversely, in a legal system with a doctrine of *stare decisis*, one can expect that a loss in influence or esteem by the judges who pronounced a precedent will have less of an impact on the precedent's authority. This follows from the fact

> Or as another [interviewee] put it: 'If a really respected group of arbitrators decides a particular set of principles, you think a lot about that. You think long and hard before you say that that does not make any sense.'

Also, see G. Guillaume, 'The Use of Precedent by International Judges and Arbitrators' (2011) 2 *Journal of International Dispute Settlement* 5, 14 (incl. n. 46), noting that, since the decisions of arbitral tribunals are of 'variable quality', it tends to be that 'the quality of the arguments and those of the arbiters are determinative'.

98 In this respect, see the analysis on this decision in Section 5.3. By way of background, the *CMS* annulment decision almost single-handedly broke what seemed like an emerging trend at the time of treating the conditions of the necessity defence, under Article 25 of the ILC's Articles on State Responsibility, as synonymous and directly applicable to state defences based on necessity found in investment treaties. More to the point, it managed to do so even without actually annulling the original *CMS* award on this ground citing instead its limited powers of review.

that the practice of following precedents in such a system is institutionalised via the *stare decisis* doctrine, in addition to being sociological in nature. Thus, one can reasonably expect that precedents will likely continue to be binding, so long as their background assumptions and statements of principle hold up to scrutiny, or so long as they do not lead to clearly undesirable results.

To summarise a lengthy discussion, four conclusions may be drawn in relation to the virtue of acquiescence in ISDS. Firstly, following a precedent is not an automatic or mechanical process. Secondly, *jurisprudence constante* in and of itself only acts as a partial constrain for future tribunals. Thirdly, and importantly, this does not preclude a tribunal from agreeing with and taking on board the *ratio decidendi* of a prior award. Yet, fourthly, the implication of the observations above is that the later tribunal should do so, not simply because the prior tribunal also did so, but rather because the solution that the prior tribunal adopted and the reasoning that it used are deemed relevant for the later tribunal as well. Acquiescence instructs that the later tribunal should take care to make the latter step clear, for instance, by showing that (and justifying why) the instant case and the prior case should be treated as analogues.[99]

7.7 The Virtues of Integrity and Candour

It may be useful to briefly recapitulate at this point. The virtue of faith instructs that doing law is an intelligible human endeavour. Still, the law's content is to some extent arguable and on occasion gives rise to ambiguity and uncertainty, which in turn gives adjudicators degrees of discretion in crafting their interpretations of it. When this happens, the virtue of humility instructs that legal reasoning is not merely an exercise in technical expertise. Too often it has distributive consequences for the parties concerned, which should be carefully taken into account. For its part, the virtue of acquiescence has capacity to lead to intersubjective agreement by acting as a partial constraint and as guide for judicial

[99] For a statement moving in this direction, see, e.g., *Bureau Veritas, Inspection, Valuation, Assessment and Control, BIVAC B.V.* v. *The Republic of Paraguay*, ICSID Case No. ARB/07/9, Decision of the Tribunal on Objections to Jurisdiction, 29 May 2009, para 58: 'Having regard to the sound administration of justice, and the need to ensure the coherence and well-being of the system of justice established by the drafters of the ICSID Convention, we proceed on the basis that it is appropriate for us to explain why we have or have not followed the approach adopted by other tribunals' (footnote omitted).

deliberation. However, it was also seen that, unlike what the case may be in domestic legal systems with a doctrine of *stare decisis*, acquiescence in ISDS is a relatively soft constraint and a gentle guide in most instances.

Given the above, Jefferson Powell has argued that integrity and candour must be included as indispensable judicial virtues.[100] The two virtues are complementary and must operate in unison. On the one hand, integrity attaches to the means and methods through which adjudicators arrive at their decisions. On the other hand, candour should accompany the way in which adjudicators present the arguments in favour of the interpretation or decision that they are advocating.

7.7.1 Integrity

As described by Jefferson Powell, the virtue of integrity instructs adjudicators to seek among the range of reasonable interpretations of the law the one that in honesty seems to them the most plausible given the law's actual text and any relevant past practice.[101] In practical terms, the virtue of integrity is incongruous with treating questions of law in an instrumentalist functional manner, which is to say, with treating them as mere tools to achieve goals one may have chosen to pursue based on external grounds.[102] ISDS decisions are frequently prone to using law in an instrumental fashion. Chapter 4 saw several examples of arbitral awards where interpretations of key treaty provisions were made on the basis of arguments about the object and purpose of investment treaties that were in turn reliant upon a particular, investor-friendly and largely policy-oriented, understanding of the treaties in question.[103]

One may counter-argue that it is perhaps easy to signal out for criticism the instrumentalism in these decisions, precisely because of their clear one-sided views on the object and purpose of investment treaties. However, the general point made here is that an instrumental

[100] See Jefferson Powell (n. 46), 87–89.

[101] Ibid., 90.

[102] Ibid., 91. According to Ralf Michaels, instrumentalism is a subspecies of a functional approach to law and a normative theory of using law for social engineering. Instrumentalism posits that the law exists to meet certain social needs. It thus argues that it is the lawyer's job to develop laws in order to meet these social needs (see R. Michaels, 'The Functional Method of Comparative Law', in M. Reimann and R. Zimmermann [eds.], *The Oxford Handbook of Comparative Law*, 2nd ed. [Oxford: Oxford University Press, 2019] 346, 350, 356–357).

[103] See Section 4.4.3.

understanding of the law could be risky in subtler ways also and even if tribunals profess to adopt a balanced approach between the interests of states and investors. Consider for example *Saluka* v. *Czech Republic* where, in discussing the content of the FET standard in the Czech Republic-Netherlands BIT (1991) in light of the treaty's object and purpose, the tribunal reasoned as follows:

> The protection of foreign investments is not the sole aim of the Treaty, but rather a necessary element alongside the overall aim of encouraging foreign investment and extending and intensifying the parties' economic relations. That in turn calls for a balanced approach in the interpretation of the Treaty's substantive provisions for the protection of investments, since an interpretation which exaggerates the protection to be accorded to foreign investments may serve to dissuade host [s]tates from admitting foreign investments and so undermine the overall aim of extending and intensifying the parties' mutual economic relations.[104]

Thus, the tribunal went on to say that the FET standard does indeed include certain duties for the state (e.g., the protection of the investor's reasonable and legitimate expectations, transparency, consistency in conduct, and non-discrimination), the extent of which must however be conditioned and counter-balanced by the state's right to regulate.[105]

The instrumentalism in the above teleological argument is subtle, yet still problematic. In brief, the tribunal's syllogism is as follows. FET should be interpreted in a balanced way because, otherwise, the contracting parties might be reluctant to admit foreign investments. This would decrease cross-border investment flows between the parties, which would then weaken rather than strengthen their economic relations. It is possible to raise two objections to this chain of reasoning. The first objection is one of institutional role. It is not the role of an investment tribunal to ensure that cross-border investment flows are kept at an adequate level or that inter-state economic relations flourish. These may be incidental policy functions that investment tribunals may or may not actually be serving in practice,[106] but they cannot be raised up to the level of being considered as proper objects of a tribunal's inquiry. The second objection

[104] *Saluka Investments B.V.* v. *The Czech Republic*, UNCITRAL Rules, Partial Award, 17 March 2006, para 300.

[105] Ibid., paras 301–308.

[106] Studies have indeed produced mixed results on this question, as shown in J. Bonnitcha, L. N. Skovgaard Poulsen, and M. Waibel, *The Political Economy of the Investment Treaty Regime* (Oxford: Oxford University Press, 2017), chapter 6.

is that the tribunal is using a policy end to justify an outcome of legal principle. This ultimately results in the tribunal's approach resting on shaky ground in the two ways outlined below.

In the first place, the 'balanced approach' to the interpretation of FET (a legal concept) is rendered contingent and thus vulnerable to potential abuse, precisely because it is based on the policy assumption that an increase in inter-state investment flows (as means) is correlative to the strengthening of the economic relations of the contracting parties to the investment treaty (as end). The tribunal's interpretation of FET would lose its moorings entirely, for instance, if compelling evidence were produced showing that there is in fact no such correlation either generally or between the particular contracting parties concerned. In other words, if a policy assumption is the sole yardstick that matters for a 'balanced' determination of legal principle, then any interpretation – whether balanced or unbalanced on either side – would be as good or as bad as the other. Evidence that the policy assumption does not hold may thus be used to justify taking a more restrictive approach to investment protection, one that would favour state sovereignty over the rights of foreign investors; or it could just as easily be used to justify a more expansive approach favouring the interests of investors over the interests of the host state. In short, if there is no evidence of cross-border investment flows and inter-state economic relations being actually affected or at stake in practice (and if this is the yardstick that matters), then why bother being balanced? Moreover, while such evidence may present states, as lawmakers, with a good reason to rethink the scope of their international investment protection policies, this is hardly related to a tribunal's job.

In the second place, even if we were to concede the validity of the policy assumption above, the undesirable outcome (i.e., a decrease in investment flows by reason of a reluctance to admit foreign investments) cannot plausibly lead as a matter of law to a decision about the proper interpretation of FET. The reason for saying this is that the teleological argument advanced by the tribunal does not seem to rest on any legal rights that investors may enjoy or any legal obligations that host states may have.[107] It rather only seeks to demonstrate that a particular

[107] Indeed, as Dworkin points out, when disputing parties ask something from a court or tribunal, they are making an argument of principle in the sense that they are asserting a right. So long as the legal norm containing this right is in force, the asserting party has said right regardless of whether one believes that the rationale behind the norm invoked

outcome would likely advance or protect a collective goal or interest of the contracting parties concerned. By contrast, the exact same argument may have stood on firmer ground if the applicable BIT provided for a general right of access of investors to the markets of the contracting parties.[108] If that were the case, then an interpretation that would affect investors' exercise of that right could provide the tribunal with a plausible argument against it. Such an argument would pertain to the rightness of a particular expected conduct (i.e., reluctance of host states to admit foreign investments), when tested against the law's text (i.e., a hypothetical BIT with a general right of establishment recognised to foreign investors). To be sure, even this hypothetical argument would likely be a weak one, as it would still rely on the doubtful validity of the key policy assumption made by the tribunal, as well as on the dubious link between an unbalanced interpretation of FET and an unwillingness by states to admit investments in their territory. But it would at least be methodologically sounder as it would attempt to establish a plausible link with a legal right of foreign investors emerging from a reasonable interpretation of the applicable law.

7.7.2 Candour

A judicial virtue of integrity in ISDS seeks to guard against the risks associated with overt or covert instrumental views of investment treaties. It instructs arbitrators to construct their interpretations by relying on

is sound or wise. Put differently, disputing parties always assert a right to win and not that their winning would be in the general interest of the community, the latter being the domain of policy (see R. Dworkin, *Taking Rights Seriously* [Cambridge, MA: Harvard University Press, 1977], 82ff).

108 Article 2 of the Czech Republic-Netherlands BIT (1991), applicable in the *Saluka* case, provided that:

> Each Contracting Party shall in its territory promote investments by investors of the other Contracting Party and shall admit such investments in accordance with its provisions of law.

However, the above provision does not create a general right of establishment for foreign investors. Rather, what this provision says is simply that foreign investors have a right that their investments be admitted into the host state under the conditions established by that state's domestic law. There is thus nothing preventing the contracting parties from refusing the establishment of an investment by a national of the other party.

See also, K. J. Vandevelde, 'Investment Liberalization and Economic Development: The Role of Bilateral Investment Treaties' (1998) 36 *Columbia Journal of Transnational Law* 501, 511.

their best assessment of the content of the available legal materials and not by attempting to impose on them extraneous policy goals. However, to be effective, integrity must also be accompanied by candour with respect to the manner in which one presents outward the arguments that justify one's decision. As described by Jefferson Powell:

> The ... virtue of candor ... goes beyond honesty about the meaning of cases and sincerity in the statement of viewpoint. It is the disposition to seek, and so far as possible to achieve, a congruity between the mind grappling with the ... issue before it and the language in which that struggle and its resolution is expressed, 'living speech', as James Boyd White has memorably described it.[109]

Stated differently, the judicial virtue of candour is about being transparent with respect to how a case ought to be decided and with respect to why it ought to be decided in one way rather than another, as opposed to merely asserting that it ought to be so.[110] In particular, it involves

[109] Jefferson Powell (n. 46), 90 (footnote omitted).

[110] For a similar view, see A. Paulus, 'International Adjudication', in S. Besson and J. Tasioulas (eds.), *The Philosophy of International Law* (Oxford: Oxford University Press, 2010) 207, 209, 221 (in the quoted passages Paulus talks about the 'integrity' of the law borrowing from Dworkin's work, yet the conclusions he draws seem to fit with what is here described as the judicial virtue of candour):

> This contribution argues that international adjudication can maintain integrity if and to the extent that the choice between different – and at times conflicting – rationales is made in a conscious and transparent manner. ...
>
> [W]hen done openly and transparently, international adjudication will still be able to remain faithful to the idea of the integrity of international law. In this event, judges should openly admit to the indeterminacy of the sources and the clash of the underlying principles and clearly distinguish between the constraints of the law and the reasons for their adoption of a particular solution and their preference for one principle over another.

Understood in that sense, candour argues against the formalistic use of legal reasoning and asks adjudicators to move beyond mere technical argumentation in their practice. To be sure, attention to legal technique and craft are necessary conditions for an argument to be considered legitimate and acceptable in the first place. Jefferson Powell (n. 46), 70, 113–114, himself points out that carefully defining the issues in dispute, identifying relevant authorities, avoiding logical flaws, and putting arguments in forms that are acceptable to the legal community are all things one expects of judicial decisions. However, absent a simultaneous commitment to the arguable character of the law, to openness, and to the requirement of persuasion, there is a risk that legal technique and craft alone may render legal reasoning impenetrable, turning it into an instrument of mere assertion and obfuscation of legitimate counterpoints. Candour seeks to guard against this.

mapping out and making explicit the pathways of one's thought process, as well as arranging these in a structure that fairly reflects the force of any opposing arguments.[111]

It follows then that candour is not only a virtue of the arbitrator's personal intellectual honesty. Rather, candour also acts for the benefit of others. It is a necessary complement to the virtue of integrity because it allows others to understand a decision's true grounds and thus assent to its correctness, or at least assent to its validity even though they may disagree with its substance.[112] A judicial virtue of candour is therefore essential if arbitrators wish for their co-arbitrators and their audience (comprising the disputing parties and the international investment law community at large) to accept their decisions as persuasive and legitimate, especially in cases when one cannot claim that a particular decision was beyond dispute.[113]

Thus understood, candour's relevance is ubiquitous. It finds application not just in the collective drafting of awards by tribunals but also in the way arbitrators should individually approach internal deliberations. The virtue of candour would, for instance, instruct arbitrators to deliberate: by making clear the way they approach the legal questions presented before them, including the way they identify and frame the question to be answered; by not avoiding controversial points but by taking care to

[111] Similarly, see J. B. White, *Living Speech: Resisting the Empire of Force* (Princeton: Princeton University Press, 2006), 73–74:

> The good judicial opinion thus takes the reader through the process of thought the judge herself engages in, with a fair representation of doubts, uncertainties, and the force of countering arguments. It should end with a conclusion that is not predetermined or shaped by considerations external to the opinion but reached by the process of thought enacted in her writing. . . .
>
> The opposite of this kind of writing is what in the law we call conclusory writing, cast in terms that bury argument and thought in one's premises, reducing it all to a set of unargued assertions.

[112] Jefferson Powell (n. 46), 90.

[113] Ibid.; similarly, H. L. A. Hart, *The Concept of Law*, 3rd ed. (Oxford: Oxford University Press, 2012), 204–205, pointing out that (emphasis in original):

> [Judges] often display characteristic judicial virtues . . . [:] impartiality and neutrality in surveying the alternatives; consideration for the interest of all who will be affected; and a concern to deploy some acceptable general principle as a reasoned basis for decision. No doubt because a plurality of such principles is always possible it cannot be *demonstrated* that a decision is uniquely correct: but it may be made acceptable as the reasoned product of informed impartial choice.

clarify and address such points if they are necessary to the decision; and by not presenting their views as axiomatic or inevitable but rather in a manner that seeks to persuade their co-arbitrators. In so doing, the chances for a tribunal to collectively arrive at a common ground solution may be increased even amid substantive disagreement among the arbitrators.

Nevertheless, the practicalities of arbitral decision-making do not always create a framework that is conducive towards arbitrators practising candour. It was mentioned above, for example, that there are no rules in place for how deliberations in ISDS should be conducted. It was also mentioned that a great deal in this respect seems to depend on the type of presiding arbitrator that each tribunal has. Overcommitment to cases further exacerbates these structural shortcomings.[114] It is not uncommon for busy arbitrators to leverage outside support for their preparation by relying on their own back-office of associates and assistants. There is a potential double impact of this practice on the quality and outcome of deliberations. Firstly, by becoming so heavily reliant on external support, busy arbitrators may devote less time to grapple with what each case is really about. Ultimately, the arbitrator's narrative and understanding of the case may not be truly his or her own but that of his or her assistants. Secondly, the same arbitrator may end up exerting an undue influence on the way the entire decision-making process is shaped simply by virtue of his or her over-preparedness.[115]

An additional aggravating factor that often remains unexplored is, interestingly, external to the tribunal itself. This is the role of counsel

[114] For a simple, yet elegant suggestion on how to manage arbitrator overcommitment and simultaneously widen the pool of arbitrators, see D. D. Caron, 'Arbitrators and the Rule of X', King's College London Dickson Poon School of Law, Legal Studies Research Paper Series, Paper No 2017-41, available at https://papers.ssrn.com/sol3/papers.cfm?abstract_id=3062537.

[115] See Tucker (n. 30), 193:

> In this model, the arbitrator accepts a large number of appointments by investors – more than he could prepare for on his own. He has 'a back-office full of people working for him full time – incredibly impressive, but unnamed people – and they do all the work for him and research. And what happens is that [such a wingman] will arrive at a deliberation with memos that have been done by his back-office'. He saves the chair from having to do this work, and is able to outmanoeuvre the other wingman by being more prepared than they are. Even if a chair is not predisposed to follow the wing arbitrator's line, the constant stream of memos subtly shapes the course of the arbitration.

in ISDS cases. Ideally, counsel should be assisting the tribunal to decide by setting out in their pleadings a clear roadmap of the case.[116] In doing so, counsel can act with candour too, by leading the tribunal through an idealised process of thought that, although arguing for a particular outcome, still gives weight and addresses any countering arguments or plausible claims arguing the other way.[117] However, party memorials in ISDS often tend to be long and undisciplined, at times resembling encyclopaedic entries rather than an exercise to distil for the benefit of the tribunal the essence of the case and the relevant points of law.[118] The consequence is that arbitrators will likely not be at the optimum position to decide when they reach the stage of deliberations.[119] Not having been afforded the opportunity to truly grasp the essence of the case, they would likely find it harder to practise candour when mapping out their way to a decision.

7.8 Conclusion

The present chapter has served a dual aim. The chapter has been a continuation of the analysis previously undertaken in Chapter 6. That chapter had argued that coherence in judicial reasoning implies a reflexive attitude from decision-makers, yet the examination of reflexivity therein did not explicitly address the collective nature of adjudication. The latter has been taken up in the present chapter as the primary object

116 T. T. Landau, 'Dysfunctional Deliberations and Effective Advocacy', in A. Menaker (ed.), *International Arbitration and the Rule of Law: Contribution and Conformity* (Alphen aan den Rijn: Kluwer Law International, 2017) 285, 297–298.

117 Cf. White (n. 111), 73–74 (incl. n. 12). To be sure, counsel's virtue of candour is different from a tribunal's but it is no less real or important because of this. Counsel are not asked to provide an answer to the question of how they would decide the case as if they were the tribunal. Rather, the question that they should be answering is what is the best argument that can responsibly be made on behalf of their client in this case given the existing legal materials. Counsel can answer this question with the virtue of candour in mind and, in so doing, provide critical help to the arbitrators who carry the responsibility of deciding.

118 See T. T. Landau, 'The Psychology of the Decision-Making Process: Arbitral Tribunal Deliberations' (2015) 17 *Asian Dispute Review* 208, 209.

119 Ibid., 213. To that end, Landau argues that tribunals should make greater use of devices such as 'Kaplan Openings' and 'Reed Retreats' and that they should hold deliberations after each day's hearing session as a matter of course. The practical effect of taking such steps, he argues, would be to 'provide for space and time at an appropriate point in the arbitral process in which information overload and the need for short-cut maps or rescue plans can both be avoided' (ibid.).

of inquiry. At the same time, the present chapter has also served as a synthesis of the arguments advanced in this book on the role of coherence in judicial reasoning in ISDS.

The search for collective reflexivity is an ever-present challenge in ISDS. This is entirely due to the fact that arbitrators do not work in isolation but come together to deliberate collectively in groups. In such a collegial setting, an individual arbitrator's process of reflection may coincide with, or differ from, another's on the same panel. Therefore, to the extent that coherence implies reflexivity, as argued in Chapter 6, it is also the panel's collective reflexivity that is at issue rather than merely the arbitrators' individual reflexivity. In other words, coherence requires both that arbitrators form their views about the outcome of a case in a manner that is individually reflective and that the tribunal as a group arrives at its conclusion in a manner that is collectively reflective. The thesis of this chapter has thus been that promoting collective reflexivity in ISDS presupposes the realisation that arbitrators bear moral responsibility over the way they discharge their duties.

It was argued in particular that moral responsibility is exemplified in a professional commitment to five judicial virtues, which, borrowing from the work of Jefferson Powell, were termed faith, humility, acquiescence, integrity, and candour. Briefly summarised: faith instructs arbitrators to regard international investment law as intelligible and as a specialised regime; humility instructs arbitrators to be cognisant of the fact that they decide matters that bear directly on the allocation of power and authority; acquiescence instructs arbitrators to take full but also critical account of past wisdom, experience, and practice in their decisions; whereas integrity and candour instruct arbitrators to not deploy legal reasoning in an instrumental manner and to be transparent about the way they approach the legal issues presented before them. A professional commitment to moral responsibility and to a series of virtues by each arbitrator on an ISDS tribunal is thus necessary if we hope for arbitrators to be able, either to convince colleagues on the same panel who may have different views, or to at least steer them towards achieving a coherent common ground solution.

Importantly, the above are not meant to be taken as a strict formula or as an equation for the courtroom. Judicial virtues are habits and mental dispositions. As such, they are meant to be taken as a framework offering guidelines and a roadmap for developing better deliberative practices in ISDS. The extent to which they will succeed in doing so will also depend on a series of structural and incidental features of international investment law and ISDS, including, the existing system's ad hoc nature, the current practice of party appointed decision-makers, the prevalence of partisanship and overcommitment to cases by arbitrators, and the strong link between the social capital of individual arbitrators and the perceived authority of arbitral awards.

Coda

Coherence and Investor–State Dispute Settlement Reform

Concerns of incoherence surrounding ISDS decisions have been widely discussed by scholars over the past several years and have moreover been overwhelmingly raised by state delegations during the UNCITRAL Working Group III discussions on ISDS reform. This book's inquiry into the concept of coherence in ISDS has taken us on a journey through aspects of epistemology, legal theory, interpretation, and the morality of responsibility. In this coda, the discussion is briefly brought back to its beginnings and the topic of ISDS reform. Are there any conclusions in relation to ISDS reform that may usefully be drawn from the discussion?

The coda proceeds in two steps. Section C.1 presents a succinct overview of the direction that the discussions on ISDS reform have taken in Working Group III as of the time of writing. Section C.2 then offers a tentative assessment of that direction in light of the preceding examination of coherence in ISDS.

C.1 ISDS Reform at UNCITRAL

A perceived lack of coherence in arbitral decisions has been called out as a key concern by virtually every state delegation contemplating ISDS reform at UNCITRAL. Further, such concern is not expressed in isolation but rather alongside related concerns over a lack of consistency, predictability, and correctness in arbitral decisions. All four of the above causes for concern are often melded together without distinction. This is to some degree understandable given that, as seen in Chapter 1, there are clear connections and linkages among the concepts of coherence, consistency, predictability, and correctness in law. However, a core aim of this book has been to point out the need to adopt a distinct understanding and treatment of each of these concepts. It has been argued, in particular that, among the four concepts, coherence is the antecedent one bearing directly upon the rest.

A critical feature of the UNCITRAL debate is that the Working Group's mandate is limited to considering only procedural ways of reforming the ISDS regime. Despite warnings by some delegations that procedural reform should go together with the substantive reform of international investment agreements and the commitments they contain,[1] the latter aspect is widely regarded as being outside the scope of the discussions. Options to address the inherently substantive concerns regarding coherence, consistency, predictability, and correctness are thus channelled principally through so-called structural reform proposals. These include proposals for the establishment of (i) a Multilateral Investment Court, comprising first instance and appellate divisions and staffed by permanent, full-time judges or (ii) a permanent stand-alone appellate mechanism with the power to review awards rendered by existing ad hoc tribunals.[2] Addressing the above concerns is also channelled, in a secondary manner, through structural proposals for the establishment of a multilateral advisory centre on international investment law (via possible functions such as state legal representation, capacity building, and the dissemination of best practices).[3]

The remainder of the coda assesses the direction of the ISDS reform debate in Working Group III, with emphasis on the concern of the perceived incoherence in arbitral decision-making.

[1] E.g., see UNCITRAL Working Group III (Investor–State Dispute Settlement Reform), 'Possible Reform of Investor–State Dispute Settlement (ISDS): Submission from the Government of Thailand', UN Doc A/CN.9/WG.III/WP.162 (8 March 2019), paras 28–29 (proposing the simultaneous negotiation of model clauses on substantive provisions); UNCITRAL Working Group III (Investor–State Dispute Settlement Reform), 'Possible Reform of Investor–State Dispute Settlement (ISDS): Comments by the Government of Indonesia', UN Doc A/CN.9/WG.III/WP.156 (9 November 2018), paras 1–2, 16 (arguing that the substance/procedure dichotomy adopted by the Working Group defeats the purpose of designing a meaningful ISDS mechanism).

[2] See UNCITRAL Working Group III (Investor–State Dispute Settlement Reform), 'Possible Reform of Investor–State Dispute Settlement (ISDS): Note by the Secretariat', UN Doc A/CN.9/WG.III/WP.166 (30 July 2019); and UNCITRAL Working Group III (Investor–State Dispute Settlement Reform), 'Possible Reform of Investor–State Dispute Settlement (ISDS): Note by the Secretariat – Addendum', UN Doc A/CN.9/WG.III/WP.166/Add.1 (30 July 2019).

[3] Ibid.

C.2 An Assessment of the ISDS Reform Debate through the Prism of Coherence

Two remarks about coherence must be reiterated at the outset. Firstly, achieving perfect coherence is improbable and likely an unattainable ideal in practice. Coherent legal reasoning is always a work in progress. Secondly, coherence has a dual dimension. It not only relates to the substance of a legal pronouncement or legal outcome but also to the process through which that pronouncement or outcome was achieved. These two remarks in turn lead to two broad, overarching considerations in relation to the ISDS reform effort. In the first place, no reform effort can ever fully succeed in securing perfect coherence in law and legal reasoning. In the second place, if it is to be even partially effective, any attempt at enhancing coherence must proceed by taking into account its aforementioned dual dimension. In other words, one needs to work from both ends – substance as well as procedure – in reforming the ISDS regime, while keeping potential risks and limitations in mind.

On the substantive end, coherence in arbitral decision-making may be promoted by ensuring that states go into investment treaty negotiations prepared. This involves having clearly defined policy goals and expectations when entering into such treaties, mapping out in advance their ideal outcomes in terms of final provisions, and identifying any negotiating 'red lines'. In more practical terms, during negotiations, states could place particular emphasis on clearer drafting for individual treaty commitments and on better treaty design overall. This could involve a variety of strategies, including (i) clarifying the meaning of any standard-like norms used in the treaty, or using rule-like norms whenever possible, in an attempt to limit (or at least guide) the interpretative discretion of tribunals;[4] (ii) introducing treaty mechanisms allowing for the easier

[4] According to K. M. Sullivan, 'Foreword: The Justices of Rules and Standards' (1992) 106 *Harvard Law Review* 22, 57–59, all legal norms fall on a continuum of discretion. Rule-like norms bind decision-makers to respond in a determinate way when in the presence of certain triggering facts. Rule-like norms thus afford decision-makers lesser discretion, by having legislators work out certain value choices in advance. Conversely, standard-like norms afford more discretion to decision-makers. In using standard-like norms, legislators still work out value choices in advance, but they do so in less detail or in very broad strokes. In so doing, they give decision-makers the opportunity to take into account all relevant principles, factors, or circumstances when deciding.

States negotiating investment treaties have sought to clarify standard-like provisions by way of introducing relevant factors (i.e., specific criteria to be assessed, weighed, or strictly applied in a situation), presumptions (i.e., ideas taken to be true on the basis of probability,

rebalancing of the contracting parties' commitments when this is deemed necessary (e.g., mechanisms for joint interpretations) or allowing for the coordination of positions as to the exact content and correct interpretation of their commitments following the emergence of an investment dispute (e.g., non-disputing state party submissions); or (iii) exploring avenues for introducing clearly defined and enforceable obligations on foreign investors. In short, carefully strategising treaty design and treaty drafting is likely to result in more coherent treaties and, by extension, more coherent interpretations of those treaties by tribunals.

Nevertheless, any effort at the drafting stage must be undertaken with two caveats in mind. The first caveat is that language, no matter how well crafted, cannot exhaust all possible meanings that may be assigned to it in the future. This is not only a result of the drafters' practical inability to anticipate and exhaustively provide for any possible future eventuality but also a consequence of the fact that negotiating parties may not always agree on substance or have the same policy priorities. Philip Allott's famous aphorism seems apt: often, a treaty is a disagreement reduced to writing.[5] The second caveat of which to be mindful is not underestimating the bigger picture of international investment law as a regime. As seen in Chapter 5, the battle of paradigms to frame and contextualise the nature, foundations, and aims of international investment law and ISDS

experience, or common-sense), or simple guidelines, acting as normative short-cuts for how tribunals should approach the interpretation of these provisions. For instance:

- examples of factors include, Article 9.4 (incl. the footnote therein and para 3 of the accompanying Drafters' Note on Interpretation of 'In Like Circumstances') of the CPTPP (2018), Article 5(1)–(2) Intra-MERCOSUR Protocol of Cooperation and Facilitation of Investments (2017), Article 8.10(2) and Annex 8-A(2) Canada-EU CETA (2016), and Article 2.5(3) Brazil-Peru Economic and Trade Expansion Agreement (2016);
- examples of presumptions include, para 2 of the Drafters' Note on Interpretation of 'In Like Circumstances' of the CPTPP (2018), Article 8.10(6)–(7) and Annex 8-A(3) Canada-EU CETA (2016), and Article 3(3) Nigeria-Singapore BIT (2016);
- examples of guidelines include Article 8.10(4) Canada-EU CETA (2016), Article 3(4) Nigeria-Singapore BIT (2016), and Article 2.5(5) Brazil-Peru Economic and Trade Expansion Agreement (2016).

However, it is to be noted that factors, presumptions, and guidelines cannot fully dispose of every case either and, as a result, do not completely extinguish arbitral discretion.

[5] P. Allott, 'The Concept of International Law' (1999) 10 *European Journal of International Law* 31, 43. He continues (ibid.): 'The eventual parties to a treaty enter into negotiation with different ideas of what they want to achieve. Negotiation is a process for finding a third thing which neither party wants but both parties can accept.'

is real and ongoing. The interests of foreign investors and host states will always be at odds, with each side advocating for a different vision for the regime. Therefore, so long as common substantive commitments or a unified overall vision do not emerge from states acting collectively, it will be up to ISDS in whatever form it takes to strike that balance case by case.

Moving now to reform efforts on the procedural end, it is evident that introducing some structure is required if one wishes to enhance coherence in ISDS. A permanent focal point taking the form of a two-tier Multilateral Investment Court or even a stand-alone appellate mechanism would help to establish, each to its own degree, an institutionalised rational point of view from which future investment adjudicators can reason. Indeed, the absence of an institutionalised rational point of view in the existing regime was identified in Chapter 7 as being among the reasons why it may be more difficult to secure collective reflexivity in the legal reasoning of arbitral tribunals at the moment. Permanent structures are also expected to address, also to varying degrees, the financial incentives that may lead decision-makers to overcommit to cases or to become partisan. Partisanship and overcommitment are incentivised in the existing regime given its entirely ad hoc nature and the fact that arbitrators are appointed by the disputing parties. As argued in Chapter 7, partisanship and overcommitment are practices that can negatively impact a tribunal's attempts at being collectively reflexive.

Permanent structures, in particular a Multilateral Investment Court, may also help promote coherence in other ways too. For instance, they could be designed to permit third-party participation thus ensuring that all affected interests (e.g., those of local communities) are considered in the litigation of an investment dispute. In the existing regime, consideration of third-party interests does not fit easily within the arbitration format given the primacy that the latter places on the principle of party autonomy. Leaving third-party interests outside the arbitral process may have a negative impact on a decision's perceived legitimacy. By the same token, it may also impact the decision's actual or perceived moral correctness.

At the same time, structural solutions come with their own limitations and drawbacks. Top-down solutions may come at the expense of bottom-up creativity. Permanent structures can quickly achieve a unified vision of the applicable law and can secure consistency and predictability. However, as understood in this book, coherence is not only about consistency and predictability but also about the moral correctness of outcomes. A fundamental point about coherence, therefore, is that it consists in more than just having decisions that nominally seem consistent. Rather, coherence is crucially also about the quality of the reasoning used. Accordingly, this book has emphasised the importance of also looking at the bottom-up dimension, especially if one is concerned with ensuring the quality and persuasiveness of judicial reasoning.[6] Related to this is an additional potential drawback of top-down solutions, especially of highly centralised ones. Even if a Multilateral Investment Court is established in the future, traditional arbitration is unlikely to completely disappear as a form of ISDS. There is a risk in this respect that centralised structures will be gradually siloed diminishing inter-judicial dialogue as a result. Inter-judicial dialogue can, however, foster the exchange of new ideas and innovative solutions that may over time lead to higher quality judicial reasoning.[7]

In conclusion, it is not only the case that securing coherence escapes the confines of strictly procedural ISDS reform but also that securing coherence is something that is more generally not amenable to perfect solutions in any event. The discussion in this book may therefore have three implications, in particular, for the delegations participating in the Working Group III discussions. Firstly, delegations may be required to reassess their conceptual understanding of consistency, coherence, predictability, and correctness. In essence, this is tantamount to reframing and recontextualising the problem that they seek to resolve. Secondly, delegations may be required to place questions of coherence at the forefront while also realising and accepting that the goal of coherence

[6] Indeed, a similar concern has also been expressed by some delegations in Working Group III. For instance, in its oral intervention during the Working Group's 35th session (23–27 April 2018, New York City), Japan expressed concern in delegating too much interpretative authority to permanent judicial bodies. Among the reasons for such concern, according to Japan, is that adjudicators in a permanent body may also produce incorrect decisions. The implication of Japan's argument seems to be that, whereas in the current ISDS system a host state can hope to persuade subsequent tribunals not to follow a prior incorrect award, doing so in a permanent system would likely be a much more difficult endeavour. Audio recordings of the Working Group's meetings are available at https://uncitral.un.org/en/audio#03.

[7] E.g., cf. A.-M. Slaughter, *A New World Order* (Princeton: Princeton University Press, 2004), 77, speaking in the context of judicial dialogue among domestic courts [footnote omitted]:

> For judges favoring the use of persuasive authority, looking abroad simply helps them to do a better job at home, in the sense that they can approach a particular problem more creatively or with greater insight. Foreign decisions are persuasive because they offer new information and perspectives that may cast an issue in a different and more tractable light.

is an elusive one. It is not matter of finding a 'silver bullet' solution but rather a matter of forming a realistic view of the expected benefits of proposed solutions, while accepting calculated risks in relation to any expected drawbacks. Thirdly, delegations may be required to also train their sights on addressing the bottom-up alongside the top-down. The bottom-up in the UNCITRAL context is the voice of the arbitrators themselves. This voice is notably missing from the formal debate. The individuals to whom states and investors entrust the resolution of their disputes may be in a unique position to offer insights that would be valuable to reforming ISDS. Particularly useful in this respect would be insights (i) about the challenges they face in interpreting investment treaty commitments, (ii) about what works and what does not work in practice in the system as it currently stands, and (iii) about possible ways of fostering a practice of judicial moral responsibility.

Epilogue

Despite an increased interest in coherence, current understandings of it are incomplete and monolithic. Coherence is typically not given an independent meaning from related, but distinct, concepts like consistency, predictability, or correctness. Moreover, most examinations of coherence are done from a 'top-down' perspective that looks, either for 'global' coherence between international investment law and other specialised regimes of international law, or for 'local' coherence within international investment law itself.

Considering the important role that ISDS arbitrators play in the case-by-case development of international investment law, the present study has eschewed a top-down approach in favour of a bottom-up one. The core question with which we have grappled has thus been in relation to the ways through which coherence manifests in ISDS. The bottom-up outlook into the subject has illuminated aspects of legal reasoning and judicial decision-making that the top-down outlook often leaves unaddressed. In brief, this book's answer to the main question is that coherence tends to manifest in adjudication in two ways simultaneously: (i) substantively, as an ideal of accuracy and correctness towards which to strive, and (ii) methodologically, as a process to be followed in order to reach and justify an outcome. The interplay between substance and method is critical for judicial reasoning, including by ISDS tribunals. Rather than being a futile endeavour, striving for coherence is a sign of professional commitment.

Delving into particulars, the book has shed light on five distinct categories of implications for judicial reasoning generally, and in ISDS particularly, which follow from a fuller account of coherence. These implications relate crucially to conceptual understandings of law, doctrine, epistemology, professional ethics in ISDS, and policy design in ISDS.

Conceptual Implications

Coherence describes the degree to which a set of legal propositions exhibit axiological compatibility, which is to say, the degree to which propositions of law are rationally related to each other and to the ordering values or ordering principles that are thought to justify them. Coherence thus describes a network, or interdependent web, among propositions and their justification, standing or falling together as a unit. This calls for abandoning existing conventional wisdom to the extent that it regards coherence as a mere formal principle or simply as synonymous with consistency and predictability in outcomes.

Once coherence is understood as an independent concept, additional implications follow with respect to how one regards the law. Coherence in its dual dimension is a central concept of the legal practice. Accordingly, two models were considered for how its two dimensions could be made to fit within legal reasoning. These models correspond to two prominent outlooks of the concept of law itself, namely, positivism and non-positivism (interpretivism). With its strict separation between law and morality, positivism leads to a bifurcated view of legal reasoning, which results in a model of 'double coherence'. According to this model, because legal reasoning is mainly technical in easy cases and mainly moral in hard cases, coherence operates as systemic consistency in the former cases and as a standard of moral congruence in the latter cases. By contrast, interpretivism does not see a strict separation between law and morality but rather regards law as forming part of morality. Accordingly, legal reasoning is a single, unified process where technical and moral arguments are intertwined resulting in a 'single coherence' model. The book has advocated for the latter model and therefore for the conclusion that coherence is not only an endemic feature of legal reasoning but also a pervasive one.

Doctrinal Implications

The above conceptual conclusions have doctrinal implications with respect to how one understands interpretation in international law. Starting with treaty interpretation, coherence is an integral component of the very structure of the VCLT rule of interpretation. It has been argued in the book that it is the combination of the VCLT's interpretative principles that yields the interpretation given to treaty provisions in each case. To do so, the VCLT's interpretative principles must be made to hang together and must be combined in a narrative of the interpretative context of each case. Still, different interpretative principles may be assigned different weights in different cases depending on the contracting parties' intentions, as reconstructed by the interpreter. This is a sign that considerations of coherence are apposite, acting as the reasons justifying the above combination and accounting for the outcome's persuasiveness.

Similar considerations apply with respect to another principal mode of reasoning in ISDS – analogical reasoning. Making a successful analogy rests on three mental processes: identifying similarities, drawing structural parallels, and devising an appropriate goal or purpose for the use of the analogy. These processes guide but also constrain analogical inferences. In so doing, they do not operate like rigid rules or like separate and independent steps. To the contrary, they are highly interdependent and at times may pull at opposite directions pressing the decision-maker to achieve a satisfactory compromise. The process of using analogical inferences thus exhibits similar attributes as the concept of coherence.

Epistemological Implications

The way in which coherence enters into legal interpretation further results in two kinds of epistemological implications in relation to legal reasoning. The first implication is that legal reasoning tracks closer to a paradigm of practical reasoning as opposed to a paradigm of theoretical reasoning. This means that reasoning and arguing about the law's content does not aim at discovering legal truth or at simply forming a belief. Rather, the aim is to formulate a reasoned opinion and to commit oneself to a specific course of action given the presence of a legal problem requiring resolution. Once legal reasoning is viewed in this light, it is possible to discern that it too exhibits coherence-related features, including (i) a web-like structure, whereby arguments severally cooperate in clusters to support a conclusion in a manner that is horizontally, rather than vertically, extensive; (ii) an understanding of rationality that does not depend only on logical connections among premises but also includes plausible connections (i.e., fit) among premises and between the premises chosen and the reasons supporting them; and (iii) a purposive character, whereby a chosen objective guides the process yet such objective is not necessarily free of ambiguities or of the need for itself to be interpreted.

The second epistemological implication for legal reasoning is that coherence is intrinsically connected with reflexivity. Reflexivity is conducive towards coherent legal reasoning and, consequently, the degree of an adjudicator's reflexivity can act as an indicator of the decision's overall coherence. As has been used in the book, reflexivity refers to a general disposition of self-awareness and self-examination, involving the critical examination of one's motivations and of how they influence one's action. Reasoning about the law is thus akin to being a researcher in a practical context, meaning that framing and contextualising are critical processes. Framing identifies the problem to be addressed, it singles out the legal question to be answered and the goal to be achieved. Contextualisation places the legal question within a larger normative context, considered to be similar in relevant respects, within which it will be addressed and which will contribute to its answering. Such context includes not only the various norms and guiding principles found in the legal system in question but also the adjudicator's appreciation of the institutional role he or she has within that system. A reflective adjudicator thus works iteratively, making judgments about the instant case and about the general theories, values, or principles that motivate his or her judgments. The idea is to achieve an optimal equilibrium between these elements, to the extent possible, before concluding the analysis and disposing of the case.

Implications for Professional Ethics in ISDS

The judicial function is a collegial function, meaning that ensuring collective reflexivity in a court or tribunal is an ever-present challenge. An individual adjudicator's process of reflection may coincide with, or differ from, another's on the same panel. Coherence requires both that adjudicators form their views about the case in a manner that is individually reflective and that the court or tribunal as a group arrives at its conclusion in a manner that is collectively reflective. A conclusion of this book has been that promoting collective reflexivity in ISDS presupposes the realisation that arbitrators bear moral responsibility over the way they discharge their duties.

Moral responsibility is exemplified in arbitrators' professional commitment to five judicial virtues called faith, humility, acquiescence, integrity, and candour. Faith instructs arbitrators to regard international investment law as intelligible and as a regime. Humility instructs arbitrators to be cognisant of the fact that they decide on matters bearing directly on the allocation of power and authority. Acquiescence instructs arbitrators to take full but also critical account of past wisdom, experience, and practice when deciding. Integrity and candour instruct arbitrators to not deploy legal reasoning in an instrumental manner and to be transparent about the way they approach the issues before them.

Importantly, these are not meant as a strict formula or as an equation for the courtroom. Judicial virtues are habits and mental dispositions. They are thus meant as a framework offering guidelines and a roadmap for developing better deliberative practices in ISDS. Structural and incidental features of international investment law and ISDS (e.g., the ad hoc nature, party appointments, partisanship and overcommitment to cases, or the predominantly sociological character of the authority of arbitral awards) will affect the degree to which this goal is achieved in practice. Nevertheless, moral responsibility and judicial virtues have been posited in this book as necessary if we hope for arbitrators to be able either to convince colleagues who may have different views or to at least steer them towards achieving coherent common ground solutions.

Implications for Policy Design in ISDS

Lastly, a series of implications relates to the ISDS reform project. Delegations participating in the UNCITRAL Working Group III discussions may be required to reframe and recontextualise the problem that they seek to resolve. They may be required to reassess their conceptual understanding of coherence and to place the latter at the forefront, while at the same time accepting that coherence is an overall elusive goal. In so doing, delegations may also be required to train their sights on addressing the bottom-up alongside the top-down. The bottom-up in this context is the voice of the arbitrators, which is missing from the formal debate. Arbitrators may be in a unique position to offer insights that would be valuable to reforming ISDS, including insights (i) about the challenges they face in interpreting investment treaties, (ii) about what works and what does not work in practice in the current system, and (iii) about possible ways of fostering a practice of judicial moral responsibility.

BIBLIOGRAPHY

Books and Monographs

Aarnio A., *The Rational as Reasonable: A Treatise on Legal Justification* (Dordrecht: D. Reidel, 1987)

Abi-Saab G., Keith K., Marceau G., and Marquet C. (eds.), *Evolutionary Interpretation and International Law* (Oxford: Hart, 2019)

Aksen G., Böckstiegel K.-H., Mustill M. J., Patocchi P. M., and Whitesell A. (eds.), *Global Reflections on International Law, Commerce and Dispute Resolution: Liber Amicorum in Honour of Robert Briner* (Paris: ICC, 2005)

Allott P., *The Health of Nations: Society and Law beyond the State* (Cambridge: Cambridge University Press, 2002)

Alston P., and Goodman R., *International Human Rights* (Oxford: Oxford University Press, 2013)

Alvarez J. E., *The Boundaries of Investment Arbitration: The Use of Trade and European Human Rights Law in Investor–State Disputes* (Huntington: Juris, 2018)

Amaya A., *The Tapestry of Reason: An Inquiry into the Nature of Coherence and Its Role in Legal Argument* (Oxford: Hart, 2015)

Andenas M., and Bjorge E. (eds.), *A Farewell to Fragmentation: Reassertion and Convergence in International Law* (Cambridge: Cambridge University Press, 2015)

Andenas M., Fitzmaurice M., Tanzi A., and Wouters J. (eds.), *General Principles and the Coherence of International Law* (Leiden: Brill/Nijhoff, 2019)

Arsanjani M. H., Cogan J. K., Sloane R. D., and Wiessner S. (eds.), *Looking to the Future: Essays on International Law in Honor of W. Michael Reisman* (Leiden: Martinus Nijhoff, 2011)

Austin J., *The Province of Jurisprudence Determined*, ed. by W. E. Rumble (Cambridge: Cambridge University Press, 1995)

Baumgartner J., *Treaty Shopping in International Investment Law* (Oxford: Oxford University Press, 2016)

Bekker P. H. F., Dolzer R., and Waibel M. (eds.), *Making Transnational Law Work in the Global Economy: Essays in Honour of Detlev Vagts* (Cambridge: Cambridge University Press, 2010)

Besson S., and Tasioulas J. (eds.), *The Philosophy of International Law* (Oxford: Oxford University Press, 2010)

Beyerlin U., Bothe M., Hofmann R., and Petersmann E.-U. (eds.), *Recht zwischen Umbruch und Bewahrung: Festschrift für Rudolf Bernhardt* (Berlin: Springer, 1995)

Bianchi A., Peat D., and Windsor M. (eds.), *Interpretation in International Law* (Oxford: Oxford University Press, 2015)

Binder C., Kriebaum U., Reinisch A., and Wittich S. (eds.), *International Investment Law for the 21st Century: Essays in Honour of Christoph Schreuer* (Oxford: Oxford University Press, 2009)

Bjorklund A. K. (ed.), *Yearbook on International Investment Law & Policy 2013–2014* (New York: Oxford University Press, 2015)

Boisson de Chazournes L., and Sands P. (eds.), *International Law, the International Court of Justice and Nuclear Weapons* (Cambridge: Cambridge University Press, 1999)

Bonnitcha J., Skovgaard Poulsen L. N., and Waibel M., *The Political Economy of the Investment Treaty Regime* (Oxford: Oxford University Press, 2017)

Bowman M. J. and Kritsiotis D. (eds), *Conceptual and Contextual Perspectives on the Modern Law of Treaties* (Cambridge: Cambridge University Press, 2018)

Broches A. (ed.), *Selected Essays: World Bank, ICSID, and Other Subjects of Public and Private International Law* (Dordrecht: Martinus Nijhoff, 1995)

Caron D. D., Schill S. W., Smutny A. C., and Triantafilou E. E. (eds.), *Practising Virtue: Inside International Arbitration* (Oxford: Oxford University Press, 2015)

Centre for Studies and Research in International Law and International Relations, *New Aspects of International Investment Law* (Leiden: Brill/Nijhoff, 2007)

Coleman J. L., Himma K. E., and Shapiro S. J. (eds.), *The Oxford Handbook of Jurisprudence and Philosophy of Law* (Oxford: Oxford University Press, 2004)

Crawford J., Pellet A., and Olleson S. (eds.), *The Law of International Responsibility* (Oxford: Oxford University Press, 2010)

d'Aspremont J., *Formalism and the Sources of International Law: A Theory of the Ascertainment of Legal Rules* (Oxford: Oxford University Press, 2011)

d'Aspremont J., and Singh S. (eds.), *Concepts for International Law: Contributions to Disciplinary Thought* (Cheltenham: Edward Elgar, 2019)

de Beaugrande R.-A., and Dressler W. U., *Introduction to Text Linguistics* (London; New York: Longman, 1981)

de Vattel E., *The Law of Nations, or, Principles of the Law of Nature, Applied to the Conduct and Affairs of Nations and Sovereigns. From the French of Monsieur de Vattel, A New Edition, Revised, Corrected and Enriched with Many Valuable Notes* (London: Printed for G. G. and J. Robinson, Paternoster-Row, 1797)

Descombes V., *Le raisonnement de l'ours: et autres essais de philosophie pratique* (Paris: Seuil, 2007)

Dewey J., *How We Think: A Restatement of the Relation of Reflective Thinking to the Educative Process*, 2nd ed. (Lexington: DC Heath & Co., 1933)

Diel-Gligor K., *Towards Consistency in International Investment Jurisprudence: A Preliminary Ruling System for ICSID Arbitration* (Leiden: Brill/Nijhoff, 2017)

Dolzer R., and Schreuer C., *Principles of International Investment Law*, 2nd ed. (Oxford: Oxford University Press, 2012)

Douglas Z., *The International Law of Investment Claims* (Cambridge: Cambridge University Press, 2009)

Douglas Z., Pauwelyn J., and Viñuales J. E. (eds.), *The Foundations of International Investment Law: Bringing Theory into Practice* (Oxford: Oxford University Press, 2014)

Duxbury N., *The Nature and Authority of Precedent* (Cambridge: Cambridge University Press, 2008)

Dworkin R., *Justice for Hedgehogs* (Cambridge, MA: Harvard University Press, 2011)

Justice in Robes (Cambridge, MA: Harvard University Press, 2006)

Law's Empire (Cambridge, MA: Harvard University Press, 1986)

Taking Rights Seriously (Cambridge, MA: Harvard University Press, 1977)

Echandi R., and Sauvé P. (eds.), *Prospects in International Investment Law and Policy* (Cambridge: Cambridge University Press, 2013)

Eisenberg M. A., *The Nature of the Common Law* (Cambridge, MA: Harvard University Press, 1988)

Fach, G. K. (ed.), *Private Actors in International Investment Law* (Cham: Springer, 2021)

Fitzmaurice M., Elias O., and Merkouris P. (eds.), *Treaty Interpretation and the Vienna Convention on the Law of Treaties: 30 Years On* (Leiden: Martinus Nijhoff, 2010)

Fuller L. L., *The Morality of Law*, rev. ed. (New Haven: Yale University Press, 1969)

Gardiner R. K., *International Law* (Harlow: Pearson Longman, 2003)

Treaty Interpretation, 2nd ed. (Oxford: Oxford University Press, 2015)

Gáspár-Szilágyi S., Behn D., and Langford M. (eds.), *Adjudicating Trade and Investment Disputes: Convergence or Divergence?* (Cambridge: Cambridge University Press, 2020)

Habermas J., *Between Facts and Norms: Contributions to a Discourse Theory of Law and Democracy*, trans. William Rehg, reprint 2009 (Cambridge, MA: Polity Press, 1996)

Harlow C., and Rawlings R., *Law and Administration*, 3rd ed. (Cambridge: Cambridge University Press, 2009)

Hart H. L. A., *The Concept of Law*, 3rd ed. (Oxford: Oxford University Press, 2012)

Heydrich W., Neubauer F., Petöfi J. S., and Sözer E. (eds.), *Connexivity and Coherence: Analysis of Text and Discourse* (Berlin: Walter de Gruyter, 1989)

Higgins R., *Problems and Process: International Law and How We Use It*, reprint (Oxford: Clarendon Press, 1995)

Holyoak K. J. and Thagard P., *Mental Leaps: Analogy in Creative Thought* (Cambridge, MA: MIT Press, 1995)

Horn N., and Kröll S. (eds.), *Arbitrating Foreign Investment Disputes: Procedural and Substantive Legal Aspects* (The Hague: Kluwer Law International, 2004)

Jefferson P. H., *Constitutional Conscience: The Moral Dimension of Judicial Decision* (Chicago: University of Chicago Press, 2008)

Jennings R., and Watts A., *Oppenheim's International Law. Volume 1: Peace*, 9th ed. (Oxford: Oxford University Press, 2008)

Koskenniemi M., *From Apology to Utopia: The Structure of International Legal Argument*, reissue with a new epilogue (Cambridge: Cambridge University Press, 2005)

Kotuby C. T. Jr, and Sobota L., *General Principles of Law and International Due Process: Principles and Norms Applicable in Transnational Disputes* (New York: Oxford University Press, 2017)

Kramer M. H., *Objectivity and the Rule of Law* (Cambridge: Cambridge University Press, 2007)

Kuhn T. S., *The Structure of Scientific Revolutions*, 2nd ed. (Chicago: University of Chicago Press, 1970)

Kulick A., *Global Public Interest in International Investment Law* (Cambridge: Cambridge University Press, 2012)

Lauterpacht E. (ed.), *International Law. Being the Collected Papers of Hersch Lauterpacht: Volume I* (Cambridge: Cambridge University Press, 1970)

Lauterpacht H., *The Development of International Law by the International Court*, rev. ed. (London: Stevens & Sons, 1958)

MacCormick D. N., *Legal Reasoning and Legal Theory* (Oxford: Clarendon Press, 1978)

Practical Reason in Law and Morality (Oxford: Oxford University Press, 2008)

Rhetoric and the Rule of Law (Oxford: Oxford University Press, 2005)

MacCormick D. N., and Summers R. S. (eds.), *Interpreting Statutes: A Comparative Study* (Dartmouth: Ashgate, 1991)

Makarczyk J. (ed.), *Theory of International Law at the Threshold of the 21st Century: Essays in Honour of Krzysztof Skubiszewski* (The Hague: Kluwer Law International, 1996)

McLachlan C., Shore L., and Weiniger M., *International Investment Arbitration: Substantive Principles*, 2nd ed. (Oxford: Oxford University Press, 2017)

McNair A., *The Law of Treaties* (Oxford: Clarendon Press, 1961)

Menaker A. (ed.), *International Arbitration and the Rule of Law: Contribution and Conformity* (Alphen aan den Rijn: Kluwer Law International, 2017)

Merkouris P., *Article 31(3)(c) VCLT and the Principle of Systemic Integration: Normative Shadows in Plato's Cave* (Leiden: Brill/Nijhoff, 2015)

Mitchell A. D., Sornarajah M., and Voon T. (eds.), *Good Faith and International Economic Law* (Oxford: Oxford University Press, 2015)

Montt S., *State Liability in Investment Treaty Arbitration: Global Constitutional and Administrative Law in the BIT Generation* (Oxford: Hart, 2009)

Muchlinski P., Ortino F., and Schreuer C. (eds), *The Oxford Handbook of International Investment Law* (Oxford: Oxford University Press, 2008)

Oberdiek J. (ed.), *Philosophical Foundations of the Law of Torts* (Oxford: Oxford University Press, 2014)

Orakhelashvili A., *The Interpretation of Acts and Rules in Public International Law* (Oxford: Oxford University Press, 2008)

Ortino F., Liberti L., Sheppard A., and Warner H. (eds.), *Investment Treaty Law: Current Issues II* (London: British Institute of International and Comparative Law, 2007)

Paddeu F., *Justification and Excuse in International Law: Concept and Theory of General Defences* (Cambridge: Cambridge University Press, 2018)

Paparinskis M., *The International Minimum Standard and Fair and Equitable Treatment* (Oxford: Oxford University Press, 2013)

Patterson D. (ed.), *A Companion to Philosophy of Law and Legal Theory*, 2nd ed. (Malden: Wiley-Blackwell, 2010)

Paulsson J., *The Idea of Arbitration* (Oxford: Oxford University Press, 2013)

Pauwelyn J., *Conflict of Norms in Public International Law: How WTO Law Relates to Other Rules of International Law*, 5th reprint (Cambridge: Cambridge University Press, 2006)

Picker C. B., Bunn I. D., and Arner D. W. (eds.), *International Economic Law: The State and Future of the Discipline* (Oxford: Hart, 2008)

Rawls J., *A Theory of Justice*, rev. ed. (Cambridge, MA: Harvard University Press, 1999)

Justice as Fairness: A Restatement, ed. E. Kelly (Cambridge, MA: Harvard University Press, 2001)

Political Liberalism (New York: Columbia University Press, 1993)

Raz J., *The Authority of Law: Essays on Law and Morality*, 2nd ed. (Oxford: Oxford University Press, 2009)

Between Authority and Interpretation: On the Theory of Law and Practical Reason (Oxford: Oxford University Press, 2009)

Engaging Reason: On the Theory of Value and Action (Oxford: Oxford University Press, 2002)

Ethics in the Public Domain: Essays in the Morality of Law and Politics, rev. ed. (Oxford: Clarendon Press, 1995)

Reimann M., and Zimmermann R. (eds.), *The Oxford Handbook of Comparative Law*, 2nd ed. (Oxford: Oxford University Press, 2019)

Ripstein A. (ed.), *Ronald Dworkin* (Cambridge: Cambridge University Press, 2007)

Rovine A. W. (ed.), *Contemporary Issues in International Arbitration and Mediation: The Fordham Papers 2012* (Leiden: Martinus Nijhoff, 2013)

Ruiz Fabri H., and Sorel J.-M. (eds.), *La motivation des décisions des juridictions internationales* (Paris: Pedone, 2008)

Schill S. W. (ed.), *International Investment Law and Comparative Public Law* (Oxford: Oxford University Press, 2010)

Schneiderman D., *Constitutionalizing Economic Globalization: Investment Rules and Democracy's Promise* (New York: Cambridge University Press, 2008)

Schön D. A., *The Reflective Practitioner: How Professionals Think in Action* (New York: Basic Books, 1983)

Schreuer C., Malintoppi L., Reinisch A., and Sinclair A. (eds.), *The ICSID Convention: A Commentary*, 2nd ed. (Cambridge: Cambridge University Press, 2009)

Schultz T., *Transnational Legality: Stateless Law and International Arbitration* (Oxford: Oxford University Press, 2014)

Searle J. R., *Expression and Meaning: Studies in the Theory of Speech Acts*, reprint 1996 (Cambridge: Cambridge University Press, 1979)

Searle J. R., Kiefer F., and Bierwisch M. (eds.), *Speech Act Theory and Pragmatics* (Dordrecht: D. Reidel, 1980)

Shapiro S. J., *Legality* (Cambridge, MA: Harvard University Press, 2011)

Sinclair I., *The Vienna Convention on the Law of Treaties*, 2nd ed. (Manchester: Manchester University Press, 1984)

Slaughter A.-M., *A New World Order* (Princeton: Princeton University Press, 2004)

Sørensen M. (ed.), *Manual of Public International Law* (London: MacMillan & Co, 1968)

Sunstein C. R., *Legal Reasoning and Political Conflict*, 2nd ed. (New York: Oxford University Press, 2018)

Sureda A. R., *Investment Treaty Arbitration: Judging under Uncertainty* (Cambridge: Cambridge University Press, 2012)

Tucker T. N., *Judge Knot: Politics and Development in International Investment Law* (London: Anthem Press, 2018)

Tupamäki M. (ed.), *Liber Amicorum Bengt Broms* (Helsinki: International Law Association, 1999)

Vadi V., *Analogies in International Investment Law and Arbitration* (Cambridge: Cambridge University Press, 2016)

van den Berg A. J. (ed.), *ICCA: 50 Years of the New York Convention* (Alphen aan den Rijn: Kluwer Law International, 2009)

van den Bossche P., and Zdouc W., *The Law and Policy of the World Trade Organization: Text, Cases and Materials*, 4th ed. (Cambridge: Cambridge University Press, 2017)

van Harten G., *Investment Treaty Arbitration and Public Law* (Oxford: Oxford University Press, 2007)

Villiger M. E., *Commentary on the 1969 Vienna Convention on the Law of Treaties* (Leiden: Martinus Nijhoff, 2009)

Viñuales J. E., *Foreign Investment and the Environment in International Law* (Cambridge: Cambridge University Press, 2012)

von Bogdandy A., and Venzke I. (eds.), *International Judicial Lawmaking: On Public Authority and Democratic Legitimation in Global Governance* (Heidelberg: Springer, 2012)

Wandahl Mouyal L., *International Investment Law and the Right to Regulate: A Human Rights Perspective* (New York: Routledge, 2016)

Weeramantry R. J., *Treaty Interpretation in Investment Arbitration* (Oxford: Oxford University Press, 2012)

Westlake J., *International Law*, 2nd ed. (Cambridge: Cambridge University Press, 1910)

White J. B., *Living Speech: Resisting the Empire of Force* (Princeton: Princeton University Press, 2006)

Zimmermann A., Tams C. J., Oellers-Frahm K., Tomuschat C., Boos F., and Methymaki E. (eds.), *The Statute of the International Court of Justice: A Commentary*, 3rd ed. (Oxford: Oxford University Press, 2019)

Articles

Akehurst M., 'Equity and General Principles of Law' (1976) 25 *International and Comparative Law Quarterly* 801

Alexy R., 'Law and Correctness' (1998) 51 *Current Legal Problems* 205
'Legal Certainty and Correctness' (2015) 28 *Ratio Juris* 441

Allott P., 'The Concept of International Law' (1999) 10 *European Journal of International Law* 31

Anscombe G. E. M., 'On Brute Facts' (1958) 18 *Analysis* 69

Arato J., Brown C., and Ortino F., 'Parsing and Managing Inconsistency in Investor–State Dispute Settlement' (2020) 21 *Journal of World Investment and Trade* 336

Baetens F., 'Judicial Review of International Adjudicatory Decisions: A Cross-Regime Comparison of Annulment and Appellate Mechanisms' (2017) 8 *Journal of International Dispute Settlement* 432

Becker L. C., 'Analogy in Legal Reasoning' (1973) 83 *Ethics* 248

Bell J., 'The Argumentative Status of Foreign Legal Arguments' (2012) 8(2) *Utrecht Law Review* 8

Brower C. N., 'W(h)ither International Commercial Arbitration?' (2008) 24 *Arbitration International* 181

Burgstaller M., 'Nationality of Corporate Investors and International Claims against the Investor's Own State' (2006) 7 *Journal of World Investment and Trade* 857

Cane P., 'Distributive Justice and Tort Law' (2001) Issue 4 *New Zealand Law Review* 401

Chasapis Tassinis O., 'Customary International Law: Interpretation from Beginning to End' (2020) 31 *European Journal of International Law* 235

Commission J. P., 'Precedent in Investment Treaty Arbitration: A Citation Analysis of a Developing Jurisprudence' (2007) 24 *Journal of International Arbitration* 129

Crawford J., 'Treaty and Contract in Investment Arbitration' (2008) 21 *Arbitration International* 351

DiMascio N., and Pauwelyn J., 'Nondiscrimination in Trade and Investment Treaties: Worlds Apart or Two Sides of the Same Coin?' (2008) 102 *American Journal of International Law* 48

Douglas Z., 'Can a Doctrine of Precedent Be Justified in Investment Treaty Arbitration?' (2010) 25 *ICSID Review – Foreign Investment Law Journal* 104

'Nothing If Not Critical for Investment Treaty Arbitration: *Occidental, Eureko* and *Methanex*' (2006) 22 *Arbitration International* 27

'The Hybrid Foundations of Investment Treaty Arbitration' (2003) 74 *British Yearbook of International Law* 151

'The MFN Clause in Investment Arbitration: Treaty Interpretation Off the Rails' (2011) 2 *Journal of International Dispute Settlement* 97

'The Plea of Illegality in Investment Treaty Arbitration' (2014) 29 *ICSID Review – Foreign Investment Law Journal* 155

Dworkin R., 'Hart's Postscript and the Character of Political Philosophy' (2004) 24 *Oxford Journal of Legal Studies* 1

'In Praise of Theory' (1997) 29 *Arizona State Law Journal* 353

'Objectivity and Truth: You'd Better Believe It!' (1996) 25 *Philosophy and Public Affairs* 87

Fauchald O. K., 'The Legal Reasoning of ICSID Tribunals – An Empirical Analysis' (2008) 19 *European Journal of International Law* 301

Fish S., 'Intention Is All There Is: A Critical Analysis of Aharon Barak's Purposive Interpretation in Law' (2008) 29 *Cardozo Law Review* 1109

Fiss O. M., 'Against Settlement' (1984) 93 *Yale Law Journal* 1073

Fitzmaurice G., 'The Law and Procedure of the International Court of Justice: Treaty Interpretation and Certain Other Treaty Points' (1951) 28 *British Yearbook of International Law* 1

'The Law and Procedure of the International Court of Justice, 1951–4: Questions of Jurisdiction, Competence and Procedure' (1958) 34 *British Yearbook of International Law* 1

'The United Nations and the Rule of Law' (1952) 38 *Transactions of the Grotius Society* 135

Fuller L. L., 'Positivism and Fidelity to Law: A Reply to Professor Hart' (1958) 71 *Harvard Law Review* 630

Gardner J., 'Legal Positivism: 5 1/2 Myths' (2001) 46 *American Journal of Jurisprudence* 199

'What Is Tort Law For? Part 1. The Place of Corrective Justice' (2011) 30 *Law and Philosophy* 1

Gazzini T., 'General Principles of Law in the Field of Foreign Investment' (2009) 10 *Journal of World Investment and Trade* 103

Gourgourinis A., 'The Distinction between Interpretation and Application of Norms in International Adjudication' (2011) 2 *Journal of International Dispute Settlement* 31

Green L., 'Positivism and the Inseparability of Law and Morals' (2008) 83 *New York University Law Review* 1035

Guillaume G., 'The Use of Precedent by International Judges and Arbitrators' (2011) 2 *Journal of International Dispute Settlement* 5

Hanessian G., '"General Principles of Law" in the Iran-US Claims Tribunal' (1989) 27 *Columbia Journal of Transnational Law* 309

Hart H. L. A., 'Positivism and the Separation of Law and Morals' (1958) 71 *Harvard Law Review* 593

Hershovitz S., 'The Model of Plans and the Prospects for Positivism' (2014) 125 *Ethics* 152

Hertogen A., 'Letting *Lotus* Bloom' (2015) 26 *European Journal of International Law* 901

Higgins R., 'A Babel of Judicial Voices? Ruminations from the Bench' (2006) 55 *International and Comparative Law Quarterly* 791

Kaufman A., 'Incompletely Theorized Agreement: A Plausible Ideal for Legal Reasoning?' (1996) 85 *Georgetown Law Journal* 395

Kaufmann-Kohler G., 'Arbitral Precedent: Dream, Necessity or Excuse?' (2007) 23 *Arbitration International* 357

Kennedy D., 'Theses about International Law Discourse' (1980) 23 *German Yearbook of International Law* 353

Kenny A. J., 'Practical Inference' (1966) 26 *Analysis* 65

Kolb R., 'Principles as Sources of International Law (With Special Reference to Good Faith)' (2006) 53 *Netherlands International Law Review* 1

Kornhauser L. A., and Sager L. G., 'The One and the Many: Adjudication in Collegial Courts' (1993) 81 *California Law Review* 1

'Unpacking the Court' (1986) 96 *Yale Law Journal* 82

Koskenniemi M., 'The Fate of Public International Law: Between Technique and Politics' (2007) 70 *Modern Law Review* 1

Kurtz J., 'Adjudging the Exceptional at International Investment Law: Security, Public Order and Financial Crisis' (2010) 59 *International and Comparative Law Quarterly* 325

Landau T. T., 'The Psychology of the Decision-Making Process: Arbitral Tribunal Deliberations' (2015) 17 *Asian Dispute Review* 208

Lauterpacht H., 'Restrictive Interpretation and the Principle of Effectiveness in the Interpretation of Treaties' (1949) 26 *British Yearbook of International Law* 48

Legum B., 'Investment Treaty Arbitration's Contribution to International Commercial Arbitration' (August/October 2005) *Dispute Resolution Journal* 71

Lillich R. B., and White G. E., 'The Deliberative Process of the International Court of Justice: A Preliminary Critique and Some Possible Reforms' (1976) 70 *American Journal of International Law* 28

Lowe V., 'Precluding Wrongfulness or Responsibility: A Plea for Excuses' (1999) 10 *European Journal of International Law* 405

'Regulation or Expropriation?' (2002) 55 *Current Legal Problems* 447

'The Role of Equity in International Law' (1988–1989) 12 *Australian Yearbook of International Law* 54

Lowenfeld A. F., 'The ICSID Convention: Origins and Transformation' (2009–2010) 38 *Georgia Journal of International and Comparative Law* 47

MacCormick N., 'Argumentation and Interpretation in Law' (1993) 6 *Ratio Juris* 16

Maupin J. A., 'Public and Private in International Investment Law: An Integrated Systems Approach' (2013–2014) 54 *Virginia Journal of International Law* 367

McCrudden C., 'Human Dignity and Judicial Interpretation of Human Rights' (2008) 19 *European Journal of International Law* 655

McLachlan C., 'The Principle of Systemic Integration and Article 31(3)(c) of the Vienna Convention' (2005) 54 *International and Comparative Law Quarterly* 279

McRae D., 'The WTO Appellate Body: A Model for an ICSID Appeals Facility?' (2010) 1 *Journal of International Dispute Settlement* 371

Meyerson D., 'Why Courts Should Not Balance Rights against the Public Interest' (2007) 31 *Melbourne University Law Review* 873

Mills A., 'Antinomies of Public and Private at the Foundations of International Investment Law and Arbitration' (2011) 14 *Journal of International Economic Law* 469

Mitchell A. D., and Munro J., 'Someone Else's Deal: Interpreting International Investment Agreements in the Light of Third-Party Agreements' (2017) 28 *European Journal of International Law* 669

Moral Soriano L., 'A Modest Notion of Coherence in Legal Reasoning. A Model for the European Court of Justice' (2003) 16 *Ratio Juris* 296

Mortenson J. D., 'The Travaux of Travaux: Is the Vienna Convention Hostile to Drafting History?' (2013) 107 *American Journal of International Law* 780

Mountfield H., 'Regulatory Expropriations in Europe: The Approach of the European Court of Human Rights' (2002) 11 *New York University Environmental Law Journal* 136

Mumford P., 'Regulatory Coherence: Blending Trade and Regulatory Policy' (2014) 10 *Policy Quarterly* 3

Obadia E., '*Banro American Resources, Inc. and Société Aurifère du Kivu et du Maniema S.A.R.L. v Democratic Republic of the Congo* (ICSID Case No. ARB/98/7): Introductory Note' (2002) 17 *ICSID Review – Foreign Investment Law Journal* 380

Paparinskis M., 'Investment Arbitration and the Law of Countermeasures' (2008) 79 *British Yearbook of International Law* 264

'Investment Treaty Arbitration and the (New) Law of State Responsibility' (2013) 24 *European Journal of International Law* 617

Park W. W., 'Arbitrators and Accuracy' (2010) 1 *Journal of International Dispute Settlement* 25

Pauwelyn J., 'The Rule of Law without the Rule of Lawyers? Why Investment Arbitrators Are from Mars, Trade Adjudicators from Venus' (2015) 109 *American Journal of International Law* 761

Petersmann E.-U., 'The Judicial Task of Administering Justice in Trade and Investment Law and Adjudication' (2013) 4 *Journal of International Dispute Settlement* 5

Polanco R., and Sauvé P., 'The Treatment of Regulatory Convergence in Preferential Trade Agreements' (2018) 17 *World Trade Review* 575

Ratner S. R., 'Regulatory Takings in Institutional Context: Beyond the Fear of Fragmented International Law' (2008) 102 *American Journal of International Law* 475

Rawls J., 'Two Concepts of Rules' (1955) 64 *Philosophical Review* 3

Raz J., 'The Relevance of Coherence' (1992) 72 *Boston University Law Review* 273

Ridi N., 'The Shape and Structure of the "Usable Past": An Empirical Analysis of the Use of Precedent in International Adjudication' (2019) 10 *Journal of International Dispute Settlement* 200

Roberts A., 'Clash of Paradigms: Actors and Analogies Shaping the Investment Treaty System' (2013) 107 *American Journal of International Law* 45

Salacuse J. W., 'The Emerging Global Regime for Investment' (2010) 51 *Harvard International Law Journal* 427

Saldarriaga A., 'Investment Awards and the Rules of Interpretation of the Vienna Convention: Making Room for Improvement' (2013) 28 *ICSID Review – Foreign Investment Law Journal* 197

Sardinha E., 'The Impetus for the Creation of an Appellate Mechanism' (2017) 32 *ICSID Review - Foreign Investment Law Journal* 503

Schill S. W., 'Allocating Adjudicatory Authority: Most-Favoured-Nation Clauses as a Basis of Jurisdiction - A Reply to Zachary Douglas' (2011) 2 *Journal of International Dispute Settlement* 353

'Deference in Investment Treaty Arbitration: Re-conceptualizing the Standard of Review' (2012) 3 *Journal of International Dispute Settlement* 577

'Enhancing International Investment Law's Legitimacy: Conceptual and Methodological Foundations of a New Public Law Approach' (2011) 52 *Virginia Journal of International Law* 57

Schultz T., 'The Three Pursuits of Dispute Settlement' (2010) 1 *Czech & Central European Yearbook of Arbitration* 227

Schwarzenberger G., 'Myths and Realities of Treaty Interpretation: Articles 27–29 of the Vienna Draft Convention on the Law of Treaties' (1968) 9 *Virginia Journal of International Law* 1

Sullivan K. M., 'Foreword: The Justices of Rules and Standards' (1992) 106 *Harvard Law Review* 22

Sunstein C. R., 'On Analogical Reasoning' (1992–1993) 106 *Harvard Law Review* 741

Tollefsen D., 'Organizations as True Believers' (2002) 33 *Journal of Social Philosophy* 395

Tollefsen D. P., 'Collective Intentionality and the Social Sciences' (2002) 32 *Philosophy of the Social Sciences* 25

Tsakyrakis S., 'Proportionality: An Assault on Human Rights?' (2009) 7 *International Journal of Constitutional Law* 468

Tucker T., 'Inside the Black Box: Collegial Patterns on Investment Tribunals' (2016) 7 *Journal of International Dispute Settlement* 183

Vadi V., 'Towards Arbitral Path Coherence and Judicial Borrowing: Persuasive Precedent in Investment Arbitration' (2008) 5 *Transnational Dispute Management* 1

van Harten G., and Loughlin M., 'Investment Treaty Arbitration as a Species of Global Administrative Law' (2006) 17 *European Journal of International Law* 121

van Harten G., 'Five Justifications for Investment Treaties: A Critical Discussion' (2010) 2 *Trade Law and Development* 19

Vandevelde K. J., 'Investment Liberalization and Economic Development: The Role of Bilateral Investment Treaties' (1998) 36 *Columbia Journal of Transnational Law* 501

Voyiakis E., 'Do General Principles Fill "Gaps" in International Law?' (2009) 14 *Austrian Review of International and European Law* 239

Wälde T. W., 'Procedural Challenges in Investment Arbitration under the Shadow of the Dual Role of the State: Asymmetries and Tribunals' Duty to Ensure, Pro-actively, the Equality of Arms' (2010) 26 *Arbitration International* 3

Waldron J., 'Fake Incommensurability: A Response to Professor Schauer' (1994) 45 *Hastings Law Journal* 813

'Judges as Moral Reasoners' (2009) 7 *International Journal of Constitutional Law* 2

Weil P., '"The Court Cannot Conclude Definitely . . ." *Non Liquet* Revisited' (1997) 36 *Columbia Journal of Transnational Law* 109

White J. B., 'Law as Language: Reading Law and Reading Literature' (1981–1982) 60 *Texas Law Review* 415

Wisdom J., 'Gods' (1944) 45 *Proceedings of the Aristotelian Society* 185

Zarra G., 'The Issue of Incoherence in Investment Arbitration: Is There Need for a Systemic Reform?' (2018) 17 *Chinese Journal of International Law* 137

International Law Reports and Documents

Draft Articles on Responsibility of States for Internationally Wrongful Acts (adopted by the ILC at its 53rd session, 23 April–1 June and 2 July–10 August 2001) (2001) Vol II (Part Two) *Yearbook of the International Law Commission*

Institut de Droit International, 'De l'interprétation des traités: Observations complémentaires et projet définitif de Résolutions, présentés par M. H. Lauterpacht' (1952– I) 44 *Annuaire de l'Institute de Droit International* 197

International Law Commission, 'Draft Conclusions on Subsequent Agreements and Subsequent Practice in Relation to the Interpretation of Treaties, with Commentaries', UN Doc A/73/10 (2018)

International Law Commission, 'Fragmentation of International Law: Difficulties Arising from the Diversification and Expansion of International Law – Report of the Study Group of the International Law Commission', UN Doc A/CN.4/L.682 (13 April 2006)

Report of the International Law Commission on the Work of Its Eighteenth Session (Geneva, 4 May–19 July 1966) (1967) Vol II *Yearbook of the International Law Commission* 172

Summary Records of the Sixteenth Session (11 May–24 July 1964) (1965) Vol I *Yearbook of the International Law Commission*

Third Report on the Law of Treaties, by Sir Humphrey Waldock, Special Rapporteur (1965) Vol II *Yearbook of the International Law Commission* 5

United Nations Commission on International Trade Law, 'Report of Working Group III (Investor–State Dispute Settlement Reform) on the Work of its Thirty-fourth Session (Vienna, 27 November–1 December 2017) - Part II', UN Doc A/CN.9/930/Add.1/Rev.1 (26 February 2018)

United Nations Commission on International Trade Law, 'Report of Working Group III (Investor–State Dispute Settlement Reform) on the Work of Its

Thirty-fifth Session (New York, 23–27 April 2018)', UN Doc A/CN.9/935 (14 May 2018)

United Nations Commission on International Trade Law, 'Report of Working Group III (Investor–State Dispute Settlement Reform) on the Work of its Thirty-sixth Session (Vienna, 29 October–2 November 2018)', UN Doc A/CN.9/964 (6 November 2018)

United Nations Commission on International Trade Law Working Group III (Investor–State Dispute Settlement Reform), 'Possible Reform of Investor–State Dispute Settlement (ISDS): Submission from the Government of Thailand', UN Doc A/CN.9/WG.III/WP.162 (8 March 2019)

United Nations Commission on International Trade Law Working Group III (Investor–State Dispute Settlement Reform), 'Possible Reform of Investor–State Dispute Settlement (ISDS): Note by the Secretariat', UN Doc A/CN.9/WG.III/WP.166 (30 July 2019)

United Nations Commission on International Trade Law Working Group III (Investor–State Dispute Settlement Reform), 'Possible Reform of Investor–State Dispute Settlement (ISDS): Consistency and Related Matters', UN Doc A/CN.9/WG.III/WP.150 (28 August 2018)

United Nations Commission on International Trade Law Working Group III (Investor–State Dispute Settlement Reform), 'Possible Reform of Investor–State Dispute Settlement (ISDS): Note by the Secretariat – Addendum', UN Doc A/CN.9/WG.III/WP.166/Add.1 (30 July 2019)

United Nations Commission on International Trade Law Working Group III (Investor–State Dispute Settlement Reform), 'Possible Reform of Investor–State Dispute Settlement (ISDS): Comments by the Government of Indonesia', UN Doc A/CN.9/WG.III/WP.156 (9 November 2018)

Courses of the Hague Academy of International Law

Abi-Saab G., 'Cours général de droit international public' (1987) 207 *Recueil des cours* 9

Broches A., 'The Convention on the Settlement of Investment Disputes between States and Nationals of Other States' (1972) 136 *Recueil des cours* 331

Habicht M., 'Le pouvoir du juge international de statuer "ex aequo et bono"' (1934) 49 *Recueil des cours* 277

Lowe V., 'The Limits of the Law – Inaugural Lecture' (2016) 379 *Recueil des cours* 9

Schachter O., 'International Law in Theory and Practice: General Course in Public International Law' (1982) 182 *Recueil des cours* 9

Verdross A., 'Les principes généraux du droit dans la jurisprudence internationale' (1935) 52 *Recueil des cours* 195

Encyclopaedia Entries

Daniels N., 'Reflective Equilibrium', in E. N. Zalta (ed.), *The Stanford Encyclopedia of Philosophy* (Summer 2020), available at https://plato.stanford.edu/archives/sum2020/entries/reflective-equilibrium/

Jay Wallace R., 'Practical Reason', in E. N. Zalta (ed.), *The Stanford Encyclopedia of Philosophy* (Spring 2020), available at https://plato.stanford.edu/entries/practical-reason/

Mitchell A. D., and Malone T., 'Abuse of Process in Inter-State Dispute Resolution', *Max Planck Encyclopedia of Public International Law* (December 2018), available at https://opil.ouplaw.com/home/MPIL

Rosenne S., 'International Courts and Tribunals, Jurisdiction and Admissibility of Inter-State Applications', *Max Planck Encyclopedia of Public International Law* (March 2006), available at https://opil.ouplaw.com/home/MPIL

Simma B., and Ortgies J., 'Deliberation and Drafting: International Court of Justice (ICJ)', *Max Planck Encyclopedia of Public International Law* (January 2019), available at https://opil.ouplaw.com/home/MPIL

Stavropoulos N., 'Legal Interpretivism', in E. N. Zalta (ed.), *The Stanford Encyclopedia of Philosophy* (Summer 2014), available at https://plato.stanford.edu/entries/law-interpretivist/

Miscellaneous Documents

Caron D. D., 'Arbitrators and the Rule of X', King's College London Dickson Poon School of Law, Legal Studies Research Paper Series, Paper No 2017-41, available at https://papers.ssrn.com/sol3/papers.cfm?abstract_id=3062537

Crawford J., and Nouwen S. (eds.), *Select Proceedings of the European Society of International Law: Volume 3* (Oxford: Hart, 2012)

International Law Association, Committee on International Commercial Arbitration, 'Interim Report: "*Res Judicata*" and Arbitration' (2004)

Kingsbury B., and Schill S. W., 'Investor–State Arbitration as Governance: Fair and Equitable Treatment, Proportionality and the Emerging Global Administrative Law', NYU School of Law, Working Paper No 09-46 (September 2009)

Report of the Executive Directors on the Convention on the Settlement of Investment Disputes between States and Nationals of Other States, in *ICSID Convention, Regulations and Rules* (ICSID, April 2006) 35

Roberts A., and Bouraoui Z., 'UNCITRAL and ISDS Reforms: Concerns about Consistency, Predictability and Correctness', *EJIL: Talk!* (5 June 2018)

Shi J., 'Speech by H.E. Judge Shi Jiuyong, President of the International Court of Justice, to the Sixth Committee of the General Assembly of the United Nations: The Internal Working Practice of the International Court of

Justice' (28 October 2005), available at www.icj-cij.org/en/statements-by-the-president

Stavropoulos N., 'Why Principles?', University of Oxford Faculty of Law Legal Studies Research Paper Series, Working Paper No 28/2007 (October 2007), available at https://papers.ssrn.com/sol3/papers.cfm?abstract_id=1023758

United Nations Conference on the Law of Treaties, First Session (Vienna, 26 March–24 May 1968), *Official Records, Summary Records of the Plenary Meetings and of the Meetings of the Committee of the Whole*, A/CONF.39/11

INDEX

For EU product safety concerns, contact us at Calle de José Abascal, 56–1°, 28003 Madrid, Spain or eugpsr@cambridge.org.

www.ingramcontent.com/pod-product-compliance
Lightning Source LLC
LaVergne TN
LVHW020325220926
848484LV00001BB/193

* 9 7 8 1 0 0 9 1 5 3 8 5 0 *